Today, sorcerers among the Nahua and Otomís
still paint paper spirits, cut paper god-dolls,
fold paper to trap ghosts, string paper infants
on the clothesline to ease childbirth, plant paper
to help crops grow, burn paper to dispel the winds
of evil, decorate paper with the drippings
of live sacrifice—the collective soul that reinvents
the universe through individual acts of superstition.

It would be best to recognize oneself as they do:
an idolator hunched spelling over blood-soaked paper,
a shaman working toward health or madness,
a vehicle for words recycled on recycled pages,
a knowledge beyond its own experience,
a symbol of itself, an image of a poet
forming in the reader's mind, or a Scheherazade, telling
story after story, just to stay alive.

Poetry in an Old Key

> "I believe that in this physical, space-time world of our experience there are things which do not fit the grammatical scheme of expression. But they are not necessarily blind, inconceivable, mystical affairs; they are simply matters which require to be conceived through some symbolistic schema other than discursive language."
>
> —Susanne K. Langer

Why, caring as I do for trees,
am I condemned to poetry? why compelled
to serve a life sentence stuttering this
syntax of desire, each poem straining
to manifest the inexpressible on paper,
a ritual offering, a superstition, a power,
prayer, seduction, clue, risk, awe, act,
as if my life depended on it?

The Aztecs knew paper as a sacred substance;
conquered towns sent millions of rolls each year
as tribute to the capital. It was not wasted
on words. Shamans painted images and soaked
the sheets with blood, provoking their divinities
to action. Under the Conquistadores, papermaking
was illegal: possession of paper was sufficient grounds
for the charge of idolatry, a sentence to be burned.

An artist (the philosopher reasons)
seeks not to arouse or convey feeling
but to portray what she knows about the nature
of feeling; once in possession of rich
symbolism, that knowledge may exceed her
whole experience. Genius (the artist shrugs
in answer) manifests itself
through attention to detail.

/ / /

A Nation Transformed by Information

*How Information Has Shaped the United States
from Colonial Times to the Present*

EDITORS

Alfred D. Chandler Jr.

James W. Cortada

UNIVERSITY PRESS

2000

OXFORD

UNIVERSITY PRESS

Oxford   New York

Athens   Auckland   Bangkok   Bogotá   Buenos Aries   Calcutta
Cape Town   Chennai   Dar es Salaam   Delhi   Florence   Hong Kong   Istanbul
Karachi   Kuala Lumpur   Madrid   Melbourne   Mexico City   Mumbai
Nairobi   Paris   São Paulo   Singapore   Taipei   Tokyo   Toronto   Warsaw

and associated companies in
Berlin   Ibadan

Copyright © 2000 by Oxford University Press

Published by Oxford University Press, Inc.
198 Madison Avenue, New York, New York 10016

Oxford is a registered trademark of Oxford University Press

Library of Congress Cataloging-in-Publication Data
A nation transformed by information : how information has
shaped the United States from Colonial times to the present /
Alfred D. Chandler, James W. Cortada, editors.
p.   cm.
Includes bibliographical references and index
ISBN 0-19-512701-3
1. Information technology—United States—History.
I. Chandler, Alfred Dupont.   II. Cortada, James W.
HC110.I55 N37 2000
338.973'06—dc21   99-049438

5 4 3 2 1

Printed in the United States of America
on acid-free paper

Preface

Americans, Europeans, and East Asians have been inundated with media coverage about the "Information Age," the "Internet," and on the "Information Highway," for more than a decade. *Time* magazine even named the computer its "Man of the Year" for 1983. The messages are similar: The Internet is new, the Information Age has suddenly arrived, everything is different. However, looking at the historical experience of the United States suggests a very different story.

A close look at the record clearly demonstrates that North Americans got on the Information Highway in the 1600s and by the late 1700s they were experiencing traffic jams. To carry the analogy further, Americans by 1800 could see highway construction underway (the U.S. postal system and roads for the mail to travel on), traffic regulations (copyright laws), and a variety of information vehicles cluttering the roads (e.g., newspapers, books, pamphlets, and broadsides). During the nineteenth century Americans applied electricity and creative tinkering to invent or highly develop key information technologies used around the world: telegraph, telephone, phonograph, and motion pictures, among others. In the twentieth century, they continued to add more vehicles to the Information Highway, most notably the computer and its smaller version, the ubiquitous personal computer. In short, Americans have been preparing for the Information Age for more than 300 years. It did not start with the introduction of the World Wide Web in the early 1990s.

The purpose of this book is to demonstrate this fact, pointing out how North Americans embraced information as a critical building block of their social, economic, and political world, and invested in the development and massive deployment of the infrastructures and technologies that made it possible for all the "hype" about the Information

Age that we read about today. Our research indicates that a historical perspective of the U.S. love affair with information and its effective deployment of these technologies have much to say about the nature of U.S. society as it does about the future of this nation. Equally remarkable is the extent to which information and its technologies were deployed in this nation. How that all happened is at the heart of this book. It is an important story, not yet fully recognized, even by specialists on the Information Age. It is one of those rare occasions where a team of researchers were able to open a door to a large new room full of insights about the United States.

But why focus on the United States? We limited our project to the United States because so much about computing in the late twentieth century focuses on the U.S. experience. While a great deal went on across all of Europe and in East Asia concerning information and its technologies, the U.S. experience is very instructive. First, there is an enormous volume of records and prior research that we could build on. Second, as we will argue in this book, information has played a very special role in American society; therefore, in order to understand this nation better, one must have a deep appreciation of the role of information and its infrastructures. Indeed, studies similar to this one should be conducted for other countries because it is obvious how little many commentators of modern society appreciate the profound role information, and its underlying technologies and infrastructures, have had on the affairs of a nation. We believe our book can serve as an example of what can be studied about other nations.

This book is an example of one of the benefits of the modern use of information management practices—namely, the ability to bring together experts from different fields—to form new perspectives, new findings, and to draw different conclusions. We believe no one individual student of the "Information Revolution" could have looked at such a broad topic. Therefore, we formed a team of experts in various aspects of the bigger story of the role of information processing in the United States to tell the story. To do that we pulled together historians, professors of business management, a management consultant, and a sociologist. They communicated in both old and new ways. They met face to face to define the project and to review findings and results. But they also used the Internet to share drafts of chapters with each other, and e-mail to conduct the necessary dialogue to make this book an integrated, cohesive view of the subject. How they worked as a team is as much a story of exploiting information technology as it is about the emerging way major topics are being explored by modern scholars.

Chapter 1 sets the context for the entire North American experience with information across three centuries. Chapters 2–8 take the reader through the details of what happened—making it abundantly clear that the run-up to the Information Age is a long one—and ends with today's situation with computing in both home and at work. Chapter 9 identifies patterns of continuity and change that have characterized the American experience.

As a team we would like to acknowledge the help of colleagues, librarians, and archivists for helping us with this project. Corporate archivists, for example, contributed illustrations as diligently as did the more traditional sources of such images, university libraries. Our students who grew up not knowing a time when there were no computers helped as well. Max Hall improved the quality of our text. Anne O'Connell, Eileen Hankins, and Teresa Hardy—all of the Harvard Business School—did a great deal of typing of this book. Kelly Porter created the charts for Richard Nolan's chapter. We also want to express our special appreciation to Herb Addison, vice president at Oxford University Press, for having absolute faith in this project and for his willingness to publish the book. It seems appropriate to publish this book with Oxford, a publisher that has been at the center of Europe's run up to its own Information Revolution for over five hundred years!

Contents

Contributors

Richard D. Brown is Professor of History at the University of Connecticut. He is the author of *Modernization: The Transformation of American Life* (Hill & Wang, 1976); *Knowledge Is Power: The Diffusion of Information in Early America, 1650–1865* (Oxford University Press, 1989); and *The Strength of a People: The Idea of An Informed Citizenry in America, 1650–1870* (University of North Carolina Press, 1996). Brown works on the social and cultural history of early America. He is presently writing a microhistory of an incest-rape case during the early American Republic.

Alfred D. Chandler Jr. is the Strauss Professor of Business History, Emeritus, at the Graduate School of Business Administration, Harvard University. He is the author of *Strategy and Structure* (MIT Press, 1962), *The Visible Hand* (Harvard University Press, 1977), *Scale and Scope* (Harvard University Press, 1990), and other volumes. He has won many prizes, including the Pulitzer and Bancroft Prizes. Chandler is currently studying the way industries have acquired and leveraged their knowledge for strategic and competitive successes.

James W. Cortada is an Executive Consultant with IBM Global Services. He is the author of a number of books on the management and history of information technology. Some of his more recent publications include *Before the Computer: IBM, NCR, Burroughs, and Remington Rand and the Industry They Created, 1865–1956* (Princeton University Press, 1993), *The Computer in the United States* (M. E. Sharpe, 1993), and *Best Practices in Information Technology* (Prentice-Hall, 1998), and, with Thomas S. Hargraves and Edward Wakin, *Into the Networked Age: How IBM and Other Firms are Getting There Now* (Oxford University Press, 1999). His primary area of historical research is on how businesses used information processing.

Margaret Graham is Founding Director of Winthrop Group, Inc., in Cambridge, Mass. She is the author of *RCA and the VideoDisc: The Business of Research* (Cambridge University Press, 1986) and with Betty Prouitt, *R&D for Industry: A Century of Technical Innovation at Alcoa* (Cambridge: Cambridge University Press, 1990). Graham is currently writing a book with Alec Shudiener on the practice of innovation at Corning Glass Works.

Richard R. John is Associate Professor of History at the University of Illinois at Chicago, and most recently, a fellow at the Woodrow Wilson Center at the Smithsonian Institution. He is the author of *Spreading the News: The American Postal System from Franklin to Morse* (Harvard University Press, 1995) and "The Politics of Innovation" *Daedalus* (1998). John is a cultural and institutional historian with a special interest in the history of communications. He is currently writing a book on American communications policy from the 1830s to World War I.

Richard L. Nolan is the William Barclay Harding Professor of Management of Technology at the Graduate School of Business Administration, Harvard University. He is co-editor (with Steve Bradley) of *Sense and Respond* (Harvard Business School Press, 1998) and *Creative Destruction* (Harvard Business School Press, 1995), and "Management by Wire," *Harvard Business Review* (1993). Currently he is writing a book on high-tech companies and how they are creating and building strategic intranents.

Lee S. Sproull is Professor of Business at New York University. She is the co-author (with Sara Kiesler) of *Connections: New Ways of Working in the Networked Organization* (MIT Press, 1991) and is co-author (with Michael Cohen) of *Learning in Organizations* (Sage, 1995). She is currently studying large electronic groups and communities.

JoAnne Yates is Professor of Management Communication and Information Studies at the Sloan School of Management at MIT. She is the author of *Control Through Communication: The Rise of System in American Management* (Johns Hopkins University Press, 1989). She has published a number of studies on contemporary electronic communications. In the area of history, she is currently studying the role of information technology before and after the arrival of the computer as used in the insurance industry.

A NATION TRANSFORMED BY INFORMATION

1

The Information Age in Historical Perspective

Introduction

Alfred D. Chandler Jr.

I begin this introduction by explaining the book's title. As it was originally conceived, the title was *The Third Industrial Revolution: The Role of Information in the Transformation of the United States from Colonial Times to the Present*. As the project progressed and the editors and contributors discussed the chapters to be written, we realized that what we were considering was not an industrial revolution but an information revolution—a revolution that evolved from the industrial world of the twentieth century. Moreover, this information revolution has transformed the industrial world of the nineteenth and twentieth centuries as profoundly as the First and Second Industrial Revolutions transformed the earlier commercial world of the eighteenth century. Of these industrial revolutions, the first, beginning in Great Britain in the late eighteenth century, transformed the processes of production; the second, beginning in Europe and the United States in the 1840s, transformed transportation and communication. For the purpose of this book a more realistic terminology appeared to be one of "ages" rather than "revolutions." We identify three—the Commercial Age, the Industrial Age, and the Information Age. Therefore, this history of the role of information in the transformation of the United States from colonial times to the present reviews that role from the centuries-old Commercial Age during the eighteenth century into the Industrial Age of the nineteenth and twentieth centuries and then the transformation from the Industrial into the Information Age in the last decades of the twentieth century.

During the eighteenth century, the economy of Britain's colonies in America was largely agricultural and commercial and its population rural. Production, transportation, and communication were powered by wind, water, human and animal muscle, and the burning of wood.

Wood was also the primary material of construction for housing, and for transportation and industrial equipment.

The Industrial Age, which had its beginnings in the last decades of the eighteenth century in Great Britain, did not reach the United States until the 1840s. Then steam power based on coal, which is fossilized wood, began to replace wind, water, and muscle and started to transform the processes of American production, transportation, and communication. In all three processes, iron and other metals—produced increasingly through the use of coal-fired heat—replaced wood as the primary material. The steam-powered railroad, supplemented by the electric telegraph and telephone, became the primary means of communication and transportation. As the Industrial Age matured at the end of the nineteenth century, the nation became increasingly urban as well as industrial. In the 1920s came a new source of power, the internal combustion engine driven by another fossil fuel, petroleum. And with this the Industrial Age reached its full fruition.

From the 1920s on, yet another new power source, electronics, began to build the infrastructure for the Information Age, by transforming the transmission and processing of information. The vacuum tube made possible wireless transmission of signals and then voice. It also added voice to motion pictures. At the same time, electronic-based devices greatly advanced the speed and accuracy of processing information. As these innovations were laying the foundations of the Information Age, city dwellers began to move to the suburbs. All these moves and a post–World War II prosperity advanced demands for a wide variety of services. So by the last decades of the twentieth century, when the infrastructure of the Information Age was being completed, the nation's economy was increasingly becoming service-oriented and its population increasingly suburban.

In the following chapters our authors (1) review the changing technological underpinnings—or, to use a modern term, infrastructure—of the means of transmitting information, (2) consider the changing nature of the recipients of the information flows, and (3) analyze the ways in which the recipients used these flows to shape and reshape U.S. business, society, and culture. Given this broad perspective, we concluded that the title *A Nation Transformed by Information: How Information Shaped the United States from Colonial Times to the Present* more clearly defined what this book is about.

This evolution of changing purveyors of information (and the information they purveyed) was, of course, embedded in a much broader historical evolution. The purpose of this introductory chapter is to provide the essential historical setting for the developments described and analyzed in the following chapters. Because the chapters have different perspectives and different themes, and deal with different time periods, this historical setting provides a way to relate one chapter to another. Moreover, because the authors intentionally concentrate on the changing nature of the recipients of these information flows and the resulting reshaping of American business, government, and broader cultural institutions, this historical overview focuses on the evolving infrastructures that enabled these transformations to take place.

The Commercial Age

Richard Brown, in chapter 2, "Early American Origins of the Information Age," reviews the initial underpinnings of information flows during the Commercial Age, that is the transmitters of information (the infrastructure) and the economic, political, and cultural arrangements that shaped the demand of the recipients (the market) for the information transmitted. His chapter falls into three parts. The first considers the expansion of the existing European (primarily British) infrastructure to its transatlantic frontier. The second evaluates the impact of the growing imperial crisis (based on the regulation of American commerce) and the resulting War of Independence. Crisis and war shaped the new nation's information infrastructure as well as its political, mercantile, and cultural institutional arrangements. The third part examines the expanding national marketplace as the new nation moved west from the Atlantic seaboard.

Although the printing press arrived with the first settlers in New England, it was used primarily by government officials, church leaders, and merchants. That is, the printed pages were produced for and read by the colonial elite. As the number of newspapers grew they increasingly carried commercial news and comments. Indeed, "the gradual pace of newspaper growth suggests that only presses that were oriented toward an elite mercantile audience could succeed," Brown notes. On the other hand, he writes, "The widespread, institutionalized Protestant belief in the importance of literacy for individual piety, conversion, and salvation" led to an exceptionally literate public. After 1760 colonial literacy exceeded 75 percent.

The British government's attempts in 1764 and 1765 to regulate the commerce of the colonies and to increase tax revenues based on that commerce led to the mobilization of public opinion in the late 1760s through newspapers and pamphlets and then after 1772 with the formation of "committees of correspondence." The resulting democratization of information moved both the transmitters and receivers of information beyond the elite. The goal of this protest against Parliamentary legislation was to create an "informed citizenry" in all walks of life and to engage them in public affairs. The culmination of this expansion in the receivers of information came with the January 1776 publication of Thomas Paine's *Common Sense*, an eloquent and passionate call to throw off British rule and create a new American nation. By the end of that year more than 100,000 copies had been sold in a country of only 500,000 households.

During and after the American Revolution the commitment to the concept of an informed citizenry became incorporated in the articles of the new state constitutions, as well as the federal Constitution, which became law in 1788 and was soon amended to protect the freedom of speech and the freedom of the press. That same commitment also led the leaders of the Revolution to finance education, both schools and colleges, and to establish an American postal system on the foundations of the royal postal system (with Benjamin Franklin as Postmaster General).

The third part of Brown's chapter considers the role of the new states and the Republic in creating a national marketplace for information through the coming of national parties, the geographical expansion of printing presses, and an expanding transportation and postal system. He stresses that, unlike Britain and France, the new United States had no metropolitan centers. "A polycentric array of state capitals and commercial centers all required presses, as well as timely access to long-distance news." They provided "a structural imperative for a competitive information marketplace." After reviewing these developments, Brown concludes by considering the challenges to the revolutionary heritage of free press, free speech, and the role of political parties in promoting the commitment to having an informed citizenry and the institutions to sustain it.

The Coming of the Industrial Age

In chapter 3, "Recasting the Information Infrastructure for the Industrial Age," Richard R. John focuses on two "recastings." The first was the swift expansion of the nation's existing Commercial Age infrastructure as the nation increased rapidly in population and territory. The second recasting, beginning in the 1840s, was based on steam and electricity. The railroad and telegraph, followed by the telephone, created the transportation and communications infrastructure for the

Industrial Age, which it matured in the 1880s and the 1890s. John calls these recastings the "first communication revolution" and the "second communication revolution." An appreciation of the significance of these revolutions requires a brief review of the basic changes of the Atlantic world between 1789 and 1815.

During the first quarter century of the American nation's existence, the French Revolution and the Napoleonic wars reshaped the political and cultural base of European civilization. At the same time, the Industrial Revolution in Great Britain—a revolution based on coal, steam, and iron machinery—began to alter that country's economic base. The United States, turning its face away from the east and Europe, began its westward march into the Trans-Appalachian West.

In 1789, when George Washington took office as president and the U.S. Congress met for the first time, the storming of the Bastille on July 14 set off the French Revolution. In 1793 the revolutionary committee executed Louis XVI and declared war on Britain and Holland. After the revolution had run its course, the war continued with Napoleon Bonaparte taking command of the troops in 1795. From then until Napoleon's defeat at Waterloo in 1815 (except for a five-month period after December 1804), Britain and France continued to battle for world dominance.

The United States was the largest neutral carrier, so its commerce became increasingly involved in what became the lucrative Atlantic trade. The American government made futile attempts to protect its commerce. Finally, the War of 1812 against Britain reduced the volume of trade, although there were still profits. This constant attention focused on the global British and French conflict for dominance in Europe—a conflict that was comparable only to the Thirty Years War in Europe in the seventeenth century and World Wars I and II during the twentieth—slowed westward expansion across the Appalachian Mountains into the Mississippi Valley. From 1796 to 1815 only two states joined the Union: Ohio in 1803 and Louisiana in 1812.

In Britain the rapid growth of factory production of cotton textiles was assured by the invention in 1785 of the "Crompton Mule" powered by James Watt's steam engine. In the United States, Eli Whitney's invention of the cotton gin in 1793 provided these textile factories with an adequate supply of raw cotton. At the same time a new abundance of coal-fired iron led to a sharp increase in the production of metal machinery and tools.

In 1815, at the end of the wars between Britain and France and between the United States and Britain, the barriers the wars had created to economic growth disappeared. Settlers surged into the Mississippi Valley. From 1816 through 1821 five western states entered the Union: Indiana (1816), Mississippi (1817), Illinois (1818), Alabama (1819), and Missouri (1821). In those same years the United States became almost overnight Britain's largest customer for the new manufactured goods—textile and metal machinery and tools—and its primary supplier of cotton.

By 1815 the Industrial Revolution in Great Britain had transformed the flows of shipping over which information traveled. After the British textile manufacturers dumped their supplies in the port of New York in that year, the trade pattern became what Robert Albion has termed the Cotton Triangle. Cotton for Britain went via New York and British textiles and manufactured goods returned there for transshipment to the cotton ports of the South as well as by road and canal to the northwest. By 1825 the political spokesman of the new West, Henry Clay of Kentucky, was urging Congress to support what he called the American System of economic growth. The South was to provide the exports to pay for the imports of manufactured goods; the West to supply the south with food and animals, including horses and mules. A tariff large enough to encourage the North to begin to compete with British manufactured goods would also provide funds for roads and canals from the Northeast to the Northwest, funds that could be used to subsidize the postal system.

John's account traces in detail the creation and evolution of the national postal system—the institution that played the critical role in the creation of the new nation's information infrastructure. The Post Office Act of 1792 created a new postal infrastructure on the foundations of the royal postal system that Benjamin Franklin had taken over as Postmaster General in 1775. The act provided that the mail service would carry the newspapers "at extremely low rates," thus ensuring the flow of printed information throughout the country. It also provided that the Congress, rather than the executive branch, was to designate postal routes, and this facilitated the proliferation of the postal routes through the westward-expanding nation. By those provisions the Congress subsidized the nation's press and the press's primary means of overland distribution, the stagecoach—and the network of dirt roads that the horse-drawn coaches traveled.

These subsidies were impressive. By 1796 newspapers accounted for 3 percent of mail service revenues, but 70 percent of the weight carried. By 1838 the figure was 15 percent revenues and 95 percent of weight carried. During the 1820s a third of the stagecoach industry's revenues came from mail contracts. The companies also received other subsidies to maintain their operations. As John notes, without government support "it is inconceivable that the newspapers could have circulated in such numbers." The support of mail coach and post roads permitted the Post Office to circulate knowledge of every kind through every part of the United States.

The Post Office not only transmitted the nation's printed and hand-written communications all the way to the edges of the settled community, but did it with increasing speed. As Figure 1.1 indicates, the time of travel from the city of New York to the rest of the country was reduced by half between 1800 and 1830.

In 1829 the British invention of the steam locomotive led to John's "second communication revolution," the second recasting of the American information infrastructure. In that year the horse still provided the fastest and most reliable power for overland transportation, as it had done since the beginning of civilization. But in 1829 at the famous Rainhill trials in Great Britain, held by the promoters of the Liverpool & Manchester Railroad (to carry cotton into and textiles out of the

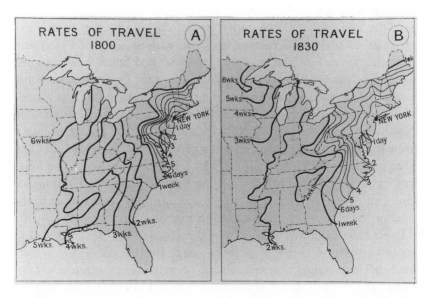

Figure 1.1 Rates of Travel. At the start of the nineteenth century, travel time was measured in days and weeks, not in hours as in our own time. Well-traveled routes were located primarily in the eastern United States. The fastest speed was that at which a horse could go. Timeliness of news was relative; six-week-old stories out of New York in what would someday be Illinois was relatively current. Source: Charles O. Paulin, *Atlas of the Historical Geography of the United States* (Washington, D.C.: Carnegie Institute and American Geographical Society, 1932), plate 138. Reprinted with permission.

Manchester factories), demonstrated that George Stephenson's Rocket was far superior to the horse in terms of speed, the number of passengers, and the amount of freight. Nevertheless, more than a decade and a half of interrelated mechanical and engineering innovations was required before Stephenson's boiler with a steam stack pulling a couple of stagecoaches became the steam-powered railroad that provided the basic transportation and communications for the coming Industrial Age.

The first American railways, built in the 1830s, were short lines that connected nearby commercial centers or supplemented existing water routes. During the 1840s, the technology of railroad transportation was rapidly perfected. Uniform methods of construction, grading, tunneling, and bridging were developed. The "Iron T" rail came into common use. By the late 1840s the locomotive had its cams, sandbox, driver wheels, swivel or bogie truck, and equalizing beams. Coal was replacing wood as the steam maker. Passenger coaches had become "long cars," carrying 60 passengers on reversible seats. Boxcars, cattle cars, lumber cars, and other freight cars were basically similar to those used on American rails a century later, though not as big.

In the mid-1840s, as the nation pulled out of a long economic depression, railroad construction began in earnest. Between 1847 and 1860 the railroad mileage operated in the United States rose from just under 5,000 miles to more than 30,000 miles, the first step in bringing a national railroad network into being. (By comparison, Britain's national network thirty years later in 1890 was 17,200 miles.) In the Old Northwest between the Ohio River and the Great Lakes, railroads grew from 600 miles in 1849 to 9,000 in 1860. By 1854 these lines had been joined to the Eastern seaboard by four trunk lines each 500 miles in length—the New York & Erie, the Pennsylvania, the Baltimore & Ohio, and the New York Central. The resulting transformation in the time of travel by 1857 is illustrated in Figure 1.2

Even before the railroad boom of the 1840s, the Post Office had to come to terms with the new technology. By the mid-1840s private mail-delivery companies were already transmitting as much as two-thirds of the commercial correspondence of the country *by railroad*. The Post Office initially responded by "vigorously prosecuting the violations of its legally guaranteed monopoly over the transmission of mail," but in 1845 it began to turn from the stagecoach to the railway. That year it canceled stagecoach contracts in the areas served by rail and reduced the basic letter rate. The rate was dropped again in 1851 to 3 cents. There it remained for more than a century, with the Post

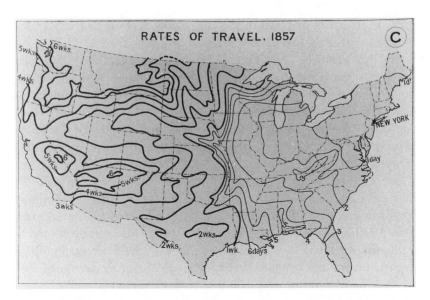

Figure 1.2 Rates of Travel. By 1857, information was being disseminated all over what would become the "Lower 48" states of the United States. The introduction of the railroad in the 1840s was beginning to have a positive effect in making it faster to move information around; however, most travel in the far western areas remained either by foot or horse. Information traveled at much faster speeds along the East Coast. This map also documents the fact that the movement of people, goods, and information interconnected from one end of the continent to the other and into Canada. Source: Charles O. Paulin, *Atlas of the Historical Geography of the United States* (Washington, D.C.: Carnegie Institute and American Geographical Society, 1932), plate 138. Reprinted with permission.

Office running a large annual deficit beginning in 1851 and continuing for decades.

The rapid expansion of the railway network from the Eastern seaboard to the Mississippi River in the decade after 1847 was hastened by a fortuitous event, the invention of the electric telegraph. Although Samuel F. B. Morse sent the first telegram on his just completed line between Washington, D.C., and Baltimore in 1844, legal uncertainties delayed the commercialization of the telegraph until 1847, just in time to provide the communication essential to operate the 500-mile, single-track trunk lines across the mountains and many of their western connections. Only single-track railroads could have been laid down over such a large area in such a short time at a viable cost. In the longer and more heavily used railroads, only telegraphic communication could prevent collisions and assure the continuing flow of two-way traffic between a large number of destinations along the track.

By 1851 when the New York & Erie reached Lake Erie, trains and traffic were beginning to be controlled through hourly and daily traffic reports. By 1854 the Erie's superintendent, Daniel C. McCallum, was using these telegraphic records as a database for determining cost, rates, and even the effectiveness of the operating management of the enterprise. From then on the telegraph increasingly became an essential handmaiden to railroad operations.

During these years this critical symbiotic relationship between the railroad and the telegraph slowly became defined by what the telegraph companies termed railway contracts. By these contracts the railroads agreed to furnish transportation and construction materials needed to string the wires and to maintain them, to operate the telegraph offices in their depots and to provide the telegraph operators. In return they received unlimited free telegraph service on their rail lines and a limited amount of services off their lines. In other words, the telegraph companies provided the wire and the telegraph departments of the railroads operated the facilities. So successful were these arrangements that in 1870, shortly after the merger of the major telegraph companies into Western Union, that dominant system had three-fourths of its telegraph offices in railroad depots, nearly 9,000 of its total 12,000 offices. That is, by 1870 U.S. railroads funded and managed two-thirds of Western Union's operations and had contributed considerably to the construction of the telegraph lines.[1]

So, by the outbreak of the Civil War in 1861, the foundations of the new transportation and communication infrastructure were in place—steam-powered and electrically supported. The four years of deadly conflict held back new railway construction. In the immediate postwar years, the destroyed Southern railroads were rebuilt and the network east of the Mississippi filled in. Finally, after the severe and prolonged economic depression of the 1870s, the nation's network of more than 200,000 miles of track was completed in the 1880s and the 1890s. With its completion railroad enterprises consolidated into giant regional systems, with each of the merged enterprises operating between 20,000 to 25,000 miles of track. By the turn of the century, two-thirds of the U.S. railroads were operated by seven such railroad groups.

Meanwhile, to take advantage of the huge and expanding rail network, postal administrators had formed the Railway Mail Service. In the 1860s the service began to have postal clerks sort mail on board railroad cars rather than merely transport it to the next distribution center in accordance with the "hub-and-spoke" sorting system that had been the backbone of postal sorting since 1800. Now the government abandoned "hub-and-spoke" altogether, and for the next eighty years the vast majority of the mail was sorted inside moving railway cars rather than in distribution centers.

This change came about as follows. In 1874 the general superintendent of the Railway Mail Service, George M. Banks, articulated for the first time the fundamental principle that the distribution of the entire mail—on railroads as well as in post offices—be coordinated through a single scheme. Toward this end, he assigned Theodore N. Vail, who at that time was the assistant general superintendent, to initiate in 1875 a high-speed and "fast-mail" train between New York and Chicago. Here Vail concentrated on developing complex systems for increasing the speed and the routing of the increasingly massive volume of letters and packages. In 1876 Vail was elevated to superintendent.

As described in chapter 3, the impact of the electric telegraph went far beyond its essential role in railroad operations. It provided flows of information with unprecedented speed, volume, and regularity. In its initial years the telegraph moved ahead of the railroad, reaching New Orleans as early as 1848 and San Francisco in 1861. Of more significance, its existence immediately transformed the dissemination of news and of commercial and financial information. As early as 1848, several New York newspapers formed the New York Associated Press for more cooperative use of the new wire services. By 1859 this forerunner of today's Associated Press "had established a truly national system for flow of public information."[2]

In the 1850s, as grain elevators were built in Chicago and at other commercial centers in the Midwest, grain exchanges appeared, providing daily prices telegraphed on different types and quantities of grain. Soon speculators were buying and selling for future delivery. The coming of the futures market permitted the commodity dealers to reduce the risk (by "hedging," or limiting financial exposure) and therefore the cost of shipping grain from the interior to the seaboard. Quickly the New York Stock Exchange and other security exchanges were using the telegraph for buying, selling, and listing securities, including those by speculators selling "long" and "short."

The invention of the telephone by Alexander Graham Bell (the patent was awarded in May 1876) added another dimension to the growing information infrastructure—the transmission of voice over extended distances. In July 8, 1877, Bell, Gardner Greene Hubbard (a Boston lawyer and close friend), Thomas Watson (Bell's technical assistant), and Thomas Sanders (who had provided funds) formed a voluntary association, with Hubbard in early 1878 as trustee. Almost immediately challenged by Western Union, Hubbard persuaded Theodore Vail, the general sperintendent of the Railway Mail Service, to become general superintendent. Vail immediately organized a strong defense of Bell's patent. He then turned to the critical issue of raising the capital essential to build a national telephone system, for from the start Hubbard had planned to lease, not sell, the telephone and its switching devices.

In July, Vail took the first step to provide the necessary funds by incorporating the Bell enterprise so that its stock could be sold to the public. Funds were raised, but by the end of the year, the company was in debt and the treasury bare. Bankruptcy seemed certain. So in January 1879, Vail and the new investors formed the National Telephone Company and in March replaced Hubbard with William Forbes, a member of the powerful Forbes group of investors, as president. That group, including leading monied men from New York as well as Boston, had financed the construction of the Michigan Central and other early Midwestern railroads during the 1850s and was funding the giant Burlington System. As Thomas C. Cochran wrote in his classical *Railroad Leaders*, the Forbes group "occupied much the same position on boards as men like J. Pierpont Morgan and George F. Baker at a later day."[3]

Vail and Forbes immediately recruited James J. Storrow, one of Boston's leading lawyers, to work with Chauncey Smith, Hubbard's patent lawyer in the litigation with Western Union over the Bell Telephone patent and patents of its rivals including Thomas Edison and others. The court's decision, based on the testimony taken during the summer and fall of 1879, was a complete victory for Bell. On November 10, Bell Telephone and Western Union signed an agreement by which the latter left the telephone business in return for 20 percent of telephone rentals for the next seventeen years. By then Hubbard and Bell had moved from Boston to Washington, D.C. The two other founders soon left the company.

As the 1880s began, the nation's most knowledgeable and most professional manager of information flows, supported by one of its most formidable financial groups, began to build the nation's first telephone network. They moved quickly. By 1881 the Bell Company had established service in all but nine of the nation's cities with population of more than 10,000.

John's chapter outlines the story of Bell Telephone System's continued growth in some detail. John notes the broad impact on information flows in the United States, emphasizing that unlike railway mail service and the telegraph, the telephone's impact was local. As late as the 1930s, only 2 percent of telephone calls were made across state lines. Until well after World War II the new electrical information technology supplemented rather than supplanted that of the Railway Mail Service.

By the end of the nineteenth century the information infrastructure for the Industrial Age was solidly in place. The railroads had consolidated their activities into a small number of large systems. Western Union continued to dominate telegraphic communication. In 1899 American Telephone & Telegraph became the Bell system's parent company. Regional companies operated the telephone exchange. Western Electric, AT&T's manufacturing arm, would soon play a central role, not only in the development of long distance telephony, but also in the creation of electronic technology on which the future Information Age rested.

The Industrial Age Matures

As its basic infrastructure was being completed, the Industrial Age had arrived. In 1890 the U.S. Bureau of Census announced the closing of the frontier boundaries between the areas of settlement moving west from the Atlantic and east from the Pacific. From the 1890s on, urban areas grew increasingly faster than rural ones. In the first years of the new century immigration from abroad soared. In six of the years between 1905 and 1914, over a million people entered the United States, providing and enlarging the working force for urban industrial centers.

Beginning in the 1880s the new Industrial Age was characterized by the rise of "big business"; that is, the development of a new economic institution, the large enterprise that commercialized, produced, and marketed goods on an unprecedented scale for national and international markets. A new subspecies of economic man, the salaried manager, emerged to operate these enterprises. The new, more reliable, high-volume, regularly scheduled, all-weather transportation and communications provided by the railroad (and steamship) and the telegraph (and cable) brought into being a new institution. This institution consisted of a managerial, integrated corporate enterprise that transformed existing industries while creating new ones, during what historians have termed the Second Industrial Revolution.

Figure 1.3, "Founding Dates of the 1994 *Fortune* 500 Companies," dramatically illustrates the coming of the managerial enterprise and its rapid growth in the 1880s and 1890s. Of the corporate leaders of 1994, almost half (244 to be precise) were established in the five decades

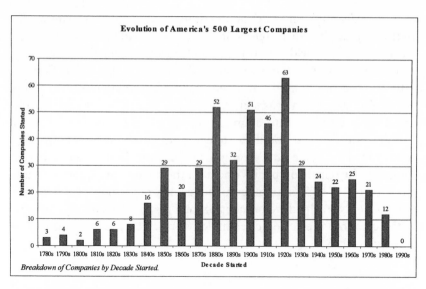

Figure 1.3 Founding Dates of the 1994. *Fortune* 500 Companies. [Modified from Harris Corporation, "Founding Dates of the 1994 *Fortune* 500 U.S. Companies," *Business History Review*, vol. 70, no. 1 (Spring 1996), p. 89, ranking based on sales.]

starting with the 1880s and ending with the 1920s. Fifty-two, or one-tenth of the total, began in the single decade of the 1880s. The burst of sixty-three new companies in the 1920s reflected the coming of the petroleum-based internal-combustion engine. That number alone is more than the fifty-eight established in the entire three-decade period of the 1960s, 1970s, and 1980s, during the formative years of the Information Age.

Figure 1.3 also tracks the rise of industrial enterprises as the steam and electrical communication infrastructure developed. The small number of present giants established before the 1830s consists largely of banks and insurance companies that supported the mercantile business of the Commercial Age. Du Pont (1802) and Colgate-Palmolive (1806) are the only manufacturing companies on the "500 list" that were founded before the coming of the railroads. Other founding dates for modern manufacturing giants are in the late 1840s; grow more numerous in the 1850s; fall off during the years of the Civil War, Reconstruction, and the Depression of the 1870s; and then rise fast in the 1880s.

JoAnne Yates's, "Business Use of Information and Technology during the Industrial Age" (chapter 4), focuses on the development of new technologies of business information and their uses by the new managerial class. She begins by describing and analyzing what she terms the "ideology" of the first generation of salaried managers as they met the initial challenges of the Industrial Age. She concentrates on manufacturing enterprises that purchased varieties of raw and semifinished materials and processed them in large volume for national and world markets, thereby creating new technological and operational challenges.

As late as the 1870s, nearly all business firms were—as they had been since the beginning of the Commercial Age centuries ago—small enterprises personally managed by their owners. They were usually partnerships that relied on personal correspondence, newspapers, and other printed commercial news for external information, and on double-entry bookkeeping to provide the needed internal data. The significant exceptions were in fact the providers of information flows— the postal system, the railroads, the telegraph, and the telephone. But as late as 1849 the directors of the twenty-six-mile-long Boston & Worcester, in their annual report, had to assure their stockholders that the company's accounts were "kept in strictly mercantile style according to the Italian method of bookkeeping."[4]

From the 1850s on, beginning with McCallum of the New York & Erie, railroad managers pioneered in providing internal corporate information needed to assure efficient low-cost operations as well as to determine short- and long-term profit and loss. But as Yates points out, their information needs differed sharply from those of manufacturing companies. These differences included the railroad's huge initial construction costs, their need to account for money received daily from thousands of passengers and hundreds of freight agents, for thousands of different types of freight items, for the variation in traffic carried, and with different physical characteristics of their geographical operating units. The resulting highly complex and control procedures were not that relevant for manufacturing companies. These differences, however, did make the railroads the initial primary market for the most complex business machines developed before World War II, the punched-card tabulators.

In the 1880s the first generation of salaried managers of the new integrated corporate enterprises, most of whom were trained as civil and mechanical engineers, began to meet the challenges of coordinating product flow through the enterprises, and those of developing costing, pricing, and depreciation accounts—data necessary both for managerial purposes and to provide consolidated income statements and balance sheets to directors and stockholders. To meet these challenges, they (in Yates's words) "began to develop and share a new management approach and techniques (presented in articles published first in engineering magazines and then in newly emerging management publications) that collectively came to be called systematic management."

These engineers/managers were thus concerned with developing cost accounting based on numerical records, routinizing and rationalizing the flow of written orders to operating staff, and sending instructions to the sales force and nonmanufacturing personnel. This growth of internal written and numerical information quickly created a need for mechanical devices to process such information—a demand that created a new office machinery industry. The first of these machines, the typewriter, initially produced in the mid-1870s by Remington Typewriter Company, provided a new device for producing the printed word. The development of carbon paper for making copies soon followed. The first machine from National Cash Register (NCR), introduced in 1882, was designed to prevent theft. After James Henry Patterson took command of the firm in 1884 those registers began to collect and record the information produced and, in time, to provide continuing data on retail sales. As they did, NCR became a national and then an international enterprise. Burroughs Adding Machine Company, established in the late 1880s, began in the early 1890s to produce modern adding machines and other calculating devices. Because these firms and a small number of competitors were established before Thomas Edison's dynamo brought electrification of home and office, all were driven not by electricity, but by mechanical means.

In the 1890s innovative makers of equipment focused more on machines for the retention and retrieval of existing printed and numerical data. A. . Dick's stencil "mimeograph" assured the producing of hundreds of copies. Vertical files improved the storage and retrieval of these copies. The increasing torrent of papers from a number of operating units led corporations to the formation of central files and the hiring of a file manager. Soon 3 in. × 5 in. cards increased the productivity of the new filing systems.

Yates, after considering the broad implications and impact of the new collectors and processors of business information, reviews the continuing growth in the use of these machines. The demand for business machines surged in the 1920s and 1930s, one reason being the needs of personnel management, needs which reflected the rise of the "human relations" school of business management. Another stimulus of the growing demand was the New Deal's labor and social security legislation.

Yates concludes her chapter by reviewing the evolution of the most complex business-information-processing instrument to be marketed before World War II, the electrical/mechanical punched-card tabulating machine. Herman Hollerith invented that device at the request of the U.S. Census Bureau to process the data collected for the census of 1890. After its success, the bureau asked James Powers to provide an alternate source. Powers thus became Hollerith's only competitor. In 1911 a Wall Street promoter, Charles R. Flint, merged the Hollerith Company with two smaller producers, one of business clocks, the other of business scales, to form the Computer-Tabulating-Recording Corporation (CTR). In 1914 Thomas J. Watson, a protégé of National Cash Register's James Henry Patterson, became CTR's general manager.

That company concentrated on the Hollerith punched-card technology, grew impressively, changed its name to International Business Machine Corporation (IBM) in 1924, and in the mid-1920s built manufacturing plants in Great Britain and France. In 1927 another financial promoter, James Rand, merged Powers Company with Remington Typewriter and a small adding-machine concern to form Remington-Rand. Two other early business-machine makers—National Cash Register and Burroughs, together with Honeywell, a maker of heat-control equipment—began exploring the punched-card tabulating business before World War II but decided that IBM and Powers were too far ahead for new entrants to compete effectively. Although IBM dominated this sector of the "office appliance" industry as it was known at the time, its rivals were clearly aware of the punched-card technology and the market for such products.

The punched-card tabulating machine differed from the other information processing devices described in chapter 4. From its start it was electrically powered. Of more importance the product was not made by a single machine, but by a system that used several devices to procure, record, and store data on cards; sort them for retrieval; perform computations; and print the resulting data in a form that could be sent to a recipient. In the beginning its markets were not manufacturers, but instead the information-intensive giant railroad systems and insurance companies and large public agencies, such as city governments and the Census Bureau and other statistical agencies. Not surprisingly, the mainframe computer that created the initial infrastructure for the Information Age evolved directly from the punched-card producers.

The next four chapters focus on the creation of the infrastructure of the Information Age. Chapter 5, by Margaret Graham, deals with the broad impact of vacuum-tube technology that brought into being radio and television. Chapter 6, by James W. Cortada, reviews the coming of the modern digital computers, the mainframe, and then the mini-computer and the profound impact they had on the processing of information. First came the mainframe, the marriage of transistor and punched-card technology for broad commercial and business markets; then the smaller, more specialized minicomputer for engineers and scientists. Chapters 7 and 8 focus on the revolutionary changes caused by the coming of the microcomputer as the personal computer replaced the mainframe and the workstation the minicomputer. Richard Nolan (chapter 7) deals with the impact of the personal computer and work-station on reshaping the processes of business information, and with it transforming business practices. Lee Sproull, in chapter 8, does the same for the impact of the personal computer on U.S. households.

The historical setting for these four chapters differs sharply from that used to relate and understand more fully the evolution of information from the Commercial through the Industrial Age. A multitude of businesses—railroads, business-machine companies, and other enterprises, many of which still dominate today's Fortune 500 list—built the larger infrastructure for the Industrial Age. Only a handful of companies brought the Information Age into being.

Indeed, the historical background for the chapters 5–8 can be presented through the history of two enterprises—the Radio Corporation of America (RCA) and IBM. RCA's story provides the linchpin for the rise and fall of the American consumer-electronics industry. IBM's story is critical to any analysis of the progenitors—chips and computers—of the Information Age, as well as understanding the significance of the microcomputer revolution.

This concentration in the commercializing—the bringing to market—innovations in electrical and electronic technology occurred worldwide. In the United States, the three companies that began to commercialize electric-based products in the 1890s, AT&T, General Electric (GE), and Westinghouse, continued to dominate electrical and electronics industries for decades. In the early 1920s, RCA was a joint venture of these three enterprises. In Europe, Siemens and Allegemeine Eleckric-täts Gellschaft (AEG), also formed in the 1890s, dominated their field. Their initial radio venture, Telefunken, was established even before RCA. During World War I, when Germany was cut off from world markets, Philips, a firm in neutral Holland that by 1900 had become Europe's third largest producer of electric light bulbs, began to compete with Telefunken. World War II hit Telefunken so hard it never recovered. After that war the Japanese leaders Matsushita and Sony built their global enterprises with products acquired from RCA, Philips, and AT&T.

As for computers, AT&T's Bell Laboratories began in 1952 to license the transistor on a worldwide basis, and the transistor soon replaced the vacuum tube as the computer's basic source of power. In the United States, Great Britain, and France, the leaders were the companies that combined the tube, and then the transistor, with the punched-card tabulator technology. In Germany and Japan, these leaders were descendants from their nation's leading industrial and electrical and telecommunications enterprises. All the Japanese computer companies received their initial electrical and communications technologies from AT&T, GE, Westinghouse, and Germany's Siemens.

Now to return to chapter 5. Margaret Graham begins that chapter describing the introduction of vacuum-tube technology, which freed the flow of information from wires and permitted it to go beyond words to provide information through sound and images. She then focuses on how the words and pictures of the new technology mobilized society by shaping public opinion in both peace and war, by enlarging consumer markets through advertising, and finally by defining an overall popular culture. This came about during two main time periods, the first between the world wars, after the advent of radio and talking films, and the second after World War II with the arrival of television.

The first period began with the formation of the Radio Corporation of America between 1919 and 1922. The corporation was created by Owen D. Young, the chief executive officer at GE, working with senior naval officers, to hold and administer "radio related patents." Its initial purpose was a military one—to assure U.S. control of the new ship-to-shore and ship-to-ship wireless technology. By the time the major patent holders had signed the final agreement, RCA had become a joint venture in which General Electric held 30.1 percent of its equity, Westinghouse 20.6 percent, AT&T 10.3 percent and United Fruit, a shipper of bananas, 4.1 percent. The just-created RCA was then suddenly overwhelmed by an unexpected flow of "radio related" patents.[5]

Even before the U.S. entry into World War I in 1917, hobbyists had been building crystal radio sets and communicating with one another, first by Morse code and then by voice. Their activities were much the same as the hobbyists in the mid-1970s who, by marketing kits for other hobbyists, initiated the microcomputer industry. In 1920 Westinghouse started operating the first licensed broadcasting station. By the end of 1922 there were 23 licensed stations, and by 1925 there were 566. Hundreds of firms making receivers were soon in business. At the same time the Justice Department, bombarded by complaints by new entrants, began an antitrust suit over RCA's controlling patents.

Between 1923 and 1927 David Sarnoff, RCA's aggressive young general manager, defined the initial structure of the new industry. He fashioned a license policy that satisfied the Department of Justice's Antitrust Division and the small competitors. RCA licensed its product at 7.5 percent of the whole value of a set. As a result of this "package licensing," royalties became a continuing source of RCA's income ($7.0 million in 1929).

In 1926 RCA's two major owners, GE and Westinghouse, completed their negotiations with the third, AT&T. The telephone company withdrew from broadcasting. In return, the historian, Hugh G. H. Aitken writes, "it would receive exclusive patent rights in the field of public service telephoning but would withdraw from broadcasting; while GE, Westinghouse, and RCA would enjoy exclusive rights in the fields of wireless telegraphy, entertainment broadcasting, and the manufacturing of radio tubes for public sale."

Sarnoff then merged the broadcasting stations received from AT&T with those that RCA owned (and would acquire) into a new enterprise, the National Broadcasting Company (NBC). He then divided NBC into two networks, the red to concentrate on commercial broadcasting, the blue on public service. In 1927, William Paley formed a competing network, Columbia Broadcasting System (CBS). In 1942, under pressure from the Federal Communications Commission (FCC), RCA sold off its blue unit, which became the American Broadcasting Company (ABC). The three remained for several decades the dominant national broadcasting networks.

After 1927 Sarnoff followed two paths to growth. One was to use the vacuum tube to develop high-fidelity recording and, in a joint venture with Hollywood producers, "talking" motion pictures. The second was to make RCA an integrated manufacturing enterprise independent of its owners, because under the 1926 agreement RCA only marketed radios and other equipment produced by General Electric and Westinghouse.

Sarnoff's first step was to convince those two companies to finance RCA's purchase of Victor Talking Machine Company, the U.S. pioneer in commercializing the phonograph. This purchase, besides bringing RCA into a closely related technology, provided it with a strong manufacturing and marketing base in Camden, New Jersey, and subsidiary ones in Japan, Canada, and Latin America.[6] In April 1930, GE and Westinghouse turned over their radio-related patents, personnel, and facilities in exchange for $6 million worth of RCA shares.

Three weeks later the government brought an antitrust suit against RCA that further propelled its independence by a consent decree in November 1930. The decree drastically reduced RCA's debts to GE and Westinghouse—debts resulting in good part from the acquisition of Victor. Both agreed to sell their equity holdings in RCA and not to compete in radio products for two and a half years.

By 1932 the now independent RCA and the radio industry were staggering through the Great Depression. Sales plummeted; radio receiver sales dropped from $842 million in 1929 to $300 million in 1934. RCA to remain solvent sold off its Canadian and Latin American (but not its Japanese) holdings that had come with Victor.

As economic recovery began in the mid-1930s, however, RCA was firmly established as the nation's only enterprise to operate successfully in several sectors of the consumer electronics industry. In radio receivers its major competitors were Philco, Zenith, Emerson, and Magnavox. In tubes and other components, Sylvania (which supplied Philco and Zenith) was the major competitor. In national broadcasting at that time it was just CBS. In motion pictures Radio Keith Orpheum (RKO) divided the sound equipment market with a subsidiary of Western Electric. Most important of all in terms of the future, RCA was leading the way in the development of television. In television RCA's base was the research unit that Westinghouse had transferred in 1930, headed by Vladimir K. Zworykin, the inventor of the basic electronic phototube. By 1932 he had sixty persons working under him in RCA's New York research laboratory.

Within this corporate framework Graham gives her detailed account of how that infrastructure was used to provide a mass medium for entertainment, to provide a national advertising medium for branded consumer products (one that supplemented the newspapers and magazines), and finally to mobilize the civilian society with the outbreak of global war. Together such societal mobilization created a definable mass culture. After the war this culture would be redefined by television—the technology that combined sound and images.

By the late 1930s television technology had been advanced enough for RCA to develop one model, and CBS (supported by Philco and Zenith), another. After a continuing battle between the two, the industry trade association in 1941 accepted the RCA standard. On July 10, 1941, NBC launched commercial telecasting. But five months later, with the Japanese attack on Pearl Harbor, the government banned commercial production of television equipment for the duration.

The coming of World War II delayed the introduction of television, but, as Graham emphasizes, it rapidly advanced the broader technology required for its commercialization. Wartime demands also profoundly transformed RCA and its competitors by bringing mass production of tubes and components and by moving the companies into production of military and industrial equipment.

With the war's end RCA turned quickly to capture the huge anticipated market for television. RCA's initial postwar move was to pin down the 1941 standard. In 1946 its management announced the firm's television technologies would be open to all. In June 1947, it invited its competitors to Camden to examine RCA's postwar product (selling at $345), and to take detailed blueprints with them.[7] This strategy worked. Television sales soared. RCA's market share of radio receiving sets dropped rapidly, but its income from licensing and tubes and other components took off. After the swift growth of hardware leveled off in the early 1950s, NBC's rising cashflow from telecasting maintained the firm's profits.

In the postwar years the industry's leaders concentrated on commercializing color TV. Again, the battle was between RCA and its competitors, led by CBS. The rivals developed contrasting types of receiving and broadcasting equipment for color. Once again RCA's standard, assisted in part by the closing down of such product development during the Korean War, was victorious in 1953.

But that victory did not assure commercial success. Much work was still to be done. RCA's competitors pulled out of the race, thus depriving the company of its income from licensing and components, but it continued (at high cost) to push on. In 1959 came its first profit from television. Zenith was the first competitor to return to color. It did so in 1961 by purchasing 500,000 RCA tubes on which RCA made a profit of $35 per tube. As the sole producer of the tricolor tube which it had recently developed and profiting from a strong pent-up demand for color—not only in television but also in motion pictures—during the 1960s RCA became one of the nation's largest industrial revenue producers (number 26), remaining the industry's dominant leader. At the same time a rapidly growing Japanese consumer-electronics industry, based in large part on licenses from RCA and those for AT&T's transistor, was becoming increasingly competitive.

From 1960 on, color television dominated electronic media for the projection of sound and images. Graham considers its impact on the existing media and then analyzes its role in the shaping of postwar popular culture, political processes, and other aspects of the role of the electronic media in the mobilizing of society.

Graham ends her chapter with a reference to the rapid transfer of RCA's technology to Japanese producers resulting from a 1957 consent decree with the U.S. Justice Department. Because that decree prohibited the use of package licensing in the domestic market, RCA focused on licensing its existing and new technology abroad, mainly to Japanese producers. At the same time it turned to markets other than those for consumer electronics.

As the Japanese were obtaining and perfecting the industry's basic technology, RCA's management embarked on a disastrous attempt to compete with IBM's System 360 mainframe computer and to diversify into unrelated products. It acquired a publishing company, a sporting goods chain, a car rental firm (Hertz), producers of frozen foods, and other enterprises.

By the mid-1970s, RCA's revenues were rapidly declining and its debts were soaring. In the early 1980s, a new management team sold off all its acquisitions, and finally in 1986 its consumer-electronics operation and NBC were sold to GE. General Electric in turn quickly sold the consumer electronics to France's Thomson Houston. The smaller producers of radio and television receivers and components had neither the scale, scope, or full line of consumer-electronics products necessary to compete in world markets. By the late 1980s, nearly all had been acquired by Matsushita, Sony, Sanyo, and Europe's Philips. Once the U.S. consumer-electronics industry had lost its RCA core, it collapsed quickly.

Chapters 6, 7, and 8 evaluate the role of the digital computer in bringing the Information Age into full flower. The authors agree on the chronology of three eras during which that role evolved: the "data-processing era" from the 1950s to the early 1980s, the "microcomputer era" from the early 1980s to the mid-1900s, and finally the "network era," beginning in 1995.

Just as RCA played a central role worldwide in providing the means of transmitting and receiving sound and images, reviewed in chapter 5, so did IBM lead in computer-based information, as covered in chapters 6 and 7. The IBM mainframe and its clones dominated world markets from the 1950s to the 1980s. IBM's "personal computers" (PCs) and its clones helped to assure continuing U.S. dominance in microcomputers after the mid-1980s.

The difference between RCA and IBM was, of course, that RCA self-destructed in the 1970s and so turned the industry over to the Japanese. IBM, after recovering from the impact of the personal-computer revolution which it did so much to create, remains today the world leader. In 1994 it was the nation's largest revenue producer in five of the seven major sectors of the computer industry. As table 1.1 shows, IBM led in large systems, midrange systems, peripherals, services, and software. Its software revenue was $11.5 billion as compared to Microsoft's $4.5 billion. IBM's revenues were a very close second to Sun Microsystems in workstations and to Compaq in PCs.[8]

As has been pointed out, the modern digital commercial data-processing computer was a marriage in the 1950s of the punched-card tabulating technology with that of the electronic tube and then the transistor. The U.S. companies that successfully made the transition from making computers for military and defense to producing them for the commercial market were the business-machine makers had had prewar experience or at least an awareness of punched-card tabulating technology. These were National Cash Register (NCR), Burroughs Adding Machine, Remington-Rand (merged with Sperry in 1955), and Honeywell. Since IBM accounted for nearly 90 percent of the punched-card tabulator market before World War II, IBM understandably jumped ahead of its competitors in the new computer industry.

As the world's leader in the production and marketing of punched-card equipment, IBM had perfected the essential capabilities needed to develop, manufacture, and sell data-processing equipment for business purposes. The new digital computers used much the same card readers, punches, and other peripheral equipment. Markets for these computers were much the same large information-intensive industries that relied on punched-card tabulators. In the early 1950s IBM enhanced its technical capabilities in electronics by increasing the number of its engineers and technicians from 500 to 5,000, and by hiring the chief scientist of the Office of Naval Research, Emmanuel ("Manny") R. Piore, to head its expanded research organization.

By 1960, IBM's revenues were twice the total of its U.S. competitors combined. By then it was producing seven different classes of "mainframes" (as these computers had become termed), ranging from more broadly based ones for corporate offices and high-powered, more narrowly focused ones for scientific purposes. These mainframes used different sets of processors, peripherals, and software and relied on outside suppliers for semiconductors and other inputs.

Thomas Watson Jr. succeeded his father as IBM's president in 1956. In December 1960 he and his senior managers decided to make the next generation of computers compatible with one another. That generation would be more than a set of new lines. It would be a system of compatible lines. The IBM System 360 would include five (later

Table 1.1 The Ten Leading American Computer Vendors in Each Industry Segment, 1994

Rank	Company	Estimated Revenues[a] ($ billions)	Rank	Company	Estimated Revenues[a] ($ billions)
Large Systems (Mainframe)			**Peripherals**		
1	IBM	5,956.8	1	IBM	8,583.0
2	Unisys[b]	1,243.2	2	Hewlett-Packard	6,336.0
3	Amdahl[c]	819.3	3	Seagate	3,465.0
4	Cray	571.4	4	Quantum	3,286.0
5	Intel	460.8	5	Xerox	3,126.8
6	Silicon Graphics	163.1	6	Conner Peripherals	2,352.0
7	Convex	76.4	7	Western Digital	1,900.0
8	Digital	40.5	8	Digital	1,620.0
9	Control Data	5.2	9	Lexmark [IBM]	1,215.0
			10	Storate Tek	1,121.2
Workstations			**PCs**		
1	Sun Microsystems	3,262.0	1	Compaq	9,018.8
2	IBM	3,206.6	2	IBM	8,775,1
3	Hewlett-Packard	2,880.0	3	Apple	7,161.8
4	Silicon Graphics	1,223.2	4	Dell	2,870.0
5	Digital	1,080.0	5	Gateway 2000	2,700.0
6	Intergraph	833.1	6	Packard Bell	2,600.0
7	Motorola	593.1	7	AST Research	2,311.0
8	Unisys	435.1	8	AT&AT [NCR]	1,718.9
9	Control Data	31.5	9	Digital	1,350.0
10	Data General	22.8	10	Hewlett-Packard	1,152.0
Mid-range Systems (Minicomputers)			**Software**		
1	IBM	5,764.7	1	IBM	11,529.4
2	AT&T [NCR]	5,042.0	2	Microsoft	4,464.0
3	Hewlett-Packard	2,688.0	3	Computer Associates	2,454.7
4	Tandem	1,538.9	4	Novell	1,901.6
5	Digital	1,174.5	5	Oracle	1,901.6
6	Motorola	616.8	6	Lockheed Martin	1,242.0
7	Data General	536.5	7	Digital	1,215.0
8	Sun Microsystems	534.8	8	AT&T [NCR]	916.7
9	Unisys	497.3	9	Lotus	873.6
10	Apple	477.5	10	Unisys	683.8

(continued)

Table 1.1 (*continued*)

Rank	Company	Estimated Revenues[a] ($ billions)	Rank	Company	Estimated Revenues[a] ($ billions)
Services					
1	IBM	16,563.5			
2	EDS	10,052.4			
3	Digital	6,345.0			
4	Hewlett-Packard	4,608.0			
5	Unisys	3,108.0			
6	Computer Sciences	3,085.0			
7	KPMG Peat Marwick	2,300.0			
8	Andersen Consulting	2,206.8			
9	Entex	1,300.0			
10	Deloitte & Touche	1,041.0			

Source: Compiled from "Datamation 100, 1995," *Datamation* (June 1, 1995): 47, 48, 57, 61, 62, 66. *Datamation* did not list semiconductors since they were used in many industries.

[a]Revenue figures represent worldwide revenues for each segment.
[b]Formed as a merger of Burroughs and Sperry-Rand in 1986.
[c]Fujitsu dominant stockholder.

six) new computing processors that would cover the overall market in terms of price and performance. They would all use the same input/output equipment, tapes, disk storage, terminals, and other peripherals. The power source would be a still untested transistor chip produced in a giant new plant. In addition, the products would have the same operating software and software applications. Since the company leased rather than sold computers (repeating the practice it had followed with punched cards), it provided regular service and repair. In addition, it would continue to supply computing services to customers who did not require the full-time use of one of its products. In other words, the IBM System 360 would incorporate within a single set of product lines much of the activity that was beginning to be carried on by a growing network of supporting suppliers and vendors.

In 1967 the System 360 began to appear in volume. Its arrival quickly defined the continuing mainframe path of learning, not only in the United States, but worldwide. In addition to the core competitors NCR, Burroughs, Remington-Rand, and Honeywell, two others—the nation's leaders in electronics, General Electric and RCA—went all-out to build similar systems. Both GE and RCA had the potential in terms of technical and managerial capabilities and the financial resources to attempt to produce a comparable line of products—a potential no other company in the world enjoyed at the time. Nevertheless, with IBM's announcement in 1970 of its next generation, the System 370, both gave up their attempts after investing an inordinate amount of time and expending massive funds in research and development. In RCA's case the cost was over half a billion dollars and a lost generation of research.

After the withdrawal of GE and RCA, the IBM System 360 and 370 became the worldwide standard for mainframe computers. The credit belongs to IBM's chief designer, Gene Amdahl. The announcement of the System 360 in 1964 turned the European computer makers, supported by their governments, to making technological alliances with IBM's U.S. competitors to produce comparable systems. The announcement of the System 370 was as great a shock to the four European and six Japanese computer makers as it was to GE and RCA. Several lost their technologically advanced U.S. partners. All understood more fully the challenges they faced. In response the Japanese Ministry of Trade and Industry (MITI) drew up a "New Series Project" that paired the industry's leaders to develop similar compatible systems. In Europe Philips (still primarily a consumer electronics producer), Siemens, and the French "national champion" CII formed Unidata to achieve the same goal.

In 1970 Gene Amdahl left IBM to start his own company to produce and sell the largest of the machines he had designed. Unable to raise the $40 million in venture capital he estimated as necessary, he contacted Fujitsu, Japan's most technologically advanced computer maker. Its management immediately responded with high enthusiasm. As Fujitsu's top manager told an assistant, if the proposal "goes well, it will be incredible!"[9]

It went very well. Fujitsu then raised the funds, primarily from the government, to acquire 20 percent of the equity of Amdahl's company. By 1974 Amdahl's Japanese factory was completed. By 1976 Fujitsu held 41 percent of its stock. Also in 1976, Fujitsu introduced its M-190, the first of an "M-series." It was a "one-to-one replacement" of the Amdahl 470-V6 which, in turn, was a one-to-one copy of the model 168 of IBM's System 370. By the end of the decade Hitachi and the NEC Corporation, as well as Fujitsu, were producing similar machines. They continued to enhance their product development and production capabilities in much the same manner as their compatriots were doing in consumer electronics, automobiles, and ships.

By 1975, the European Unidata project had collapsed. Germany's Siemens then turned to Fujitsu, asking to be supplied with its

M-series on an Original Equipment Manufacturing basis (OEM), that is, selling another company's product over its own name. By 1978 it was receiving the same M-190 IBM clone. In 1981 Fujitsu agreed to supply Great Britain's International Computers Limited (ICL) on much the same basis. Hitachi then did the same for Italy's Olivetti. The fourth European company, France's Machines Bull, made comparable arrangements in 1982 with NEC. Thus by the early 1980s Europe was getting its mainframe technologies from the United States via Japan.

At home during the late 1960s and early 1970s, two entrepreneurial start-ups became significant competitors to the IBM mainframes. Each developed its product line on the edges of IBM's System 360 line. The first start-up, William Norris's Control Data (CDC), introduced a supercomputer for scientists in 1966, but its market remained highly specialized and limited.

On the other hand, Kenneth Olsen's Digital Equipment Corporation (DEC) commercialized the first minicomputer and thus opened up a small but increasingly lucrative market. Olsen's high-powered PDP series, with no advanced technological peripherals and with customers supplying much of the software, sold at unprecedented low prices. In the early 1970s a small number of firms began to follow Olsen's lead in producing minicomputers. The most successful were Data General (established by Edson DeCastro, the designer of Olsen's PDP series), Hewlett-Packard, and IBM itself. By the early 1980s IBM's minicomputer revenues were larger than those of Digital.

The stream of IBM's System 360 and Digital's PDP series quickly broadened the data-processing infrastructure for the Information Age. Between 1968 and 1972 a burst of new enterprises appeared to meet the rapidly increasing demand for peripherals, packaged software, computer services, and, most important of all, chips.

The central role of chips in information processing is described by James W. Cortada in chapter 6. The initial chip manufacturers were not the large tube makers like RCA and Sylvania; instead they were small specialized firms that had acquired Bell Laboratories' transistor license. Another set of chip companies appeared a decade later to meet the demands of the late 1960s. The early set of small specialized firms included Texas Instruments (TI), makers of geodetic instruments used in the exploration for oil; Motorola, producers of car radios; and Fairchild Semiconductor, established in 1954 in Palo Alto by Gordon Moore and Robert Noyce, and others.

Of these three, Texas Instruments proved the most innovative. After receiving its license in 1952, TI signed a contract with AT&T to produce a transistor radio. It then led the way in developing silicon-based chips, becoming IBM's semiconductor supplier in 1959. That same year Jack Kilby, one of TI's engineers, patented the integrated chip that, by placing several transistors on a single silicon wafer, became the central power source for computers. TI then began to expand aggressively overseas.

Though less innovative, Motorola quickly followed TI in building a multinational enterprise with manufacturing facilities in Europe and Asia. By 1965 TI had fifteen operating plants in ten countries, and Motorola was not far behind. One missing market was Japan. Here TI negotiated with Sony from 1963 to 1968 and finally paid the price of entry into Japan by licensing its Kilby patent to all Japanese firms. On the basis of that patent, Japanese firms quickly moved forward in the volume production of semiconductors as they were already doing in consumer electronics.[10]

Fairchild was a highly innovative enterprise but far less financially successful than TI or Motorola. One of its partners, Robert Noyce, patented an integrated chip in 1959, the same year as Kilby did. Fairchild's problem was that it produced entrepreneurs not products. Gordon Moore, one of Fairchild's founders and director of its research, has written: "The fact that new ideas [from his unit] were spawning new companies rather than contributing to the growth of Fairchild was immensely frustrating."[11] So Moore, Noyce, and a younger man named Andrew Grove decided to leave Fairchild to form Intel. Grove had joined Fairchild in 1963 after receiving his Ph.D. from the University of California.

In 1967 and 1969 two other entrepreneurial firms, National Semiconductor and Advanced Micro Devices, began operations near Fairchild and Intel in what was becoming California's famous Silicon Valley. Since then, in the 1990s, these six—Intel, TI, Motorola, Fairchild, National Semiconductor, and Advanced Micro Devices—still dominate the U.S. production of chips for computers.

Although during the 1970s TI and Intel concentrated on Dynamic Random Access Memory (DRAM) chips primarily for mainframes (as did other U.S. firms), both companies pioneered in commercializing the microprocessor, the "computer on a chip" that so transformed the industry in the 1980s. During the 1970s, however, the new microprocessor was used primarily to improve the performances of machinery, appliances, automated assembly lines, and the like. By the end of the decade all the U.S. chip makers were suffering from the increasingly powerful Japanese competitors.

By the late 1970s the infrastructure of the "data-processing era," based on large computers used by business, government, education, and other institutions had been completed, as told by Cortada in chapter 6. Cortada describes in detail the creation of this infrastructure and its effect on the U.S. economy. After considering the impact of the transistor and the integrated chip and tracing the evolution of IBM's Systems 360 and 370, Cortada carries the story further in terms of the evolution of hardware and software, and the resulting increase in computing power and the types of information processed. He indicates the extent of the deployment of data-processing technology through the broad sectors of the economy (manufacturing, retailing, and financial services), and its impact on the nature and the composition of the nation's working force. He also calls our attention to the speed with which this deployment of computing technology occurred, demonstrating yet another example of America's appetite for useful technologies.

But the drama of the evolution of computing technology and its deployment continued. The data-processing era was completed only to be dramatically reshaped in the early 1980s by the unanticipated onslaught of the personal computer.

This event brought about the computer world as we know it today— a world of microcomputers (personal computers and workstations) powered by microprocessors and used by individuals, connected with each other through networks. In expediting the microcomputer revolution, IBM played as critical a role as it did in creating the large computers of the data-processing era in the 1950s and 1960s.

The personal computer (PC) era had been foreshadowed in 1977 when Apple, Commodore, and Tandy introduced the first commercial microcomputers, which quickly replaced the pioneering kits assembled by hobbyists for hobbyists. But the PC industry's explosive growth began with IBM's entry in 1980 when the laboratory director of the company's Entry Level Systems Unit, William C. Lowe, at the explicit direction of IBM's senior management, sent a task force to Boca Raton, Florida. His charge to the task force was to design a microcomputer, build a factory to produce it in volume, and create a national and worldwide marketing and advertising organization for the mass-produced consumer product—and all this was to be accomplished *within a year*.

To meet the assigned schedule, the new computer would have an "open architecture," not protected by patents as were those of its competitors. Peripherals were to be purchased from sources that could supply the equipment immediately in volumes needed for mass production. Software was to be developed separately from the central processing unit. For their processor the Boca Raton team chose a low-powered 8-bit Intel chip. For its operating system the task force's managers chose Gary Kildall, who had written what was by 1981 the dominant operating system for microcomputers. When Kildall refused to sign a nondisclosure agreement, they turned to William Gates, whose enterprise in Seattle was producing a version of the programming language BASIC for microcomputers but had not yet built an operating system.

IBM's Boca Raton team completed the product on schedule. By autumn 1981 the mass-production facilities were complete. By then the managers had signed contracts with retailing chains, including ComputerLand and Sears Business Centers, and built a national (later international) marketing unit to support a network of franchise dealers. In 1982, the first year of full production, IBM's microcomputer revenues were $500 million. In 1985, the fourth year of full production, revenues had soared to $5.5 billion, a record of revenue growth unsurpassed in industrial history.

Consider the profound, but largely unintended and certainly unexpected, consequences of the Boca Raton venture.

First, it revealed a mass consumer market for computers. Hitherto the market had been institutional—corporations, government offices, universities, research laboratories, and the like.

Second, by making its PC an open system, IBM created an unprecedented opportunity for both existing and start-up companies to enter this new market, an opportunity denied by Apple and the other existing proprietary systems. The clones indeed poured in. As *Business Week* reported in July 1986, "Now more than 200 clone suppliers using the same software and working with the same hardware" were challenging the standard's progenitor.[12] IBM's entry into the microcomputer business profoundly changed the structure of the computer industry in barely five years.

Third, because the development of the chip and the operating system were so intimately connected—one could not be created without the other—Intel and Microsoft had received the franchise to produce for this new unexpected multi-billion-dollar market. They quickly became the microcomputer industry's two major players. By the early 1990s their near monopolistic position provided them with far greater funding for continuing research and development than any of their competitors.

Fourth, the swift proliferation of desktop computers created a demand for new types of packaged software written for individuals in offices and also at home rather than for corporate information technology managers. First came spreadsheets, designed by VisiCalc and Lotus, then database management systems, graphic word processing, and other types of application software offered by such firms as Oracle, Computer Associates, and Borland. Software for personal computers became the industry's fastest-growing sector. By the 1990s, it had become a major U.S. industry by itself, with some vendors' stock values (but certainly not revenues) exceeding venerable U.S. manufacturers (e.g., Microsoft over General Motors).

Fifth, the sudden appearance of personal computers on a multitude of desks within corporations and other institutions demanded creation of internal enterprise networks to connect individuals within and between operating units. As early as 1983 start-ups Novell and 3Com were providing software for what had become termed the local area networks (LANs). Others soon followed.

Sixth, because the personal-computer industry was not created in the normal evolutionary manner, with the successful pioneers developing their proprietary systems, these new and unexpected demands led to a burst of entrepreneurial start-ups in the United States. This did not occur elsewhere. Foreign competitors, primarily Japanese, were quickly left behind. From its start, U.S. firms dominated the microcomputer industry worldwide.

During the mid-1980s the entrepreneurial start-ups in personal computers were IBM clones—Dell, Gateway 2000, Packard Bell, and AST Research had begun as innovators in marketing rather than technology. In 1994 the leading producers of PCs were Compaq (the first successful IBM clone, which shipped its first production in 1983), IBM itself, and Apple (the one remaining producer with a proprietary operating system), followed by the four marketing pioneers (see Table 1.1). In peripherals the largest revenue producers included two 1980 start-ups, Quantum and Conner, while Hewlett-Packard became one of the world leaders. Indeed by 1994, Hewlett-Packard was a major player in five of the industry's sectors, excluding large systems and software. In chips, however, Intel became and remained the ruling firm. In 1994, of the worldwide production of microprocessors by U.S. makers, Intel had 74 percent, Motorola (then working with IBM) 12 percent, Advanced Micro Devices (IBM's second source for IBM Boca Raton venture) 7 percent, and Texas Instruments 3 percent.

Because IBM's clones dominated the PC market, Microsoft's operating system (powered by Intel chips) controlled the gateway to application software development. Gates quickly used that advantage to attack aggressively Lotus, Oracle, Computer Associates, Borland, and Novell, and other new producers of applications and networking software. By 1994 approximately 63 percent of Microsoft's income came from application software, 34 percent from operating systems, and 4 percent from hardware. As the Information Age came into its own, U.S. firms accounted for 87 percent of packaged PC software worldwide. In Japan, U.S. vendors accounted for 50 percent of the application software and Microsoft provided 70 percent of the operating systems.

Nevertheless, the Intel/Microsoft combination of chip and operating system did not completely dominate the new microprocessor industry, for during the 1980s the PC had increasing competition from the workstation using a different combination. By the mid-1980s the makers of minicomputers—IBM, Hewlett-Packard, Digital, Apollo (which emerged from the earlier out of Prime Computer, Inc.), and the innovative start-up Sun Microsystems—used proprietary RISC (Reduced Instruction Set Computing) microprocessors and UNIX operating systems (initially developed by AT&T) to manufacture workstations that met the needs of their existing customers in engineering and scientific fields. Their success lay in developing a highly effective intra-enterprise network technology by which high-powered "servers" stored information and then transmitted it on call to "clients" (desktop computers) to be analyzed and manipulated in order to obtain the information required. In 1993 Gates moved Microsoft into the workstation market with his Windows NT. At the same time Microsoft was challenging Novell's much improved NetWare file/server for PC local and wide area networking.

By the early 1990s most major U.S. companies were using one network technology or the other—or a combination of them—to build their own intra-enterprise networks, or intranets. At the same time they were beginning to tie their intranets to the growing external Internet. Richard Nolan, in chapter 7, provides an excellent brief review of the Internet's evolution from the government's Advanced Research Project Network, the ARPANET. This was first used by government agencies and universities to communicate with one another and then by corporations, interest groups, and other associations to do the same.

However, to connect enterprise intranets with those of other enterprises and with the larger Internet required the development of a specialized hardware and software, the router and the browser. With that connection the Information Age had arrived.

Cisco, a company formed in 1984, introduced in 1986 the router, a selector of the most effective routes for data to flow from one network to another. Cisco's initial markets for these routers were universities and research centers and other groups using the ARPANET. By 1988 its major customers had become mainstream corporations that communicated internally through private local and wide area intranets. As the pioneer, Cisco continued to enjoy 50 percent of that market through 1994.

The final step uniting the intranets to the internet was Mosaic, the initial "browser" software, written at the University of Illinois, Champaign–Urbana, for expediting the connecting of the intranets and the Internet. In 1994 the university licensed Mark Andreesen, one of its creators, who formed Netscape. Its Navigator software became the dominating browser for the World Wide Web, whose initial code for the public Internet was written in 1990. At the same time, another one of Mosaic's creators formed Spyglass, whose license was acquired by Microsoft in 1995 and then bundled free of charge as Internet Explorer with Windows 95. As versions of Mosaic software came on stream, Cisco's income from its hardware and services shot up from $650 million in 1993 to $2 billion in 1995.

In chapter 7, "Information Technology Management, 1960–2000" Richard Nolan focuses on the changes in IT management in business enterprises from the data-processing era through the microcomputer revolution and then to the challenges IT managers face with the coming of the network era in 1995. Nolan does this by relating the firms' IT architecture to corporate organizational structure.

Nolan first considers how the budgeting and managing techniques developed in the data-processing era reflected the needs of large vertically integrated, multidivisional enterprises. Next he reviews how these needs were transformed by the impact of the explosion of information that accompanied the coming of the personal computer, considers the tensions that this created for data-processing managers, the resulting shaping of IT management, and the coming of new benchmarks for organizational performance. Finally the chapter considers the challenges for IT management caused by the marriage of intranets and the Internet "to coordinate the thousands of computers that made up their internal networks, as well as tens of thousands of computers with which the organizations communicated through various connections with other Intranets of suppliers and customers and the overall Internet." Nolan then describes and evaluates the resulting impact on the enterprises' working forces, on their methods of resource allocation and management, and on other business and managerial concerns.

In chapter 8, "Computers in U.S. Households, 1977–1997," Lee Sproull reviews the evolution of the home computer "from a sociological point of view." The computer, of course, appeared in the household only after the coming of the personal computer. Sproull divides the ensuing evolution into three periods.

The first period, from 1977 to 1984, was one of standing machines, acquired primarily for two purposes, entertainment (games and hobbies) and self-improvement, both educational and for home office work using VisiCalc spreadsheets. The second period began in 1984, as the output of personal computers soared, and continued until 1994. In that ten years the household machines became connected with a variety of databases such as airline schedules, news wires, financial services, entertainment, and self-education. Because the home computers were unable to store much data in permanent form, "on-line service companies" were formed to provide that access via a modem and a telephone call with charges paid for each call. Although such firms as Prodigy, Delphi, and America Online began operations in the 1980s, they had limited use until the late 1980s when the ARPANET was turning into the Internet. Sproul's third period began when the router and browser, by linking the Internet to other networks, marked the arrival of the full-fledged Information Age.

After covering the chronological development of the home computer, Sproull reviews its impact on society in terms of social status, gender, income, and race. She considers its impact on children and family dynamics, on the changing boundaries between the household and office, between home and markets (including on-line purchasing transactions), and those between home and government, and then the differences between rural, suburban, and inner-city dwellers in the defining of these boundaries. Particularly intriguing is Sproull's analysis of the role of the home computer in changing family and personal relationships, in bringing individuals and interest groups to communicate with each other via the Usenet, and later the Internet—including communication between people who have never met face to face. As the chapter ends, "One of the most amazing features of the *information revolution* has been its character as a *people's revolution*, once the household computer went on-line."

But let us begin the story with the Colonial Period, because it is in this era that some of the fundamentals of the American experience started late in the Commercial Age.

2

Early American Origins
of the Information Age

Richard D. Brown

The Ancien Régime of Information Diffusion
in the British Colonies

During the nineteenth century a dynamic, innovative information culture emerged in the United States, one in which the production of print and oratory, and systems for their diffusion, came to set the pace for much of the world. In global terms this was an astonishing development, especially in light of the condition of British North America during the Colonial Period. Colonial society had been by European standards relatively crude, even backward: its population was thinly spread in a vast landscape, and there was a general scarcity of social and economic infrastructures and the capital to develop them. Information and transportation infrastructures were only beginning to grow, and they lagged far behind Britain. Whether one counts printing presses and associated industries such as papermaking, typefounding, and bookbinding, or libraries, roads, and canals, the American colonies were a raw, frontier society when measured against England. Indeed, colonists relied more on the British information infrastructure than on anything their own settlements could muster for much of the eighteenth century. The American starting point was not especially promising.[1]

It is true that Europe's most advanced information technology came early to the colonies. The Puritan stronghold, Massachusetts-Bay, imported a press into Cambridge in 1638, and thereafter sponsored a printer. But the purpose of this government-controlled press was limited to printing the laws of the colony, such religious works as the leading magistrates and clergymen thought necessary, and job-printing for the government and Harvard College. Almost forty years would pass before a commercial press was allowed to operate in Boston, and even then it produced only a handful of titles in its brief existence. By 1700 a couple of presses were at work in Massachusetts, as in Connecticut, but the output was meager. The only other colonial presses were located in New York and Philadelphia, which each had a single press that subsisted chiefly on government jobs.[2]

The significance of these early presses is not that they show the American information revolution in its infancy, but precisely the reverse—they show the power and pervasiveness of European tradition. Not only did colonists import many more printed pages than these presses ever produced, these one-man shops were emblematic in that they eked out their survival within the restrictive censorship policies of the mother country and Europe in general. Parliament required that all publications be submitted in advance to the government censor before they could be licensed for printing. After this legislation lapsed in 1695, prior censorship ended and the English (and colonial) press became "free," but laws against seditious and blasphemous libel remained in force and served as significant restraints on publication. Newspapers, whose continuous publication began in Boston in 1704, would continue to require government approval until 1720. Together, economic and political constraints inhibited the development of colonial printing although, as commerce grew, printing gradually became established in all the colonies and would, by the time of independence, supply a substantial infrastructure of experienced personnel and distribution networks.[3]

The initial purpose and function of printing in the colonies was, after all, to reinforce the top-down model of information diffusion that was characteristic of seventeenth-and eighteenth-century societies. Printed goods were scarce and expensive commodities, almost always intended to serve the needs of magistrates, merchants, and the learned professions, as well as the pleasures of the gentry. Popular imprints never supported a colonial press, but by the mid-eighteenth century almanacs in particular were a staple for printers and laid a foundation for popular secular reading distinct from devotional and prayer books. Although the objectives of printing were defined by the elites who sponsored and supported print shops in the colonies as in Britain, the press did come to have a lively popular dimension.

This was much less true for most colonial information systems. The men who conducted the public affairs of the colonies, and who ran their religious and educational establishments, all assumed that most information whether it concerned transatlantic events or the cultures of science, letters, and theology, was properly confined to the better sort. Magistrates and clergymen, and even the press, diffused information discreetly, as needed, for purposes of governance and piety. The most well-informed men in the colonies, whether Boston's Samuel Sewall at the turn of the eighteenth century or Virginia's William Byrd a generation later, saw no reason why cosmopolitan information and learning should be widely accessible.[4]

The restrictive character of information systems is manifest in the newspapers, which were the broadest, most nearly popular disseminators of information of the era. Their circulations were limited to a range of 600 to 2,000 subscribers, and until 1750, most colonies had no more than one or two papers in operation at any one time. On their two- or four-page weekly (later biweekly) sheets, they included news of court politics, European warfare and diplomacy, British and colonial statutes, and transatlantic and coastal commerce, in addition to shipping notices and advertisements. This was as close as colonial America came to mass communications—and it was not very close. With subscriptions costing several pounds per year (more than the average man's monthly wage), and with timely circulation limited to the environs of the ports and capitals where the newspapers were printed, the audience was limited. At least 80 percent of the colonial population saw newspapers seldom or intermittently. The gradual pace of newspaper growth suggests that only presses that were oriented toward an elite mercantile audience could succeed.[5]

Colonial education moderated this restrictive approach to information only slightly. Most instruction, whether tax-supported in New England or tuition-based in the other colonies, aimed only at the literacy and numeracy that were required for Christian piety and managing a farm or a craft. Grammar schools and academies sought to educate the few who aspired to gentry status and to attend college—inasmuch as advanced learning, algebra, Latin, history, and natural philosophy (science) was linked to political leadership and the learned professions. When colonies sponsored colleges, as over half did before independence (Massachusetts, Virginia, Connecticut, New York, Pennsylvania, New Jersey, and Rhode Island), the purpose was to supply a locally trained leadership cadre, not to discover or disseminate information more broadly.[6]

The single potentially revolutionary element of the colonial information infrastructure was the widespread, institutionalized Protestant belief in the importance of literacy for individual piety, conversion, and salvation. Owing to this commitment, European settlers in colonial America—British, German, and French alike—were more widely literate than the peoples of France or Germany, and at least as literate as those of Great Britain. Although the inhabitants of the southern colonies lagged those of the north, and although female literacy rates trailed male rates everywhere, colonial literacy after 1760 exceeded 75 percent. In New England overall literacy approached 90 percent on the eve of independence—higher than England or Wales, and comparable to Presbyterian Scotland.[7] This broad-based literacy supplied a human social and cultural infrastructure of people who were technically and psychologically prepared to move beyond the informational status quo of colonial society.

Revolutionary Foundations

The pace of growth for information-related activities in the colonies was arithmetic, and correlated with the increasing population, territory under settlement, and acres cultivated until the 1760s when the Revolutionary era began. Then, and only then, did Americans begin to lay the foundations for the Information Age, ideologically and institutionally. But this outcome was more the secondary by-product of political conflict than it was intentional. In the early stages of opposition to British measures, the men who would later be called "revolutionaries"—Samuel and John Adams, Benjamin Franklin, Patrick Henry, and George Washington—wanted nothing more than to preserve the status quo. It was only as a part of their efforts to block English alterations of that status quo that they turned to mobilizing the "people" through their aggressive use of information and ideology, what some have called "propaganda." Information had nothing—and everything—to do with the imperial crisis of the 1760s and 1770s.[8]

The ideas that underlay this remarkable turn of events had grown out of seventeenth-century English political strife. During the mid-century Civil War and Commonwealth period, republicans such as John Milton had advocated the public necessity of free speech in order that the public good could be defined truly, according to principles of reason and justice rather than selfishness and prejudice. Expressing the soaring confidence in reason that would later characterize the Enlightenment, Milton proclaimed: "So Truth be in the field. . . . Let her and Falsehood grapple; whoever knew Truth put to the worse in a free and open encounter?" Milton joined this faith in the necessity of free speech to a belief that "the common people" should be informed. No matter if there was controversy and conflict, he said, since "knowledge thrives by exercise." In Milton's view, only "popish places," homes to the "most tyrannous inquisition," made popular ignorance their policy.[9]

Fifty years later a policy resembling Milton's rhetoric became embedded in English politics owing to the Glorious Revolution, the passage of the Bill of Rights, and the termination of official censorship through the expiration in 1695 of the licensing act. After generations of deadly conflict, Britain's acceptance of religious toleration and parliamentary competition gave free speech a vitality and prominence in everyday public affairs.[10] Though few shared Milton's enthusiasm for controversy as a sign of healthy inquiry, Britain supported a multitude of controversialists in an era when the London and provincial press and pamphleteers enjoyed a golden age of activity.

Colonists took their cue from British public affairs, both because the empire required that they conform to English law, and because England was their cultural as well as commercial metropolis. All colonies were now required to practice religious toleration, and the same principles of free speech that prevailed "at home" belonged to the colonies. The idea that the public good required an informed citizenry had some critics, but it became a routine convention of British public life without much fanfare. After all, an informed citizenry normally referred only to the 5 to 10 percent of English men who were freeholders qualified to vote for parliament. Its impact on ordinary politics was slight, and reinforced the status quo. Although the idea of an informed citizenry could have been viewed in a more inclusive manner during the first half of the eighteenth century, practically no one chose to do so, and none did who were highly placed politically. But this complacent outlook toward free speech and an informed citizenry changed swiftly during the 1760s. As certain opposition leaders in both Britain and the colonies turned to the people for support and sought to mobilize them with newspaper and pamphlet information as well as public speech, the idea of an informed citizenry took on radical, even revolutionary, implications.

In the American colonies the transition began to appear in 1764 and 1765. Heretofore, when colonial leaders opposed British measures, they sought adjustments or repeal through private letters to well-placed English allies or, at most, through a letter from the legislature to the relevant officials at Whitehall. Sometimes this worked, sometimes not; but the people at large were not encouraged to protest. With rare exceptions, colonial householders were spectators to an imperial politics that belonged to elite cadres of planters, merchants, and magistrates.

In 1764 Boston merchants broke out of this convention by leading the Boston Town Meeting, a popular local assembly, to vote protest resolutions against Parliament's Revenue Act.[11] A year later the merchants, planters, and printers in many colonies would call on all freemen to protest and to nullify the Stamp Act. In retrospect this first attempt to inform and mobilize the colonial citizenry at large was a momentous event.[12] Almost simultaneously British radicals made the case of John Wilkes a cause célèbre for mobilizing the unfranchised London masses, because Parliament had convicted Wilkes of printing seditious libels and nullified his election to the House of Commons.[13] On both sides of the Atlantic, activists energized by radical whig or republican ideology engaged common people in public affairs. An ancien régime, buttressed by statutory franchise restrictions, the unreformed Parliament, and entrenched class politics, blocked British radicals; in contrast, in America high levels of property-holding, enfranchisement, and literacy among white men created a politics conducive to change. In Britain, Wilkes's supporters' only recourse was street demonstrations—and they failed to gain their objective. In America the men who mobilized the many on behalf of colonial rights took over one legislature after another, winning control of provincial and local government. In Britain the movement to extend the boundaries of the informed citizenry beyond gentlemen freeholders was hotly contested until 1832 and after; in the colonies property was so widely distributed that the old statutory restriction of a 40-shilling freehold had already enfranchised a majority of household heads by 1750.

The political logic of the imperial conflict powerfully intensified the drive to inform Americans. Although friends of Parliamentary policy, as supporters of top-down government, did not believe in mobilizing popular engagement in politics, their patriot opposition did. Proponents of colonial rights could only succeed by mobilizing the many to obstruct the new laws. Consequently the rhetoric of colonial rights and citizen activism overwhelmed administration apologias in the press.

One of the most significant landmarks for the activation of informed citizens was the 1767–1768 series of newspaper articles (later consolidated into a pamphlet) entitled *Letters from a Farmer in Pennsylvania to the Inhabitants of the British Colonies*. Published serially in twenty newspapers up and down the Atlantic seaboard and reprinted seven times as a pamphlet, this was the most popular political treatise that had ever been published in the colonies and perhaps in the English-speaking world. The author was a learned Delaware attorney and gentleman farmer, John Dickinson, who argued that the empire had been just fine before the recent Parliamentary meddling, and would be so again if Britain would recognize that since the colonists were not represented in Parliament, only their own legislatures (as well as towns or parishes) could properly tax them. As author, Dickinson portrayed himself as a genteel informed citizen who used his leisure to read history and law. He was a model with whom thousands could identify, and from whom tens of thousands took instruction.[14]

Four years later, in 1772, the colonists passed another milestone when the town of Boston created a Committee of Correspondence as an agency to organize a public information network in Massachusetts. The immediate issue that prompted this innovation (opposition to a Crown takeover of judges' salaries from the legislature) was much less important for the Revolution than the response it elicited. Led by Samuel Adams, James Otis, and Joseph Warren, three experienced debaters, the Boston Committee of Correspondence drafted a pamphlet and a covering letter to circularize the province's 260 towns and districts, instructing them in current politics and inviting each to express its views publicly. No such public effort had ever been attempted anywhere before, so when dozens, scores, and, over the ensuing months, a total of over 140 towns responded, it was evident that the commitment to an informed citizenry was widespread and concrete.[15] In scores of towns, community leaders had read the "Boston pamphlet" aloud to the inhabitants, who had then discussed and debated whether and how to respond. And if they chose to reply (as most did), a local committee was selected to draft the town's response, which was then read publicly and voted upon. In summary, the process initiated by the Boston Committee of Correspondence constituted a short (and partisan) course in imperial politics for the majority of Massachusetts voters, demonstrating that they could and should be politically informed.

Publishing these town political pronouncements in the newspapers magnified the lesson of informed political engagement throughout New England and beyond. Moreover, even though the region was more literate than others, the responsiveness of its people was not exceptional. Three years later the householders of the middle and southern colonies demonstrated that they, too, envisioned themselves as active political participants by embracing Thomas Paine's pamphlet *Common Sense*, published anonymously.

The American response to *Common Sense* was the single most important manifestation of the communication revolution of late eighteenth-century America. Before 1776 was over, Thomas Paine's pamphlet was published in nineteenth American editions and achieved a circulation exceeding 100,000 copies in a country that possessed no more than 500,000 households.[16] There was no precedent for such massive popularity for a tract, not in America, not Britain, not the Continent.

Paine's direct, pungent, uninhibited diction—familiar enough to readers of London polemics—was new to American political discourse, and it ignited enthusiasm in the shops of craftsmen, at the hearths of farmers, and in the taverns where men of all ranks congregated. The sedate prose of John Dickinson and the spare style of the Boston Committee of Correspondence pamphlet paled beside Paine's angry and sarcastic rhetoric. Moreover, the timing of *Common Sense*, which circulated just after news of the King's proclamation of the colonies' rebellion and Parliament's prohibition on American trade, gave the argument for independence an irresistible pertinence for contemporaries.

But however necessary the style and relevance of *Common Sense* was for its broad appeal, its success also rested on a communication infrastructure that would produce and disseminate tens of thousands of pamphlets swiftly, and on the fact that the mentality of Americans led them to demand personal copies of Paine's work. The gradual growth of a decentralized colonial press—at least one in each colony—and its attendant distribution networks, as well as the conviction that citizens must be politically informed so as to defend their rights and interests, created the conditions that permitted the publishing phenomenon that was *Common Sense*. Such an episode would not be repeated, but the fact that it did occur awakened a new sense of the possibilities of information politics in a society where every free man, and more than a few women and youth as well, might be included in the circle of the politically informed.

So long as the Revolutionaries concentrated their efforts on opposing the expansion of British power—what they called "tyranny"—they emphasized their rights as Englishmen and later their rights according to natural law. The foundation of the mobilization of the many, whether by the press, by committees, or by popular demonstrations invariably rested on the rights and liberties that the people were said to possess. But once Americans declared independence and began to construct state governments to sustain their resistance and to provide order, their political discourse became more complicated. Now, together with the rights of citizens, they began to articulate notions of citizens' responsibilities. Whereas the rhetoric of rights had strong popular and grassroots appeal, the discourse of civic responsibility came from elite gentlemen, often public officials.

It was a citizen's duty to be informed, American leaders argued, both in order to select wise governors and to assure that officials and governments remained within their legal and constitutional boundaries. Because corruption naturally infected all governments, even their own, only the continuous vigilance of an informed citizenry could protect liberty. The preservation of hard-won rights depended on the responsibility of citizens to be alert and informed defenders of those rights. Though this doctrine long predated the Revolution, it was never before so salient in public affairs. With this objective of an informed citizenry in view, the new state constitutions encouraged information development by their declarations in favor of free speech and press and by making provisions for schools and universities.[17]

At the moment of Revolutionary climax in 1776 the Massachusetts provincial congress declared that "a government so popular can be supported only by universal knowledge and virtue, in the body of the people," and therefore it was "the duty of all ranks to promote the means of education."[18] Soon after, Pennsylvania and North Carolina promoted public schools and universities with explicit provisions in their new constitutions.[19] The value of developing an informed population and the infrastructure necessary to sustain it was universally acknowledged by Revolutionary leaders who, as early as 1775, had created an American postal system on the foundation of the royal colonial service.[20]

But in light of the military crisis and the fragility of public finance during the war, governments confined themselves to encouragement and exhortation rather than expenditures. They guaranteed a free press and they granted school and university charters. Thomas Jefferson drafted a "Bill for the More General Diffusion of Knowledge" for Virginia (introduced in 1779), and John Adams wrote a provision for the Massachusetts Constitution (1780) that sought to develop a mixed infrastructure of "private societies and public institutions"—including the university, seminaries, schools, and other agencies—all with the ultimate objective of assuring that "the body of the people" would be informed and instructed.[21] In the 1780s the United States Congress itself moved hesitantly in the same direction, not by revamping or expanding the post office or by creating a national university, but by using its vast landholdings in the Northwest to subsidize local public schools in the region.

Developing a National Information Marketplace

The reorganization of government dictated by the Constitution (1787) profoundly shaped information-related activities and institutions from the 1790s onward. While the ideological commitment to an informed citizenry remained true to its formation during the Revolutionary era, the geopolitical and institutional character of the United States moved toward a new sort of national integration. In place of the old imperial system, which had integrated colony government and administration more with Britain than between and among the colonies, and in place of the wartime Articles of Confederation government that allied the individual states, the new constitutional government actively developed a national political infrastructure and administration. Still, individual states remained powerful and centralization came slowly and incompletely in many areas of government, but politics after 1789 created a national marketplace and a variety of associated institutions—such as national political parties, a national press, and an expanding transportation and postal infrastructure. Internal American communications, heretofore secondary to transatlantic exchange, now became crucial for American politics and economy.

But unlike the former mother country or America's great wartime ally, France, the United States possessed no metropolitan center. No London or Paris dominated the political, economic, and information infrastructure of the new nation. Instead, along with the national capital (which moved from New York City to Philadelphia in 1791, and a decade later to the new federal city of Washington), a polycentric array of state capitals and commercial centers all required presses, as well as timely access to long-distance news. The decentralized character of the United States' political structure, a decentralization that increased with the repeated addition of new states—Vermont in 1791, Kentucky in 1792, Tennessee in 1796, and Ohio in 1801—created a structural imperative for a competitive information marketplace. No one center could achieve dominance; no one organization, not even the United States Post Office, possessed an unchallenged monopoly status.[22]

The information marketplace that took shape was remarkably complex, with competition operating on at least four levels. First, there was the partisan competition of political parties and their newspapers, most prominently Federalist and Antifederalist during the ratification of the Constitution, later Federalist and Jeffersonian, and then Whig versus Jacksonian. Second, there was competition among political and commercial centers such as New York, Philadelphia, Boston, Baltimore, and later Washington, D.C. Third, there were voluntary associations, political, cultural, and reformist. Finally, there was the competition among entrepreneurs, printers and publishers, and proprietors of circulating libraries. Because of the ever-increasing size of the United States, its political structure, and its numerous ports and river systems, the most the national government could do was provide ground rules and some subsidies in an ongoing competition among information centers and agencies.

Competition became a leading characteristic of the American information system. Not one major printing center emerged as a consequence of national union; there were at least three—Philadelphia, New York, and Boston, joined later by Washington, D.C., and Cincinnati. In every state, government contracts helped to sustain the publishing industry, and by the 1830s presses in scores of countries—north, south, and west—were issuing newspapers, pamphlets, and books. Ever-expanding markets nurtured this competition and gave the information system its vitality.

From 1776 to 1860 high birthrates and growing immigration were doubling the size of the U.S. population every generation. Because people widely believed that republican government required an informed citizenry, they scrambled to make sure that they, and often their neighbors, were properly informed. In a land of numerous political and economic (as well as ethnic and religious) constituencies—often scattered across a broad landscape—competition for political and cultural influence assured that markets would expand. Bottom-up demand for improving and entertaining print and public speech combined with top-down efforts to instruct, indoctrinate, and proselytize, so as to support a vast postal system under national auspices, as well as a transportation infrastructure of roads, canals and, after 1830, railroads.[23]

Except for the national postal system, the role of government in creating this cornucopia of information production and dissemination was primarily indirect and enabling, rather than active or prescriptive. So far as public policy was concerned, nonprofit religious ventures like the vast publication and distribution efforts of the American Tract Society and the American Bible Society were no different from either the secular marketing of *Davy Crockett Almanacs* and the *Works of William Shakespeare* or the unfettered dissemination of political information in electoral campaigns.[24] The connection between liberty and the free flow of information was asserted so often and so broadly in American public life that the commitment to democracy included the culture of informed citizens.

Nevertheless, notwithstanding the First Amendment's guarantee that Congress should make no law "abridging the freedom of speech or of the press," Americans could be restrictive when free speech seemed to pose a threat to the security of society and its institutions. While there are many examples of the suppression of free speech and press in localities and states, sometimes by law and sometimes by vigilante violence, at the national level two events—the Sedition Act of 1798 and the 1835 blockage of the abolitionists' postal campaign—illustrate the boundaries that national officials could impose on the free traffic in information. In the first case a partisan congressional majority of Federalists sought to repress their Jeffersonian opposition in time of war; their temporary policy of prosecuting newspaper editors expired just as the Federalists were leaving office in 1801.[25]

In the second case, President Andrew Jackson's postmaster general acted to prohibit abolition newspapers, periodicals, and tracts from entering slaveholding states via the United States postal system. Inaugurating a policy that would endure until the Civil War, Amos Kendall, a member of the president's cabinet who had sworn to uphold the laws and Constitution of the United States, publicly set law aside and, with President Jackson's blessing, declared that in exceptional circumstances federal officials had a "higher" responsibility to local communities than to national law.[26] Congress, which might have reprimanded Kendall or even impeached Jackson over the issue had this repressive policy not been so popular, gave its silent assent, and in the national election the following year, Jackson's party and the cause of anti-abolition triumphed. When the new Congress met in 1837 it in effect extended the postal ban to the floor of Congress by instituting the "Gag rule," which forbade members from reading publicly the abolition petitions of their constituents. No matter how rational and eloquent the speeches of Congressman John Quincy Adams on the subject, when it came to slavery, free speech was too subversive for national protection.[27] Congress and successive administrations, Whig as well as Democrat, believed that Americans must be politically informed—but not on the subject of slavery and abolition. This restriction on information was national policy.

But although abolitionists were everywhere in the minority and suffered mob attacks from time to time, in the free states no court or legislature acted to enforce any national gag rule. The decentralized character of U.S. institutions meant that even when there was a disposition to curb free speech, it was next to impossible to do so on a national scale. The culture of civil society became so widely developed in the decades after 1790, with so many voluntary associations patronizing so many printers, that virtually every voice, popular or not, found a public outlet for advocacy.[28]

Beyond the particular question of free speech for potentially subversive political and religious views, there were real differences concerning information policy more broadly. Democrats, for example, maintained a laissez-faire approach in which the marketplace, states, and individuals exercised responsibility. Whigs, in contrast, used public resources to promote an informed citizenry and the institutions to sustain it. In the states Whigs advocated tax-supported, tuition-free public schools from the 1830s onward. In the Northeast and the Great Lakes states Whigs scored their greatest successes, where their civic and economic arguments for developing an informed citizenry won majority support.[29] When the Republican party took control of the national government in 1861 and most of their Southern opposition seceded, Republicans went on to pass the Morrill Act (1862), which used public lands to subsidize agricultural and mechanical colleges in every state.

Republicans, like Whigs and Federalists before them, wanted the whole body of citizens educated and informed. Experience showed that when this mission was left to the private responsibility of individuals, too many of the poor and near poor saw education as a luxury, rather than a social necessity; therefore, Republicans wanted to use the state and its revenues to support schools and the information infrastructure generally. To Democrats, with the important exceptions of Jefferson and Madison, individual liberty and low taxes were regarded as even greater necessities. All agreed, however, that encouraging an informed citizenry was central to public policy. This commitment, dating from the Revolutionary era, supplied a foundation for the information revolution in America.

Conclusion

The Information Age that Americans created in the first half of the nineteenth century represented a major break from earlier information systems in the colonies, in Britain, and in Europe. At its core lay the belief and the reality of the mobilization of the many, first manifest in Americans' astonishing response to Thomas Paine's *Common Sense*, and subsequently institutionalized by the United States' polycentric, competitive political and economic order. The United States was national without being centralized, so there was little support for top-down, monopolistic information practices. Too many competing elites were demanding access to information to permit closed information systems in politics or the economy.

The result was a remarkably open, democratic information system which served to reinforce the vitality of a civil society that, as Tocqueville observed, had no rival in the old world.[30] So open was it, that even the most marginal people in society exploited the opportunities that easy access provided. Free African Americans, for example, were socially despised by many whites, and they were generally poor. But even though they were widely excluded from voting, they pooled resources and generated newspapers, published pamphlets, and engaged in public speech and politics all across the Northern states. Women, too, might elicit scorn when they made public pronouncements, whether in print or from public platforms—but that did not stop them from actively engaging in information politics, even though they were everywhere barred from voting.[31] Minority religious sects were also subjected to derision or worse, but they spoke out and published vigorously. Free speech was not always and everywhere honored, especially in the slave states, but free speech and open access to America's information system was the normal expectation, the system's "default" position, to use a twentieth-century term.

In the competitive social, political, and economic environment of the United States, information activity was a self-intensifying process. For example, because anti-abolition forces could not silence their opponents—notwithstanding anti-abolition control of the national government and its agencies—they were forced to answer abolitionists in print and public speech, which in turn generated more abolition declamations. Likewise, evangelicals could not suppress worldly publications, so using stereotype printing plates and rotary steam presses they flooded the nation with the holy scriptures and purifying tracts.[32] There was no end to Americans' resort to information in a system built on the Miltonic principle of open competition to establish truth in people's minds. The closed information system model, where monopoly and suppression were guiding principles, was in retreat in the mid-eighteenth century, and by the early republican era all such efforts—such as the Sedition Act and the Gag Rule—failed. The institutions and expectations required to sustain a closed system did not survive in the early republic, whereas the agencies and beliefs connected to an open, competitive system were flourishing extensively.

By the middle of the nineteenth century, key foundational principles of the information age were securely established. First, Americans recognized that in a majoritarian political system and culture it was vital to persuade not merely the few, but the many, and that making information broadly available and packaging it attractively was essential to achieving that goal. Second, in cases of competition or conflict, information and rhetoric were the major weapons of partisans. Finally, owing to generations-long exposure to and participation in such an information environment, Americans of all descriptions, enfranchised or not, had—unlike their colonial predecessor—come to expect an open system where abundance and competition, not scarcity and monopoly, ruled. Their sense of entitlement was embodied in the growing number of United States post offices, which went from 69 in 1787 (one for every 58,000 people), to 4,500 in 1820, to 13,500 in 1840, to 28,000 post offices in 1860 (one for every 1,100 people, about one for 580 free adults).[33] Only in a nation where the free flow of information was generally recognized as an essential priority, could such an establishment be justified and self-supporting. Even before the consolidation of national power in the Civil War, Americans had created the infrastructure for the information age—on the ground, in their organized activities, in their embrace of information technology, and in their customs, habits, and expectations.

3

Recasting the Information Infrastructure for the Industrial Age

Richard R. John

In the century and a quarter between the framing of the federal Constitution in 1787 and the outbreak of World War I in 1914, the United States evolved from a struggling commercial republic on the margins of Europe into one of the most powerful industrial nations in the world. Accompanying the rise of the United States to world power was a comparable transformation in the informational environment. The period witnessed an unprecedented expansion in printing and publishing, the emergence of information-intensive industries such as credit reporting and life insurance, and the elaboration of major innovations in science, technology, and education. Each of these developments could furnish the theme for an essay on the role of information during the "long nineteenth century" that stretched from 1787 to 1914.

Yet there was one development that may well have been the most fundamental. This was the recasting of the facilities for transmitting information cheaply, reliably, and on a regular basis throughout the country and around the world. Challenged by the size of the territory to be spanned, emboldened by a highly competitive institutional setting, and inspired by an irrepressible popular demand for more and better information, government administrators, business leaders, and ordinary Americans joined together in a grand collaborative project that would have been unimaginable in any prior age. The central institutions in the information infrastructure during this period—the Post Office Department, the Railway Mail Service, Western Union, and the Bell System—may seem rudimentary today. Yet, at the time, they played a major role in U.S. business and public life.

The first communications revolution of the long nineteenth century began in the 1760s, with the emergence of an organized opposition to the Crown, and culminated in the 1820s with the establishment of a national postal network. The second began in the 1840s, with the expansion of the railroad and the commercialization of the telegraph, and culminated in the 1910s with the completion of a national telephone grid.

It is one of the themes of this chapter that the speed with which it was theoretically possible to convey information from place to place—by, say, stagecoach, railroad, telegraph, or telephone—was merely one dimension of a complex social process. In part, this is because the transmission of information involved then—as it does now—not only its conveyance but also its routing. Indeed, for many information users, the speed with which information was transmitted might well have been less valued than its cost and accessibility, and the regularity and reliability with which it was conveyed. It is also worth remembering that speed is a relative concept. From the standpoint of a merchant in the 1830s, a mounted horse express that traveled at ten miles an hour was moving extremely fast. After all, with a few minor exceptions, at no prior time had information ever been conveyed at a more rapid pace.

The concept of an *information infrastructure* is somewhat novel, and for this reason it deserves a few words of explanation. The phrase highlights the fact that the transmission of information has long been coordinated by a constellation of institutions, rather than by a single government agency or business firm. Often these institutions were complementary rather than mutually exclusive. Telegraphy supplemented mail delivery, and telephony supplemented telegraphy, without rendering either mail delivery or telegraphy obsolete. When Andrew Jackson won the presidency in 1828, the principal elements in the information infrastructure were the postal system, the stagecoach industry, and the newspaper press. On the eve of the Civil War, in 1861, the infrastructure had expanded to embrace the railroad, the telegraph, the wire service, and the commodity exchange. By World War I, it had expanded once again to include the railway mail service and the telephone grid.

The concept of an *informational environment* is also worth a brief comment. Although this phrase may seem at bit abstract, it draws attention to a familiar enough phenomenon: namely, the far-reaching yet often subtle ways in which the information infrastructure has shaped, and continues to shape, institutional patterns and cultural norms. In this way, it reminds us of the legacy of decisions made long in the past. Like the French countryside, the present-day informational environment is the product of an ongoing partnership between purposeful human agents and an institutional setting that is so pervasive that it is easily mistaken for a natural world. Just as the farming techniques of medieval agriculturists left their mark on the physical environment of early modern Europe, so, too, have the actions of government administrators, business leaders, and information users of all kinds shaped the informational environment of the early twentieth-century United States.

Reorienting the Information Infrastructure of the Commercial Republic

Ever since the 1760s, Americans have hailed an informed citizenry as a civic ideal. Yet it was not until after the framing of the federal Constitution in 1787 that this ideal was finally translated into law.

From an institutional standpoint, the world of the framers of the Constitution remained an informational ancien régime.[1] The early history of the American postal system is a case in point. Established in 1775 by the Continental Congress shortly after the start of the War of Independence, the system remained a small and uninfluential institution for the next seventeen years. As late as 1788, the American postal system had a mere sixty-nine offices, virtually the same number that its colonial counterpart had in 1765.[2]

The first postmaster general was Benjamin Franklin, a logical choice since, in addition to being a prominent supporter of the colonial cause, he had previously spent more than two decades as an administrator in the royal postal system. Franklin shared the faith of the Revolutionary generation in an informed citizenry. Yet, as postmaster general, he merely sought to replicate, under American control, the institution that he had helped administer when the postal system had been under the Crown.

Franklin held the postmaster generalship for only a few months before giving it over to his son-in-law, Richard Bache. Bache ran the institution—with indifferent success—for the duration of the war. Bache's successor, Ebenezer Hazard, compiled a decidedly better administrative record. It was Hazard, for example, who in 1785 enlisted stagecoach contractors for the first time to convey the mail on a regular schedule—a practice that, in later decades, would prove influential. Yet Hazard lacked the authority—and the Continental Congress lacked the will—to institute any permanent changes in policy.

When the founders of the American republic met in Philadelphia in 1787 to establish a stronger national government, they had little reason to anticipate the full magnitude of the changes in communications policy that were about to occur. Communications policy had figured little on the debates over the drafting of the new constitution and received scant attention in the *Federalist* essays that James Madison, Alexander Hamilton, and John Jay wrote to help build support for its ratification in the pivotal state of New York.

Only in the years after the framing of the federal Constitution would it become evident that the government had an obligation to keep the citizenry informed on a regular basis about the affairs of state. With the adoption in 1788 of the Constitution by popular consent, this ideal acquired the force of a categorical imperative. Now that popular assemblies had demonstrated their sovereignty in the most unequivocal way by deliberating upon, and approving, a fundamental charter of law, it seemed incontrovertible that the citizenry had, at the very least, a right to remain well informed.[3] Since the postal system was the only long-distance communications technology, this put its expansion high on the political agenda.

Key figures in the subsequent restructuring of the information infrastructure included Benjamin Rush and James Madison. As Rush explained as early as 1787, to adapt the "principles, morals, and manners of our citizens to our republican forms of government," it was "absolutely necessary" that the government circulate "knowledge of every kind" through every part of the United States. To fulfill this ambitious mandate. Rush looked to the postal system, the "true non-electric wire of government," and the "only means" of "conveying light and heat to every individual in the federal commonwealth."[4] Madison editorialized in 1791 that Congress had an obligation to improve the facilities of communication by encouraging commerce, national improvements, an opposition press, and, most important of all, the "*circulation of newspapers through the entire body of the people*" in the mail.[5]

The policy innovations that Rush and Madison championed helped inspire the passage of the Post Office Act of 1792. This law included no ringing preamble to invite detailed historical scrutiny—and thus is often overlooked even by specialists in the field. Yet it deserves to be remembered as a key event in the history of information in the United States. No single legal enactment—not the free press guarantee in the First Amendment, not even the provisions for public education that Congress mandated in the Northwest Ordinance—did more to institutionalize the communications revolution that traced its beginnings back to the struggle against the Crown.[6]

The Post Office Act of 1792 had three main provisions. First, it barred government officials from opening personal letters to monitor domestic subversion; second, it admitted newspapers into the mail at extremely low rates; and third, it transferred control over the designation of new post routes from the executive branch to Congress. While these might seem like arcane procedural matters, in practice they established institutional mechanisms that had broad-ranging practical import. The first provision safeguarded civil liberties by establishing a precedent for a right to privacy, while the second and third provisions guaranteed that, as the area of settlement expanded from the Atlantic seaboard to the Trans-Appalachian hinterland, the government would provide a far-flung citizenry with subsidized, time-specific information on business and public affairs.

For a time, the expansion of the postal network was constrained by the international tensions that culminated in the War of 1812. With the ascendancy following the Treaty of Ghent in 1815 of a younger generation of nationally minded public figures that included Henry Clay, John Quincy Adams, and John McLean, these constraints receded. Together, these national republicans, as they were commonly called, promoted an "American System" that fostered the interregional movement of agricultural staples, manufactured goods, and information of all kinds. As postmaster general between 1823 and 1829, McLean played a particularly conspicuous role in this ambitious government-sponsored project. Fittingly, it was during his tenure in office that the postmaster generalship was elevated to cabinet rank. After all, in the 1820s the postal system first became widely known as one of the largest, most politically powerful, and most administratively complex organizations in the country. The rapid rise of the postal system to national prominence in this decade was symbolized by President Andrew Jackson's decision, shortly after his inauguration in 1829, to elevate the institution to the status of a government department, a distinction it would retain for the next century and a half.

The expansion of the postal network in the early Republic was a remarkable achievement that could not have been anticipated by any of the statesmen who had drafted the Constitution in 1787. While in 1788, the postal system had fewer than 100 offices, by 1800 the total had increased to 903, and by 1820 the number was 4,500 (see table 3.1). The speed at which this network grew struck some contemporaries as nothing short of astonishing; one Washington editor remarked in 1826 that the expansion was so rapid as "almost to stagger belief," and "did we not know its history to be true, it might pass and be received as a romantic tale, having no foundation but in the regions of fancy, in the wanderings of imagination."[7]

Table 3.1 The Expansion and Geographical Penetration of the Postal Network, 1790–1840

Year	Post Offices	Population per Post Office	Settled Area per Post Office (square miles)
1790	75	43,084	3492.7
1800	903	4,876	339.3
1810	2,300	2,263	180.2
1820	4,500	1,796	116.3
1830	8,450	1,289	75.5
1840	13,468	1,087	61.4

Source: Richard R. John, *Spreading the News: The American Postal System from Franklin to Morse* (Cambridge, Mass.: Harvard University Press, 1995), 51.

Note: Population excludes Indians and slaves.

By 1828, the postal network was complete. At that time, the United States, with its 7,500 post offices, had by far the largest postal system in the world. From an international perspective, this fact highlighted the distinctiveness of the American case. At a time when the United States boasted seventy-four post offices per 100,000 inhabitants, Great Britain had seventeen, and France four.[8]

Perhaps the most revealing measure of the magnitude of the government's achievement was the extent to which the postal network had kept pace with the westward expansion in the area of settlement. Between 1790 and 1840, the settled territory over which the federal government presided increased by a remarkable 300 percent; even so, the postal network expanded at an even more rapid rate. In 1790 there had been one post office for every 3,500 square miles of settled territory; by 1840, there was one post office for every 61 square miles, an increase of almost 600 percent (see table 3.1).[9]

As the postal network expanded, so too did the volume of information that it conveyed. In 1800, the postal system transmitted 1.9 million newspapers and 2 million letters. By 1840, it was transmitting almost 39 million newspapers and more than 40 million letters (see table 3.2). The newspaper totals, postal authorities agreed, were significantly understated, since accounting procedures were notoriously lax. It is also worth remembering that, in this period, newspapers were almost invariably read in groups—almost never by solitary individuals, as is the custom today. Although it is impossible to say for certain, there is a good deal of anecdotal evidence to suggest that, on average, an indi-

Table 3.2 Letters and Newspapers Transmitted by the Postal System, 1790–1840

Year	Letters (millions)	Letters Per Capita	Newspapers (millions)	Newspapers Per Capita
1790	0.3	0.1	0.5	0.2
1800	2.0	0.5	1.9	0.4
1810	3.9	0.7	n.a.	n.a.
1820	8.9	1.1	6.0	0.7
1830	13.8	1.3	16.0	1.5
1840	40.9	2.9	39.0	2.7

Source: John, *Spreading the News,* 4.

Note: Population excludes Indians and slaves; the newspaper total for 1790 is based on data for 1791; the newspaper total for 1800 is based on data for 1799.

vidual copy might well be read—or listened to, as the case might be—by as many as a dozen different people.[10]

The expansion in newspaper conveyance was particularly impressive, since newspapers accounted for the great bulk of the mail. Throughout this period, newspapers made up as much as 95 percent of the weight of the mail, while accounting for no more than about 15 percent of the revenue. In the absence of the newspaper subsidy, it is inconceivable that newspapers could have circulated in such numbers or on such a geographically extensive scale.[11]

Just as the government subsidized the transmission of newspapers, it also subsidized the cost of gathering news. Throughout the early republic, the government permitted every newspaper editor to receive, free of charge, one copy of every other newspaper in the country. Newspaper editors came to depend on this privilege for much of the material they used to fill their columns. In conjunction with the low postal rates, this policy made newspapers editors—including the editors of the burgeoning country press—one of the most privileged occupational groups in the United States.

Other favored classes of information included magazines and government documents. Magazines enjoyed preferential postal rates beginning in 1794, while government documents passed through the mail free of charge, provided only that they bore the signature, or frank, of an authorized agent, such as a postmaster or congressman.

The rapid expansion of the postal network in the early Republic owed much to the determination of ordinary Americans to maintain close ties with the wider world. Better mail delivery was one of the few tangible benefits that Congress had the authority to bestow, and individuals quickly grew expert at lobbying their representative for new routes and more frequent service.

The principal constraint upon postal expansion was the reluctance of fiscally prudent congressmen to authorize any improvements in service that might run the institution into debt. Indeed, for a time postal administrators actually returned to the treasury a modest annual surplus. Congress achieved its dual mandate of service and self-sufficiency by keeping rates on letter postage artificially high. In effect, Congress imposed a hidden tax on merchants, the great majority of whom lived in New England and the Mid-Atlantic states, in order to subsidize the transmission of newspapers and the maintenance of the postal network in those parts of the country that could not cover the cost—in particular, in the South and West. In some instances, as critics did not fail to point out, Congress authorized the establishment of routes that could not bear one-hundredth of the expense.[12]

The information infrastructure in the early Republic owed little to steam power, and nothing to the railroad, which was still in its infancy in 1828. As late as 1840, several years after the railroad had begun to carry the mail, the horse remained the primary motive power. Though postal administrators occasionally arranged to transport the mail by steamboat, the stagecoach remained the principal means of conveyance. This fact provides a revealing glimpse of how far a sophisticated information infrastructure can operate without any dependence on fossil fuel.

Among the most important organizational innovations in the information infrastructure of the early Republic was the establishment in 1800 of a network of distribution centers to facilitate the routing of the mail. For the next sixty years, this "hub-and-spoke" sorting scheme, overseen by a team of middle managers, was a cornerstone of postal administration. No longer was it necessary for postmasters to open every mail sack at each office, as they had prior to 1800. Surprisingly, resilient, this hub-and-spoke sorting scheme was little altered by the coming of the railroad; it remained a pillar of the information infrastructure from 1800 until after the Civil War, when it was gradually supplanted by the continuous sorting scheme known as railway mail.

Equally innovative was the willingness of postal administrators to subsidize stagecoach service in order to establish a rudimentary system of public transportation. By the 1820s, postal administrators had grown accustomed to awarding stagecoach firms sums that significantly exceeded the cost that they would have had to pay post riders to carry the mail. With the possible exception of the newspaper press, few enterprises were more dependent on federal largesse. According to one estimate, fully 33 percent of all stagecoach industry revenue came from this single source.[13]

Since the government provided no comparable bonus for road-building, the stagecoach subsidy helps to explain why travelers like the English writer Charles Dickens complained so frequently about the bumpiness of the ride. In effect, the public investment in the means of passenger conveyance had outstripped the capacity of the transportation infrastructure over which the passengers were conveyed.

The Informational Environment of the Commercial Republic

The completion of the national postal network reoriented the informational environment of the early American Republic from the Atlantic seaboard to the Trans-Appalachian hinterland. In conjunction with a rudimentary national banking system, a burgeoning trade in agricultural staples, and a competitive and dynamic commercial sector, the postal network hastened the emergence of a national market for information. In its absence, it is hard to imagine the rise of geographically extended, information-intensive industries such as credit reporting and life insurance, or nationally oriented organizations such as the voluntary association and the mass party.

The rapid, regular, and reliable transmission of information was of particular importance to merchants engaged in long-distance trade. Postmaster General McLean declared in 1828 that "no inconsiderable amount of the active capital of the country" was transmitted through the postal system every year.[14] Each year, one knowledgeable insider estimated in 1855, some $100 million was transmitted in this way.[15]

Much of this money took the form of bank notes and other forms of negotiable currency, all of which went uninsured. Surprising as it might seem to us today, it was by no means uncommon for merchants to send through the mail as much as $10,000 in cash. While some of this money was stolen or lost, the vast majority reached its intended destination. Had theft been endemic, after all, merchants would not have continued to rely on the postal system to this extent to settle their accounts. Indeed, there can be few better measures of the effectiveness of the institution in this period, or of the high regard in which it was held.

In cities, towns, and villages throughout the United States, the arrival of the mail was a major event. Post offices were almost always located in the heart of the business district and were often thronged with merchants anxious to hear the latest news. In Rochester, New York, merchants continued to congregate daily at the post office until well after the Civil War. This was true, interestingly enough, even on Sunday, the one day when virtually every other commercial establishment was obliged by law to shut down. Though convention proscribed women from visiting the post office on this day, the lobby was almost invariably thronged with men who had stopped by to chat, discuss the week's events, and pick up their mail (see figure 3.1). Only in 1912 did the Post Office Department close its offices to the public on this day, ending a practice that dated back to 1810.

If an individual received anything in the mail, it was far more likely to be a newspaper than a letter. Prior to the major letter-rate reductions in 1845 and 1851, letter writing remained confined mostly to mer-

Figure 3.1 Post Office, Rochester, New York. Throughout the nineteenth century, the post office was a popular place to meet friends, transact business, and catch up on the news. This photograph shows the businessmen of Rochester waiting in line to pick up their mail. They are assembled in Reynolds' Arcade, an indoor gallery in the heart of the city's business district. The date is Sunday, March 25, 1888. According to federal law, the post office had to be open for business every day of the week—including Sunday. The absence of women was no accident. Tradition decreed that on Sundays the men were to have the post office to themselves. Note the proximity of the telegraph office—another key element of the informational infrastructure of the industrial age. Courtesy of the Rochester Historical Society.

chants, the well-to-do, and public figures who enjoyed the franking privilege, which permitted them to send or received an unlimited number of letters free of charge. Postage was customarily borne by the recipient, rather than the sender, and could sometimes total 50 cents, a substantial sum in an age when many laborers made $1 a day. Newspapers, in contrast, were relatively cheap to transmit, and could be sent anywhere within the United States for less than 2 cents a copy. The vast majority circulated within an area of, at most, a few hundred miles. Only a few—including *Niles's Register*, the *National Intelligencer*, and, in a slightly later period, the *New York Tribune*—reached an audience that aspired to be genuinely national in scope.

Like so many features of American society in the early Republic, the newspaper market was polycentric. Though Washington was the political capital—and therefore a major publisher of government documents—it hosted few influential organs of public opinion, a situation that would have been inconceivable in Great Britain or France.

The novelty of the informational environment sparked a good deal of contemporary comment. When the mail arrived, observed one English visitor in 1814, the townspeople hurried to the post office, where they "formed a variety of groups round those who were fortunate enough to possess themselves of a paper." This was true, the visitor added, not just in the cities, but throughout the countryside. "I am of the opinion," he elaborated, "that this general circulation of newspapers throughout America, tends very much to the instruction of the country people, and divests them of that air of ignorance and rusticity which characterizes the greater part of the peasantry in Europe." The information that newspapers conveyed might be "superficial," but it gave men a "general acquaintance with the world":

It sets before them the actions of their countrymen, and the government under which they live; it renders them familiar with the transactions of foreign nations; and though confined to a small spot themselves, yet at one view they become acquainted with every section of the globe. Without a knowledge of what is passing in the world, man may be said to be an isolated being; but with a newspaper before him, he mixes with society, hears the opinions of others, and may communicate his sentiments upon men and things to all parts of the world.[16]

The democratization of the informational environment struck a special chord with painters, who documented its social implications in a series of memorable genre scenes. One of the earliest painters to dramatize this theme was John Lewis Krimmel. In "The Village Tavern," completed in 1814, Krimmel demonstrated how the arrival of the mail during the War of 1812 provided artisans and gentry alike with up-to-date news from the front, challenging the gentry's monopoly over public affairs. The popular appetite for information had simply overwhelmed the constraints on its widespread circulation. Never again, Krimmel seemed to imply, could the gentry presume to monopolize access to news from afar (see figure 3.2).[17]

Among the most evocative renderings of the voracious public demand for information was Richard Caton Woodville's "War News from Mexico" (see figure 3.3). Woodville set his political parable in a post office during wartime—in this case, the Mexican War. At the center of Woodville's canvas is a group of men eagerly scanning a newspaper for the latest military dispatches. Hovering on the periphery is

Figure 3.2 "Village Tavern." John Lewis Krimmel completed this painting of the interior of a village post office in 1814, toward the end of the War of 1812. The view depicts the arrival of newspapers with up-to-date reports about the course of the war. Information is freely available to everyone—including women, children, and artisans. Note the obvious discomfort the gentleman in the middle of the room; no longer will the gentry be able to block the flow of the news. Note also the newspaper-filled portmanteau that is draped over the shoulder of the mail carrier in the doorway. Courtesy of the Toledo Museum of Art.

Figure 3.3 "War News from Mexico." Painted in 1848 by Baltimore artist Richard Caton Woodville, this scene illustrates the importance of newspapers as a source of information about the wider world. The setting is a hotel that also houses the post office, a common arrangement in the 1800s. Note that the news is being read aloud, a customary practice at the time. On the margins are a women (partially visible in a window) and several African-Americans. They, too, are cusious about the latest news. Yet they are plainly overshadowed by the white men who, in this period, dominated American public life. Courtesy of the American Antiquarian Society, Worcester, Mass.

a woman and a free black; Woodville seems to imply that as the public sphere expanded beyond the gentry, it has rendered increasingly marginal the participation of anyone who could not claim to be white and male.

The democratization of the public sphere was, as these paintings suggest, not without its ironies and unintended consequences. The morally ambiguous character of this process was pointedly revealed in 1835 when, to appease the South, Postmaster General Amos Kendall blocked the transmission into the slaveholding states of information dealing with the slavery issue. The resulting information embargo had the full approval of President Jackson, and it remained in place until the Civil War, significantly exacerbating the growing sectional rift between the North and the South. Kendall's conduct struck many as of questionable legality, and raised howls of protest in the North. "I denounce it," declared Massachusetts Congressman John Quincy Adams seven years after the event, "as a violation of the freedom of the press, as a violation of the sacred character of the post office, and of the rights and liberties of all the free people of the United States."[18] The embargo remains to this day as one of the most thoroughgoing peacetime assaults on the freedom of the press in U.S. history. The willingness of the Jacksonians—long praised as apostles of political democracy—to embrace this action underscores one of the paradoxes that accompanied the institutionalization of the civic rationale for communications policy that the founders of the republic had so earnestly espoused.

The Railroad and Telegraph Recast the Information Infrastructure for the Industrial Age

The second communications revolution of the long nineteenth century was set in motion in the 1840s with the rapid expansion of the railroad and the commercialization of the telegraph. The advent of the telegraph is often hailed as a decisive turning point in the history of communications; in certain respects, however, the telegraph was less significant than the railroad, which emerged, during this decade, as an important means of conveyance for the mail.

The potential of the railroad for mail delivery had first been glimpsed in the 1830s by Postmaster General Kendall. Just as Kendall found himself unable to mediate the growing conflict between North and South, he also found it impossible to resolve the thorny conflict between the government and the railroad over the appropriate contracting terms. Kendall readily conceded the railroad's superiority as a mode of conveyance. Yet he warned that existing legislation made it extremely difficult for postal administrators to secure satisfactory arrangements, and he even hinted that Congress might be obliged to raise postal rates to cover the cost. "Certain it is," Kendall declared, "that if the demands of railroad companies are to be satisfied, most of whom are not willing to serve the public as they serve individuals, and seem to think that the Government is bound to make their investments profitable, there will be little left of the means of this department to pay for the conveyance of the mails on other lines, much of the interior of the country must be deprived of them altogether, and the rates of postage, instead of being reduced, must be increased."[19]

The crux of the problem was the unsuitability of the existing contracting methods. In the stagecoach era, it made sense for postal administrators to advertise for bids to transport the mail, since it was relatively easy to start up a new line. In the railroad era, however, this assumption no longer made sense, since competition between two railroads on a single route was unknown. As a consequence, railroads were free to charge what they wished, and to run their trains in accordance with their best interests, even if their scheduling significantly slowed the carriage of the mail.

To help resolve this dilemma, Kendall urged Congress to establish a maximum rate for railway mail pay. Though Congress obliged, railroads quickly found various ways to evade this restriction. Kendall also briefly experimented with a special horse-express—which he justified, in large measure, as an attempt to outpace the railroads. In addition, he tried, without success, to secure for the government its own special mail train.[20]

Kendall's failure to contain contracting costs led his successor, Charles Wickliffe, to propose a different approach. To gain control of the right-of-way and to help limit expenses, Wickliffe urged Congress to award the leading railroad lines a long-term mail contract, in the form of a substantial lump sum payment. Had Congress supported Wickliffe's proposal, the government would have committed itself to making a substantial investment in the completion of the railway network. Yet Congress refused to take Wickliffe's advice, leaving him (and his successors) with little recourse but to pay the railroads whatever amount they might deem to be fair.

The failure of Kendall and Wickliffe to work out satisfactory contracting terms had major implications for mail delivery. Unlike their counterparts in Great Britain, France, and most of the other European countries, U.S. postal administrators never secured control over the scheduling of the railroads that carried the mail. This failure significantly complicated the establishment of advantageous routing arrangements and marked a sharp departure from the stagecoach era, when postal administrators had routinely coordinated stagecoach schedules to minimize unnecessary delays.

The failure of the government to adapt to the railroad created a market niche for the private expresses, a new kind of business enterprise that sprang up between 1839 and 1845 in New England and the Mid-Atlantic states on the most heavily patronized routes. These firms took advantage of the means of conveyance that the railroad provided to transport small parcels, including money and letters, in competition with the Post Office Department, and in violation of the laws undergirding the postal monopoly. The first private express was established in 1839 by William Harnden, a young man of modest means who had previously worked as a conductor on the Boston and Worcester Railroad. By 1845, at the height of the boom, dozens of entrepreneurs had joined Harnden in transmitting information of all kinds. Though it is difficult to know just how much mail these firms conveyed, one congressmen calculated that—in conjunction with other, more informal means of conveyance—they were probably transmitting as much as two-thirds of all the correspondence in the United States.[21]

The private expresses proved popular with merchants and received a generally favorable reception in the press. In large measure, this was because they charged significantly lower rates than the Post Office Department. This proved to be relatively easy, since they operated exclusively on routes where Congress had for half a century kept the rates on letter postage artificially high.

The rise of the private expresses confronted the Post Office Department with the greatest administrative challenge in its history. Determined to destroy the competition, Wickliffe vigorously prosecuted violations of what he firmly believed to be the government's legally guaranteed letter-mail monopoly. Government attorneys instituted dozens of suits against individual expressmen, such as James W. Hale, who quipped at one point that he was the "most arrested man in the world."[22] Within Congress, Wickliffe's tactics met with broad bipartisan support. During the extensive debates over postal policy between 1839 and 1845, no congressman proposed the abolition of the postal monopoly, and few praised the private expresses as a laudable example of private enterprise. Indeed, the very notion that mail delivery might be privatized still remained somewhat exotic, since the concept of private enterprise had yet to acquire the positive moral connotation that we now take for granted.

Outside of Congress, the private expresses enjoyed a broad base of popular support. Newspaper editors in Boston, New York, Philadelphia, and Baltimore championed their cause, as did merchants in New England and the Mid-Atlantic states. In 1845, Congress bowed to the inevitable and significantly lowered the basic letter rate to 5 and 10 cents, depending on the distance that the item was conveyed. Subsequent legislation in 1851 reduced the basic letter rate even further for most domestic destinations to a flat 3 cents—where it remained with minor modifications for the next hundred years.

The independent mail delivery boom hastened the recasting of the information infrastructure to accommodate the railroad as a means of conveyance. In 1845, Congress eliminated most of the subsidies that stagecoach firms had traditionally enjoyed. In 1851, it abandoned the presumption that the postal system should remain self-supporting, making it possible to draw on general revenue to cover the cost of railroad transportation. By this time, the railroad had emerged as the principal means of conveyance on the most heavily patronized routes. Yet it was not until the Civil War that postal administrators would finally begin to scrap the long-outmoded, stagecoach-based, hub-and-spoke sorting scheme and replace it with the train-based, continuous sorting scheme that would come to be known as railway mail.

To take full advantage of the routing possiblilities that the railroad afforded, Postmaster General John Creswell established the Railway Mail Service in 1869 as a distinct and largely autonomous branch of the Post Office Department. Under the leadership of a succession of able superintendents—George A. Armstrong, George N. Bangs, and Theodore N. Vail—railway mail quickly established itself as a central information infrastructure of the industrial age.

The Railway Mail Service was one of the first enterprises to coordinate the routing of information throughout the length and breadth of the United States. Its mission was deceptively simple: to transmit the mail from sender to recipient as rapidly as a passenger could travel between these two points. To achieve this goal, railway mail managers promulgated an entirely new set of administrative protocols and entered into complex and ongoing negotiations with the postal distribution centers and the railroads. No other administrative entity transmitted such an enormous number of items, and only Western Union operated on a comparable geographical scale.

At the core of railway mail was an elaborate administrative apparatus that was overseen by a superintendent and a staff of geographically based division heads with the assistance of a team of roving inspectors.

The sorting itself was performed by a cadre of highly trained clerks who were much admired for their reliability, accuracy, and esprit de corps.[23] These men routed the mail for the entire country as they traveled about in specially equipped railroad cars fitted with custom-built wooden sorting cases subdivided into pigeonholes. To help insulate the railway mail clerks from the debilitating effects of patronage politics, Congress decreed early on that none were to be subject to partisan dismissal—a striking departure from the norms that prevailed in the rest of the department.

The most ambitious project that railway mail administrators sponsored during the early years of the service was the "Fast Mail." The Fast Mail was a special high-speed train, staffed by railway mail clerks, that ran day and night between New York and Chicago on a fixed schedule at the then extraordinary speed of forty miles per hour. Far more than merely an experiment in high-speed transportation, the Fast Mail was a showcase for advanced routing techniques, and a goad to all the mail contractors whose lines bisected the New York–Chicago route. Inaugurated during the tenure of Superintentent Bangs, the Fast Mail was supervised by Bangs's assistant, and soon-to-be successor, Theodore N. Vail (see figure 3.4). Vail relished the challenge that the Fast Mail provided, and he used it to better coordinate not only the government's own operations, but also the railroads that the government relied on to carry the mail. Indeed, at one point Vail went so far as to propose, unsuccessfully, that Congress grant the Post Office Department "absolute power" to determine which trains should carry the mail, and how much room they should provide to facilitate its sorting.[24]

The Fast Mail proved to be expensive, making it a perennial target for congressional critics. Yet during its brief heyday in the 1870s, it provided its managers with an invaluable lesson in the possibilities of administrative coordination. Indeed, to an extent that no one could possibly have imagined at the time, it may well have provided Vail—who would later go on to a distinguished career in telephony—with a foretaste (and, perhaps even a template) for the kind of managerial innovations he would later implement at American Telephone & Telegraph (AT&T).

While the Railway Mail Service marked a new major departure in the routing of information, it remained dependent on the existing transportation-based means of conveyance. For this reason, it has rarely been accorded the respectful attention that is routinely lavished on the telegraph, the first electrically based communications technology.

Figure 3.4 Theodore N. Vail. Vail was the architect of the 'Bell System" and a founder of AT&T. This picture was taken in 1878, the year Vail began his career as a telephone executive. Vail had just completed a highly successful stint as superintendent of the Railway Mail Service—a key element in the information infrastructure of the industrial age. Vail's work for the government taught him a good deal about the management of complex systems, knowledge he would later put to good use at AT&T. Courtesy of AT&T Archives.

The telegraph industry in the United States began in 1844 with the establishment by Samuel F. B. Morse of a forty-mile line between Washington and Baltimore. Morse's project, like most technological breakthroughs, had been subtly shaped by preexisting assumptions and norms. In particular, it owed a good deal to the well-known system of optical telegraphy that Claude Chappe had devised in the 1790s in revolutionary France.

Chappe's telegraph consisted of a chain of towers that had been fitted up with a pair of wooden shutters that could be arranged in a variety of positions. Under normal conditions, it could transmit a detailed message in less than three minutes over a distance of 100 miles. The French government invested heavily in the new technology and soon established an optical telegraph network that linked all the country's major cities. It remained a mainstay of French communications for fifty years.[25]

Chappe's telegraph popularized the idea that information could be transmitted at long distances at an almost instantaneous speed. Indeed, Chappe coined the term "telegraphy"—which meant, literally, "writing at a distance"—to characterize his invention, even though, strictly speaking, it was not a recording medium, since it left no written record and relied entirely on sight. Though no comparable system was ever established in the United States, merchants in Boston and New York soon established telegraphs on similar principles to hasten the transmission of information from sea to shore.[26] By 1820, more than forty newspapers had incorporated some variant on the word "telegraph" into their title. A few years later, it would even find its way onto the masthead of Andrew Jackson's leading campaign newspaper in the election of 1828. Popular interest in the new technology was widespread. "It must . . . be evident to the most common observer," declared one optical telegraph enthusiast, "that no means of conveying intelligence can ever be devised, that shall exceed or even equal [its] rapidity . . . for, with the exception of the scarcely perceptible delay at each station . . . its rapidity may be compared to that of light itself."[27]

Optical telegraphy held a special fascination for postal administrators, since it offered the possibility of beating out any potential competitor in the transmission of information. Ever since the 1820s, when John McLean had proclaimed his determination to outpace any private express, a generation of postmasters' general had preached the gospel of speed. McLean briefly debated the merits of a government-sponsored optical telegraphy, as did Amos Kendall, who at one point was reputed to have hailed it as "just the thing" to supersede a high-speed horse express that he had established between Washington and New Orleans.[28]

Morse echoed these sentiments, and took it for granted that his telegraph should be regulated by the federal government, preferably under the control of the Post Office Department. The electric telegraph, Morse explained, was but "another mode" of accomplishing the "principal object" for which the Post Department had been established, "to wit: the rapid and regular transmission of intelligence."[29] To help bring this about, Morse lobbied Congress to purchase his patent. Only when it became obvious that Congress had no intention of buying him out did he proceed to develop the new technology as a private enteprise.

Even critics of federal largesse favored governmental control. "In the hands of individuals or associations," warned the notorious fiscal conservative Cave Johnson, the electric telegraph might become the "most potent instrument the world ever knew to effect sudden and large speculations—to rob the many of their just advantages, and concentrate them upon the few. . . . The use of an instrument so powerful for good or for evil cannot with safety to the people be left in the hands of private individuals uncontrolled by law."[30]

To Morse's chagrin, Congress refused to purchase his patent, obliging him and his partners to seek private funding. Jumping at the chance, a swarm of promoters began to string telegraph lines between the leading commercial centers, inaugurating what one nineteenth-century telegraph historian called an era of "methodless enthusiasm."[31] By 1848, telegraph lines linked New York to both New Orleans and Chicago. By 1850, 12,000 miles of wire had been strung; by 1853 the total had almost doubled, to 23,000 miles.[32]

Wartime is often a catalyst for innovations in communications technology, and the Civil War was no exception. Shortly after the fighting began in 1861, telegraph promoter Hiram Sibley completed the first transcontinental telegraph line between Omaha and San Francisco. Sibley's line rendered obsolete the Pony Express, a transcontinental horse express that had been established the previous year. The transcontinental telegraph owed its impetus less to commercial considerations than to political fiat, and, in particular, to a construction subsidy that Congress wrote into the Pacific Telegraph Act of 1860. For a time, it seemed as if Sibley might well extend the telegraph to Europe by way of the Bering Strait and Siberia. The construction of a trans-Siberian line actually began, only to be abandoned in 1866, when the news came of the successful completion of a cable under the Atlantic between the United States and Great Britain.

During the Civil War, the military leaders of both the Union and the Confederacy found the telegraph to be an indispensable logistical aid. While the telegraph had already been used in various European conflicts—most notably, in the Crimean War—it had never before been deployed in wartime on such a geographically extensive scale. Union military officers proved particularly skilled in putting it to good use. By the end of the war, they had authorized the construction of some 15,000 miles of line. President Abraham Lincoln relied on a steady stream of telegraph dispatches to keep open the lines of communication with his commanders in the field. According to military telegrapher David Homer Bates, the president spent more hours during these years in the telegraph office at the Department of War than in any other place, with the exception of the White House itself.[33]

Military mobilization proved particularly advantageous for telegraph firms, such as Western Union, that maintained an extensive telegraph network inside the Union lines. Western Union officials worked closely with the Union army during the war, and, following a brief flurry of mergers, emerged in 1866 as the first industrial combine to operate on a scale that was at all comparable to the Post Office Department. By 1880, Western Union transmitted 29.2 million messages over a network of 244,000 miles of wire and boasted a network of more than 9,000 offices (see table 3.3.). Three-quarters of Western Union's offices were located in railroad stations, a testament to the pivotal importance of the railroad in the information infrastructure of the Industrial Age.

Western Union officials gained valuable administrative experience from the unprecedented mobilization of men and material that had

Table 3.3 The Expansion of Western Union, 1866–1910

Year	Telegraph Offices	Miles of Wire (thousands)	Messages Handled (millions)
1866	2,250	76	n.a.
1870	3,972	112	9.2
1875	6,565	179	17.2
1880	9,077	234	29.2
1885	14,184	462	42.1
1890	19,382	679	55.9
1900	22,900	933	63.2
1910	24,825	1,429	75.1

Source: U.S. Bureau of the Census, *Historical Statistics of the United States* (Washington, D.C.: Government Printing Office, 1975), 2:787–788.

taken place during the war. Many Western Union telegraphers had served in the military telegraph corps, an experience that instilled in them a preoccupation with speed and accuracy and a vivid appreciation of the power of the state. These habits of mind proved surprisingly enduring and would shape Western Union's business strategy for the next thirty years.

Of the many Western Union officials to have been shaped by the wartime mobilization, perhaps the most enterprising was William Orton, the first president of Western Union following its consolidation in 1866. Though Orton had no formal background in telegraphy, he had earned high marks from telegraph investors for his energetic stint late in the war as commissioner of inland revenue in the Department of Treasury. At Western Union, Orton put to good use the legal, administrative, and political skills that he had deployed so effectively as a public administrator. In addition to promoting the vigorous expansion of the firm's core business, the long-distance market, Orton dedicated Western Union to providing its customers with information in a reliable and impartial way. In this way, as one longtime colleague would later recall, Orton strove to elevate the horizons of the enterprise to embrace "considerations of citizenship" rather than mere "questions of simple profit and loss."[34]

Western Union dominated long-distance telegraphy during the Gilded Age. To be sure, at various points company officials faced serious challenges from the Baltimore & Ohio Railroad, the Postal Telegraph Company, and the financier Jay Gould. In each of these contests, Western Union emerged victorious—although, in the case of Gould, at the cost of according him a dominant voice on the board of directors, which Gould retained from 1881 until his death in 1892.

Western Union's position in the intraurban market was considerably more precarious. Here it competed with a multitude of firms that employed different types of electrical signaling devices, such as fire alarms, stock tickers, and call boxes of various kinds. By 1870, thirty-eight municipalities had fire alarm systems; by 1880, this total had increased to 103; by 1902, to 764. Western Union intraurbans included the Gold & Stock Company and the American District Telegraph Company. In 1885, American District had fifty-two offices and 12,000 subscribers, and it responded to 6,000 calls a day.[35]

To strengthen Western Union's market position, Orton expanded its manufacturing capabilities and briefly sponsored a program of research. In 1871, he helped acquire for Western Union a controlling interest in Western Electric, a major supplier of telegraphic equipment. At roughly the same time, Orton hired a number of inventors—including Thomas Edison and Elisha Gray—to increase the capacity of Western Union's wire network. Orton's research program culminated with Edison's quadruplex telegraph, a device that could transmit four messages simultaneously over a single wire.[36]

The greatest threat that Western Union confronted was not economic but political. With its consolidation in 1866, the firm became the first industrial combine to transcend decisively the boundaries of the individual states. Predictably enough, Congress found this situation unsettling, and in response it passed the Telegraph Act of 1866. This legislation granted those telegraph firms that consented to its provisions the right to string wires along every post route in the country. In return, it obligated these firms to permit Congress to purchase all their telegraphic assets at a mutually agreed upon price, should Congress so decide.

The Telegraph Act marked a compromise between Western Union, telegraph entrepreneurs who sought a national charter, and reformers who favored the outright nationalization of the industry. These Western Union critics were soon joined by several congressmen and Boston reformer Gardiner Greene Hubbard who would quickly emerge as Western Union's most determined foe.

Hubbard was a lawyer with extensive experience in public utilities and a tireless promoter of projects intended to promote the public good. Beginning in 1868, he lobbied Congress for several years to charter a "postal telegraph" that would compete with Western Union by reducing rates and expanding public access. Hubbard's ideas are of interest, since, in the following decade, he would become a key backer of the Bell Company, the progenitor of the Bell System and AT&T.

Hubbard lost few opportunities to chastise Western Union for its failure to realize the democratic potential that he believed to inhere in the new technology. From his standpoint, Western Union's rates were too high, its service too limited, its technology too primitive, and its offices too few. In articulating a position he had held for fifteen years, Hubbard declared in 1883: "As a telegraph for business, where dispatch is essential and price is of little account, the Western Union system is unrivaled; but as a telegraph for the people it is a signal failure."[37]

Hubbard was a keen student of communications policy, and his views were strongly reminiscent of the arguments that postal reformers such Joshua Leavitt had deployed in the 1840s in urging a reduction in the basic letter rate. Like Leavitt, Hubbard firmly believed that the American people had a God-given right to communicate with each other, and that existing institutions were impeding the free flow of information. If Western Union would not perform this public service, Hubbard believed, then Congress had an obligation to fill the void.

Neither Orton nor his successor Norvin Green found Hubbard's arguments persuasive, and they rebutted these arguments at length in a series of reports, magazine articles, and congressional hearings. The controversy ranged widely over many topics that included the technical innovativeness of Western Union; the funding and administration of telegraphy in Belgium, Switzerland, and various other European countries; and the advantages and disadvantages of government control. One key disagreement involved differing perceptions of the social utility of the new technology. Hubbard firmly believed that telegraphy, like mail delivery, was a democratic medium with an enormous potential to transform social relations. Orton and Green did not. If Western Union reduced its rates to the level of postage, Green predicted in 1890, he did not believe that 10 percent of the people would prefer telegraphing their sentiments to communicating by mail. This was because, Green explained, the telegraph was "essentially" an "adjunct of commerce and speculation, requiring immediate communication and answer," rather than a vehicle of popular communication.[38] It was, in short, a private enterprise that served a limited market, rather than a public utility that met the needs of the public at large.

Though Congress never established a postal telegraph, Hubbard's critique had a subtle yet far-reaching influence on Western Union's business strategy. For the next quarter century, Western Union officials remained convinced that, at some point in the near future, the government would purchase Western Union's assets and nationalize the industry—just as the government had in Great Britain, France, and every other leading industrial nation. To forestall this as long as possible, Western Union officials did their best to make the case for private control. Ironically, this business strategy encouraged Western Union officials to narrow their time-horizons, focus on short-term profits, and downplay the long-term competitive challenge that was posed by new communications technologies such as the telephone.[39]

The Informational Environment during the Transition from Commercial Republic to Industrial Nation

Few events in the nineteenth century raised greater expectations than the advent of telegraphy. The new technology was an agency of "almost superhuman facilities," or so declared one of Morse's business partners in 1845: "Every interest, political, social, commercial, and industrial, will find the use of the telegraphic facilities sine qua non. . . . It is destined to effect a revolution in the business, the social, political, commercial and industrial relations of men, such as neither the more potential physical power of steam, nor the noiseless influence of the compass, has developed, gigantic and sublime, to the contemplative mind, as the results of each have been, and are, and are to be. . . ."[40]

The actual development of the new technology was decidedly more prosaic. Early telegraphy was often irregular and could be surprisingly slow. Storms often interrupted service, and even in good weather operators were bedeviled by technical difficulties that stemmed from poor insulation. To make matters worse, telegraphy had to compete with mail delivery, which by 1844 had attained a high level of service. It was hard to convince Americans to patronize the new technology; in the words of one telegraph promoter, looking back on the early days of the industry, the Post Office Department already "served every purpose of ordinary intercourse."[41] Long after the telegraph had become an established institution, a postal clerk could still report that the arrival of a single letter could still could "convulse the market" and create a "commotion" at the commercial exchange.[42] It was not until the 1880s that the number of telegrams Western Union transmitted would equal the number of letters that the Post Office Department had delivered in 1840—which was prior to the passage of the Post Office Act of 1845.

Mail delivery remained particularly important in the sparsely settled and newly developed regions of the West. Here, as one postal administrator noted in 1880, the "comparative scarcity and expensiveness" of the telegraph rendered merchants entirely dependent upon the Post Office Department.[43] Even journalists were slow to make the transition. In the period between 1844 and 1860, for example, only 8 percent of news stories in American newspapers originated as telegraphic dispatches, while 46 percent still came by mail.[44]

The advantages of mail delivery were especially evident following the passage of the Post Office Acts of 1845 and 1851, which it made possible, for the first time in U.S. history, to send a letter without worrying about the cost. Telegrams, in contrast, remained relatively expensive throughout the century. Though rates varied widely, depending on a number of factors, including the competitive situation, a ten-word telegraph message almost never cost less than 50 cents. In 1876, it cost $2.00 to send a ten-word telegram between New York and San Francisco. In contrast, it cost a mere 3 cents to send a letter this distance—and the letter might contain hundreds, or, conceivably, even thousands of words.[45]

The limited facilities that Western Union provided further constrained its utility. As late as 1880, for example, Western Union had a mere 9,000 offices, far fewer than the 43,000 offices in the postal network. And, as critics like Hubbard were quick to point out, three-quarters of these offices were in railroad stations—which, unlike post offices, were often inconveniently located far from the center of town.

Perhaps the best index of the relative importance of the Post Office Department and Western Union was the size of their operating budgets. At no time did Western Union's annual revenue exceed that of the Post Office Department. Between 1870 and 1890, the operating budget of the Post Office Department was, on average, three times as large as that of Western Union. In 1880, for example, the Post Office Department had $33.3 million in operating revenue; Western Union, $10.6 million. In 1900, the gap had widened, with the Post Office Department bringing in more than $100 million, and Western Union, a mere $23 million (see table 3.4).

Through data on telegraphic usage are hard to come by, several generalizations can be ventured. Few Americans ever had occasion to send a telegraph—far fewer than wrote letters or received a newspaper in the mail. A mere 2 percent of the American people, estimated Western Union President Norvin Green in 1887, ever had had occasion to send a message by wire. Fully 87 percent of all the messages that Western Union did transmit, Green added, were business-related. Of

Table 3.4 Relative Expenditures on Mail Delivery, Telegraphy, and Telephony, 1866–1920

Year	Post Office Department operating revenue (millions of dollars)	Western Union operating revenue (millions of dollars)	Bell System operating revenue (millions of dollars)
1866	14.4	4.6	0.0
1870	18.9	6.7	0.0
1880	33.3	10.6	3.1
1890	60.9	20.1	16.4
1900	102.4	22.8	46.1
1910	224.1	30.7	164.3
1914	287.9	45.9	224.5
1920	437.2	n.a.	448.2

Source: U.S. Bureau of the Census, Historical Statistics, 2:785–786, 787–788, 804–805.

the remainder, 8 percent were news-related, and the remaining 5 percent personal. Many of the business-related telegrams were frankly speculative—or, as Green put it, had been occasioned by the buying and selling of goods where "no transportation and often no delivery is ever made."[46]

A substantial fraction of this speculation took place outside of the regular commercial exchanges, in the so-called "bucket shops." These controversial, often precarious, and sometimes clandestine businesses permitted small operators to speculate in agricultural commodities and corporate securities without having to work through a mercantile exchange. Bucket shops, Green observed, generated a "considerable percentage" of Western Union's total revenue, by "selling and buying, forfeiting margins when they expired, settling, when the customers shall demand, at the quoted price at the instant, and no delivery is ever pretended to be made."[47]

Among the heaviest telegraph users were merchants trading in agricultural staples such as cotton and wheat. Since these staples had a ready market in Europe, price information was a valuable asset, particularly in commercial entrepôts located far from the Atlantic seaboard, such as the cotton ports of New Orleans and Mobile and the wheat-processing marts of Buffalo, St. Louis, Minneapolis, and Chicago. A business editor remarked in 1854 that before the coming of the telegraph, traders had taken advantage of advance information to speculate in agricultural staples on an enormous scale. Each year, the editor estimated, planters had lost some forty million dollars in this way—a sum that, since the telegraph, had been reduced to probably one-twentieth its former magnitude.[48]

While the telegraph hardly eliminated speculation, it did change its character. Now that price data were transmitted telegraphically, traders lost the ability to capitalize on advance knowledge of price differentials in distant locations. Instead, they began to speculate about the likely price of staples at specific future dates. Time, as it were, supplanted space as the great unknown. Before long, this practice led to the establishment of the futures market. Odd as it might seem, traders began to purchase crops that had yet to be harvested—and even that had yet to be planted. Planters and farmers found this arrangement advantageous, since it enabled them to sell their crop at a predictable price, protecting themselves against an unexpected market downturn. Traders hoped to profit from unanticipated increases in market demand, and sometimes they tried to drive up the price by purchasing a large fraction of the available contracts and refusing to sell.

To coordinate these complex transactions better, merchants established the modern mercantile exchange. The Chicago Board of Trade dated from 1848, the same year the telegraph reached the city. In the next few years merchants set up similar institutions in several other leading commercial centers, including St. Louis, Minneapolis, and Buffalo.[49] Often these exchanges were located at quite a distance from the site of production. The principal cotton exchange, for example, was located in New York City rather than Mobile or New Orleans.[50]

Mercantile exchanges transformed agricultural staples into easily quantified abstractions that could be bought or sold. For the first time, it became possible to purchase a given quantity of a specific agricultural staple in a distant market without having to rely on middlemen with first-hand information about local conditions. In the process, agricultural staples became commodities, something they had never been in nature.[51]

Telegraphy had analogous consequences for the transmission of news. To regularize news transmission, several New York editors joined together in the 1840s to form the New York Associated Press. Before long, the Associated Press became a newsbroker, and information a commodity.[52] Telegraph officials granted newsbrokers various privileges, including special rates and—most important of all—preferential access to the telegraph wires. The ability of newsbrokers like the Associated Press to coordinate the distribution of time-sensitive information gave them an influence that many regarded as politically dangerous, and which embroiled the industry in a number of public controversies in the Gilded Age.

Few firms used the telegraph more intensively than the railroad. Indeed, there is more than a little truth to the nineteenth-century commonplace that the railroad and the telegraph marched together across the continent as the "Siamese twins of commerce" (see figure 3.5).[53] Telegraphic train-dispatching helped managers prevent accidents, coordinate operations, and generate the data necessary to monitor traffic flows. Financier Jay Gould declared that without the active cooperation of the railroads, the telegraph system, "in its broadest and most popular features" had no financial basis "by which it could exist, as a valuable enterprise, for an hour."[54]

During the early years of telegraphy, the relationship of the telegraph and the railroad was hardly self-evident. Had the railroad never been invented, the first decade of commercial telegraphy would have been substantially unchanged. After all, the primary users of the new technology were merchants dealing in agricultural staples, and the primary

Figure 3.5 American Progress. This lithograph was based on an 1872 painting by John Gast. According to its caption, it represents the "grand drama of Progress in the civilization, settlement, and history of this country." Emblematic of this progress was the "Star of Empire," the robed woman who hovers over the westward movement. Among her gifts is information. In her right hand she carries a book (the testimonial of our national enlightenment"), in her left, a telegraph line ("to flash intelligence throughout the land"). Source: *Crofutt's New Overland Tourist and Pacific Coast Guide* (Chicago: Overland Publishing, 1879–1880), 2:12–13. Courtesy of Robert Dalton Harris.

axis linked New York and New Orleans—a route that the railroad had yet to traverse.

The slow adoption of telegraphic train dispatching was particularly surprising since, in the United States—in contrast, for example, to Great Britain—most railroads were single-tracked. Single-tracking cut down on capital costs, yet it greatly increased the risk of collision and enormously complicated the administrative challenge of coordinating routine operations. "The telegraph is rarely seen in America running beside the railway," remarked one English editorialist in 1854, "for what reason we do not know; the consequence, however, is that locomotion in the United States is vastly more dangerous."[55]

The first American railroad to experiment extensively with telegraphic train-dispatching was the New York & Erie. Station managers relied on telegraphy to regulate train movements as early as 1851, though the procedure does not seem to have been systematized for a number of years.[56]

The Erie's general superintendent, Daniel McCallum, wrote a report that in 1856 describing the new uses for the telegraph. McCallum was one of the first managers to clearly delineate the lines of authority on a major railroad and he regarded the telegraph as an indispensable managerial tool. "It would occupy too much space," McCallum declared, "to allude to all the practical purposes to which the telegraph is applied in working the road; and it may suffice to say, that without it, the business could not be conducted with anything like the same degree of economy, safety, regularity, or dispatch. . . ."[57] McCallum required station managers to transmit by telegraph hourly reports stating the precise position on the line of every passenger train and every important freight train. Should a train run significantly behind schedule—ten minutes for a passenger train, thirty minutes for a freight train—McCallum required the conductor to report the cause of the delay to the telegraph operator when he reached the next station. The operator, in turn, was responsible for transmitting regular reports to the general superintendent. At this point, it was transcribed, as fast as it was received, on a "convenient tabular form," that showed, "at a glance" the "position and progress of trains, in both directions, on every division of the road."[58]

McCallum used the data generated by the telegraph to hasten what business historian Alfred D. Chandler Jr., has called "control through statistics." McCallum's goal was not simply to improve safety, but also to coordinate more effectively the deployment of resources. Indeed, McCallum went so far as to contend that a single-tracked railroad that relied on telegraphy to coordinate the movement of its rolling stock was actually superior to a double-tracked railroad that continued to rely on more rudimentary methods.

Within a few years, McCallum's example was emulated by most of the other leading eastern railroads—including the Baltimore & Ohio, the New York Central, and the Pennsylvania. During the 1860s, telegraphic train-dispatching became commonplace throughout the United States. In the West, the Chicago, Burlington, & Quincy led the way, followed by the Illinois Central.[59] The first telegraph superintendent on the Illinois Central was hired in 1862; a few years later managers issued a printed rule book that included an extensive section on "Movement of Trains by Telegraph."[60] Other lines soon followed their lead, often at the instigation of Western Union officials.[61]

Telegraphic train-dispatching benefited both the railroad and the telegraph. Railroads received an unlimited amount of free telegraphing on the road and a certain amount of free telegraphing throughout the rest of the network. Since railroad managers could telegraph free of charge, it is difficult to know just how much information they transmitted; in all probability, the volume was enormous. Telegraph firms secured free office space and telegraph operators, as well as the free transportation of poles, wires, and other materials. Most important of all, they received an exclusive right to transmit messages over the railroad's right-of-way, forestalling competition and ensuring themselves a reliable conduit for their own long-distance traffic.[62]

Just as the telegraph facilitated the administrative coordination of the railroad, it also became a key managerial tool in manufacturing. Beginning in the 1850s, a number of industrial firms began to place unprecedented demands on the information infrastructure. These enterprises were typically much larger and more complex than any institution in the period prior to 1840, with the exception of the Post Office Department. Had these firms' managers not been able to rely on the fast and reliable means of communication that the telegraph provided, it would have been more difficult, if not impossible, for them to have attained the administrative coordination of production and distribution that was such a key feature of the business enterprise in the industrial age.

Firms adopted telegraphy selectively. In credit reporting agencies, the telegraph proved to be a less important technological innovation than the typewriter—since, unlike the typewriter, it was used primarily in unusual circumstances, and never for the routine transmission of information.[63] Telegraphy played an equally modest role in iron and steel, presumably because managers did not find it necessary to maintain tight control over their stock.[64]

In businesses that specialized in perishable products, such as meatpacking, telegraphy quickly became indispensable. By the 1880s, two leading Chicago meat packers, Armour and Swift, required daily telegraphic reports from their East Coast agents on the state of the market. In an average year, the total cost of these dispatches came to $200,000, a substantial sum.[65] Meat spoiled rapidly, and the packers regarded it as extremely vital to know how much they could safely ship. "The head offices are in constant telegraphic communication with the branch houses and commission agents during the progress of the sale of each carload of beef, obtaining information and giving advice." declared one government observer.[66]

The Telephone Completes the Information Infrastructure of the Industrial Age

In February 1876, Alexander Graham Bell secured the first in a series of patents for a device to transmit the human voice by wire. Bell's patents became the legal cornerstone of the American Bell Telephone Company, the progenitor of American Telephone & Telegraph, which American Bell established in 1885 as a subsidiary to develop the long-distance market. Following a reorganization in 1899, AT&T became the parent firm, with full control over the federation of manufacturing facilities, operating companies, and research and development laboratories that together came to be known as the Bell System. By World War I, the Bell System had become the final element in the information infrastructure of the Industrial Age and one of the largest and most innovative technological systems in the world. As late as 1910, however, AT&T's annual operating revenue had yet to match that of the Post Office Department. But by 1920, AT&T had decisively pulled ahead (see table 3.4). Much like the completion of the postal network in the 1820s, the rise of the Bell System elicited a fair amount of editorial comment. As one journalist declared, the telephone was "unquestionably" the "greatest industrial and commercial achievement of the American people."[67]

Prior to the breakup of the Bell System in 1984, AT&T executives often described the telephone network as the most complicated machine ever built. While this claim is somewhat self-serving, it does highlight the abiding preoccupation of Bell executives with what historians have come to call the "network mystique." In recent decades—in particular, in the 1960s and 1970s—Bell managers spent a disproportionate amount of time and energy in an ultimately futile attempt to protect their communications empire from outside assault. Yet, in the early years of the industry—especially in the period preceding World War I—this distinctive mindset, which combined a disparagement of competition with a faith in public oversight, systems integration, and technical expertise, provided a generation of talented business leaders with a mandate that helped to make AT&T a highly innovative firm.[68]

Few today would question the utility of telephony in the home as well as the office. Yet when Bell secured his patent, it remained uncertain just how the new technology would be used. Unlike the telegraph—which, from the start, met the needs of merchants dealing in agricultural staples—the telephone did not fill an obvious market niche. According to Elisha Gray—a respected authority on electrical applications, and himself the inventor of an early telephone—the new technology had limited commercial value and was merely a "scientific toy."[69]

The successful commercialization of telephony in the United States owed a good deal to the creative leadership of its early champions. Particularly influential were promoter Gardiner Greene Hubbard, inventor Alexander Graham Bell, and manager Theodore N. Vail.

Hubbard's involvement in telephony grew directly out of his own prior experience with telegraphic reform. Though Hubbard was no inventor, he was well aware of the commercial value of an acoustic telegraph that, like the quadruplex, could transmit multiple messages over a single wire. He was thus understandably intrigued when he learned that Bell was experimenting with just such a device.

Hubbard bankrolled Bell's experiments in the expectation that Bell would invent an improved telegraphic instrument that Hubbard could sell to Western Union. Bell had other ideas. Far less interested in multiple telegraphy than in voice transmission, Bell hoped to invent a machine that could transmit human speech. Hubbard initially regarded Bell's research on telephony as a distraction, and did all he could to keep Bell focused on the multiplex. Bell refused to give up his work on the telephone, even though he had good reason not to alienate his patron (among other things, he had fallen in love with Hubbard's daughter, Mabel, whom he hoped to marry).

Hubbard was initially reluctant to commercialize the new technology himself. Just as Morse had hoped to sell his telegraph patent to the government, so Hubbard tried at first to unload the telephone on Western Union. Toward this end, at some point in the fall of 1876 Hubbard arranged an interview with William Orton. Precisely what the two men said to each other during their conference remains a matter of speculation, since no first-hand account has survived. Many years later, one of Bell's closest associates, Thomas A. Watson, recounted that Hubbard had offered Western Union Bell's telephone patent for $100,000, and that Orton had declined.[70]

Orton's refusal to purchase Bell's patent is often cited as one of the worst decisions in the annals of U.S. business. Yet it is not hard to understand why he acted as he did. Hubbard had long been one of Western Union's most outspoken critics, and Orton was, quite naturally, reluctant to reward his longtime adversary with what was, at the time, a quite substantial sum. It was Orton's "repugnance" toward Hubbard, one telegraph official later reminisced, that prevented him from acquiring for Western Union a "controlling interest" in Bell's invention at a "very low cost."[71]

Once Hubbard discovered that there was no easy way to cash in on Bell's patents, he set about to commercialize the telephone himself. On July 9, 1877, Hubbard formally drew up papers to establish the Bell Telephone Company as a patent association. Two days later, Bell married Mabel Hubbard in Hubbard's front parlor.

Hubbard had long criticized Western Union for its narrow focus on the business market and aspired to establish the telephone industry on a broader, more inclusive foundation. Middle-class Americans such as himself (Hubbard frequently presented himself as such in his numerous essays on telegraphic reform) constituted a potentially enormous market for communications that Western Union had conspicuously neglected.[72]

Bell shared Hubbard's idealism, and in 1878 prophesied that the telephone would one day become an everyday medium of social communication on a nationwide scale. At a time when telephony remained limited for technical reasons to a distance of twenty miles, and a host of related issues had yet to be resolved, this was an extraordinary claim. Explaining his beliefs to one group of investors, Bell said that in the future telephone wires would unite the "head offices" of the telephone company in different cities, making it possible for individuals to communicate over vast distances by "word of mouth." Bell conceded that such ideas might appear "Utopian and out of place." Yet he remained confident that "such a scheme" would be the ultimate result of the commercialization of the new technology, and urged investors to at all times keep this "end in view," so that "all present arrangements of the telephone may be eventually realised in this grand system."[73]

Bell focused, like Hubbard, on the middle-class market, broadly conceived. In particular, he envisioned the telephone replacing the speaking tubes, bell pulls, and other devices that the well-to-do relied on to maintain contact with their household staff. Once householders became accustomed to the new technology, he reasoned, they would urge its extension to stores and offices and push for the establishment of a central exchange. In an age when even modest middle-class households employed one or more servants, this was an ingenious strategy, and one that was well calculated to help insure that the arbiters of taste and fashion would soon come to regard the new industry in a favorable light.

This expansive vision of the potential of the new technology shaped its commercialization in several ways. To encourage homes as well as offices to install telephones, Hubbard offered residential users special low rates. And to promote its widespread use, he offered subscribers unlimited monthly service for a single fee. This rate structure had the advantage of being relatively simple to administer. Other pricing schemes, based on message units, could have been devised—and some were, particularly in Europe.

Equally innovative was Hubbard's development strategy. Fearful that poor-quality service would raise doubts about the soundness of the new technology (and also intent on securing a steady return), Hubbard refused to sell telephones outright. As an alternative, he licensed promoters to establish operating companies in specific localities. Typically, Bell licensees solicited subscribers in a relatively small geographical area, such as a city or town, whom they then connected to a central switchboard or exchange. Few of these exchanges interconnected, at least at first, since technological constraints limited a telephone conversation to a range of no more than about twenty miles. Notwithstanding these limitations, Hubbard's development strategy furnished a key precedent for two key tenets of the Bell System: namely, that the parent firm would maintain technical standards among the operating companies and that it would control the manufacturing of the necessary equipment, including the switchboards and telephones.

Hubbard's greatest administrative achievement was his recruitment of Theodore N. Vail as Bell's first general manager. Hubbard first met Vail in 1876 during a trip that Hubbard took across the country as the chairman of a special government commission on railway mail pay. Hubbard was much impressed by the vigor, breadth of vision, and organizational acumen that Vail brought to the superintendence of the Railway Mail Service, and he urged Vail to cast his lot with the fledgling telephone industry. Vail, for his part, found Hubbard's enthusiasm for telephony infectious, and, frustrated by congressional opposition to his ambitious plans for the Fast Mail, jumped at the chance to make a fresh start.

Vail's greatest administrative challenge at Bell came during the very first year of his appointment. The antagonist, predictably enough, was Western Union. Now convinced of the merits of the new technology, President Orton decided in late 1877 to enter the telephone business. Since Western Union had already established a subsidiary in intraurban telegraphy, it proved relatively easy to set up the American Speaking Telephone Company as a rival to Bell.

For a brief moment in the late 1870s, Western Union seemed poised to dominate the telephone industry and relegate Alexander Graham Bell to a footnote in the annals of invention. In addition to its own telephone patents, Western Union had at its disposal a formidable array of administrative and legal talent, an almost unlimited supply of capital, and an ownership stake in Western Electric, the largest man-ufacturer of electrical equipment in the country. American Speaking Telephone established operating companies faster than Bell and se-cured a beachhead in several major cities, including New York and Chicago. (The firm even had, in its secretary, James D. Reid, its own corporate historian. When, for example, Reid described in 1879 the newly emerging telephone industry in the first edition of his history of telegraphy, he treated the American Speaking Telephone Company in some detail, while omitting from his discussion any mention what-soever of Hubbard or Bell.[74])

Though Bell's defenders could not hope to match Western Union's resources, they were not without some key assets of their own. In addition to Bell's patents and Hubbard's zeal, they had in Vail a skillful tactician with a keen grasp of the relevant issues. As his first official act as general manager, Vail sent every Bell licensee a copy of Bell's first patent, with a note enjoining them to keep up the fight against Western Union. In the ensuing months, Vail worked diligently to secure for the licensees the funding necessary to stave off the compe-tition, and to force Western Union onto the defensive by suing it for infringing on Bell's patent rights.[75]

Most important, Vail helped convince Boston financier William H. Forbes to invest in the firm.[76] Forbes quickly became the leader of a group of Boston investors who provided the Bell Company with a much-needed infusion of cash. In the absence of the financial resources that the Boston group provided, it is hard to imagine how the fledgling Bell Company could have met the challenge that Western Union posed. In recognition of this contribution, in early 1879 Hubbard renamed the firm the National Bell Telephone Company, and persuaded the Massachusetts legislature to increase the amount of capital that it was legally entitled to raise.

Hubbard and Bell had assumed that the National Bell stockholders would chose Hubbard as the first president of the reorganized firm. To their surprise, the investors settled on Forbes. Forbes's appoint-ment curtailed Hubbard's authority, and deeply worried Bell, who feared that Forbes might cut a deal with Western Union that would tarnish his scientific reputation. Yet as it turned out, neither had much cause for concern, since Forbes fully shared their determination to battle Western Union.[77]

In November 1879, following extended negotiations, Forbes emerged triumphant, having persuaded Orton's successor, Norvin Green (Orton had died in 1878), to cede the telephone market to National Bell. This agreement, Vail later observed, was "the most important single event in the history of the telephone business."[78] For its part, Western Union promised to stay out of telephony, and to transfer to Bell its telephone assets—including its operating companies and every one of Edison's and Gray's patents. In return, Bell agreed to turn over to Western Union all of the interurban telegraph messages originating in Bell telephone exchanges, and to pay Western Union a generous royalty for the next seventeen years on every telephone it leased.

In retrospect, Green's abandonment of the telephone industry seems no less shortsighted than Orton's refusal to purchase Bell's patent. Yet, at the time, it too made a certain amount of sense. Preoccupied with the long-distance business market—and resigned, as Orton had been before him, to the eventual government takeover of Western Union's assets—Green concluded it was simply not worth the effort to embark on a new venture that might not realize its full commercial potential for another twenty-five years. Green's lawyers had advised him that Bell's patents would prove hard to contest, and Green lacked the stomach for a fight. Though Green's negotiations with Forbes did occur during the same months Green was immersed in a fierce competitive struggle with the financier Jay Gould, there are few hints in Green's correspondence that Gould's threat influenced Green's decision to sell out. Far more important was Green's revulsion at the prospect of a long, drawn-out competitive struggle. In the end—as Green explained to Forbes, after the final settlement had been reached—Western Union had been willing to compromise for the sake of "peace and harmony" and to avoid the "trouble, loss, and expense of a wasteful competition."[79]

The acquisition of Western Union's telephone business significantly augmented Bell's burgeoning network of operating companies. By 1881, as Forbes took care to point out in Bell's first published stockholder's report, Bell and its licensees had established telephone service in all but nine of the nation's cities with a population of more than 10,000.[80] Since telephony was a mere five years old, this statistic demonstrated an impressive record of growth.

Following the Western Union settlement, Forbes and Vail moved swiftly to consolidate their rapidly expanding telephone empire. In 1881, they once again increased the firm's legal capitalization, and changed the firm's name, this time to the American Bell Telephone Company, a moniker it would retain for the next twenty years. In addition, Bell lawyers redoubled their efforts to protect Bell's patent position, which from the outset they had defended with great skill. Between the granting of Bell's first patent in 1876 and the expiration of Bell's last major patent in 1894, Bell lawyers found themselves embroiled in 600 separate legal disputes; they never lost a case.[81]

Of particular importance for the future was Vail's 1881 acquisition of a controlling interest in Western Electric—a leading manufacturer of electrical equipment that, for the past ten years, had been affiliated with Western Union. The following year, Western Electric became an exclusive supplier of Bell telephone equipment, a position it would long retain. Interestingly, Western Electric's owners fully supported the takeover; they reasoned that, if the company remained independent, Bell might well enter into an exclusive manufacturing agreement with some other firm.[82]

The acquisition of Western Electric helped make American Bell one of the first business enterprises to promote continuing research in the production and development of electrical equipment. In this way, Bell executives established a tradition that would culminate in 1925 with the establishment of Bell Labs, a key element in the information infrastructure of the Information Age.

Vail left AT&T in 1887 following a quarrel with the Boston investors over financial policy, but by this time he had established the firm on a foundation that it would maintain for the next 100 years.[83] One early milestone came in 1884, when, under Vail's leadership, American Bell established the first commercial telephone service between Boston and New York, a distance of several hundred miles. Slowly but steadily, Bell-funded engineers were making advances in transmission technology that made it possible to link the various operating companies in a single interconnected network. No longer would telephony remain restricted to a mere twenty miles. Vail's preoccupation with transmission technology occasioned his appointment, in 1885, as the first president of American Telephone and Telegraph (AT&T), a wholly owned subsidiary with a mandate to focus on long-distance transmission. Eight years later, following Vail's departure, AT&T achieved another technical breakthrough when, for the first time, it extended service from New York to Chicago.

With the expiration of Bell's last major patent in 1894, Bell executives suddenly confronted a host of newly chartered telephone firms. In the following decade, some 6,000 independents sprang up throughout the United States. These firms offered rudimentary, inexpensive telephone service not only in urban centers, where Bell was already well established, but also in many rural regions that Bell had yet to tap. Independent strongholds included St. Louis, Rochester, New York, and countless smaller cities in the South and Midwest. By 1907, non-Bell firms operated half of the telephones in the United States (see table 3.5).

The independents greatly expanded the market for telephony and forced Bell to extend its network at an unprecedented rate. In 1891, several years prior to the expiration of the Bell patents, fewer than four of every 1,000 Americans had a telephone. By 1910, fifteen years after the rise of the independents, the number of telephones had increased to 82 per 1,000 Americans (see table 3.6). In the period between 1894 and 1914—the first two decades of competition—Bell installed ten times as many telephones as it had in the period between 1876 and 1893.

Though the independents provided little long-distance service, few customers cared. Far more important, at least initially, was their ability to offer low rates and a reasonable level of service. In large measure, the ability of these firms to underbid Bell can be explained by the simple fact that, on account of their relatively small subscriber base (compared to Bell), they had little need to make a comparable investment in switching technology. This was because in telephony, in contrast to mass-production industries such as steel or automobiles, expanding the scale of operations led to an increase, rather than a decrease, in unit cost. The larger the number of subscribers, the greater the problem. Or, to put it somewhat less abstractly, as the network expanded, it became relatively more expensive to provide the necessary facilities to enable a user to make a call.[84]

The rise of the independents forced Bell Telephone executives to

Table 3.5 Telephone Usage Patterns, 1876–1920

Year	Number of Telephones[a] (thousands)	Telephones Per 1,000 Population	Telephone Calls[a]	
			Local (millions)	Toll (thousands)
1876	3	0.1	n.a.	n.a.
1880	54	1.1	0.2	2
1890	234	3.7	1.4[b]	10[b]
1893	266	3.9	1.9	34
1900	1,356	17.6	7.7	193
1910	7,635	82.0	35.3	862
1920	13,273	123.4	50.2	1,607

Source: U.S. Bureau of the Census, Historical Statistics of the United States, 2:783–784.

[a]Bell System and independent companies.
[b]Totals for 1889.

Table 3.6 Competition in Telephony, 1893–1920

| | Number of Telephones | | | Percentage | |
Year	Bell System (millions)	Independent (connecting) (millions)	Independent (nonconnecting) (millions)	Connecting	Nonconnecting
1893	0.3	0	0	100	0
1900	0.8	0.02	0.5	63	37
1905	2.3	0.3	1.6	61	39
1907	3.0	0.8	2.3	63	37
1910	3.9	2.0	1.8	77	23
1912	4.8	2.5	1.4	84	16
1920	8.7	3.8	0.7	95	5

Source: U.S. Bureau of the Census, *Historical Statistics of the United States,* 2:783–784.

rethink their business strategy. Following the lead of E. J. Hall, a key figure in Bell's expansion in the South, they entered into a variety of sublicensing agreements with firms that remained outside of their direct control. Sublicensing proved particularly advantageous in peripheral regions like the South, because it enabled Bell to expand its network at a minimum cost.[85] Unlike the Bell operating companies, the sublicensees lacked direct financial ties to the parent company, yet they could interconnect with the Bell network, provided that they maintained certain technical standards.

Hall also cultivated support for high technical standards among sympathetic government officials, particularly in state legislatures and state regulatory commissions. Hall's skillful political entrepreneurship significantly raised barriers to entry in the industry, since it obliged Bell's competitors to meet its exacting operating requirements. Just as the judiciary had shielded Bell from competition between 1876 and 1894, so the state governments helped it fend off potential challengers between 1894 and World War I.[86]

Bell strategy assumed a heightened coherence in 1907, when a New York banking consortium headed up by J. P. Morgan gained control of AT&T and appointed Vail to the presidency. Back in power, Vail picked up where he had left off two decades before.

The cornerstone of Vail's business strategy was his commitment to universal service. Universal service for Vail was soaring ideal that, at times, assumed an almost utopian cast. Like Bell and Hubbard, Vail had a visionary streak, and he was firmly convinced that, at some future time, AT&T would provide a basic level of telephone service to every household in the country. This was, however, a highly unrealistic objective at a time when telephones could be found in fewer than 10 percent of American households. In the interim, he aspired to the less ambitious, yet still quite challenging, goal of interconnecting every existing telephone controlled by Bell. To popularize interconnection, Vail launched a public relations campaign that was by far the largest effort of its kind to have ever been mounted by a U.S. corporation.[87] Its theme was "one system, one policy, universal service," which succinctly expressed Vail's vision of an integrated telephone network under the supervision of AT&T.

Vail's strategy was predicated upon a close working relationship with the New York investors under J. P. Morgan. In addition to providing AT&T with the capital it needed to buy out selected independents, the Morgan group was determined to block the creation of an independent long-distance network. Confident that AT&T could always outspend the competition, Vail followed Hall's lead and encouraged state legislatures and state regulatory commissions to mandate high technical standards for telephone firms operating within their jurisdictions—establishing, by no means inadvertently, barriers that the more poorly capitalized independents found difficult to meet.[88]

One area in which Vail proved unwilling to innovate was in switching. Though AT&T's competitors had begun in the 1890s to introduce automatic switching, before 1920 virtually every telephone call made with Bell equipment had been connected manually by a telephone operator—almost always a young woman known as a "hello girl." Vail was reluctant to move ahead in this area for several reasons. AT&T had a huge investment in mechanical switching equipment and Vail was understandably hesitant to write it off as obsolete. Technical challenges also loomed large. Automatic switching raised a host of perplexing operational problems, especially in a network as large as the Bell System. Still, had Vail made automatic switching a priority, it seems likely that AT&T could have moved a good deal faster in this area than it did (see figure 3.6).

Vail's business outlook posed a further constraint. Automatic switching violated the principle of "user transparency"—that is, the notion that telephony should be kept so simple that subscribers would not even have to dial a number. Like Hubbard and Bell, Vail remained sensitive to the fact that most telephone subscribers hailed from the middle or upper classes and had come to regard telephone operators as a logical extension of their household staff. The decision to use the telephone—or so Vail assumed—should be analogous to ringing a maid

Figure 3.6 Telephone Operators. This is a very early photograph of telephone operators, dating from 1883. Taken in Boston, it shows men and women working together at a switchboard. The operators connected calls by attaching the caller's line to the appropriate slot in the plugboard that is mounted against the wall. Within a few years, this job would be reserved for women, the famous "hello girls." Automatic telephone switching became commonplace in the 1920s, after having been long resisted by AT&T. AT&T executives worried that customers would resent having to dial calls themselves; they also sought to protect the firm's enormous investment in manual switching equipment. Courtesy of AT&T Archives.

to hand-deliver a personal note. "The telephone operator," Vail declared, was the "servant of every subscriber, as though she was in his office or in his direct employ. . . . There can never be, in my opinion, any way devised to get rid of the 'intelligence' which at some point in making up the connection is apt to be required."[89] Not until the 1920s, with the widespread introduction of the dial telephone, would Bell democratize telephony by permitting subscribers to hold a telephone conversation without having to rely on the assistance of a Bell System operator to complete the connection.[90]

Vail proved far more committed to solving the problem of long-distance telephony. Though the market for long-distance service remained quite limited, Vail was driven by what one historian has aptly termed an "almost irrational commitment" to interconnection.[91] The invention by Bell engineers in the 1880s of the loading coil and in the 1900s of the audion (an early vacuum tube) were major steps toward the realization of this goal. So was the advent, in 1915, of telephone service between New York and San Francisco, which demonstrated for the first time the feasibility of telephony on a truly continental scale.

The New York–San Francisco connection was a major technical triumph, since it had required the use of the audion, one of the key innovations of the Information Age. In the following years, AT&T built on this breakthrough by experimenting with the audion in wireless telegraphy, or what would soon come to be known as radio.

AT&T's foray into the new technology was short-lived. Fearful of possible legal action under the Sherman Anti-Trust Act, Bell pulled out of radio as a precaution. This decision drew on a certain fund of experience—in the years preceding World War I, AT&T had found itself embroiled in a related lawsuit aimed at contesting its control over the telephone business. This legal action was abandoned in 1913, when, to the surprise of many observers, AT&T Vice President Nathan Kingsbury and U.S. Attorney General James C. McReynolds devised an out-of-court settlement that made major concessions to the independents. Had McReynolds and Kingsbury failed to work out the compromise that became known as the Kingsbury Commitment, the Bell System might well have been broken up or even nationalized. The Kingsbury Commitment required Bell to provide access to its long-distance lines to independents that sought such a connection; the settlement also promulgated a set of principles that would structure relations between AT&T, the operating companies, and the independents for more than seventy years—until the court-mandated breakup of the Bell System in 1984.

Given the present-day deregulatory climate, one might assume that the Kingsbury Commitment was a clear victory for monopoly over competition. After all, it weakened the independents, and left the Bell System intact. Yet this was not how it was commonly understood at the time. Far more important to contemporaries was the role of this agreement in defusing pressure for the nationalization of the entire telephone industry—which was, as one popular magazinist aptly observed, one of the "big, smoldering issues" of the day.[92] Government ownership of telephony was an established fact in Great Britain, France, and every other major industrial country; in the 1910s, such ownership had the support of many U.S. public figures, including Postmaster General Albert Burleson. In such a political setting, the independents quite understandably supported the Kingsbury Commitment as the lesser of two evils. Indeed, one historian of the independents has gone so far as to credit the endorsement of the agreement by these firms as a major reason the industry escaped the evil of government ownership. "It is fair to say," this historian observed, that if the Kingsbury Commitment had not "broken the ice" and convinced both the independents and AT&T that they had an equal stake in the status quo, the "public ownership zealots" in Washington might have been able to "put over" on a "disunited and internally bickering industry" a much more intrusive regulatory scheme.[93]

During World War I, the federal government did, in fact, briefly assume control of the telephone industry. Yet Congress proved disinclined to perpetuate this experiment once the hostilities ceased, and in 1919 it swiftly returned the industry to its investors. It may well be that this outcome owed more than a little to the collective ability of AT&T, the government, and the independents to devise a politically acceptable regulatory regime.

Vail's business strategy proved so successful and enduring, that it is tempting to speculate a bit about the organizational models upon which he drew. One possible source of inspiration was, of course, the telegraph industry. Vail had briefly worked for Western Union as a telegraph operator in his youth, and was familiar with the prominent role that his cousin, Alfred Vail, had played in the 1840s in helping Samuel F. B. Morse's to set up the Washington–Baltimore line.

Yet the influence of telegraphy on Vail's managerial style is easily exaggerated. In several key respects, Vail's leadership of the Bell System differed from Orton's and Green's administration of Western Union. Unlike Vail, Orton and Green lacked a commitment to systems integration, opposed all forms of government control, and, with the exception of a brief moment in the 1860s and 1870s, displayed scant interest in technological innovation.[94]

A far more plausible, though often overlooked, organizational seedbed for Vail's ideas was the Post Office Department. Ever since the passage of the Post Office Act of 1792, postal administrators had striven, in one way or another, to provide the citizenry with universal access to up-to-date information about commerce and public affairs. Though this goal differed in several ways from Vail's commitment to universal service, it did share with it an unambiguously civic cast. Even more direct were the lessons that Vail may have drawn from the Railway Mail Service, over which he had presided in the 1870s. Particularly suggestive was Vail's involvement in the Fast Mail. This project, after all, was a major experiment not only in high-speed long-distance transmission, but also in interconnection, technical standard-setting, and the administrative coordination of a highly decentralized federation of operating units. Without wishing to push the analogy too far, it may well be that it furnished Vail with at least some of the ideas that he would later deploy with such effectiveness at AT&T.

The Informational Environment of the Industrial Nation

"What strikes and frightens the backward European almost as much as anything in the United States," declared one English visitor in 1912, is the "efficiency and fearful universality" of its telephone service:

> Just as I think of the big cities as agglomerations pierced everywhere by elevator-shafts full of movement, so I think of them as being threaded under pavements and over roofs and between floors and ceilings and between walls, by millions upon millions of live filaments. . . . the European telephone is a toy, and a somewhat clumsy one, compared with the inexorable seriousness of the American telephone.[95]

The Englishman's observation was borne out by comparative data. At the turn of the twentieth century, there was one telephone for every sixty individuals in the United States; one for every 115 individual in Sweden; and one for every 1,216 individuals in France.[96] In 1909, there were more telephones in the hotels of New York City than in all of Spain.[97]

Telephony shaped U.S. business in a variety of ways. By facilitating interpersonal communication within localities and inside buildings, it reduced the demand for messenger boys. And by providing senior-level administrators with a tool for overseeing foremen, middle managers, and other subordinates, it encouraged the physical separation of the factory floor from the executive suite, a necessary precondition for the emergence of the central office district. Bell engineer John J. Carty observed: "It may sound ridiculous" to hail Alexander Graham Bell and his successors as the "fathers of modern commercial architecture—of the skyscraper." Yet, Carty added, the relationship between telephony and the multistory office building was impossible to ignore. "Suppose there was no telephone and every message had to be carried by a personal messenger. How much room do you think the necessary elevators would leave for offices? Such structures would be an economic impossibility."[98]

The emergence of the skyscraper significantly augmented the authority of the central office. So did the novel requirement that sales representatives report back to headquarters every day when they were on the road. To meet this demand, hotel owners installed telephones in the guest rooms of establishments that catered to business travelers, an innovation that at this time distinguished U.S. hotels from their counterparts in the rest of the world.

The speed with which the telephone transformed social relations within the firm is easily exaggerated. At no point did telephony entirely displace written communication, or render obsolete any of the other information-related technologies that were beginning to come into widespread use. In certain large firms—such as the Metropolitan Life Insurance Company, in New York—the telephone faced stiff competition from pneumatic tubes, an ingenious mechanical delivery system that had the advantage of leaving a written record. In the late nineteenth century, Metropolitan employees within the firm's New York headquarters were transmitting pneumatically some 5,000 messages a day.[99]

Executives sometimes tried to compensate for the absence of a written record by mounting two phones on their desks—one for their own use, and one for their stenographer (see figure 3.7). Yet this expedient was awkward and expensive, and it rarely caught on. Outright resistance to the new technology was by no means unknown, particularly when its introduction was unaccompanied by any related changes in organizational design. A manager of a medium-sized manufacturing firm in Connecticut in 1917 complained, "Time is lost, confusion results and money is spent in endeavoring to locate executives [for telephone calls] when they are out in the plant."[100]

For many Americans—in particular, those in the middle and upper classes—the telephone provided a useful substitute for a face-to-face exchange, just as Bell and Hubbard had hoped. Storekeepers large and small quickly came to recognize it as an indispensable business asset. Telephony proved especially valuable for individuals whose cultural authority rested on technical expertise or verbal skill. This was particularly true of the lawyers, bankers, doctors, ministers, and civic leaders who made up such a vital part of the professional middle class.

By World War I, many middle- and upper-class households had come to regard the telephone as a necessity. But it was hardly inexpensive. The

Figure 3.7 Office Telephone. By 1904, when this photograph was taken, telephones were a common feature in business offices. But, as this photograph reveals, some businessmen continued to prefer to mount them on separate tables, rather than on their desk. Note that the telephone has two transmitters. This made is possible for a stenographer to record the conversation. Telephone service quickly spread to private residences and, by the First World War, was widely available throughout the United States. Courtesy of AT&T Archives.

average residential rate for a Bell telephone in 1895 was $4.66 a month, or $66 a year—which put it well out of the reach of the working poor.[101] It is hard to come up with comparable totals for later decades, since Bell began to give households the option of choosing between metered service and a flat monthly rate. In addition, households could sometimes secure more inexpensive service from the independents, or by sharing a party line that enabled several families to share a single circuit. Long-distance telephony was especially expensive. In 1919, for example, it cost $16.50 to make a three-minute call between New York and San Francisco, and $4.65 to make a three-minute call between New York and Chicago.[102] Not until well after World War II would it become at all common to make long-distance calls from one's home, and, as late as the 1930s, less than 2 percent of all telephone traffic crossed state lines.[103]

Prior to the expiration of the Bell patent monopoly in 1894, few farms had telephones. With the rise of the independents, rural telephony was born. In 1903 less than 3 percent of farm households had telephones, at a time when the national household average was 10 percent. By 1912, fully 30 percent of farm households had at least some form of telephone service, which was surprisingly close to the national average of 35 percent. For a time, the overwhelmingly rural state of Iowa had one of the highest rates of per capita telephone usage in the United States.[104]

Many hoped that rural telephony would slow the migration of farm children from the country to the city. "With a telephone in the house, a buggy in the barn, and a rural mail box at the gate," predicted one rural booster, "the problem of how to keep the boys and girls on the farm is solved."[105] The reality, however, was more complex. The telephone notwithstanding, farm regions continued to lose population—and, between 1920 and 1940, the number of rural telephones users actually declined.[106] Not until after World War II would rural telephone penetration once again approximate the national average. This upsurge owed less to private competition than to public policy—in particular, the government-mandated cross-subsidization of telephone service and the cheap loans and technical aid provided to thinly settled portions of the country by the Rural Electrification Authority. Just as political fiat had spurred the expansion of the information infrastructure in the commercial republic, so too would it continue to shape its development in the industrial nation.

Summary

This chapter reminds us that the prehistory of the present-day Information Age antedates the invention of the computer by a century and a half, and, in fact, is older than the United States. Beginning in the 1760s with the emergence of an organized opposition to the Crown, and accelerating in the 1790s with the expansion of the postal network, information has always figured prominently in American life. In conjunction with the seemingly insatiable demand of Americans for more and better information, the transformation of the information infrastructure during the long nineteenth century goes far toward explaining why a faith in the emancipatory potential of communications has long been one of the most distinctive, and enduring, of American cultural traits.

Between the adoption of the Constitution and World War I, two distinct yet partly overlapping communications revolutions recast the informational environment in the United States. The first of these revolutions received its initial impetus in the 1760s, when large numbers of Americans came for the first time to regard the creation of an informed citizenry as a valued ideal. This cultural imperative found an institutional embodiment in the postal system, which, after an uncertain beginning in the 1770s and 1780s, acquired a discernibly modern form with the passage of the Post Office Act of 1792.

The first communications revolution reoriented the informational environment of the commercial republic from the seaboard to the hinterland. No longer would the primary information flows be transatlantic, as they had been in the informational ancien régime that existed prior to 1787. By 1828, a Trans-Appalachian, land-based informational environment had come to supplement—though never altogether to supersede—the Atlantic, maritime informational environment that had once yoked the United States to Great Britain.

The second communications revolution recast the informational environment for the Industrial Age. This revolution began in the 1840s with the expansion of the railroad and the advent of the telegraph, and accelerated in the 1870s with the elaboration of the Railway Mail Service and the coming of the telephone. By World War I, this information infrastructure was complete. In many ways, it would become the foundation of the information infrastructure of the present-day Information Age.

This second communications revolution shaped the informational environment in a variety of ways. In its first, transitional phrase, it fostered major institutional innovations in commodity trading and news reporting and improved internal communications within business enterprises that operated on a geographically extended scale. In its second (and final) phase, it eased rural isolation and hastened the rise of the modern central office district and the professional middle class.

The history of the information infrastructure in the United States cannot be fully understood by focusing exclusively on the interplay of technology and markets. No less important have been the cultural norms that decision-makers relied on to shape the course of events. The ideal of an informed citizenry inspired postal administrators such as John McLean; the ideology of private enterprise constrained telegraph officials such as William Orton and Norvin Green; and the ethos of universal service guided telephone executives such as Theodore N. Vail. Political considerations have also proved significant. Congressional opposition stymied competition in mail delivery; the specter of government control narrowed time horizons at Western Union; and various kinds of government regulation have shaped the contours of the telephone grid.

While competition has often been a catalyst for change, it remains undeniable that the communications sector has been dominated for long periods by a relatively small number of large institutions—the Post Office Department, the Railway Mail Service, Western Union, and the Bell System. To a remarkable extent, it was these institutions—each a first mover in its respective realm—that, in conjunction with the constant demand of countless Americans for more and better information, best explains the transformation of the American informational environment in the long nineteenth century that began in 1787 with the framing of the Constitution and closed in 1914 with the start of World War I.

4

Business Use of Information and Technology during the Industrial Age

JoAnne Yates

We have seen that democratic ideology encouraged U.S. demand for information in the eighteenth century, and that technologies such as the printing press allowed and encouraged increased dissemination of such information. The continued growth of demand for information, combined with new communication and transportation technologies and evolving organizational forms, encouraged the development and support of information infrastructures such as the postal system, the railroad, the telegraph, and the telephone in the early and mid-nineteenth century. During the period from 1880 to 1950, the nonfarm sectors in the U.S. economy, especially manufacturing, expanded rapidly, with manufacturing overtaking agriculture as the dominant sector in the private economy.[1] The rapid growth of manufacturing both encouraged and was built on the extensive use of information to control business processes and outcomes; this appetite for information in turn encouraged the diffusion of technologies—including both office equipment and bureaucratic techniques or systems that supported information use.[2] These information processing technologies spread into other, often information-intensive sectors such as financial services and retail selling, adding further to the demand for information processing technologies. By 1950, the uses and technologies of business information had evolved to a considerable extent, putting U.S. business on the threshold of what has become known as the Information Age.

This chapter will first consider the period of growth in markets, production, and firms from 1880 to 1920. I will discuss the systematic management ideology that emerged in response to problems of managerial control—and the ways in which this philosophy of system and efficiency encouraged new uses of information, along with increased office work and the development and/or adoption of new supporting technologies for handling information. Many aspects of this managerial philosophy were anticipated earlier among railroad managers, but it emerged into popular business awareness in manufacturing, then spread to other sectors and types of work, including office work itself. In the final decades of the nineteenth century and the initial ones of the twentieth, systematic management encouraged the adoption of a wave of office equipment and bureaucratic systems and techniques— including, for example, typewriters, carbon paper, filing systems, adding machines, and graphic representation—that supported recording, storing and retrieving, analyzing, and communicating the increased amount of information being gathered.

The depersonalization characteristic of systematic management was supplemented and tempered by the human resources and personnel movement beginning around World War I and building up to 1950. This managerial ideology involved yet more gathering and analyzing of information, which was further encouraged in the first half of the twentieth century by increased regulation concerning organizational employees. In the early twentieth century, a more complicated information processing system—punched-card tabulating—had emerged and was adopted by businesses such as railroads, financial service firms, and manufacturing companies to support large-scale, back-office information operations involving multiple information processes, from recording, storing and retrieving, and analyzing to printing out for communication. These information operations reflected growth in information-intensive organizations and in the information component of other types of organizations, the adoption of personnel departments, other aspects of the human resource approach to management, and New Deal regulation. This technology continued to evolve up to the 1950s, paving the way for the introduction of computers into business.

Growth, Ideology, and Increased Information Demand, 1880–1920s

In the early and mid-nineteenth century, most U.S. manufacturing businesses were quite small—generally consisting of one or more owner/manager(s), perhaps a small number of skilled artisans or foremen, and a few unskilled workers—and operated on the basis of informal and ad hoc management methods.[3] In such small firms, the owners and skilled artisans could generally coordinate and manage activities through informal oral exchanges. Typically, only external transactions were recorded, using the double entry method of bookkeeping. Even in the textile factories that appeared in New England in the first half of the century, managerial methods did not change very much, with skilled artisans running primitive "departments" of the factory as they might have run independent shops.

With the growth of the railroads from small local lines to large regional and national transportation systems, new managerial methods began to emerge; initially this occurred in the railroads themselves, even before the transportation they provided had fostered growth in other sectors. As railroads started to grow into the first large-scale U.S. businesses around mid-century, their inherent geographical dispersion increased, and issues of safety and profitability arose.[4] Railroad managers responded first to train wrecks (with their accompanying loss of life, property, and reputation) and then to diseconomies of scale by developing the earliest modern managerial techniques. In the 1840s, they addressed safety issues, instituting strict requirements that only *written* orders and regulations be used to govern train movement and setting up rudimentary reporting systems to allow them to learn from their mistakes.

Starting in the 1850s and 1860s, leading railroad managers such as Daniel C. McCallum of the New York & Erie Railroad attempted to improve efficiency and profitability in the growing railroads by developing many accounting techniques, including refining financial accounting and inventing capital and cost accounting.[5] Such techniques required new and extensive internal flows of documentation to collect and store information, and elaborate systems for analyzing and communicating it. These techniques were widely publicized among railroads in railroad magazines such as the *American Railroad Journal*, in business journals such as the *Commercial and Financial Chronicle*, and even in more general publications such as *Atlantic Monthly*,[6] but the cost accounting techniques, in particular, were fairly specific to the size and nature of the railroad business, and thus were not adopted more broadly. Although the literature of systematic management discussed here reveals similar general goals of system and efficiency, it makes almost no reference to the accounting techniques developed in the railroads.

The final decades of the nineteenth century saw rapid growth in manufacturing output.[7] The establishment of the new U.S. communication and transportation infrastructures opened larger markets, production technology improved, and postbellum economic growth in general promoted increased production. Manufacturing output expanded, both in mass-production, high-throughput businesses and in customized and batch-oriented specialty production.[8] As the quantity and diversity of their products grew, firms began to encounter the problems of internal coordination and control railroads had encountered a few decades earlier. What one contemporary manufacturing engineer referred to as "the old slipshod way of our forefathers"[9] did not provide adequate coordination in larger firms. As hierarchies grew vertically (with additional layers of management) and horizontally (with larger numbers of units and workers at the bottom levels), new mid-level managers (mostly engineers by training) felt that they had lost control over production processes and that the lack of coordination was resulting in chaos and inefficiency. Firms producing an array of specialty or customized products, even those only moderate in size, sought better ways of establishing costs for those products and of producing such variety efficiently enough that buyers were willing to pay prices that resulted in profits for their manufacturers. In response to all these pressures, engineer/managers gradually began to develop and share new managerial approaches and techniques (presented in articles published first in engineering magazines and then in the newly emerging management publications) that collectively came to be called "systematic management."[10]

The systematic management philosophy or ideology, more amorphous than Frederick Taylor's much narrower but better publicized "Scientific Management" (a shop-floor management system), reflected the broader societal search for order during this era.[11] The emergent philosophy of systematic management centered around the use of what was designated "system" to achieve managerial control and efficiency. In particular, the systematizers who developed and spread these notions had two common themes: (1) the need to transcend individuals, whether owners, managers, or workers, by systematizing and documenting duties and procedures; and (2) a systematic approach to gathering and analyzing information as the basis for coordination.[12] The principles of systematic management favored written over oral communication, as indicated in this quote from an early advocate of the new management philosophy:

> Even if entire honesty and sincerity prevailed at all times in all business transactions, the mere differences due to variations in individual understandings of orders would render it impossible to conduct any business of magnitude on verbal specifications.[13]

One of the earliest engineer/managers, Captain Henry Metcalfe, speaking at the 1886 meeting of the American Society of Mechanical Engineers, put this principle more eloquently:

Now, administration without records is like music without notes—by ear. Good as far as it goes—which is but a little way—it bequethes [sic] nothing to the future. Except in the very rudest industries, carried on as if from hand to mouth, all recognize that the present must prepare for the demands of the future, and hence records, more or less elaborate, are kept.[14]

Many different specific schemes for systematizing manufacturing were proposed by different advocates, with managerial innovation in specialty production focusing more on the need to create order in variation, and innovation in mass production focusing more on the need to improve efficiency through standardization of products.[15] In general, however, "system" and "efficiency" became watchwords of manufacturing managers of all types, increasing the demand for systematic, primarily written, information about roles, processes, and outcomes. Managers established more or less elaborate systems of information collection, analysis, and use in firms to fill this demand.

One notable arena of innovation spurred by systematic management was cost accounting, which was extensively developed as a managerial tool during this period from its very sketchy beginnings in pre-1880 cost management.[16] Several of the leading writers about systematic management, including Metcalfe, Slater Lewis, and Alexander Hamilton Church, made significant contributions to cost accounting. During the period from 1875 into the 1930s, a range of specialized accounting positions were created in firms, as shown in table 4.1. Attempts to calculate the cost of manufacturing standardized or customized items (and, where possible, to compare the performance of different units) were full of difficulties posed by such issues as how to allocate indirect costs. Moreover, dependence primarily on numerical data carried dangers as well as advantages, since numerical data were, by definition, abstracted from their context and could be used in ways

Table 4.1 New Accounting Positions Created between 1875 and 1930s

Controller	Production Controller
Chief Cost Accountant	Financial Controller
Cost Accountant	Auditor
Sales Controller	System Manager

Source: J. Brooks Hechst, Accounting Systems: Design and Installation (New York: Ronald Press, 1936), 473–477.

inappropriate to that context. For example in *Relevance Lost*, H. Thomas Johnson and Robert S. Kaplan make this argument with regard to cost accounting data, and others have made it more broadly.[17] The emergence into prominence of cost accounting and other uses of quantitative data related to systematic management practices called for the recording, storing and retrieving, analyzing, and presentation of large amounts of numerical information within companies. Effective managerial use of these numerical data required an understanding of the source and nature of the data and intelligence in using it.

Another notable area of development was in the downward flow of written orders, instructions, and rules—both in handbooks and in frequently issued orders and circular letters. Managers used such documentation to standardize processes and jobs. Independent sales agents, for example, were often replaced by salaried employees (often the same individuals) and whether they were salaried employees or not, they were given sales manuals intended to help the firms standardize prices, terms for sales, and the sales process itself.[18] Managers following systematic management principles often favored jobs that were more narrowly defined and routinized.[19] Analogously, horizontal flows of interdepartmental correspondence to document coordination (or failures of coordination) for the record also developed. Finally, reports analyzed cost and data and other data flowing up the hierarchy as the basis for monitoring and for recommending policy.

Thus the managerial appetite for information, both non-numerical (e.g., reports or interdepartmental correspondence) and numerical (e.g., cost accounting data or sales analysis data), in specialty and mass-production manufacturers grew enormously as production quantity and variety grew and managers sought to improve control over them. This systematic management philosophy spread through mechanisms including the engineering and early management journals (one of which was entitled *System*) and consultants, often called systematizers.[20] In fact, this managerial philosophy of system, with its emphasis on collecting and using information, was also adopted by smaller manufacturing firms and by nonmanufacturing businesses.[21] One well-known systematizer, William Henry Leffingwell, focused solely on the application of the principles of systematic management to the office setting (whether the office was part of a manufacturing firm or a law firm).[22] The increased appetite for information also contributed to rapid growth in the number of clerical workers to handle it, from a mere 74,200 in 1870 to 2,837,700 by 1920 (a jump of 3700%).[23] This rapid growth occurred during a period that also witnessed a rapid growth of information technologies, discussed in the next section, suggesting that during this period the two trends reinforced each other. These clerical workers were only some of the new positions that depended on the new internal information being collected. Table 4.2 shows the new information-dependent jobs added after 1875, according to one book on office management.

The Technology of Information: Office Equipment and Bureaucratic Techniques

With growing firms, information flows, and clerical staffs in the decades around the turn of the century, it is not surprising to find a growing office supply industry that provided the information technologies of this period. Getting a handle on the size and growth rate of this industry (if it is even appropriate to call it a single industry) is difficult, because the technologies of information processing could be defined broadly to include office machinery (then typically referred to as office appliances) such as typewriters and adding machines, furniture products such as filing cabinets, stationery products such as preprinted forms and carbon paper, and a plethora of small items such as paper clips.[24] To give just one indication of growth, total capital in office appliance manufacturing firms alone increased by 2700% between 1879 and 1919.[25] The increasing demand for information encouraged growth in the supply of information technology for handling it. Moreover, as Leffingwell noted in explaining the growth of the office machinery industry:

When business method was individual and self-centered and business aims narrow and secretive, there was little incentive for inventive genius to burn the midnight oil in the search for business machinery.

Table 4.2 New Positions Relying Primarily on the Collection and Processing of Information, 1875–1918

Office manager	Typist
Office workers	Stenographer
Statisticians	Vice President of Sales
Mailing Clerks	Filing Clerks

Source: The Editors, *Office Management* (New York: Alexander Hamilton Institute, 1919).

The demand for mechanical office appliances did not exist because there was no similarity of method. But as similarity of method spread through the exchange of ideas, the possibilities for mass production attracted some of the keenest minds in the country, who turned to making machines and devices that would simplify the mass of problems crowded into the business man's day. As a result, an immense industry has been created—an industry which produces office machines and devices for the entire world.[26]

As Leffingwell suggested, standardization of methods and of office supplies and equipment in a range of businesses further spurred manufacturers of the latter to supply this demand, often through cheaper mass-production methods. Moreover, the use of such office equipment (a term I will use to include both machines such as typewriters and specialized office furniture such as filing cabinets for vertical and card files) and techniques or systems (e.g., the system by which papers or cards were organized in the filing cabinets) came to be associated with the "modern," systematic management approach, so its symbolic value also reinforced demand for it.[27]

In the final decades of the nineteenth century and the first decades of the twentieth managerial firms adopted many information technologies, including both office equipment and bureaucratic techniques or systems of all types, newly developed or adapted to new uses, to aid in recording, storing and retrieving, analyzing, and communicating information within firms.[28]

Recording

Until the mid-1870s, and in spite of many unsuccessful attempts to mechanize the recording of information, the recording process was a laborious, pen-and-ink operation. In 1874, the first mass-produced typewriter came out of the Remington factory, aimed not at the business market, but at a specialist market of authors and court reporters.[29] During the late 1870s sales mounted, although initially relatively slowly, as typewriters gradually spread into the broader business world, reaching a sales total of 4,000 machines in the first five years. By 1880, the business market had overtaken the niche market, manufacturing growth and the systematic management philosophy were increasing the business appetite for information, and one competitor had entered the market, the American Writing Machine Company. Sales of typewriters now picked up rapidly. By 1884, ten years after the first typewriting machines came off the production line, Remington had four competitors in the typewriter market (all using different patents), and by 1886, *Scientific American* estimated that a total of 50,000 typewriters of all makes had been manufactured.[30] Growth continued to accelerate, with almost 150,000 typewriters sold in 1900 alone.[31] This rapid takeoff of the typewriter business reflects strong demand for efficient recording of information, encouraged by the increasing use of information within firms, previously discussed.[32]

From the point of view of the businesses buying the typewriters, these new machines created, for the first time, a way of recording text or numerical information that was faster—more than three times faster with a trained typist—than handwriting.[33] The appeal of such a device was clear, and the timing excellent, because it reached production just in time to help handle the rapid increase of documentation in firms. As we have seen, the typewriter did not prevent a rapid increase in clerical labor during the same period; based on the relative speed of the two modes of recording information, however, an equivalent amount of recording activity without the typewriter's aid might have increased clerical demand (if not supply) at three times its actual rate of growth. The result would have been either a much increased work force (and correspondingly higher costs), or a change in some of the methods then evolving to depend less on written documentation.[34] With the proliferation of typewriters there also came a separation and specialization of clerical jobs, with traditional secretaries (typically males doing a variety of work and with the potential to rise in the firm) often replaced by typists and stenographers, job categories with narrow and specialized duties that rapidly came to be dominated by females at lower wages and with little chance to rise above that position.[35] Typewriters became a fixture in the office (see figure 4.1).

While the typewriter was the most widely adopted advance in recording technology during this period, there were other innovations, both in office equipment and bureaucratic techniques. During this period, the time clock, a more specialized technology for recording a particular type of information, was adopted for recording (and controlling and standardizing) employee time, either in total or on a given job.[36] The cash register emerged as a means of collecting sales information in retail establishments. The cash registers first sold by John H. Patterson starting in 1884 helped reduce clerical pilfering by registering sales amounts, but they did not record these sales in a reusable form. By the turn of the century, however, cash registers included features such as adding and printing, and, according to historian James Cortada, "by World War I, Patterson's machines had evolved into accounting-like devices that trapped information and went beyond

Figure 4.1 Tabulators and Typewriters. This picture suggests how massive an effort it was to conduct a Census. The first U.S. Census to make extensive use of tabulating equipment (seen on the left side of the picture) occurred in 1890. This picture, taken in 1910, shows the results of twenty years of experience with information handling equipment at the U.S. Bureau of the Census. As quickly happened in commercial offices, women came to dominate many jobs requiring the operation of "office appliances." Courtesy the National Archives.

simply keeping clerks honest."[37] Thus cash registers collected, recorded, and eventually performed preliminary calculations with retail information.

The demand for recording methods also included demand for small-scale document copying, for uses such as making copies of outgoing and internal correspondence and reports for the firm's internal records. Firms had long undertaken small amounts of copying, particularly for important outgoing correspondence. In the early nineteenth century, such copying was done just as the recording was: by hand into bound blank books. By the mid-nineteenth century, U.S. firms began to replace hand copying with press copying.[38] This process used special ink, moisture, and a mechanical press to take an impression of a document on a page of a bound volume. While messy, inconvenient, and generally limited to a single readable copy, this process was faster than hand copying and could be done by unskilled and even illiterate office workers. With the growing production and widespread adoption of the typewriter in the closing years of the century, carbon paper, an older technology heretofore used only in very limited ways, was adapted to a major new application.[39] Using carbon paper, a typist could make several (unbound) copies at the same time the original was created. Carbon paper thus solved any efficiency problems posed by the increased numbers of outgoing and internal documents of which copies were needed.

Finally, forms were a bureaucratic recording technique that spread rapidly during this period. Railroads had used preprinted forms with blanks to be filled in by hand since at least the middle of the nineteenth century, and they were the major business users by the turn of the century. The use and popularity of forms spread to other businesses by the start of the twentieth century, as demonstrated by the many articles in engineering and early management journals about sets of forms designed for particular uses.[40] Forms reduced time spent to record information and encouraged its consistency. Such forms could also be used in conjunction with typewriters, further speeding the process of recording numerical or otherwise structured information. It was also easier for clerical workers to extract and compile data from forms, in order to pass this information to higher levels. Typically the forms were designed for a specific purpose and sent to a printer's shop to be printed.

All of these office appliances and bureaucratic techniques helped speed up and reduce the cost of increased recording of information, further stimulating business demand for information.

Storing and Retrieving

Internal business documents, relatively rare before the 1880s, were stored haphazardly (if at all) in an array of devices. The increased numbers of documents flooding firms at the end of the century, however, were only useful for managerial purposes as delineated by the systematic management ideology if they could readily be retrieved. The systems for storage and retrieval of business documents and data in the mid-nineteenth century were adequate to the small volume common at that time, but they posed several problems when they were scaled up to handle the greatly increased volume of documents at the end of the century. In mid-century storage systems for business documents of that day (consisting primarily of external correspondence), related incoming and outgoing correspondence was divided between two differently organized systems.[41] Bound, chronologically organized press books with primitive indexes held copies of outgoing correspondence, and pigeonholes, letter boxes, or flat files, organized by correspondent, geographical area, or even subject, held incoming correspondence. As the numbers and types of documents increased, and as firms filled more and more bound volumes and letter boxes each year, it became increasingly difficult for managers to find documents when they sought them later.[42] Carbon copying, which became popular as the typewriter was widely adopted, allowed the creation of loose, rather than bound, copies and consequently made it possible to combine the two storage systems (for incoming and outgoing documents) into a single system.[43] In the 1880s, however, managers' notions of storage still generally involved bound books, so such loose copies were often bound into chronological books.

Ultimately, vertical filing, first presented to the business community at the 1893 Chicago World's Fair (where it won a gold medal), became the accepted solution to the problem of storage and retrieval of paper documents.[44] From the beginning, vertical files were presented as a way of combining all documents (incoming, outgoing, or internal) in a single system organized by subject, location, or any categorization appropriate to the business. Thus the technology included not just file drawers and folders to hold papers; it also included the bureaucratic technique of organizing the papers into folders and the folders into drawers by an appropriate and accessible filing system. Both the filing system and the office equipment and supplies to house it (what we might now call the software and the hardware) had roots in the library world. The first commercially available vertical filing cabinets were made by the Library Bureau, a firm founded by Melvil Dewey to market the card indexes developed for use with the Dewey Decimal System, introduced in 1876.[45]

Vertical filing, still ubiquitous (if no longer quite taken for granted) in offices today, was seen as an important development by business people in the 1890s. Indeed, articles on filing appeared in management periodicals, and textbooks focused wholly or partially on filing proliferated, as filing systems became closely associated with systematic methods.[46] Businesses adopted such systems relatively rapidly. An interesting, unintended consequence of the adoption of vertical files was the proliferation of decentralized, departmentally and individually maintained files, in spite of the widespread recommendations of filing experts to maintain centralized files.[47] Individual managers and even even some workers seemed to desire control over local files. Such decentralized files in turn seemingly spurred additional internal documentation (especially lateral communication related to areas of contention among departments or units), contributing to its growth in firms. Finally, filing led to the emergence of yet another job category, that of file clerk, with narrow, routinized duties in accordance with the tendencies of systematic management.

While vertical filing of business documents worked well for correspondence (internal and external) and for reports, it was less satisfactory for storing large quantities of numerical data in rapidly retrievable form. For accessible data on such matters as production, sales, and costs, card files—also adopted from libraries and using appropriately preprinted cards (tables, forms, etc.)—became a popular mode of storage.[48] Metcalfe urged the adoption of cards instead of ledgers for accounting data, because such systems made:

> each card a representative unit, capable of combination with others, according to any one or more of their common features; thereby attaining by the mechanical operation of sorting, the results otherwise achieved only by the tardy and laborious processes of book-keeping.[49]

Although loose-leaf accounting ledgers with rings became the preferred form for keeping regular accounts (replacing old-fashioned bound ledgers), card systems were used extensively and for a wide variety of purposes.[50] The business of selling such card systems, typically using standardized sizes of cards (e.g., 3 in. by 5 in. cards), became a large and important one, including firms such as Rand Kardex, which would become part of Remington Rand, the firm that marketed the first commercially available computer in the United States.[51]

Although managers wanted internal information recorded and stored primarily for relatively immediate use, the presence of such internal documentation in filing cabinets and card systems soon raised the issue of mid- and long-term storage. In Du Pont, for example, the Sales Record Division kept central card records of sales for all sales offices for a moderate period of time; this turned out to be particularly useful in replacing records for the San Francisco sales office lost in the city's 1906 earthquake, for example, and in refuting erroneous data presented in antitrust suits.[52] In 1907, the Sales Record Division and other Du Pont statistical offices were supplemented with a central, long-term storage facility known as the Hall of Records. Here, records managers (another new job category created by the changes in internal business use of records) sifted through records, with the official mandate of discarding what were considered unimportant records and keeping ones considered to be important—whether for documenting the history of the firm, defending patents, or fighting antitrust suits—even if no longer in active use. Of course, by the later twentieth century, businesses in general had learned that firm records could sometimes be used against them in antitrust suits, and many records managers have become as active in discarding what corporate lawyers see as potentially dangerous records as in saving valuable ones.

The techniques and equipment that facilitated storage and retrieval of documents and data, including card and paper files and short- and long-term storage facilities, were key to making information accessible and thus potentially useful to managers. Although recording technologies such as typewriters seem from a distance to be more important innovations in information technology than vertical files, the latter were equally important to the overall information system developing to support the growth in production and systematizing of firms during this period.

Analyzing

The new emphasis on gathering and analyzing quantitative data as the basis of controlling processes and monitoring efficiency created growing demand for aids to speed up analysis of such information. Analysis included sorting, counting, and calculating. On the simplest level, the card systems just discussed were often embellished with devices such as notches, tabs, or punched holes, which, by their particular positions, indicated some characteristic. The user working with such card files could separate out and count cards identified by one or more chosen characteristics. Where analysis consisted primarily of understanding the relationships between categories (e.g., in breaking down sales data by region and product), and the quantity of cards was not overwhelming, such systems were particularly useful. Of course, they became less efficient as the number of cards grew, as in some of the information-intensive businesses (e.g., life insurance) that became lead users of the tabulating systems (discussed in a subsequent section).

Most analysis involved numerical calculations, and as the flow of data in firms grew, so did demand for mechanical adding and calculating devices that could speed up the work of performing numerical calculations (as the typewriter had sped up the recording of information). Such early, dial or lever-based calculating devices as Arithmometers—which had been commercially available since 1820 and were sold in small numbers to scientists and to actuaries—were not considered very useful for bookkeepers in firms because of their extremely slow speed and lack of reliability.[53] Technological developments occurred and additional producers of such devices entered the market during the middle of the nineteenth century and after, but the adding and calculating machine business really took off only at the end of the nineteenth century and in the early twentieth. In the mid-1880s two technological innovations that made the machines more suitable for business use were introduced to the market, innovations probably induced in part by the increasing demand of firms for aid in processing quantitative information, made.[54] Felt & Tarrant Manufacturing Company began marketing the Comptometer, a calculating machine that used keys rather than dials or levers to enter numbers, thus speeding up use enough to allow the skilled Comptometer operator (yet another new clerical position, but one that would disappear into the broader category of office machine operators) to calculate more rapidly than a skilled accountant could calculate mentally (see figure 4.2). At around the same time, the predecessor of the Burroughs Adding Machine Company introduced an adding-listing machine that printed out the numbers as they were entered and the totals as they were added, providing a way to record and verify the calculations. Subsequent developments in both adding and calculating machines (the former devices only added, while the latter also performed other arithmetic functions) followed, in interaction with the growing market for such machines.[55]

Adding and calculating machines were joined by more specialized billing and bookkeeping machines (in addition to accounting and tabulating machines, discussed in a later section) to aid in analyzing the floods of numerical information being collected and processed by the early twentieth century.[56] Operators of such machines entered quantitative information on a keyboard, simultaneously registering it for use in calculations and posting it on specialized loose-leaf ledger pages or other forms; then these operators used the machines to perform various calculations on the entered data and post the results in the appropriate location. The adoption and use of all such machines was spurred by the withholding of taxes from individual paychecks, made mandatory by federal legislation in 1913, and by the further expansion of corporate taxes during World War I.[57]

These new technologies facilitated use and reuse of numerical data (whether appropriate or inappropriate use), contributing further to managerial demand for quantitative data concerning all aspects of their operations, including processes as well as output.

Figure 4.2 Calculating Accountants. Nothing so profoundly changed the job functions of an accountant, or did more to expand the types of accounting that could be developed and applied, than the humble adding machine. In this picture, the Comptometer, the most popular calculator among accountants of the period 1900–1930, is used by members of the audit team at the Pennsylvania Railroad. The Comptometer was particularly useful in conducting a variety of basic mathematical functions in large enterprises. Manufactured by the Felt & Tarrant Company, it was the most important competitor to another great American firm, the Burroughs Adding Machine Company. From the private collection of James W. Cortada.

Communicating

In addition to being recorded, stored and retrieved, and analyzed, the rapidly increasing flood of information needed to be communicated to those who would use it. Communication occurred in the early stages, as recorded information was transmitted up or across the hierarchy, or at later stages, when information was communicated to its users up, down, and across the hierarchy. Thus communicating the information involved transmission, dissemination, and/or presentation, orally as well as in writing (though the systematic management ideology favored written communication).

Transmission of written documents within a location tended to operate primarily via interdepartmental mail systems, which emerged in larger firms during this period.[58] Such systems were the subject of attention in management magazines, and the memo heading that differentiated internal from external correspondence emerged during this period to facilitate interdepartmental delivery and subsequent filing of documents. In some settings, more specialized technologies (including, e.g., the pneumatic tube system) were adopted for rapid internal transmission of information.[59] Transmission of written material from location to location took place primarily through two of the infrastructures discussed in chapter 3: postal service (via railroad and other transportation means) and telegraph. Telegraph codes became a popular way of transferring information on relatively standard topics through the telegraph system from sales agencies or offices to headquarters, for example, while reducing cost and assuring privacy of the information.[60]

As we have seen, the systematic management ideology favored written over oral forms of information transmission, but the telephone, introduced to the American public in 1876, was also used to facilitate informal transmission of information. Its earliest installations, even before the development of the telephone exchange two years later, were often point-to-point lines linking the office and factory of a single firm, allowing informal oral contact between owner/manager and factory foremen, even when they were not in the same location.[61] Beginning in the 1890s, many larger firms adopted private branch exchanges to link locations within a large or dispersed facility, as well as to connect with outside exchanges.

When written instructions and procedures needed to be disseminated to large numbers of employees, mass copying was needed.[62] To the extent that instructions were mass distributed before the 1880s, they had to be typeset at a printer's shop, making such dissemination slow, expensive, and inconvenient. In the final decades of the nineteenth century, two methods of making larger quantities of copies right in the office became available. Hectograph methods used an original written or typed with aniline dyes together with a gelatin bed to make up to 100 copies of a document.[63] Stencil methods used a stencil master perforated with tiny holes allowing ink to pass through to make up to 1,000 copies. Edison introduced the first stencil method to the United States in the form of his electric pen and stencil duplicating press in 1876; by the 1890s stencil masters for use with typewriters had appeared, and rotary "mimeographs," stencil copiers produced by A. B.

Dick, had replaced handwritten stencil masters and flat-bed copiers for more rapid production of hundreds of copies. These copiers filled the need for a quick, convenient, and inexpensive way to make multiple copies of documents intended for wide dissemination. Of course, some types of documents, such as sales manuals, were still sent to printers for higher quality mass reproduction. These manuals were often illustrated and were issued relatively infrequently to large numbers of sales agents or employees, in some cases with the knowledge that they would be shown to customers to show the firm's products.[64]

Developments in bureaucratic techniques also facilitated oral dissemination of information. Shop conferences, the subject of a monthly column in *Factory* magazine starting in 1916 ("Getting More Out of Shop Conferences") and of articles in other management magazines, brought together the foreman and/or department heads regularly for a variety of purposes. Based on a questionnaire sent to twenty-five executives, *Factory* classified such meetings into two types, good will and supervisory. While the former promoted "team spirit" among lower-level managers (and were early indicators of the human resource philosophy discussed later in this chapter), the latter promoted downward and lateral dissemination of ideas about efficiency and system, as well as facilitating monitoring of processes and comparison of results across units to assure that such new ideas were being implemented.[65] Such oral dissemination often involved written documents or visual aids. In addition to shop conferences, specific to manufacturing settings, other types of managerial meetings took place to promote goals of systematizing. For example, when DuPont consolidated a set of previously independent and geographically dispersed dynamite plants within its High Explosives Operating Department (HEOD), the executives in charge of the department adopted regular plant superintendents' meetings to accomplish similar goals at a higher level than the shop conference.[66]

Techniques were also introduced to facilitate effective presentation of information. As the amount of information being gathered and processed increased, the decision makers in the larger firms were faced with problems of information overload—they needed information to be selected and presented in a way that reduced that overload and highlighted critical information. Tables and forms were efficient for gathering structured numerical data, and they presented the data more compactly than text, but they took time to absorb and interpret. Graphical representation was a bureaucratic technique for displaying data in an easy-to-absorb form that highlighted comparisons among units, change over time, and other such critical factors. This technique had been developed centuries earlier but had been used more by scientists than by managers.[67] In the early twentieth century, this technique for presenting data was widely advocated by systematizers and adopted by managers of many "modern" firms.[68] Of course, graphs were open to manipulation (e.g., of the scales) for the presenter's purpose. DuPont's Executive Committee established a specialized room for the display of large-sized graphs of what they deemed to be critical data, updated and presented monthly in a prescribed standard form to avoid managerial manipulation.[69] Demand for more efficient presentation of textual information was also growing, and new techniques (e.g., elimination of wordy formula text from traditional letter-writing style, addition of subheads, tables, and graphs into textual documents) were introduced in response.[70] In fact, internal efficiency or system departments, which were started in many firms adopting the methods of systematic management, sometimes began by systematizing the internal systems for communicating information.[71]

Thus communication, including the transmission, dissemination, and presentation of information, was a final area of information handling to benefit from improvements during this era.

Importance of This Wave of Information Technologies

This brief examination of some of the office equipment and bureaucratic techniques for handling information that entered widespread use beginning in the 1880s suggests that both the demand for and supply of information in firms increased during this period, with the latter aided by the widespread adoption of information technologies. Information demand, spurred by growth and the systematic management ideology, seemingly took the lead, although supply and demand reinforced each other. As we have seen, some of the technologies (e.g., adding machines and carbon paper) had existed but had not yet been adapted to business uses, and technological developments related to these and newer devices seem to have been encouraged by growth and by the systematic management ideology. The widespread adoption of bureaucratic techniques such as forms and graphs also points to the key role of demand generated both by economic and firm growth, on the one hand, and by the wide adoption of the systematic management methods, on the other.

By 1926, the *Office Appliance Manual*, edited by William Henry Leffingwell and sponsored by the National Association of Office Appliance Manufacturers, included sections on all of the office appliance types discussed here, plus dozens of others. The list of product categories (compiled from chapter titles in his book), shown in table 4.3, reveals the incredible range of such devices. One category of office machine, designated "accounting and tabulating machines" by Leffingwell, is particularly highly developed and important as a predecessor of computer-based information technology. A subsequent section below examines the emergence and use of this tabulating technology. First, however, we must consider some new sources of demand for information in the period from World War I to 1950.

Additional Information Demands: Human Relations and Regulatory Change

While systematic management, along with continued growth in the quantity and variety of products produced by firms (especially during

Table 4.3 Categories of Office Appliances in Use by 1926

Adding Machines	Duplicating Machines
Calculating Machines	Photo-Copying Machines[a]
Billing Machines	Addressing Machines
Bookkeeping Machines	Mailing-Room Equipment
Accounting and Tabulating Machines	Shipping-Room Aids
Check Protectors and Writers	Scales
Check Certifiers, Endorsers,	Time-Recording Devices
Cancelers, and Signers	Intercommunicating Systems
Coin-Changing Devices	Miscellaneous Office Appliances
Coin-Handling Devices	Safe-Keeping Records
Autographic Registers	Filing Methods
Autographic Cash Registers	Filing Equipment
Cash Registers	Visible Index Systems
Credit Registers	Finding and Filing Devices
Adding Machine-Cash Registers	Office Furniture
Adding Machine-Cash and Credit Registers	Loose-Leaf Accounting Records,
Dictating Machines	Equipment, and Systems
Typewriters	Billing-Machine Forms
Typing Aids	

Source: William Henry Leffingwell, ed., *The Office Appliance Manual* (National Association of Office Appliance Manufacturers, 1926).

[a]1926 was well before the advent of plain paper photocopying; the photocopy machines referred to here were large devices with a camera, coated paper, and developing fluids, used to take photographs of documents. Applications for this slow, expensive process were limited.

the two world wars), continued to fuel information demand in U.S. firms throughout the first half of the twentieth century, another managerial ideology, the human relations school, and the related personnel management function, began to emerge early in the century in response to labor unrest and a broader societal movement toward humanitarian reform. This managerial thrust acquired definition and initial momentum during World War I; it continued to gain adherence through the added impetus of the New Deal and World War II. Under its influence, many firms added personnel departments, which collected, analyzed, and used new types of information. Like systematic management, human relations encouraged the appetite for information among managers in U.S. firms. At the same time, changes in regulation that accompanied the twentieth century world wars and the Great Depression also imposed added informational demands. Although these were not the sole factors in the adoption of back-office tabulating technology discussed in the following section, they were additional contributors to the increased information processing demands that supported its adoption, as well as continued growth in the office appliances and techniques already discussed.

The human relations or industrial relations ideology had multiple roots. It grew in part out of the industrial welfare movement that emerged around the turn of the century as a strand of the broader Progressive Movement of the era, with the humanitarian goal of bettering the lives of workers.[72] From early on, managers and owners also saw this movement as a way of combating what they saw as common labor problems, from sloth or soldiering (pretending to work) to labor unrest and strikes, by bringing back some of the personal element and family feeling that had been lost in larger, systematized firms. Techniques associated with industrial welfare included employee clubs, inhouse publications, and morale-building shop conferences. Another contribution to the ideology came from academics in the social and behavioral sciences who, as part of the professionalization of these fields, sought to demonstrate the power of their approaches in business applications such as industrial psychology.[73] With the emphasis on their disciplines as *sciences*, academics justified their work to firms through metrics such as reduced turnover and increased efficiency, as well as improved industrial harmony. Meanwhile, personnel management was just beginning to emerge as a professional function in business, both a contributor to and a result of the emergence of the human relations ideology itself. This management philosophy advocated working for system and efficiency among the human, as well as nonhuman, elements of work.[74]

All these developments began to converge in the early twentieth century. In the years leading up to and through World War I, labor unrest and strikes increased, and managers became increasingly concerned more with the practical goal of replacing worker conflict with worker cooperation than with the purely humanitarian goals of the welfare movement. In David Noble's words, the corporate reformers "remade the innovations of welfare workers into elaborate industrial-relations programs, to try to foster a spirit of voluntary cooperation among workers, to transform the energy of potential conflict into a constructive, profitable force within a larger corporate framework."[75] A recent reading of the labor movement sees the labor unions as cooperating with this development, in the interests of establishing a consumption-based notion of wages, the so-called living wage.[76] Whether this new managerial philosophy was a managerial plot or a labor triumph, it would fuel additional increases in information processing demand in firms.

A key indicator of the progress of the human relations ideology is the establishment of personnel departments in firms. Beginning before World War I but accelerating during the war and associated labor shortages and unrest, such departments were established in some of the largest firms. The department transfered much authority over personnel decisions from foremen to managers specializing in personnel management, and provided a base for the practical applications of the techniques of human relations.[77] By 1927, 12 percent of all firms (and 34 percent of firms with 250 or more workers) had personnel departments.[78] This institutionalized presence continued to increase, spurred by federal and state legislation responding to the Great Depression (including the Social Security Act, the establishment of workman's compensation, unemployment insurance, and the minimum wage). By 1935, after most of the requisite legislation had been passed, 32 percent of all firms had personnel departments (including 62 percent of firms with 1,000–4,999 workers and 81 percent of firms with 5,000 or more workers). The labor shortages and wage controls of World War II spurred even more expansion of the personnel function, so by 1946 the proportion of firms with personnel departments had grown to 63 percent of all firms (including 86 percent of firms with 1,000–4,999 workers and 81 percent of firms with 5,000 or more workers). Another indicator of the spread of this human relations approach appears in business school curricula. Courses entitled "Personnel Management" began to appear in the business curriculum of universities in the 1920s, although the human relations school would become even more prominent in the academy during and after World War II.[79]

These indicators suggest that by the 1920s the human relations ideology had a secure foothold in larger firms, and that it continued to expand its influence through World War II.

This spread of the human relations ideology and of legislation surrounding employment brought a proliferation of techniques that depended on the gathering and analysis of new categories of information.[80] Wage data, once the province of foremen, were now gathered by personnel departments, systematized into wage classification systems, monitored, analyzed, and (in some cases) reported to government bodies. Jobs were similarly systematized and classified. Personnel managers compiled and tracked turnover rates and costs; they used reductions in turnover to justify the establishment of new policies, reinforcing systematic management's emphasis on cost accounting and adding new categories of data. They also tracked morale by survey. Employment records became more extensive, and some firms instituted selection tests as part of the hiring processing. Managers maintained, expanded, and further systematized the employee communication methods initiated during the early corporate welfare movement to convey corporate policy around employment. Thus this new human resource ideology, along with increasing regulation of employment matters, further encouraged the spread of information-processing technologies and techniques, including both those discussed previously and the large, back-office tabulating systems discussed next.

Large-Scale, Back-Office Information Systems: Tabulating Technology

We turn now to the most elaborate of the precomputer information processing technologies. With a few exceptions, most of the technologies adopted between 1880 and 1920 to aid in the processing of increasing amounts of information were associated primarily with one of the information processes previously discussed—recording, storing and retrieving, analyzing, or communicating. Moreover, the office appliances were generally stand-alone machines, purchased singly or by the hundreds, depending on the purchasing firm's size and needs. Only the most sophisticated of the bookkeeping machines were customized to a particular firm's needs and rented or sold with an "application" and with a long-term relationship that involved training and maintenance.[81] Punched-card tabulating technology was the major exception to these common characteristics of office equipment. From the very beginning, it involved multiple machines used in sequence together to manage large-scale, elaborate uses of information. These installations of machinery did not fit on desks and were not typically visible to the public in front offices, but they were used to handle large-scale, back-office work of various sorts. Although punched-card technology was introduced in embryonic form before the turn of the century, it came into more extensive use beginning in the 1920s. As the most direct predecessor of the computer in terms of scale, scope of information functions handled, commercial market, applications, and vendors (IBM and Remington Rand were the only U.S. vendors of tabulating equipment and both made the transition into computers in the 1950s), tabulating technology and its use deserves a closer look. It represents an approach to information processing technology and its use that points toward the post-1950 computer era.

On the demand side, in this case manufacturing firms did not lead the way. The pioneer users of early punched-card technology, around the turn of the twentieth century, tended to be first in large railroads and then in information-intensive businesses such as life insurance.[82] As discussed earlier, railroads had developed their accounting methods and supporting information systems quite early, starting in the 1850s and 1860s. By late in the nineteenth century two other developments had increased their appetite for information. In 1887 the Interstate Commerce Act had created the Interstate Commerce Commission and given it powers to collect data from all railroads, inducing expansions in the data-gathering of some firms.[83] In addition, railroads had gone through a period of system building in the final two decades of the century that combined individual lines into huge systems, making the quantities of information needed to perform existing information functions, especially cost accounting, even larger.[84] Finally, railroads had, from early on, sought increasingly sophisticated information systems and technological aids to support them.[85] They were always on the lookout for new methods of handling data.

Information-intensive businesses such as life insurance also had increasing demands for information. These financial service firms were based on information and produced no physical output other than documents, both external (e.g., customer bills and printed policies) and internal (e.g., management reports and actuarial and accounting data). By the end of the nineteenth century, the largest such firms had more than one million industrial insurance policies (small policies for which premiums were collected weekly by door-to-door insurance agents) and more than 100,000 ordinary insurance policies (larger policies that were billed by mail monthly).[86] Simply carrying out the necessary billing functions for all of these policies involved vast numbers of documents, the specifics of which varied by policy. Moreover, they were regulated on a state-by-state basis, with regulations requiring yearly reports to each state on a variety of financial and other measures. Although Prudential Assurance Company, the British insurance firm, had shown that high-volume information processing could be achieved through entirely bureaucratic, nonmechanized systems,[87] American insurance firms were part of a wider U.S. business culture that favored systematic management in offices (as well as factories) and were more interested in keeping up with the new developments in office technology, often tied to the systematic management ideology in works such as Leffingwell's. Moreover, they were concerned about keeping costs down, particularly because the Armstrong Commission Hearings of 1905 in the New York Legislature had exposed corruption in insurance and had drawn attention to their practices (as well as inducing, in its aftermath, more insurance attention to providing a quasi-public service at the lowest cost possible).[88] Information processing was clearly the major task of insurance firms. Thus there was still business demand for faster and less labor-intensive methods of processing information, eagerly awaiting and encouraging developments such as that of punched-card tabulating technology.

Herman Hollerith developed electromechanical punched-card tabulating technology to enable information collected in the 1890 U.S. Census to be processed and published more rapidly than by manual methods used previously.[89] By the turn of the twentieth century, the technology had reached its characteristic early form, consisting of three devices—card punch, sorter, and tabulator—plus the cards used in them (see figure 4.3). Operators used a card punch to record information onto standardized cards, punching holes in particular positions (by the early twentieth century, the most standard cards had forty-five columns). Then operators placed cards in a sorting machine that sorted cards by the numerical value registered in any of their columns. Finally, they used a "tabulator," wired as needed for a particular operation, to count cards or to accumulate the quantities encoded in a designated column of the card (e.g., to add the quantities in a specified column for all cards that had a certain value in another position). Operators could rewire the tabulator as needed to perform different operations. In spite of Hollerith's continuing development of the technology, for political reasons, the U.S. Census sought an alternative supplier in the early years of the twentieth century, ultimately setting up James Powers in competition against Hollerith. Powers became Hollerith's sole com-

Figure 4.3 Census-Taking as Big Business. In this 1910 photograph we see the main working room at the U.S. Bureau of the Census, loaded with Powers's Automatic Electric Card Punch equipment—the arch-rival of the Hollerith Tabulating Machine Company—along with some of Hollerith's smaller devices, such as the Pantograph Punch on the table in the lower foreground. What is important to note in this picture is the extent of the commitment to information technology that a government agency had to make in order to do one task—in this case, census taking—while other agencies were also embracing the new technology. Courtesy of the National Archives.

petitor in the United States, and the competition between the two men's firms contributed to the fast pace of innovation in this technology.

Hollerith early on saw the potential for commercial customers, and, he made a few limited contacts with prospects such as railroads and insurance firms in the 1890s. After he lost the business of the U.S. Census around the turn of the century, however, he focused his attention on developing the commercial market.[90] That market was interested, but it was also demanding. He worked with the New York Central Railroad to establish a system for processing waybills, and in the process he standardized the cards and developed the tabulator's accumulating (or adding) function to supplement its initial ability to count cards.[91] Insurance customers pressured him to improve his system for sorting cards, which he did.[92] In the early twentieth century, he also expanded his commercial market to manufacturing (a cost accounting system for the Pennsylvania Steel Company), retail (a sales analysis system for Marshall Fields), utilities (a system for verifying and analyzing operating revenues for the Edison Electric Illuminating Company, predecessor of the New York Edison Company), and payroll applications (the forerunners of more complex personnel and payroll systems) in a variety of businesses.[93] Meanwhile, Powers also began to address this commercial market.

Under pressure from these commercial customers and in competition with each other, Powers and Hollerith continued to develop the equipment, speeding it up and adding a variety of capabilities.[94] Most important, in the 1910s and 1920s both manufacturers added printing capability to their systems, allowing them to print first numerical data (both as it was entered and in totals) and later alphabetic text. This capability made almost all applications more useful, but especially those involving documents sent to customers (e.g., insurance and utility billing), accounting records (since most accountants were not willing to adopt the technology until it could provide a printed audit trail[95]), and personnel records (which especially benefitted from the alphabetic printing capability which allowed the printing of names. By the 1920s, then, tabulating equipment could record and store data on cards, sort the data for retrieval, perform computations with the data, and print data and results out on forms for communicating them with whomever needed it. Unlike a typewriter or an adding machine, tabulating technology was a punched-card *system*, including several machines and procedures for using them to handle entire applications, such as insurance premium billing. In his chapter on "Accounting and Tabulating Machines"[96] in the 1926 *Office Appliance Manual*, Leffingwell explained the appeal of such systems in terms of efficiency and accuracy:

Wherever the classifying and analyzing of statistics or the compiling of reports is part of the daily routine of any business enterprise, there the tabulating machine can be of invaluable service. It is of major importance because it will serve more economically and with greater speed and accuracy than a large clerical force. It removes the possibility of "human error." Today accounting and tabulating machines are recognized as the most dependable means of analyzing such facts as develop in the every-day operation of manufacturing, insurance, transportation, or other businesses.[97]

By the end of the 1920s, IBM had introduced a new eighty-column standard card; this card held almost twice as much information as the earlier forty-five-column standard and would remain in use for decades, in computers after tabulators. IBM and Remington Rand, the successors to the firms started by Hollerith and Powers, controlled the tabulator market by 1930, with IBM dominating Remington Rand eight to one in installations. Still, this segment of the office appliance industry accounted for less than 13 percent of total industry sales in 1930.[98]

Tabulating equipment continued to evolve and to expand its market in subsequent decades. It went from being a small piece of the office appliance market to a somewhat larger piece but still did not dominate it in sales figures. Further developments in tabulating technology, all made by the vendors in interaction with customers, were introduced during the 1930s and 1940s. The automatic carriage and high speed printers using continuous forms expanded printing capabilities and made printing more reliable, while the introduction of multiplying units increased the speed of calculations.[99] Uses of these systems evolved as well. A few insurance firms, for example, developed integrated premium billing and accounting applications that used a single set of cards for several connected operations.[100] Manufacturers even found ways to link machines electrically to eliminate some transfers of cards from one machine to another, anticipating the much greater integration of functions that would emerge in the computer age.[101] During the Depression, while other firms in the office appliance industry languished, IBM survived and thrived, due in great part, to "the 'rent-and-refill' nature of the punched-card business."[102] The machines were rented rather than sold, so while not many new installations were established during the Depression, firms with large installations tended to continue renting existing installations and to buy cards as needed, a profitable part of IBM's business. Moreover, New Deal legislation such as Social Security increased the market for such machinery, both in the government and in businesses.

Tabulating technology is a particularly important forerunner of computers because the users of tabulating machines would be the first adopters of computer technology in the 1950s, and because tabulating technology and its use would shape the early commercial computer market, technology, and uses. Still, we can also see the continuities between it and the office equipment and bureaucratic techniques discussed in the previous section. The keypunch, the ability to print, the cards for storing and sorting data—all had analogues in the information technologies already discussed. Thus tabulating technology is an important link between precomputer and computer-based information technologies.

Summary

During the period from 1880 to 1950, the demands of growth, of the resulting new ideologies of management, and of regulation all encouraged increasing use of information within firms. Technology was adopted to facilitate this information-handling and to signal the "modern" nature of a firm through its offices. The nineteenth-century office, still alive and well in 1880, had given way by the early decades of the twentieth century to a more modern office with many of the elements recognizable in the office of 1980 (before the advent of the personal computer). Moreover, by mid-century, back-office technology that handled multiple stages of information processing (recording, storage and retrieval, calculation, and even printing for presentation), sometimes even combined into entire applications, was also well established. The stage was set for the business adoption of early computers after 1950. But first, it is important to note developments in electronic mass communication that were occurring at the same time as these developments in business use of information and information technology.

5

The Threshold of the Information Age
Radio, Television, and Motion Pictures
Mobilize the Nation

Margaret Graham

In previous chapters we have seen how the rise of large bureaucratic structures in the early decades of the twentieth century, enabled by a national communications infrastructure and driven by the needs of systematizers, created a voracious appetite for information and information processing technologies. At roughly the same time, in what we will term the Vacuum Tube Era, communications technologies in the United States came to be adapted to broader social purposes, on a national scale. These changes, driven in the first instance by the imperatives of national defense, involved creating a new communications infrastructure based on incorporating vacuum tubes into preexisting technologies. The result of this new combination was not only an enhanced communications infrastructure, but one that was concentrated under the control of a few large enterprises, loosely but effectively aligned with the federal government.

From the 1930s through the 1960s, vacuum-tube–based communications in their various forms made the United States into an increasingly mobilized society, that is, a society that could be motivated to achieve broad national purposes. Chief among these purposes were the search for national economic recovery through consumption; a culture unified, or at least socially homogenized, through mass entertainment; and broad public support for war aims. Some semblance of this "national unity culture" endured through World War II and the Korean War, continuing well into the 1960s when both the concentrated control of the infrastructure and the broad cultural consensus disintegrated.

The mobilized society began its slow erosion in the late 1950s, becoming simultaneously media-rich and self-conscious. Government policy toward technological changes introduced greater competition among different forms of mass media, supporting competing alternatives to a national cultural consensus. Radio, television, and movies all still had national "reach" and some had even attained international reach, but for the audience the experience had changed. With the advent of the transistor it was possible to foresee the arrival of truly individualized (or at least customized) information, and with that a resulting fragmentation of the collective experience.

The Vacuum Tube Era (1907–1967)

If we think of the Information Age, beginning with the spread of automated information processing in the late 1950s, as the time when social and economic activities began to be organized according to the logic of information flow rather than materials flow, then vacuum-tube–based technologies defined the threshold of that age. The Vacuum Tube Era began with twin related inventions—the Fleming valve, or diode vacuum tube (1904) and the de Forest triode or audion (1906). It ended with the triumph of the transistor, which was introduced in the 1950s for defense and commercial technologies but did not replace vacuum tubes in consumer electronics until the 1960s. (Indeed, it has yet to replace cathode ray tubes for most types of television displays even today, although portable computer displays are already mainly solid state.) As the ultimate "radio–related" technological devices, vacuum tubes both enabled and manifested a new scientific understanding of electrons as particles, and of "electronics" as an emerging practical branch of applied physics.[1] Even as the British physicists at the Cavendish Laboratory were uttering their famous toast: "To the Electron, may it never be of any use to anybody," early cathode ray tubes were serving as tiny laboratories in which the behavior of electrons could be observed, as well as used, to good effect.[2]

As we have seen in earlier chapters, the newspaper was the earliest form of mass communications that could be said to have reached a national audience long before the turn of the nineteenth century. By the time vacuum tubes were invented, the Hearst papers reached audiences in cities across the United States and had already been blamed for whipping up public support for the Spanish-American War in an orgy of sensationalism and misinformation. Point-to-point electrical communication already existed in the form of the telegraph and the telephone, and some people even envisioned the telephone as the basis of a mass entertainment system.[3] But the telegraph required expert operation by operators who were skilled at Morse code; the telephone was still a local matter, and expensive.

Many of the communications technologies that eventually used vacuum tubes predated the invention of the vacuum tube by decades. Crystal sets, the precursors to vacuum-tube–based radios, were in widespread use by amateurs before World War I, but it was by no means evident at that time that radio had the potential to challenge newspapers. Mass entertainment in the form of silent films was also already in existence, but because the industry was dominated by cheap, bawdy entertainment for working-class audiences that could not afford vaudeville, film could hardly be viewed as a potential instrument for effecting social revolution. Vacuum tubes not only dramatically changed the direction of these information technologies, they also shaped their subsequent development and their collective interaction as components of a national communications infrastructure able to mobilize a national audience for various collective ends.

Some scholars have seen the Vacuum Tube Era as the "the control revolution," that is, the last episode in the Industrial Revolution. Here, while the chief basis of the economy was still material, electronic communications media enabled the regaining of market "control" at a national level after early phases of the industrial revolution had undermined market control at a local or regional level.[4] Greater purposes than control of commercial markets were engaged in the Vacuum Tube Era, however. Information conveyed by means of electronic media came to pervade every aspect of U.S. national culture. Vacuum-tube–based technologies were rightly credited with defending, perhaps even preserving, American freedoms; at the same time they also helped to curtail a few freedoms. They were also responsible for a mass national culture characterized by electronic sound and image, and a mass consumer society homogenized by the 1950s to the point that its members came to do their laundry, eat, dress, and amuse themselves in similar ways all over the country. By the 1960s, so pervasive was this development and so media-rich the society that Marshall McLuhan could point to the medium itself as "the message."[5]

Vacuum-tube–based communications technology well illustrated a familiar reciprocal principle evident in the evolution of most infrastructural technologies: while technology in its material form was shaping social phenomena, the material form itself was being shaped by social forces.[6] There were many mediators of this reciprocal relationship—some individual, many more institutional. They included not only the inventors and producers of the electronic hardware systems and their programming or content producers, but also their early users, their competitors, and their opponents. All these parties participated in laying the foundations for the Information Age that was to accompany transistor-based information processing in the 1960s and 1970s with sight and sound communication first created by the vacuum tube.

The Tube as Enabler and Controller

The American Lee de Forest's invention of the audion, the ancestor of all later vacuum-tube devices, has been called "one of the 'great divides' in the history of radio technology," and we might add, of all radio-related technologies as well.[7] The tube, or "valve" as it was known in England, revolutionized both the transmission of radio signals and the ability to detect or receive them. It increased the capacity of signal systems to handle far more information, greater "bandwidth," and thus to accommodate sound and images as well as simple blips. It also made it possible to repeat and refresh a signal traveling over wire or cable, enabling wired transmission over long distances and ultimately making it possible to hook up national networks. As we shall see later, it was the U.S. defense establishment that early recognized radio and related technologies as the most powerful munitions and that provided the impetus for pushing their performance capabilities.[8]

Had it not been for a prior connection between the English inventor Ambrose Fleming and the English company Marconi de Forest's invention of the triode would have given the U.S. communications giant American Telephone and Telegraph (AT&T) undisputed postwar control of radio, and perhaps of subsequent radio-related technologies as well. Lee deForest had come up with his device by modifying the Fleming diode. The decisive advantage of the triode was in its grid structure, which de Forest could not have created without Fleming's prior discovery.[9] AT&T purchased de Forest's rights to his invention in 1912. The telephone company made the triode purchase initially for use as a telephone signal repeater, but it quickly also recognized its broader applicability for general wireless communications, and with that the potential threat to its own wired system.[10] American Marconi's control of the Fleming technology, however, gave it the ability to block AT&T's use of de Forest's device for most purposes, and with that the potential to challenge AT&T's U.S. communications monopoly.

To keep the battle between various radio-related patents from blocking the development of wireless as a strategic defense technology during World War I, the U.S. government effectively took control of strategic patents during the war and mandated cooperation among those who owned them, promising to indemnify them afterwards for any infringement.[11] After the war, the problem of sorting out competing patent positions threatened to plague all forms of electronic communication in the United States and was to involve several major disputes between the government and various industry patent combinations in motion picture sound, radio, and television before the communications infrastructure based on vacuum tubes achieved maturity. To keep patent conflicts to a minimum, the government collaborated with the General Electric Company (GE) to set up the Radio Corporation of America (RCA), effectively using a commercial enterprise to coordinate the evolution of radio-related technology on the government's behalf.[12]

As we have seen, with the exception of radar, most of the communications technologies that used vacuum tubes were already in existence in more primitive forms, but incorporation of the first electronics gave them the much greater power and performance they needed to be agents of mobilization. Movies acquired sound, radio receivers could be precision tuned and amplified, radio networks could use telephone lines to reach nationwide audiences, and local radio stations could transmit live radio programs originating from outside their studios; when these developments occurred, it was possible to reach a mass, national, networked audience—to inform, to persuade, to entertain, to reassure, and to sell. In the era of the Red Scare, after World War I, and the rise of totalitarian regimes abroad, with social unrest and militant labor unions at home, the potential for nationwide communications to fall into the wrong hands was recognized as a serious threat to U.S. national security. One way of dealing with the threat was to concentrate this potential under the technological control of a handful of companies allied or at least aligned with the U.S. government. This, then, was one reason that the Federal Communications Commission (FCC) could lean toward interpreting its legitimate regulatory role as ensuring corporate stability against upstart new technologies. Corporate stability in a time of general instability was one public interest it was defending. Moreover, by enabling corporate concentration in the media it could indirectly control a force that it could not afford to control openly.[13]

However potent the radio art might be, it was limited by its material form. One producer of glass envelopes for vacuum tubes referred to the cathode ray tube (CRT) as the "glass heart" of any radar system.[14] In fact, with the coming of vacuum-tube technology all radio–related devices had numerous vital organs made of evacuated glass bulbs. These typically contained large amounts of lead oxide, which was a heavy, expensive, and scarce ingredient. By the 1930s they could also be made of ceramic material combined with metal, or of metal alone. The glass enclosures, which were at first simply physical clones of lightbulb enclosures[15], were fragile, expensive, tough to make, and difficult to transport. When assembled into tubes they were by far the most expensive of the components that made up all electrical and electronic communications devices. Though smaller, weaker sets might get by with one tube, even early high–performance sets in kit form required four or five tubes of different sizes. Sold separately, each tube retailed for about $5.[16]

Glass bulbs enhanced electronic devices, for glass had beneficial electrical properties in its own right.[17] At the same time glass also imposed powerful physical constraints on the usability of all vacuum-tube devices. Any "set" using vacuum tubes, whether radio, radar, or (later) television was heavy, bulky, prone to interference and sudden failure, and voracious in its use of power. Indeed, early radio sets had high-drain filaments and required rechargeable storage batteries, like today's car batteries, which ran from $15 to $30. So-called "farm radios" and military portables were designed to run solely from dry cells, while standard radios were eventually adapted for household current.[18] These physical characteristics placed constraints on the social uses radios could serve. Vacuum-tube radios required expert maintenance and service to test and replace failing components. Their prodigious consumption of electricity made battery power a limiting proposition for a long time.

In 1922 when all components had to be assembled by the buyer and tubes came separately, radio set prices ranged from $18 to $350. By 1927 all radio components (including power supply and speakers) were sold in one box, and even then the buyer had to string an outdoor antenna when installing the radio. Tubes were still unreliable and prone to failure. It was quite possible for the novice installer to make a mistake in hooking up a radio that would knock out a whole set of tubes. A power surge, common to early power systems, could knock out the radios of a whole neighborhood. In 1927 radios began to look less like physics experiments and more like attractive pieces of furniture, with prices ranging from $82.75 to a luxurious $2,000 (at a time when Fords and Chevrolets sold for as little as $600).

At such prices there was unlikely to be more than one set to a household in all but the most affluent households. Radios were hard to hear at first, owing to the twin problems of static and "birdies" (the shrill whistles emitted when neighboring sets interfered with each other). These characteristics accounted for the way radios were used at first. As depicted in advertisements from the 1920s, an entire family would cluster around the radio, which would be located in the living room or kitchen, all generations listening intently to the same program.

Although tubes never overcame many of their main physical defects completely, they did improve dramatically as to performance and operating expense. Owing to their dual use character (i.e., parallel military and commercial uses), military requirements, especially for missile systems, pushed tube design improvements toward higher performance, while commercial requirements for low cost, ease of use, and improved sound drove other aspects of tube development. A cumulation of small interrelated innovations by the bulb makers, the device makers, and the set makers would gradually produce significant changes in radio design and operation.

Improvements in the ability to mass produce receiving tubes reduced prices for tubes and components (speakers, power supplies etc.) in the 1930s. Tube makers included not only the members of the so-called Radio Trust—General Electric and Westinghouse—but also AT&T, Hygrade (later Sylvania), Dumont, and many smaller enterprises. The capital-intensive part of tube making was glass bulb manufacture. Automatic bulb-making equipment capable of producing millions of bulbs a year from one machine first came into production in 1926. By the 1930s most smaller vacuum tubes were produced by a few very large automated machines owned by General Electric, Coming Glass Works, and Libbey Glass. The resulting improvements in manufacturing productivity reduced radio costs dramatically. The bulb producer, Corning Glass Works, jumped from a theoretical capacity of 40,000 handmade bulbs per man-year in 1910, to 640,000 per man-year in 1912 (on semiautomated equipment) to more than 300 million receiving bulbs per man-year in 1932.[19] As a result of all the changes by tube and bulb makers, radio set prices went from an average of $133 in 1929 to $87 in 1930, $35 in 1933, and as little as $10 (for the "peewee" model) in the middle of the Depression.[20] Tubes that were optimized for increased signal output and reduced power-consumption also gave off less heat, thus allowing table top models to be made of lower-quality, lighter-weight materials such as pressed metal and moldable plastics.[21]

Similar physical considerations affected sound in movies where vacuum tubes were also key to improving performance. Movies equipped with sound were only possible when sound could be amplified to fill a large space, and when microphones and recording devices could produce soundtracks on film. The vacuum tube was essential to making these developments possible. The incorporation of sound into movies was technically feasible years before it was tried. But movie studios incurred huge capital expenses both for their studio production equipment and for modernizing the theater chains that they owned.

Radar sets also had tube-based physical limitations when they first came into use during World War II. Cathode ray tubes could not be mass produced in the same manner as other less complicated receiving bulbs. Display units used in wartime radar sets—3 in., 7 in., and 9 in. round screens made of heavy leaded glasses—had to be made by hand for most of the war. Their invention and introduction had been so sudden that there had been no time to find either new glass compositions to make them lighter or tooling modifications to make them easier to produce. For many wartime radar applications, portability was a desirable attribute, but it was hard to achieve. It was a sign of just how valuable the devices were to the war effort that despite their weight and bulk they not only found a home on shipboard in World War II, but were jammed into airplane cockpits.[22] The attempts to master radar's physical limitations came too late for wartime service, but they were in time to benefit television mass-production after the war.

Key innovations by component suppliers also helped enable the introduction of black-and-white television after World War II at a price low enough ($375) for rapid market penetration (90 percent in ten years). Tube makers like RCA, Westinghouse, Dumont, and Hygrade/Sylvania worked with glassmakers Corning Glass Works and the Owens-Illinois Kimble Division to develop new lead-free glasses as well as finding new ways to mass produce CRT bulbs. In contrast, the innovation that produced color television ten years later was a much more radical jump from black-and-white to color than black-and-white had been from radar. It involved inventing, designing, and (hardest of all) finding ways to produce an all-electronic color picture tube (the shadow mask) that was very large and that required precise machining and alignment; in addition, the picture tube emitted radiation and therefore required lead to be reintroduced into the glass as protection.[23]

Television stations and consumers were slow to adopt the new technology. Color television was introduced in 1954, but it was ten years before color achieved the market penetration that either radio or black-and-white had achieved in half that time. Early color televisions sold at much higher introductory prices ($695 to $1,100, plus a mandatory service contract of more than $100) than black-and-white televisions. They were as hard to adjust and keep in adjustment as early radios had been. Sales were also limited by the problem that there was relatively little color programming. Not only the networks but also the local stations had to be able to originate color programming, and this involved a major investment in new production equipment. Sales were so poor (only 50,000 for all manufacturers in the first year), that GE, CBS, and Zenith withdrew from the market and essentially boycotted color, leaving RCA, RCA's licensees, and RCA's NBC network to keep the business going on its own. The rest of the industry charged that RCA's timing was dictated mainly by its need to renew its licensing income, for a large number of radio-purpose patents, including many having to do with black-and-white television, expired in 1954. This situation continued for seven years, until in 1961 Zenith finally broke the color boycott as black-and-white sales fell off.[24]

In the 1950s and 1960s developmental work on microwave electronics and other powerful electronics used for weapons and aircraft stimulated economic growth in several high-technology areas of the country. In New York City and California both the electronics and the entertainment industries were engines of the economy, whereas the leading-edge weapons work went on around the campuses of MIT, Stanford University, and Princeton University. Companies like Varian, located on the fringes of the Stanford campus, grew rapidly because of their contributions to radical increases in the performance of specialized vacuum tubes. Ironically, although silicon gave the place its nickname, it was glass and metal that gave Silicon Valley its original shape and character.[25]

Radio: The Unforeseen Dual Use Technology

Even though wireless was at a primitive stage when World War I began, it was vital to U.S. interests both before and during U.S. entry into the war. Great Britain, an ally but also a commercial competitor, controlled the other major international form of communications—the international telegraph cables. Britain defended its interests by cutting the cables between the United States and Germany when the war started. This action caused an international incident, for the United States, as yet not a belligerent, had its commercial dealings with Germany substantially disrupted. It was clear that to have a commercial policy independent of the British even after the war, the United States needed its own capability in ship-to-shore wireless technology. Nor was the Navy the only branch of the service interested in radio. As early as the late 1910s the Army Signal Corps developed a portable radios that could be carried on a donkey or in a cart.[26]

In addition to buying hundreds of thousands of tubes, and thousands of radio sets for ship-to-shore and battlefield use during World War I—and thus stimulating new radio tube production methods—the U.S. government intervened in the development of radio-related communications by helping to sort out the intellectual property maelstrom just described. After the war, the U.S. government's concern was to keep the British from obtaining vital radio technology via British Marconi's subsidiary, American Marconi—and also as we have seen, to sort out the radio patent situation. These concerns led the Navy to sponsor, with Owen D. Young (president of General Electric), the formation of RCA. The company was set up as a joint holding company to hold and administer all "radio-related" patents on behalf of its corporate owners, which originally included General Electric, Westinghouse, United Fruit, and AT&T but gradually narrowed down to GE and Westinghouse, known as the Radio Trust. By sanctioning what amounted to a patent monopoly in radio-related patents, the government kept destructive competition from slowing down the post-war development of wireless technology as a vital part of the military arsenal.[27]

Commercial broadcasting was a largely unanticipated consequence of these arrangements. Neither the government nor RCA's corporate owners had anticipated the popularity of commercial radio, or that RCA would also become the sales and marketing arm for large quantities of commercial radio equipment made by GE and Westinghouse. Focused on other mostly industrial markets, GE and Westinghouse could not initially see how to make money out of a broadcasting service though they could anticipate the returns from selling apparatus. Left to their own devices they would almost certainly not have mass-marketed radios at the relatively low prices needed to achieve rapid mass penetration of households. But latent demand was already there, and the government had unwittingly cleared the last obstacle keeping commercial radio broadcasting from leaping forward.[28]

Amateurs at work before World War I had been using crystal sets to send and receive radio signals. Their numbers had multiplied into the thousands, with 13,000 radio licenses issued in 1917 alone. By establishing a climate of experimentation conducive to invention and by attracting entrepreneurially oriented immigrants to the field of communications, these enthusiasts had laid the groundwork for regular radio broadcasting.[29] Budding young self-taught engineers, eager to build the best apparatus, shared tips and accomplishments in popular radio magazines. Some were known as the "distance fiends," competing to see who could detect signals from furthest away. But crystal sets were limited by the ability of the operator to assemble the device in the first place, the ability to master Morse code to broadcast and receive comprehensible signals, and skill at tuning in a signal that continually appeared and disappeared.[30]

Commercial radio broadcasting, which began in 1920 (soon after the end of a three-year wartime hiatus in amateur listening), had fewer limitations and appealed to a much different type of audience. It broadcast real voice and sound in the form of analogue signals. Rank novices could tune in and hear comprehensible, if not high-fidelity, programming—music and talk—without special training, though they still had to fiddle frequently with their dials.

David Sarnoff, RCA's general manager and formerly of American Marconi, was an immigrant entrepreneur, more akin to the young proto-engineers among the radio amateurs than he was to his superiors at GE. He flung RCA at the opportunity of radio broadcasting, and the new start-up soon found itself at the core of an exploding commercial radio business and the founder of one of several rapidly expanding broadcasting networks. Westinghouse's pioneering station KDKA (established in 1920) was soon joined by RCA's WJZ and AT&T's WEAF (the most overtly commercial of all three), each offering regularly scheduled broadcasts of live talent to urban audiences.[31]

A struggle ensued between the amateurs who preferred the old kind of point-to-point wireless with little more than occasional programs and regularly announced call letters to be heard, and the powerful commercial interests backed by the large equipment makers who recognized greater potential in a passive audience that wanted to be entertained and amused by regularly scheduled programming. In 1924 the latter party prevailed, pushing the "distance fiends" off the air and marginalizing other small opponents and competitors, such as stations run by small local feedstores or variety stores, but also educational radio stations run by schools and universities.[32]

The Radio Act of 1924, unlike earlier acts which dealt with military uses of radio, was the first to regulate commercial broadcasting by giving the U.S. secretary of commerce the power to issue radio licenses. This was resisted by many and taken to court by Zenith, allowing the problem of wave jumpers and pirates to worsen until 1927, when Congress created the Federal Radio Commission (FRC; later the FCC). Among other provisions the FRC was empowered to assign radio frequencies by type of station. "B" class stations, which received the larger, more select area of the spectrum, were those that had abundant resources and commercial interests related to the advance of commercial radio broadcasting. They included not only the radio apparatus manufacturers GE, Westinghouse, and RCA, who needed steady programming to keep up their sales, but also many stations owned by newspapers and department stores. By 1923 these included both of the Detroit dailies, the Kansas City *Star*, both Rochester papers, the Atlanta *Journal*, the St. Louis *Post Dispatch*, the Chicago *Daily News*, and the Los Angeles *Times Mirror*, as well as Wanamakers in Philadelphia, Gimbels in Pittsburgh, and Bambergers in New York.[33]

B class stations had to meet certain highbrow programming conditions in order to receive their choice spectrum space. One condition was live entertainment, not just the broadcasting of phonograph records. This prohibition on recorded music was observed more in the breach than the observance by the most powerful stations, and was later dropped altogether; it served, however, as an effective means of stabilizing broadcasting under the control of the larger stations and the networks they were creating.[34]

In the 1920s both RCA and AT&T had started and acquired multiple powerful radio stations, linking them together in what were to emerge as the first broadcasting networks. As early as 1921, stations were linked over telephone lines for single event, but permanent networks with centrally scheduled programming offered for some part of each day awaited an agreement between AT&T and RCA, which came in 1926. AT&T kept for itself the transmission system, and with it the revenues generated by providing telephone line transmission for the nationwide linkage. It left the broadcasting business to RCA and its National Broadcasting Company (NBC) "red" and "blue" networks. Another network, the Columbia Broadcasting System (CBS), emerged in 1927, to be taken over and built to prominence by tobacco magnate William S. Paley; Dumont had a third network that floundered badly and disappeared before World War II.[35]

This move to consolidate radio broadcasting was portrayed as a triumph for the forces of order, a chance to make use of the airwaves for cultural and educational purposes, and to quell some of the more unruly aspects of amateur transmissions. There is little doubt, however, that the chief impetus for networks was the need to spread the high cost of programming, while what kept the networks in place was the substantial revenues that accrued when network advertising was introduced in the late 1920s.[36] There was considerable rural and regional opposition to the centralizing moves and as we shall see, some elitist opposition to the intrusion of advertising into the home. Without the role of gradually evolving regulatory agencies, especially the FCC, siding with network promoters, more democratic, entrepreneurial, diverse models might have prevailed. But a centralized or at least concentrated communications system was essential to defense purposes, increasingly desirable for political and economic purposes, and certainly in the public interest to sort out the chaotic state of the airwaves on some organized basis.

Despite the initial predominance of urban audiences drawn to the broadcasting of their local entertainments and consumer interests in such commercial centers as New York, Pittsburgh, and Chicago, the other force that made radio's development so rapid was the unforeseen demand for information and entertainment among segments of the new audience outside urban areas. Farmers, thinly spread across the U.S. frontier and isolated by distance and weather, were able to get vital weather news and agricultural information. This service was begun by amateurs who relayed their information in encoded form to other amateurs in outlying localities who would translate it and spread the news.[37] Residents of outlying areas who were neglected as uneconomic customers by the telephone companies—and in some regions by the electric power companies as well—were able to feel part of a larger community. Sports fans were able to follow their teams on radio even when the fans lived nowhere near the ballparks, while people for whom even a quarter was too much to pay for a movie embraced radio's free entertainment.

Newspapers, more than 2,200 of them read by 20 million readers in 1910, had fed this need for information, entertainment, and connectedness before[38], but they had required a literate readership and they suffered from the limitations of text. Now radio offered the far more accessible modes of speech and music. So important did radio sets become to the U.S. population that they could be found in 14 million households by 1930, a rate of household penetration far in excess of that achieved by either household electricity or the telephone.[39] The nearly universal use of radios during the Depression, at a time when disposable household income was drastically diminished—when even attendance at motion pictures was off by a third—showed how important radio had become to a large and growing audience.

Sound in Motion Pictures

The addition of sound to films was a technological revolution that was even more devastating to existing interests than the revolution in wireless, because there was already a well-established film industry in place before World War I, albeit not one that received much respect from the social establishment. Having originated with peep shows and arcade amusements, silent films had developed into something of an antiestablishment force before World War I. Early film was a low-cost medium abounding in small studios and independent producers, with flexible distribution. It was possible under such conditions for films to be made about all kinds of social problems.[40]

After World War I the climate changed. The rise of Hollywood and the studio system combined with conservative reaction to the Red Scare and heightened postwar antiunion sentiment to virtually eliminate radical filmmaking. In the early 1920s film graduated from being a pillar of working-class entertainment to serving a larger and more socially varied audience. Studios thrived from their investments in picture palaces, and from promoting the colorful lives of flamboyant Hollywood stars like Douglas Fairbanks, Mary Pickford, and Mae West. As films became more expensive, risky productions were harder to make. With the emergence of downtown movie palaces came "cross-class" films that stressed harmony among the classes. The picture palaces and the pictures they showed promoted "conservative visions of consumption and class interaction," including films that depicted love between men and women of different classes, replacing themes of social problems with those related to social mobility.[41]

In the late 1920s, however, partly in response to the emergent Russian film industry that threatened to undermine the American studios' dominance of programming worldwide (and spreading socialist revolutionary fervor), the industry made a sudden jump to "talkies." Two relatively unknown U.S. studios, Fox and Warner Brothers, took the pioneering step of adding sound to motion pictures, thus gaining a lead on the rest of the industry. In the space of a year Warner Brothers came out of nowhere to gain control of more than 700 theaters.[42]

Talkies, what one motion picture historian has called the "technological counterrevolution of sound technology" put the familiar mode of capitalist commercial cinema firmly back on center stage. The American sound monopolies, RCA's Radio Keith Orpheum and the competing Westrex system from AT&T's Western Electric (marketed by AT&T's ERPE), could shut out the Soviets by controlling all the relevant technology.[43] For a time it appeared that a struggle over sound patents might block a speedy transformation until AT&T stepped in and forced an agreement.[44]

However controversial they might have been in establishment terms, silent films had developed a formula that made vast sums of money for U.S. capitalist enterprises at home and abroad. The changeover to sound was costly, involving new moviemaking facilities in acoustically protected studios, different actors and actresses, different methods of production, and new theaters with elaborate sound systems.[45] Ultimately, the shift was effective in keeping American enterprises at the forefront of filmmaking internationally, but the timing caused serious short-term upheavals in the film industry.

Silent film producers had adopted a regime of moderate moral self-censorship in the mid-1920s, but the risqué and the bawdy reasserted themselves when sound pictures came in, because studios needed to attract large audiences to their new theaters. Success seemed assured at first, but with the onset of the Depression audiences diminished. The large sums of capital the studios owed put even such giant studio empires as Paramount Pictures into bankruptcy court when revenues dropped in the early 1930s. For a while financial control of the industry devolved on a few key Wall Street enterprises controlled chiefly by the Morgans and the Rockefellers. However, artistic control soon returned to the people who had started the earlier studios and who knew the business. Eventually many of the outsiders who had begun their careers in the era of silent film returned to head the large studios, some of them well into the 1960s.

Although movie revenues achieved some fabulous peaks among their valleys, the movie story was never as rosy as popular mythology would have suggested. Movie-going never equaled the popularity of radio once radio became well established. In surveys cinema ranked well behind both newspapers and radio as a form of wartime information, even though, as discussed later, the movie industry received special dispensations for war work. Attendance and revenues peaked for the last time in 1946 when market research appeared to show that movies had finally achieved the audience of their dreams. This impression soon turned out to be illusory. In the late 1940s movie attendance fell off for several reasons: locations of theaters in declining urban areas, postwar changes in lifestyle, and, by 1950, an audience preference for television. Eventually television would give all other media a run for their money, though at first it seemed to be a victim of a serious "chicken and egg problem"—equipment sales depending on programming availability and programming availability depending on equipment sales. Owing to the necessary "lock and key" nature of its transmission and reception, far more constraining than radio, television could not benefit from thousands of amateurs putting out their own pictures over the airwaves in the way distance fiends had prepared the way for radio.[46]

The Transition to a Mobilized Society

The transition to a newly mobilized society, characterized by at least a superficial cultural unity, occurred from the 1920s to the 1940s. The transition occurred in several arenas simultaneously—the shaping of public opinion for political purposes, the expansion and manipulation of a mass market through electronic media advertising, and the transformation of a civilian society into a society permanently mobilized for war. To a great extent these arenas were interdependent.

A Culture of National Unity

Radio broadcasting's potential to reach a large mass of newly connected people was quickly apparent. Wireless in the hands of amateurs had already revealed a latent and growing need for a way to communicate over distance and to form bonds among people with similar enthusiasms.[47] The rapid creation of nationwide leagues of amateurs in 1914 and 1915 manifested this impulse, though amateurs were sometimes viewed with the same ambivalence as computer hackers today, as a potentially rebellious and incendiary force.[48] The problem radio broadcasting seemed to address even more effectively than wireless was an immigrant and mobile culture gripped by feelings of anomie and isolation. The United States had become a population of newcomers, whether to the country itself or just to a new part of the country, radio could hasten their cultural adjustment by keeping them in touch.

To those who sponsored it at the start, radio seemed to be a vehicle for a new national unity of a superior kind, consciously purveying programming of a much more upscale variety than older forms of entertainment like vaudeville and silent film. In radio's formative period the goals of cultural unity and homogeneity were held up repeatedly as matters of the highest importance.[49] NBC's stated mission explicitly committed the organization to provide the "best programming," or again, to provide machinery to insure the national distribution of national programs, "of the highest quality."[50] Consistent with a general attitude of paternalism among big business leaders, an ad from the National Carbon Company proclaimed, "The air is your theater, your college, your newspaper, your library." Underneath it all, though not as explicitly stated, there was a perceived need to reach people who might not be able to read, and a desire to combat the "transgressive forces" that seemed to be showing up in the aftermath of World War I—including the disruptive forces associated with large groups of blacks migrating north and women asserting themselves to claim voting rights.[51]

Leaders of large companies like GE and Ford were adopting the role of corporate statesmen in the 1920s. To paraphrase Keynesian biographer Robert Skidelsky, on both sides of the Atlantic leaders had shown what could be done in mobilizing their countries' resources for war, and they wanted to believe it was possible to mobilize for constructive peacetime purposes as well.[52] A particular emphasis was on acculturating immigrants. To this end large companies adopted progressive benefits, and they viewed radio as yet another means to accomplish some of the same ends.[53] As one scholar has observed, listeners tuning in by the tens of thousands to one specific program airing at a specific time created an even more intense version of the imagined community, with its "shared simultaneity of experience," than has been claimed for the daily newspaper. Indeed, chain newspapers were actually far more local in their impact than network radios.[54] Radio promoters were confident that they knew what cultural standards ought to be, but the culture of the Eastern elites turned out not to be a realistic set of norms for their purposes. New types of entertainment were needed that would appeal to a broad range of people, transcending social class and pocketbook, and helping to build through shared experience a culture of national unity that created common ground among people of widely differing ethnic backgrounds.

Inside the home, radio offered another kind of shared experience. Indeed, as mentioned earlier, it entered the private domain of the family in a way that was potentially more intrusive than any previous medium. Playing in the bosom of the family it reached everyone within earshot, young and old alike; unlike print media, it could be heard and understood by young and old alike. This intimate aspect of radio broadcasting was not lost on its promoters; it was one of the reasons that there was at first so much reluctance to use radio for advertising. Although it was undeniably possible for the listener to switch off or tune out a program if it took an offensive turn, it certainly was more risky to broadcast programming that might give offense than it was to print it.[55]

It soon became apparent that programming that appealed to Eastern elites was not the programming the general public wanted to hear. Promoters like Lee de Forest and David Sarnoff envisioned programming around patriotic themes and highbrow cultural entertainment such as operas and recitals. deForest emphasized bringing opera to the airwaves, though he also spoke of a broad mix of news and comedy; Sarnoff originally spoke of a public service kind of broadcasting that would be supported by philanthropists. As discussed later, these promoters initially shunned advertising, but it was advertising that would help to sort out mismatches between the goals of program selectors and those of their audience. For the first several decades of radio the white middle-class family image of radio prevailed. As radio stations proliferated, this image was diluted. After television replaced radio as the dominant networked medium, other social groups would also find in radio a way to get their voices heard in the larger community.

By far the most popular program in the early years of broadcasting was *Amos 'n' Andy*, which began in Chicago in 1926 as *Sam 'n' Henry* and later switched to NBC, which nationally broadcast the program. The program was indicative of many of the concerns that were shared by the broader populace, though it portrayed them through the adventures of two Southern black men who had moved to Chicago to seek their fortunes. By 1931–1932 *Amos 'n' Andy* was estimated to be reaching an audience of 40 million Americans. At a time when minstrel shows were still the stock-in-trade of most local live entertainments, this program could hardly be construed as the voice of a genuine black culture. Its writers and actors were two white male actors, Freeman Gosden and Charles Correll, and their dialogue as well as their plotlines undoubtedly reinforced racial stereotypes. Nevertheless, immigrants of many stripes identified with the hilarious experiences of two newcomers having to cope with a complex and unfamiliar urban setting beyond their control.[56]

Critics soon rose to denounce radio on cultural grounds. They complained that the networks, bolstered by government regulation and by strong local affiliates, were refusing to represent a broad spectrum of cultural interests. To radio's claim that requests for educational programming were slighted because advertisers would not pay for it, they replied that radio had aligned itself with government regulators to repress social dissent. College stations were in fact being squeezed by the FRC into poor and noisy channels; their spectrum assignments seemed to get worse each time the radio spectrum was reallocated.

Allocation of the radio spectrum remained an area of tremendous controversy, intensifying when in the late 1930s frequency modulation (FM) band radio and National Television Standards Committee television began to contend for the same area of the radio spectrum. Of course most critics had their own axes to grind. Their complaints about the debasing of public taste arose out of their fears that radio posed a destructive form of competition for other better cultural institutions. Nevertheless they could point to the government radio systems of Great Britain and Canada with their explicit educational aims as superior alternative models.[57]

Movies offered another approach to solving the problems of social isolation and loss of community. Films were less ephemeral than radio broadcasts; viewed repeatedly, they could reinforce taste and standards, and embed certain material ideals in the collective psyche. Since their storytelling depended as much on image as on sound, they also provided a chance for immigrant groups to learn the language. Unlike radio, which began as highbrow and therefore exercised fairly strong self-censorship from its start, movies grew out of a silent film culture that had had more than a few run-ins with the arbiters of taste and decency. In the mid-1920s the movie studios adopted their own half-hearted self-censorship to head off a Roman Catholic church push for government censorship. After a rash of gangster movies and other celebrations of offbeat heroism in the 1920s, Hollywood took a much more aggressive and deliberate stance toward influencing the national culture as young movie producers and directors assumed a new mantle of respectability. Three men in particular, David Selznick, Irving Thalberg, and Darryl Zanuck, transformed the very nature of Hollywood's pictures by making numerous dignified, elevated, and respectable (and often very expensive), movies set in the past, many based on literary classics—films of *Hamlet, Romeo and Juliet, Anna Karenina, David Copperfield, Les Miserables,* and *A Tale of Two Cities.* Later the trend moved to making films of the best contemporary works like *Gone with the Wind* and *Rebecca.*[58]

F. Scott Fitzgerald and other writers, who were cultural heros in the 1920s, sensed more of a threat than an opportunity in these Hollywood developments. They saw serious movies as a more critical challenge to the literary life of the nation than the silent films had ever been, because they portended a narrowing of the cultural life. The economics of movie production and distribution, and for that matter of all vacuum-tube–based communications technologies, were such that there came to be less and less room for opposing views, or alternative visions of what life in America was like. In what one movie historian has called "the first fully conscious era of cultural mythmaking," the middle-class culture of those who attended movies, and who could first afford radio and television, became identified in the 1930s both domestically and internationally as the U.S. national culture.[59]

Mobilizing Public Opinion   Electronic media were hardly the first mass media to be used by politicians and other national figures to mobilize public opinion. Newspapers, aided by the telegraph, had already proven effective in stirring up their mass audience. President Woodrow Wilson had acknowledged the effectiveness of mass print advertising campaigns when he appointed the Curlee Commission to help raise volunteers for World War I. The commission had mounted an effective national advertising campaign to persuade the U.S. populace of the rightness of U.S. entry into the war.

Nevertheless, radio clearly improved the prospects for engaging the U.S. populace more immediately in the political process. The very first radio broadcast on KDKA in Pittsburgh aired the Harding–Cox election returns on November 2, 1920, heard by at most a few thousand people. In 1923, Calvin Coolidge became the first president to use networked radio broadcasting. President Herbert Hoover used it to mark national milestone events such as the fiftieth anniversary (in 1929) of the invention of Edison's lightbulb. But Franklin D. Roosevelt perfected the use of radio for political purposes with his "fireside chats," which bypassed commentators and journalists to go directly to the people.[60] In the depths of the Depression these intimate addresses broadcast to citizens—whom he addressed as "my friends"—reached roughly 16 million households, nearly half of all Americans.[61] They were credited with raising morale and stabilizing a potentially explosive social situation, where millions were unemployed and desperate. The Roosevelt administration also borrowed an idea from the British government by employing filmmakers to educate the people about the government's goals. Pare Lorentz organized government film units to produce such notable documentaries as *The Plough that Broke the Plain* (1936), *The River* (1937), and *Power and the Land* (1938). These films used powerful sound tracks and lyrical images to convey their messages about the need for agricultural electrification or the manmade causes of what were previously thought to be simply natural disasters.[62]

The public purposes to which radio was put in its first three decades were generally of this unifying and stabilizing sort, partly because it was the sitting politicians who had access to the media. The potentially dangerous power of radio to influence the public was not lost on radio's critics, however. James Rorty, a prominent spokesmen for opponents of radio, warned in the early 1930s that "the control of radio means increasingly the control of public opinion."[63]

Newspapers, whose opposition to radio was obviously motivated by fear of competition, tried to keep radio from broadcasting news in the mid-1930s by refusing to allow the news they gathered to be broadcast. The networks retaliated by founding their own news bureaus, which caused advertisers to worry that the still stronger newspapers would shut them out. An agreement signed in late 1933 ended the dispute by limiting the time slots in which the radio networks could broadcast the news and getting the networks to do news on an unsponsored basis. Radio also agreed to limit their news to analysis or commentary, rather than reporting. As discussed later, the distinction between analysis and reporting helped to prepare the public for the special requirements of wartime news broadcasting.

After World War II, electronic media would come to be used in a more divisive and partisan way. In 1946, young John F. Kennedy of Massachusetts was one of the first aspiring politicians to buy radio time for his personal radio ads. Kennedy built up a broadcasting per-sonna that would serve him well when he became one of the first two presidential candidates to conduct televised debates, in the 1960 election. The networks began routinely to broadcast party conventions and election nights as a public service, and they also broadcast the political show trials of the House Unamerican Activities Committee under Senator Joseph McCarthy.

Mobilizing the Mass Market   Though the advertising profession was well established when radio broadcasting began, early radio promoters, with the exception of AT&T, were mostly averse to advertising on radio. One scholar attributes this to the perception of radio as a high-brow medium, starting as it did with affluent buyers and gradually spreading to the less well off.[64] No less a personage than Secretary of Commerce Herbert Hoover commented that it would be "inconceivable that we should allow so great a possibility for service to be drowned in advertising chatter."[65] Even leading members of the advertising profession fulminated against allowing commercialism to intrude on the "sanctity of the home." There was the fear in the advertising community that if advertising were allowed to invade this new medium there might be a consumer backlash against all advertising.

But radio posed significant challenges to advertisers, as well as to the advertising agencies that served them.[66] The practice of advertising in print media was well understood, and it was relatively easy to calculate how many people a particular ad might reach and what kind of people they were. In this sense early radio was a big unknown,[67] and preparing copy to be heard in the privacy of the home was perceived to be a delicate matter. Radio advertising went through several quick stages in the 1920s. First came "sponsorship only," simply identifying the name of a sponsor with a program, allowing the audience to infer that the National Carbon Company must be sponsoring the *Eveready Hour* because radios were such large users of batteries. Next, the advertising came to be blended with the program content in a fairly subtle way. A character in a situation drama or a comedy might refer to the brand of tea he was drinking, for instance. Later on, programming and advertising were interwoven, as advertising agencies began influencing content. Even styles of performance, such as the crooning of Bing Crosby and Rudy Vallee, were favored because crooning was the style of music deemed most likely to prepare the listener to be receptive to a commercial message.

Gradually advertisers deduced from favorable, though not necessarily representative, correspondence that the audience did not object to advertising of an even more overt sort despite being in the privacy of the home. Especially in the daytime hours when women tended to be at home working, listeners seemed to welcome a helpful, often educational "message from our sponsors."[68] Ironically, opera of a kind also came to form the basis of daytime programming in 1933 when the large packaged goods companies became some of the earliest enterprises to discover the advantages of getting their message to masses of women. The vehicle for this was the "soap opera," so-called because it was invariably sponsored by detergent manufacturers, who knew that their target consumer was the housewife. More than 70 percent of women could be relied upon to be at home in the afternoon hours; they bought the products without consultation and were known to be loyal to brands.[69]

By 1930 advertising on radio was reaching $60 million annually, and by 1940 it had jumped to $600 million. By 1935 some 12.5 percent of the whole advertising market had moved from newspapers and magazines to radio. It was evident that in spite of hard times generally, the networks were doing very well. *Fortune* magazine, part of the print media that was struggling to stay afloat, noted with envy that in the year 1930–1931 NBC's profits increased from $20 million, to nearly $26 million, while the smaller CBS increased from $8.5 million to $11.6 million.

Small wonder that newspapers felt the need to acquire radio stations.[70] Some newspapers bought stations as a defensive move, while others saw them as additional sources of advertising revenue. In some cases they fought back in other ways, refusing to carry radio schedules and giving bad reviews to programs that were commercially sponsored. At first they saw these moves as countering the very real threat to their revenue base, but after a while they realized that publishing radio schedules was more likely to sell papers than not and capitulated into peaceful coexistence.

In the 1920s, even before the economy had fallen into depression, some corporations had begun to think of themselves as conducting business as a public service. Prominent among these companies were GE and AT&T, both major players in the radio industry. Then the economy went into depression, and Roosevelt's New Deal came in with a philosophy quite different from the probusiness philosophy of the Republican administrations of the 1920s. At that point, many corporations faced the shocking prospect of a growing public hostility. To counter some of the bad press, companies sponsored radio programming intended to show their public-spiritedness—special concerts, dramatic shows, and so on. At this period advertising agencies began producing their own shows, a practice that would continue for a time with television.

Movies, which were held in about the same low regard by the advertising community as were the tabloids, had played a relatively small role in advertising in the era of silent films. Even this small exposure—a few spots before a film began—was lost with talking pictures. Movies were likely to portray a world of conspicuous consumption and to stimulate interest in it, but they were not likely to become a direct advertising medium. Consumption, decreased though it was in the 1930s, was nevertheless a form of recreation. And in the 1930s consumption was also public-spirited. The New Deal government, believing that consumption was imperative to get the national economy moving again, was disinclined to oppose any efforts the advertising community might make to stimulate it. The old dichotomy was gone. Increasingly the population was drawn together as a culture more by what has been called a "democracy of goods" than they were by a democracy of ideas.[71]

Mobilizing a Civilian Society for War. "Radio is the one channel of publicity which has not previously been available in a great international crisis. It lends itself with singular effectiveness to the creation of morale on a national scale," claimed the Treasury Department in one of its 1941 bulletins. Treasury was early among U.S. agencies to try to mobilize public opinion with its Defense Savings Bond program. But outside the government other organizations had already been using radio's considerable powers of influence to raise consciousness about Nazi atrocities and to fight anti-Semitic activities in the United States. The Council for Democracy, formed in 1940 to fight all forms of prejudice in "our national consciousness" whether it was directed at minority groups or the foreign-born, relied heavily on the mass media, especially radio. It also worked with government agencies including the Justice Department, and later with the House Unamerican Activities Committee reporting on the activities of subversives who were sympathetic to the Nazi regime. Such groups were ready to give assistance, and even lend their personnel, when the government moved to mobilize public opinion in favor of the war in 1941.[72]

Before the United States entered World War II, the country was divided in its sympathies toward the belligerents and also toward the idea of U.S. involvement. As it had during the depths of the Depression, the Roosevelt administration once again turned to radio to move public opinion to support its program, this time on behalf of the Allies. Radio broadcasts and newsreels of the Battle of Britain helped contribute to the sense of urgency and national purpose as well as to the need to make funds available for war materiel under the Lend-Lease Program. Roosevelt's use of the radio to persuade the populace of the necessity of his course of action allowed him, in the face of considerable congressional opposition, to violate the spirit, if not the letter, of the Neutrality Acts by diverting war materiel to Great Britain. Soon radio was asked to help in recruiting men and women for military service, and women for war work at home.

Radio was no longer restricted from broadcasting news, immediacy being viewed as an advantage to keep the populace informed. Indeed, the familiar voices of such radio personalities as Lowell Thomas and Edward R. Murrow did much to bring home the reality of the devastation overseas and the need for the United States to intervene. More than a dozen manufacturers had begun turning out portable radios from late 1938, when Sylvania's introduction of new battery tubes— tubes that made smaller, less expensive radios possible—coincided with increased tensions in Europe. Demand for them was created almost entirely by listeners eager to hear war reporting.

War coverage moved into high gear as soon as Germany invaded Poland in 1939. *Newsweek* reported that broadcasting studios adopted twenty-four-hour emergency schedules, and "armies of correspondents and commentators were mobilized" creating such a "stream of war-and-peace confusion . . . that Americans were left almost as tense and groggy" as those who were actually experiencing air raids. So excessive was some early war coverage that the three networks (the three included the American Broadcasting Company "red network," which RCA had been forced to divest in 1942) worked with the FCC to draw up a code governing wartime news dispatches. It held that every effort consistent with the news itself should be made "to avoid horror, suspense and undue excitement."[73] One important matter was to distinguish clearly between fact and fiction when broadcasting news. Radio had made such a practice of embedding its messages in story and skit form that it was necessary to make a very clear distinction for news formats.

After the United States entered the war, President Roosevelt commissioned the Bureau of the Budget under Milton Eisenhower to propose a better approach to coordinating the government's information functions, which often seemed to be working at cross purposes. The new Office of War Information, headed by Elmer Davis, a well-known journalist and radio commentator, was directed to facilitate the development of an informed and intelligent understanding of the government's wartime activities at home and abroad, and to coordinate and review all federally sponsored programming intended for radio broadcast or motion picture.[74] The advertising agencies offered their services through an effort that circulated an average of three messages a week involving timely themes to be incorporated into programs at the discretion of producers. Unlike the massive orchestrated efforts of the German propaganda machine, all such activities on the part of the U.S. broadcasting, motion picture, and advertising industries were strictly voluntary, and the government's role remained officially one of coordinator rather than originator of the information. These efforts were often chaotic at first, and the bureaucratic apparatus involved (though reorganized from time to time) never achieved the effect of a well-oiled machine.

Nevertheless, mass media were employed at all levels for training, civil defense, and information dissemination purposes.[75] The Motion Picture Committee Cooperating for the National Defense, which officially came into being on December 12, 1941, comprised six divisions; some parts such as the Hollywood Division, employed tens of thousands of workers throughout the war. The Distributors Division managed more than 300 film exchanges in thirty-one cities to handle releases of approved films at no expense to the government. The Newsreel Division, which consisted of five major newsreel companies and the March of Time, took responsibility for filming the war in all of its theaters, at home and abroad. Between 1942 and 1945, one of Hollywood's most distinguished directors, Frank Capra, produced the important twelve-part military-training film series "Why We Fight." Combining "stock footage, newsreels, and specially produced film."

This series attempted to explain to U.S. servicemen and women why the United States was at war. Meanwhile John Ford, William Wyler, and others produced films for the different armed services that aimed to inspire patriotism and resolve in the population at large; they created such moving war stories as *Memphis Bell* for the Air Corps, *The Battle of San Pietro* for the Army, and the *Battle of Midway* for the Navy.[76]

The Office of War Information, formed in 1942, took as its mandate the need to broadcast information from the various agencies concerned with defense mobilization about the state of business–government co-operation. The office was ineffective because there were no clear guidelines as to whether its primary mission was to build morale and create unity, or conversely to shine light on the problems arising in the arena of government–business cooperation. More effective was a branch of the Office of Civil Defense, called the Office of Facts and Figures (organized under the leadership of then Librarian of Congress Archibald MacLeish), to provide public opinion samplings and to give Americans an accurate and coherent account of government policy while striving to avoid the appearance of propaganda. This office had a radio division, headed by former CBS programming vice president William Lewis, "to give guidance to government departments and agencies and to the radio industry as a whole" and "to handle certain government programs on the networks within the U.S."[77]

Media executives like David Sarnoff of RCA, William Paley of CBS, and James Galvin of Motorola received wartime commissions commensurate with their peacetime status and were enlisted in the cause of adapting broadcasting and communications activities of all kinds to wartime missions. Rapid advances in emergent electronic communications technology were considered so important for military purposes that the government funded civilian communications and electronics research via the Office of Scientific Research and Development and kept it free of military control even as the war was progressing. This extreme deviation from previous practice put millions of dollars into research at a long list of radio and electronics firms and also supported mammoth university–industry–government cooperative efforts such as the Radiation Laboratory at MIT.[78] One key wartime development was the image orthicon, a significant improvement by RCA of its old orthicon tube, and one that had important implications for guided missiles and reconnaissance.[79] In addition to performing large amounts of high-priority research, the large integrated companies, such as GE, Westinghouse, and RCA, were converted to manufacturing military communications equipment and electronic weapons. Among the technologies that emerged during this very fertile period, though it drew on work already under way in the 1930s, was solid state electronics, which involved electrons flowing through solids rather than through gas or vacuum or conductive metals. When it became apparent that it would not be possible for the country to return to the peacetime status quo after the war, the military–industrial complex that formed at this time would continue even stronger in the postwar period. Pillars of this complex were the integrated electronics and communications companies, now joined by many other companies who could rely on continued postwar government funding and who would rise to challenge, ultimately successfully, the way the largest companies had previously been allowed to dominate broadcasting and communications.[80]

Television and Radar: The Planned Dual Use Technology

Although television as an invention was as old as radio, it was World War II that prepared the way for it to become a thriving commercial medium in its own right. Television had been under development before World War II in several companies—of which RCA, CBS, and Dumont (an entrepreneurial firm cross-licensed to RCA from 1938) were the most significant. Vladimir Zworykin, a Russian immigrant, had invented the iconoscope camera tube in 1923 while working at Westinghouse before its radio-related research transferred to RCA, and then later with funding from fellow Russian immigrant, David Sarnoff at RCA. Zworykin was a student of another Russian inventor, Boris Rozing, who in 1907 had already patented a cathode ray tube (CRT) television receiver.[81] The ingenious but unlucky Philo Farnsworth was the first to demonstrate a complete prototype television system, in the late 1920s. In the late 1930s Corning Glass Works supplied enough experimental CRTs for RCA to run several major pilot tests of television in New York City. In 1937 the Radio Manufacturers' Association (RMA)—generally regarded as a "tool" of the RCA because the corporation dominated the tube market and still controlled radio technology through its licensing arrangements—made recommendations to the FCC for a workable all-electronic television standard. The rest of the radio industry feared another RCA monopoly over television. Led by CBS, which was promoting its own partly electronic television system, RCA's industry opponents appealed to the FCC, and a National Television Standards Committee (NTSC) was formed in 1940 to produce one set of universal standards agreeable to the entire industry. A year later the FCC agreed to a set of NTSC standards calling for 525 lines and the use of FM for the audio portions of the broadcast. RCA began broadcasting on this standard in July 1941, only to have it come to a halt five months later with the Japanese attack on Pearl Harbor.[82]

Because of its lock on critical materials and devices, the war diverted the nation's capacities for the duration. This hiatus in television broadcasting turned out to be of incalculable value to television manufacturers and broadcasters, because World War II prepared the way for television in innumerable ways. It provided the means and the focus for significant improvement in key electronic devices like the image orthicon; it made inexpensive radar plants available for television tube manufacturing; it trained servicemen in electronics; and it created a pent-up demand for consumer goods. Radio had enjoyed this type of advantage to some extent in World War I, as wireless operators came back having benefited from training and field operations, but World War II made much greater use of electronic equipment in numerous forms. Radar, the top-secret weapon, gave the Allies the incalculable advantage of superior information about enemy whereabouts, guarded U.S. airfields, sailed aboard U.S. naval vessels, gave eyes to U.S. submarines, and even flew on U.S. bombing runs.[83] Once again, as with radio, the bulb makers were the high-volume producers with many more tube companies manually assembling the finished tubes. Television receivers, using the same small round CRTs, were also used in primitive form in wartime, though the military form was still rudimentary enough to have limited application, mostly for training.[84]

When World War II was over it was in almost everyone's interest to see that television came into being as a regular broadcasting service as quickly as possible. The war had pulled the country out of the Depression, but it was generally recognized that it would be necessary to reprime the pump of national consumption if prosperity were to continue. After two decades of austerity, postwar Americans looked forward to a future of new homes, new cars, and countless conveniences. The consumer electronics industry employed tens of thousands of people, and pent-up demand could move many radios and televisions. Nevertheless, the industry was sharply divided in the postwar period as to whether it should be improved radio transmission and better radio receivers, or the new (but less well-developed) medium television, that should be allowed to benefit most from postwar demand. Here RCA prevailed, though only by overcoming stiff opposition from competitors led by CBS.[85]

The industry battle over television standards, now for both black-and-white and color, resumed on two fronts: in the FCC, which had a larger role in television standard-setting than it had in radio, and in the marketplace, where RCA began selling black-and-white television receivers before the standards questions were settled. In the spring of 1947, CBS was pursuing a petition with the FCC for a revised color television system broadcast in the ultra high frequency (UHF) part of the spectrum, thereby creating uncertainty as to whether television would be a "go" or not. Under pressure from RCA, which warned that the stagnation of television would be ruinous to a potentially shaky economy, the FCC gave provisional approval to RCA's prewar NTSC standard for black-and-white and deferred judgment on the color standard. It had been James Fly, chairman of the FCC, after all, who had written, "I think it quite likely that during the post-war period television will be one of the first industries arising to serve as a cushion against unemployment and depression."[86]

CBS continued to direct its efforts toward convincing the FCC to adopt its constantly improving "field-sequential" color television standard, which employed spinning color wheels in both camera and receiver. The advantage of CBS's system was that it would free the very high frequency (VHF) part of the spectrum for FM radio. This would appease those radio manufacturers that had already been producing high-fidelity FM radio, which had been successfully introduced by Edwin Armstrong in 1939. The disadvantage would be that it would render obsolete all existing black-and-white television sets.

However provisional it was intended to be, FCC's decision in 1947 was the encouragement black-and-white television sales needed to explode. *Nations's Business* noted in the summer of 1947 that television was "something the average American family has just about decided it cannot do without."[87] RCA and more than 100 smaller existing and new entrepreneurial television receiver makers were selling enough black-and-white television sets on RCA licenses—table models, consoles, television-phonograph combinations—to impose a de facto standard on the marketplace.[88] RCA's combined revenues soared from licensing, tubes, receiving sets, professional broadcasting equipment, and the sale of other components, providing support for the development of television programming and the next advances in color television technology.

RCA's television system occupied the VHF channels, preempting the original FM radio band, and limiting severely the number of television stations that could operate in any given metropolitan area, making television broadcasting more concentrated—and television stations even more valuable than radio stations. The FCC's decision necessarily affected FM as well. It reallocated FM radio to a new part of the spectrum, and cut back FM's power, rendering obsolete half a million receivers and forty prewar FM stations. This action raised a storm of controversy that would make it unthinkable to do such a thing again.

By 1950 television had already entered ten million households—at an average price of well over $200. The Korean War intervened to stop all production of television receivers, as users of scarce materials that were needed for weapons. When the Korean action was over, the FCC and the industry were forced grudgingly to accept RCA's NTSC standard not only for black-and-white television, but also as a starting point for the color television standard which now had to be compatible. FM survived as a system, used for the sound in television, but RCA and its many licensees flatly refused to pay Armstrong, FM's creator, the licensing fees he should have received for its use. Worn out by court battles, even though they were ultimately decided in his favor, Armstrong committed suicide in 1954. His FM radio system straggled along, only picking up adherents in the 1960s when classical radio stations, benefiting from static-free sound, became one of many multiplying radio formats.

Unlike radio, which had had to start largely from scratch as a broadcasting medium, television had the good fortune to follow radio, which it was able to mimic and to steal from in many different ways. Studios were adapted as well as assembly plants. Performers and writers moved from radio to television. Often shows appeared on prime time television that had developed their audience on radio. And many formats that had been developed for radio were adapted for television. Even the extremely popular morning programs that eventually anchored all three television networks were actually imitations of Mary Margaret McBride's very successful women's program on radio, which after a run of twenty years was reaching eight million listeners per day by 1954. Though hailed at the time as original breakthroughs in programming, with a magazine format largely directed toward men, they were actually derived from McBride's magazine format for women. Many radio soap operas, and situation comedies, made a similar rapid transition.[89]

What television could not adapt directly from radio, however, was the ability to hook up long-distance network broadcasting over the telephone lines. Multiple stations could see the same programming over stations all owned by the same company in Philadelphia and New York, but otherwise shared programming had to be transferred on film, an expensive and inferior procedure. Because of the greater bandwidth required, television networking had to await the construction of a nationwide coaxial cable transmission system chat was not in place until 1951. It was only a short time after the coast-to-coast hook-up occurred, marked by Edward R. Murrow standing on the Golden Gate Bridge, that both prime-time radio programming and large-scale radio advertisers moved en masse to television.[90]

Media Coexistence

Judged solely in commercial terms (i.e., dollars expended on advertising), one generation of vacuum-tube–based technology rapidly displaced another. Radio, having stolen revenues from newspapers at such impressive rates, was in turn displaced by television as a bigger revenue generator from advertising. Nevertheless, despite predictions to the contrary, all of the vacuum-tube–based forms of communications technology continued to coexist, and gradually became complementary to each other. Radio, having created the major national audience, retrenched and decentralized to become a more local medium serving niche markets. Although low yield at first, these franchises became more and more profitable as radio discovered a new programming format that aimed different kinds of specialized music at different audiences—developing whole new genres of music or news or talk shows in the process.

Movie studios meanwhile made up for the loss of their primary audience by renting their film libraries to television, and later to cable television. Beginning with Howard Hughes's sale of the RKO film library in 1955, pre-1948 Hollywood productions flooded into television network libraries in the late 1950s. Certain studios, like Columbia Pictures' Screen Gems (starting in 1952), developed long-range relationships with the networks to make "telefilms," that is, made-for-television movies, in a format that would become extremely profitable for all parties involved. The studio would make a thirty-nine episode prime-time series that could be shown twice for the initial licensing fee, after which it would go into syndication both domestically and internationally. Ironically, even as television was arguing publicly that the ability to show live drama and current events was an important justification for having centralized networks, it was in the process of shifting almost entirely to film-based programming to maximize revenues from seasonal reruns. By 1957 live drama on television was coming to be a thing of the past.[91]

The coexistence of all the electronic media with print gave rise to cultural self-consciousness about the effects of different media on their

audiences and on the culture at large. Previous commentators, especially educators, had certainly questioned the legitimacy of broadcasting content and the effect of commercialism on the culture, but one
question had yet to be considered. Were there unique effects from the
media themselves, irrespective of content? Canadian professor Marshall McLuhan was one of the first public figures to raise this question.

In a keynote speech to the annual convention of the National Association of Educational Broadcaster (NAEB) in Omaha, Nebraska, in
1958, McLuhan used a phrase that was to generate public discussion
throughout the 1960s: "The medium is the message." McLuhan told
the NAEB and anyone else who would listen—including countless
gatherings of communications industry executives from companies like
GE and IBM—that his concern was the "mutational powers," the
"various and often contradictory qualities and effects" of media.[92] For
the remainder of his career McLuhan developed his theories about the
human "sensorium" and the ways different media extended the human
senses causing the other senses to interact with each other in ways
unique to each medium.[93] In his book *Understanding Media,* McLuhan
got to the implications of his theories. The media, he said, were capable
of "imposing their own assumptions" on the people who used them,
or indeed creating their own world. Unless people were aware of this
and understood the nature of electronic media in particular, McLuhan
warned, they were in danger of losing all the traditional values of
literacy and Western civilization.

In 1960 when a number of U.S. events became media events—the
U2 spy plane capture and the Kennedy–Nixon debates—McLuhan
asserted with justification that the media had transformed North American current events and politics into a branch of the entertainment
industry. Of the Kennedy administration he commented that a four-
year stint in the White House was "no longer easily distinguishable
from something arranged by a booking agency." And when Kennedy's
assassination in 1963 was seen over international television, closely
followed by his murderer's murder seen live, McLuhan entitled his
comments "Murder by Television."[94]

McLuhan's theories led naturally to serious attempts to assess which
medium was most effective for which kinds of advertising. Time Life
employed McLuhan to offer his insights into the matter, and then used
the skills of a young psychologist, Daniel Yankolovich, to test them.
Yankolovich found that television advertisements were more effective
at exciting emotional responses, whereas print was more effective at
conveying information. The conclusion was that products that needed
their buyers to have more information were better sold through print

media, whereas products that depended on visceral appeal were more appropriately advertised over television. By 1964, when his *Understanding Media: The Extensions of Man* was published, McLuhan could irritate a whole seminar of assembled publishers by predicting the imminent obsolescence of the hardcover book.[95]

Looking at the interaction of the different media, McLuhan saw each new medium as more than a cultural add-on. Instead it transformed the use of all previous media, "creating its own environment which acted on human sensibilities in a 'total and ruthless' fashion." To McLuhan a medium was not just the thing itself, but all the habits that collected around it, as well as the energy it created. The new environment created by a new medium rendered the old media and their environments newly visible, just as *The Late Show* made old movies into a self-conscious art form. McLuhan predicted that because television appealed to the innate American visual sense it would be all-engulfing, eventually turning print objects into little more than museum artifacts.[96]

Major human dislocations had indeed attended each generational change in technology and more were to follow. Many skills from the pre-electronic forms did not transfer, nor did the skills needed for one necessarily transfer to the other. The technical skills needed to show silent motion pictures, for example, had not transferred to "talkies" and 10,000 technicians from the silent era were thrown out of work, not to mention the musicians and the live acts that accompanied silent films. Moreover, the economic consequences of each shift in media generations were great. The manufacture of each generation of receiving sets tended to follow a dramatic life cycle—from introduction to saturation followed by layoffs of factory workers—until the next generation of set came along. The consumer electronics business employed tens of thousands of people in manufacturing, and was famous all during the 1950s and 1960s for laying them off in vast numbers a week or so before Christmas. The advantage of the large integrated communications concerns was that their control of networks' steady earnings countered the cyclicality of the business on the manufacturing side. All this would change when U.S. companies lost the consumer electronics business to off-shore, primarily East Asian, manufacturers. The layoffs that occurred then, in the consumer electronics recession of 1970, differed in one important respect: they turned out to be permanent.

The Cultural Extremes of Mobilization

The 1950s version of popular culture was outwardly as homogeneous in the broader society as the gray flannel suit was in business. Partly a consequence of the other developments in communications that originated well before World War II, partly a consequence of shared wartime experience, the society leaned toward a stripped-down "high-tech" material order made of modern technology-based materials—aluminum siding, glass blocks, glass ceramic oven ware, and, above all, plastics, promoted in the media as wartime spin-offs. In style and spirit these products were designed and promoted to match the ultra-plain architecture and furnishings of the modernist era.

In other eras this degree of social conformity—typified by loyalty oaths, pledges of allegiance, and security clearances, and in more sinister ways by the televised activities of the House Unamerican Activities Committee—would have been taken as the surrender of freedoms that it certainly was. In the face of the Soviet threat, however, many considered it to be a necessary cultural defense to narrow the bounds of social tolerance. Few in either Hollywood or the broadcasting studios of New York rose to oppose Joseph McCarthy or even objected to the blacklisting of hundreds of prominent members of the entertainment industry on both coasts. On the other hand, the vast media-based credibility of communications giant Edward R. Murrow, built up during his many wartime broadcasts, was one of the few forces powerful enough to break the spell of McCarthyite demagogery.[97] Murrow's interview of McCarthy on *See It Now* did much to discredit the self-appointed inquisitor in the eyes of the public. By the late 1950s, however, commercial pressures did what political pressures could not do. Even Murrow's brand of televised dissent became intolerable to the advertisers and they used their considerable clout to push his *See it Now* program off the air.[98]

The Costs of "Free" Media

The rhetoric of the mobilized society had barely begun to slacken after World War II, when renewed international tensions brought it once again to the fore. Starting with the Russian atomic tests of 1948 and continuing through the Korean action into the Cold War, the networks seized on the need for continued vigilance as a rationale for perpetuating the concentration of broadcasting power. No longer was it simply open warfare that justified living in a state of constant alert; now it was a matter of civil defense in peacetime. In 1956 CBS's Frank Stanton told a group that the threat of intercontinental nuclear missiles demanded an instantaneous civilian mobilization which could only be assured by means of network television. "It seems to be providential," he said, "that we are thus able—at this pivotal point in world history—to reach into nearly every home in America simultaneously and at a moment's notice."[99] Providential or not, there was of course a tremendous irony here, for although CBS and others argued that their "free"—in the political and legal sense—commercial system of broadcasting was obviously preferable to government control, it was a governmental agency, the FCC, that effectively perpetuated the concentration of broadcasting control in the hands of a very few powerful, and highly profitable, broadcasting networks. Regular local stations were highly resentful of the networks' privileged positions, as were the aforementioned independents such as local educational stations. Even as they were touting the value of free networks, the networks were overstepping their bounds commercially.

In the 1960s the networks' control of programming and advertising revenues made them so profitable and so powerful that they behaved arbitrarily toward even the largest local affiliates. Knowing that loss of network affiliation could halve a local station's revenues overnight, the networks exercised almost total control. Their behavior set in motion a rebellion on the part of local stations that would ultimately result in regulatory action to reduce their programming role. Meanwhile alternative forms of transmission (such as cable), and alternative entertainment formats (such as pay-TV) slowly moved into position to challenge the networks' hegemony, though they would take two decades to make a serious dent in network profitability. The agitation that began against the networks' dominance of programming would ultimately lead in the 1970s to Nixon administration antitrust rulings that would deprive the networks of their programming rights.[100]

The Loss of Alignment between Government and Industry

Paradoxically, though the full effects would not be felt for almost a decade afterward, it was in the late 1950s that the informal but potent alignment between the U.S. government and the large companies that controlled the national networks was beginning to unravel. Not the result of deliberate government policy toward communications as such, it came about because government antitrust policy undercut the pragmatic policy that had for so long justified RCA's quasi-sanctioned monopoly of radio-related technology.

RCA had felt the first effects of governmental antitrust action directed against it in 1940, when it had been forced to divest one of its two broadcasting networks and turn its smaller B network into the independent, and at first very shaky, American Broadcasting Company (ABC).[101] Then throughout the 1950s, responding to complaints by the broader industry about high-handed tactics on the part of RCA/NBC, the government launched an antitrust case against RCA. Although for years it had sanctioned RCA's control of radio-related technology for its own national defense reasons, the government charged that RCA's practice of package licensing its consumer electronics technologies was a predatory practice leading to unfair monopoly of the technology. The rest of the consumer electronics industry had long bitterly resented RCA's dominance of its technology even as it benefited from the standards it helped to set, and even though RCA was losing large sums of money keeping color broadcasting alive alone until the other producers broke the industry boycott on color in the early 1960s.[102] It had not escaped the industry's attention that RCA had hired a former head of the FCC as an NBC executive when his term of public service had come to an end—presumably as a reward for help in once again giving RCA the edge, this time in the standards battle for color television.[103]

In 1954 RCA had managed to renew its licensing position when its radio-related patents ran out by persuading a large number of domestic licensees to give its color system a try. It had spent well over $100 million developing television, especially color, and it looked on licensing as one reliable way to recover its investment. But the renewal was to be short-lived. In 1957 RCA signed a government consent decree, thereby agreeing to license the technologies it controlled, individually and at minimal cost, to all its domestic competitors.[104]

This marked the beginning of the end of the U.S. consumer electronics industry. In 1958, to maintain the substantial stream of licensing revenues that it had come to rely on (and would surely lose under the new arrangement), RCA began the practice of package licensing its proprietary consumer electronics technologies overseas, especially in Germany and Japan. Europe had other contenders, such as Philips, offering licenses, but in Japan RCA's technology packages were eagerly purchased by a number of licensees. In a few years David Sarnoff received the highest award ever given to a foreign businessman, the "Order of the Rising Sun, 3rd class," for his substantial contributions to fostering the Japanese consumer electronics industry. Japanese pocket radios using primitive transistors had been coming into the United States since 1954, because Japanese producers had been able to license transistor technology from Bell Labs after AT&T had signed a similar consent decree earlier in the decade. But RCA's licensing involved much more complete and advanced technology packages, embracing the entire field of consumer electronics. Advanced television technologies, advanced display technologies, and advanced recording and pickup devices would all be included in the packages offered each succeeding three years to international licensees throughout the 1960s and 1970s. By the late 1960s, RCA had begun to abdicate its own leadership in technology to the Asian competitors it had helped to create. Distracted by financial pressures and diversification strategies, and plagued by declining manufacturing capabilities in what it regarded as "mature" technologies, RCA would delay introduction of new consumer electronics products that its dealers and its industry followers needed to keep their business on track. Meanwhile the offspring of RCA's (and Philips's) internationally licensed technologies would flood back into the United States spelling the beginning of the end for the U.S. industry. Japanese companies Matsushita, Sony, Sanyo, and the like, became powerful enough to make short work of most U.S. firms in a very few years.

RCA, with its NBC network, had been hated and feared by many in the consumer electronics and related industries. But although there were many opponents, a pattern had developed when RCA controlled the radio purpose patents that served as an effective pathway to innovation. RCA was a fully integrated company that controlled all parts of the entertainment system, from consumer and professional equipment manufacturing, a dedicated dealer network, and research and development, to entertainment producing and broadcasting. With the sometimes reluctant concurrence of the government RCA had been able to carry through a complete innovation cycle from beginning to end. No other U.S. Company was in a position to do this single-handedly. When RCA faltered, therefore, in the 1960s, no other company was in a position to step into its shoes.[105] Almost unnoticed, "control" of the communications infrastructure—and in particular of the pace and direction of innovation—slipped out of the grasp of institutions closely aligned with the U.S. government in a breakdown of control not unlike the one that occurred in the middle of the Industrial Revolution.

Conclusion

There exist many historical studies of mass communications technologies, but few have treated these technologies in concert, as we have portrayed them here—the communications infrastructure of a society that by the second half of the twentieth century had become media-rich and media-dominated partly through alignment with multiple government priorities (though not, as in other parts of the world, direct government control). If, as, U.S. broadcasting moguls like William Paley were fond of pointing out, these media, especially the broadcasting media, were indeed "free" of government control in a way that such media were not in other countries, they were still willing servants of government interests. Government aligned and government assisted through regulatory channels, and shaped in other ways by repeated antitrust actions when they failed to conform, the media behaved as important instruments of national purpose both culturally and economically. Partly because of the tremendous capital cost of setting up vacuum-tube–based systems that were integrated enough to innovate and reach a national audience, these media were also highly concentrated.

A consequence of the peculiar brand of freedom the media enjoyed in the United States was the bias toward information in the form of entertainment. Entertainment was of course a powerful conveyor of information—cultural and political—and because of the ubiquity of advertising as the prime source of funding (movies being the exception here), U.S. media purveyed their information in the form that the largest, or the most affluent, segments of its audience found most entertaining. This was, of course, not new with the electronic media; it merely continued a long-established connection between newspaper sales and sensational reporting. But it ought to remind today's reader that the postwar professionalism of journalism is more of an historical aberration in the United States than a norm from which current standards can be said to have departed.

There are interesting parallels between the Vacuum Tube Era and the current era, when once again several powerful emerging information technologies are threatening the established media and vying for public acceptance. As we shall learn in the following chapters, in the Internet we once again have the rise of a socially and culturally integrating technology that has the power to mobilize those who are connected by it in all the ways that occurred in the early twentieth century, though this time the scope appears to be global. Once again it has not been the large companies who have invested so much to develop and merge computer and telecommunications technologies, but the amateurs, now known as hackers, who have quite suddenly transformed the technology from a defense-related form of communication (the ARPANET of the 1970s and 1980s) to an infrastructure that other interests can recognize as being rich with commercial potential.

It remains to be seen what role the U.S. government, necessarily both interested and involved in this tool for mobilization purposes, will take. Few could argue that the public interest does not need defending in some way as these new communications technologies combining computers and telecommunications evolve. But once again the definition of public interest remains a matter of much controversy, although little direct public debate. Issues have already arisen around the allocation of the broadcast spectrum and its use by high definition television, and here the government's chosen role is clear. Once again, existing broadcasting interests are being aided in their modernization, based on an economic rationale. As with FM radio, if present plans continue, we can expect to see television receivers in vast numbers of consumer households rendered obsolete by the new technologies. In both cases only one lesson of history can be relied upon to come true: It is safe to predict that the old media, as distinct from old technology, will not be replaced, but will transform themselves in new forms of complementarity. It remains to be seen how different elements of society will then work to adapt and reconfigure these technologies to their own unforeseeable patterns and uses, but we can be sure that they will.

6

Progenitors of the Information Age

The Development of Chips and Computers

James W. Cortada

Ground zero and the first minute of the Computer Revolution occurred at 9:00 A.M., April 21, 1952, at Bell Laboratories in Murray Hill, New Jersey. Representatives from more than thirty companies gathered for a six-day seminar on the transistor, learning about what would become the heart of the computer. The companies had paid a $25,000 fee for their representatives to attend, and with that attendance to sign up for the right to manufacture the transistor. If one had to pick the one time, place, and item that heralded the arrival of the computer, this event is as good as any because the key to understanding why the computer was such an American story depended more on appreciating how this machine was diffused than on how it was invented. The initial development of the computer for primarily military purposes occurred simultaneously in Great Britain and the United States, with smaller projects underway in Germany and in Poland, but the transistor was clearly a U.S. invention that we can precisely document as having been created at Bell Labs in the 1940s. It was the decision of American Telephone & Telegraph (AT&T) to license this technology to other firms that made it possible for the transistor to work its way out of one company into many, and therefore to be used in ways unanticipated in the beginning. One of those unanticipated uses would be as the heart of this new machine we call the computer.

AT&T recognized that by sharing the rights to manufacture the transistor it would fulfill a traditional commitment as a nationally regulated utility in disseminating knowledge useful to the public while generating revenues from licensing agreements. This act would also stave off real concerns about what the Antitrust Division of the U.S. Department of Justice might do; at that moment, government lawyers were pondering the massive market power of AT&T. Management also recognized the strategic importance of the transistor to the nation, however. For example, in its first formal seminar on the transistor, held at Bell Labs on September 17–21, 1951, the firm worked with the U.S. Department of Defense to determine who should attend.[1]

The conference was highly successful in stimulating interest in rights to manufacture the transistor. Before the end of the year, nearly three dozen firms had signed up and by 1960, there were several hundred. The vast majority were U.S. companies, with a smaller representation of West European firms. By the end of the 1950s, companies from around the world had also become licenses. Of the original list of licenses from 1952, we can see firms that in very short order became manufacturers of computers or their components: Minneapolis Honeywell, Raytheon Manufacturing, Texas Instruments (TI), General Electric (GE), International Business Machines (IBM), NCR, and two important European firms: Philips, and with Melchip, Siemens & Halske.[2] Diffusion of rights meant dissemination of information about transistors, more advanced manufacturing techniques for electronics, and creating the base for the knowledge this nation needed to develop, manufacture, apply, and distribute the computer chip in the 1960s— which ultimately became the true power base and generator of the Information Age that so many like to speak of today.

Previous chapters have demonstrated how individuals and organizations in the United States had long exhibited a penchant for exploring new scientific and technological insights and then immediately applying them in practical ways. The themes of speed of application, the hunt for economic return, and the utopian optimism that a market and a need existed at the end of a technological rainbow—all these applied to continued evolution of electronics and deployment as a prime mover of information through the U.S. economy. The open flow of information about the science of electricity and its derivative technologies, such as transistors, microelectronics, and semiconductors, in turn facilitated further evolution of practical forms of electronic devices for manipulating and moving of useful information. The AT&T conference represented yet another example—if to be sure a very dramatic one—of the historic process of inventing, discovering, sharing, disseminating, and exploiting information-centric technologies.

In this chapter we explore briefly how the computer came into being, and the industrial and economic infrastructures required to make this new engine, which historians Martin Campbell-Kelly and William Aspray aptly label the "Information Machine."[3] It is the story of American innovations leading to the creation of a hidden infrastructure in the U.S. economy. That hidden infrastructure is the "chip" in everything from microwave ovens in our homes to the palmheld computers that Americans are buying at the rate of more than two million a year. Going from the nearly accidental invention of the transistor in 1946 to an environment where well over 75 percent of all United States homes have computer chips of one sort or another by the end of the 1980s is a remarkable story of transformation. It is a story of invention, deployment, and acceptance.

Arrival of the Transistor and the Chip

American fascination with and adoption of new information technologies can be explained in part by a long-standing history of good experiences with innovation. But Americans are a practical people who will not embrace the next great technology unless it meets several criteria. First, the new technology must perform at least as well as the current technology. Second, it must not cost more than the current alternative unless it has new function or capacity. In other words, it must be cost-effective. Third, it must be as reliable as an existing alternative, or very close; risk is tolerated if one of the other two criteria are compelling. Often a combination of the three criteria is evident in the decision to acquire any technology. A fourth criteria, the one that often initially trumps the first three is new functionality, that is to say, the ability to perform a task that could not be done with an existing alternative technology. Of course, in hindsight we can explain how managers made a decision to acquire a system. At the time, everyone was learning how. As John Diebold, a leading expert on computing in the 1960s, puts it, "naive standards are used in justifying and evaluating the machines which so greatly extend our analytical powers."[4] Perhaps too harsh? Managers did use common sense and sound judgment. An auditor from the same period, L. Fred Boyce Jr., explained:

One of the reasons advanced for adopting electronic data processing is the expectation of savings in data processing costs. The ability of the company to use the computer at a level close to capacity is a major factor; idle capacity costs can devour estimated savings in a voracious fashion. Another justification offered is that it will be possible to provide more timely and useful data that may enable management to achieve significant reductions in operating costs.[5]

The practical bent was no stranger to these important decisions.

It is to the fourth alternative that we can also attribute the importance of the transistor and the integrated circuit. But what is a transistor? A chip? Definitions are complicated by the fact that many types of devices have been developed since the 1940s. Figure 6.1 (pp. 182–183) lists key types, their definitions, capabilities, and when they were used. But we can speak about these base technologies generically as transistors and chips. The most widely consulted dictionary of computer terms defines the transistor as "a small solid-state semiconducting device than can perform nearly all the functions of an electronic tube, including amplification and rectification."[6] The key concept is the idea that a device, using a material capable of enhancing (amplifying) an electrical signal can carry or transmit predetermined electrical impulses which can then be interpreted as numbers or data. The word *chip* is shorthand for an integrated circuit (IC). The same dictionary defined an IC as "a combination of connected circuit elements inseparably associated on or within a continuous substrate."[7] The first device looks like an old piece of chewing gum with several wires sticking out of it, the second like a well-jeweled square with little lines and layers of materials. Originally, the first device could only amplify electronic signals coming into it because of the physical characteristics of its its material (e.g., silicon or germanium), while the second came to house built-in instructions to perform mathematical calculations, take readings, and issue instructions to other devices. The difference between the functionality of the first and the second device was less than twenty years of development, all done in the United States. But both became the "brains" of computers. Engineers used transistors in computers throughout the second half of the 1950s. By the late 1960s every manufacturer had moved to the cheaper, more versatile integrated circuit, which remained the bedrock of a computer's technology for more than thirty years. We cannot, therefore, appreciate the effect of the computer on U.S. society and business without understanding the transistor and the computer chip. The interdependence of technology with its uses and consequences is clearly explained in the next chapter.

The technical history of the transistor and the computer chip has been well documented and need not detain us here. Again, an American story: Walter Brattain, John Bardeen, and William Shockley worked in the nurturing environment of Bell Labs. In 1956 the Nobel Prize Committee recognized this great American achievement by awarding all three the Nobel Prize in physics.[8] Ultimately more important than the pure science that made the transistor (or the Nobel Prize) possible are characteristics of the U.S. economy that encouraged this kind of development. We have already suggested one in this chapter, the existence of organizations with engineers and scientists who could work on these kinds of projects. Bell Labs is a good example. At the time Bell Labs was studying solid state physics and invented the transistor, it had 5,700 employees, 2,000 of whom were some of the nation's best scientists and engineers. They came from universities that had quietly invested in the study and transmittal of scientific and engineering knowledge over the previous eight decades. Bell Labs continued to invest in science and technology; in the late 1970s, for instance, it had more than 17,000 employees earning over 700 patents each year.[9] But Bell was not an isolated case. Other corporations, such as GE, IBM, NCR, and RCA also had substantial development labs, while the U.S. government had a collection of national laboratories. Nothing quite like this extensive complex of facilities existed anywhere else in the world.[10]

As the semiconductor business grew in the 1950s, a whole industry came into existence to develop, manufacture, market, and improve semiconductor technologies. A strong tradition of patent protection in the United States, dating back to the founding of the Republic, provided economic incentives to develop innovative products. Creation of a computer industry and demand for its products generated additional opportunities for more microprocessors. Availability of a growing pool of engineers, scientists, and experts on semiconductors made possible the prerequisite trained brain power. The physical proximity of developers, manufacturers, and vendors of this technology proved important as well. The bulk of this industry clustered (in descending order of size) in California, Connecticut, Massachusetts, and Texas, with more than a third located in a small area in northern California that has come to be called Silicon Valley.

Proximity allowed companies to share, collaborate, compete, recruit employees from each other, provide venture capital, and speed up development and sale of their products.[11] Yet, in a seeming contradiction, the industry also located elsewhere in the nation. In 1972—midpoint in our history of the chip—semiconductor plants existed in 120 U.S. counties and by 1982, in 182, suggesting that semiconductor manufacturing was expanding slowly through many sections of the nation. A similar pattern existed with computer and peripheral manufacturers: facilities in 203 counties in 1977, with many counties not having both types of high-tech in them, proof that computational "high-tech" sites existed in more than 300 communities. By the late 1990s that number was greater, due especially to Personal Computer

Figure 6.1 Evaluation of Computer Chips, 1947–1993

Type	Features	When Invented	Who invented	Year in Use	Uses	Significance and Facts
Germanium Transistor	Germanium	1947	Bell Labs	1951–Early 1960's	Hearing Aids, Radio, Computers, Rockets, Telephone Routing	Early use of science-based R&D; Dominant type of transistor until 1955; That year IBM introduced its first transistor-based computer
Silicon Transistor	Silicon	1954	Texas Instruments	1954–Early 1960's	Same	In 1950's over 600 types of transistors were in use. In 1956, 26 firms were sending commercial transistors
Various Transistors	Silicon 400–799 Mhz	1956–62	Over 40 Firms	1950-Mid 60's	Military, Computers, TV, Space, Aircraft	6,000 transistor types produced until 1962; variety drops after that date
Integrated Circuit	Multiple functions could be done on 1 chip Germanium	1959	Texas Instruments	1963–Present	Hearing Aids, Digital Watches, Mili, Space, TV, Cars, Home Appliances	Replaced transistor by end of 1960's massive miniaturization and cost reduction occur all through 1960's–70's
Single Chip Calculator	Semi-conductor memory calculator functions	1960's	TI, Intel, Various electronic firms	1970's–Present	Computers, Appliances	Massive expansion of computer capacity, speed and reliability; Replaced older ICs and transistors
Intel 4004 Micro-processors	4-bit length words	1971	Intel	Early 70's		Called "micro-programmable computer on a chip" the first microprocessor the heart of all future computers

Name	Specification	Year	Company	Period	Use	Description
Intel 8008	8-bit length words	1972	Intel	Early 70's	Various portable intelligent electronics	Considered the standard first generation 8-bit processor, the workhorse of the early micro-processor. 40 types of micro-processors available by mid 1970's
MOS Technology	Faster, Smaller	1975	Intel Motorola Texas Instr.	1970's	Computer Mem Org	Computer memory workhorse technology 1970's, early 1980's
16-Bit Processor	16-Bit Processing	1974	National Semiconductor	1970's	PCs Compatibles	
8086	Same	1978	Intel	1970's–1980's		
64K DRAM		1979	Fujitsu	1980's		1st major Japanese micro-processor
APX432	32-Bit processor 200,000 in 3 chips	1982	Intel	1980's		Processing power of an APX432 was equal to that of a mainframe computer
80286	16-Bit	1982	Intel	Early Mid-1980's		Workhorse of early IBM PC Also called the 286
	256K		Intel, Hitachi, Fujitsu			Chip innovation truly international
80386	386K	1985	Intel			3X faster than 80286
80486	486K	1989	Intel			1st micro-processing chip to have 1.2 million transistors
Pentium	3M Transistors 300 MIPS at 100 Mhz	1993	Intel			Workhorse of PCs (1990's) Speed microprocessor improved by over 100 times since 1982

(PC) and semiconductor manufacturing in the upper Midwest, throughout the South, and the Southwest.[12] The implications are clear: over time the spread of information technology skills and economic activity diffused throughout the American economy.

During the 1950s and early 1960s an embryonic semiconductor industry developed. By the end of the 1960s, when computer chips were THE brains of all computers, in the United States alone the semiconductor industry had become a $1.5 billion business. As figure 6.2 shows, enormous growth occurred in those years when the computer moved rapidly throughout the American economy almost like a technological wave passing through all major and mid-sized organizations.

The social and managerial practices of this industry have long been fairly consistent and contributed to the flowering of this sector of the economy. Perhaps the practice most obvious to its members is the mobility of personnel. For example, in Silicon Valley one can easily move from one company to another without changing homes. More important, as one member of this community put it, "We all know each other. It's an industry where everybody knows everybody because at one time or another everyone worked together."[13] Critical mass and synergy, compounded by growing knowledge of the technology, made

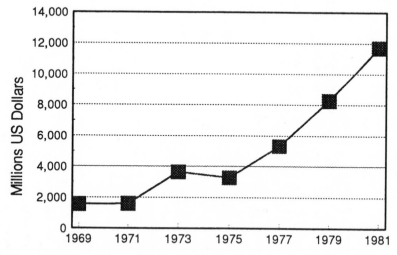

Figure 6.2 Value of US Semiconductors, Selected Years, 1969–81. *Source:* Derived from various data in Manuel Castells, *The Informational City* (Oxford: Blackwell, 1989): 108.

possible a dynamic industry that could adapt quickly to chase technological innovations with the resources required to exploit economically the opportunities these presented.

Economic results were very positive. Between 1967 and the end of 1980, double-digit percent growth in consumption of this industry's products occurred in nine out of fourteen years; single-digit growth occurred only once, in 1968 (4.7 percent). There were four negative growth years, which came during periods of national recession.[14] In the 1980s and 1990s, growth rates in demand of 30 percent per annum were not uncommon. In the same period, the industry expanded rapidly around the world as well, often as offshoots of U.S.-based firms, with the result that globally in 1995, sales surpassed $140 billion, with expectations that it would more than double by the end of the century. Over one million Americans were employed in this industry. In addition to feeding a national appetite for digital chips, these plants exported roughly one-third of their production, about the same percentage all U.S. office vendors had done with their products over the previous thirteen decades.[15]

While we will have more to say later about how computers were used (applications), critical mass of knowledgeable workers and improving technology are never enough to drive any product deeply into an economy. Applications is the name of the game. For the most part, throughout the history of the U.S. semiconductor chip, demand had come from three sources: the computer, personal computer, and telecommunications. By the late 1990s, chips amounted to about 40 percent of the cost of a personal computer—the largest source of new demand for ICs during the late 1980s and throughout the 1990s. As U.S. corporations became more dependent on chips, they continued to demand more capacity and price performance. This set of demands occurred simultaneously as the cost of developing new types of chips rose along with the enormous expense of constructing factories that could manufacture these devices. In the United States the industry responded to this problem by creating consortia and alliances, sometimes funded and frequently encouraged by the U.S. government. NexGen and IBM, Hewlett-Packard and Intel, and SEMATECH are high-profile examples. As a result of expanded capability to develop new products, the number of classes of application continued to increase.[16] One survey done in 1994 demonstrated that computers used 47.9 percent of all chips (down from more than 90 percent in the mid-1960s), industrial and instrument manufacturers another 10.3 percent, communications 14 percent, consumer electronics 21.9 percent (the largest growth area in the 1990s), automotive 4.9 percent (the largest growth area in the 1980s), and then the government and military about 1 percent. Later in the decade, in the United States, about two-thirds of all chips went into computers—which should be of no surprise since this is the nation with the largest computer manufacturing industry in the world. By the end of the 1990s, PC manufacturers had become the largest computer manufacturing industry in the world. By the end of the 1990s, PC manufactures had become the largest users of semiconductors.[17]

The simple little transistor of 1946–1947 also launched a process of product diversity that has yet to be fully documented. While we can catalog all the new chips that increasingly came out each year from the 1950s to the present, less understood is the enormous variety of single-purpose and multipurpose semiconductor products. By the 1990s, there were literally tens of thousands of variations of semiconductor products. In the mid-1990s, National Semiconductor Corporation, only one of a few in the industry, had more than 40,000 products in its catalog. However, all ICs are characterized as one of four basic types: memory chips, micro components, logic, and mixed-signal and analog devices. Around the world more than 300 firms made such products, but sixteen accounted for 80 percent of the market. Since the mid-1980s, twenty U.S. firms dominated the industry. To put things into a global perspective, Americans accounted for 31.7 percent of all semiconductor sales in 1995, making them the largest consumers. That year, Japan consumed 29.7 percent, Europe 19 percent, and the Asia-Pacific market an additional 19.7 percent.[18] In short, as had been the case for nearly a century with other information-processing technologies, Americans used more of this class of information-handling devices than anyone else, as measured by either raw quantities purchased or percent consumed.

Development of the Computer

When thinking about computers, computer chips also pop into our heads—as they should, because both are tied together. Andrew Grove was named man of the year by *Time* magazine in December 1997 not because he served as CEO of a computer manufacturer, but because he was the CEO of Intel, the largest producer of computer chips. As Norman Pearlstine, editor-in-chief of *Time* put it, Grove had become the symbol of a much larger transformation at work:

. . . an acknowledgment of the culmination of an ongoing process. Intel's chips have been around for nearly three decades, but 1997 was the year Grove's life's work reached full flower. It was the year cell phones, Web sites and E-mail became ubiquitous, the year the global economy, for good and ill, became an undeniable reality. Intel chips hum at the center of everything from coffee machines to Hollywood's special effects to Wall Street's trading desks.[19]

Hyperbole? National pride? Perhaps, but nonetheless a very mainstream acknowledgment that the chip had become an important building block of the modern economy. If better informed historically, Pearlstine could have realized that the situation he described as ubiquitous had come about before 1997, the result of a process of deployment with a very long past.

While Grove was a child, and before the transistor, and its sequel, the integrated circuit (chip) had been developed, engineers in Europe and in the United States had been busy developing what in time came to be known as the computer. More than any other device, it gave economic purpose to the development of the microprocessor, or, as most people would call it, "the chip." That is why our story began with the development of the transistor and then the chip. Now we move to the computer which provided the devices into which these components—transistor and chip—went. It is both a story of the integration of these basic building blocks of the Information Age and their deployment through the economy.

In chapter 4, JoAnne Yates explained the enormous spread in the practical uses of mechanical aids to calculation, such as adding machines tabulators, and punched cards, that took place across the entire U.S. economy in the late nineteenth and early twentieth century. That deployment gave users in large corporations, national government agencies, and engineering departments at leading universities additional insight to the potential of even greater machines.[20] But more specifically, one must turn to the engineering community in a handful of universities for the next phase in the long history of computing, because they had access to the scientific and engineering knowledge prerequisite to development of the computer. Their sources of knowledge included (a) an understanding of the rapidly evolving scientific knowledge about electricity (see table 6.1), (b) new tools to solve complex mathematical problems for the scientific and military community, and (c) construction of components to build calculating devices between the 1920s and 1940s (see table 6.2). Without developments in

Table 6.1 Key Events in Electricity Affecting Information Technology

1750s	Benjamin Franklin conducts world-class basic research
1820s	Michael Faraday builds first electric motors
1830s	Michael Faraday builds first electric generators
1837	Samuel Morse applies for his patent on the telegraph
1840s	Joseph Henry conducts research on electromagnetic relays, stepping up voltages
1876	Alexander G. Bell makes first telephone call
1880s	Vacuum tube becomes building block of new electronic industry
1890s	Herman Hollerith determines how to build electric punch-card equipment
1903	Nikola Tesla patents first electronic logic circuits
1919	W. H. Eccles and R. W. Jordan invent flip-flop electronic switching circuit
1936	Alan M. Turing (British) proves mathematical possibility of building a digital computer
1939	Bell Labs builds one of the first electronic relay computers
1942	IBM engineers use electronic relays instead of vacuum tubes to perform mathematical calculations
1946	Transistor is developed at Bell Labs
1951	William Shockley introduces first reliable junction transistor
1952	Color television introduced as a commercial product
1959	Jack Kirby at Texas Instruments and Robert Noyce at Fairchild Semiconductor independently create the integrated circuit, the bedrock of all future computers
1969	MOS semiconductors become possible, allowing chips to function as a calculator
1972	Intel introduces the 4004 and the 8008 chip, triggering the microprocessor revolution in electronics

all three areas, creation of the computer in the mid- to late 1940s would not have been possible. Once the possibility of new machines became clearer, developers and users learned how to turn them into more practical uses. In the beginning, it was a new period of discovery and the unknown.[21] An Wang, one of the researchers at Harvard working on computers in the 1940s, recalled that "Those of us working on computers in the late 1940s enjoyed the sense of purpose and creativity of the times, but I suspect that most of us did not have a sense that we were making history."[22]

Almost all the early work in the United States took place at universities. In the 1920s and 1930s an enormous amount was done by Professor Vannevar Bush and his students and colleagues at the Massachusetts Institute of Technology (MIT), building a variety of calculating devices using mechanical moving parts, vacuum tubes, and

Table 6.2 Key Scientific Milestones on the Way to the Modern Computer

1830s	Electricity applied to telegraphic basic research
1850s	Boolean logic introduces concept of zeros and ones
1920s	Electrical analog machines are built
1920s	Use of radio and electricity spreads in the United States
1930s	Wireless telephone becomes practical
1940s	Claude Shannon's works on information theory and the role of electricity applied to Boolean logic
1940s	John von Neumann describes the modern architecture of the computer
1950s	First large commercial digital computers become possible
1960s	Digital computers are built using integrated circuits; go on-line
1970s	Super computers come into their own commercially
1980s	Massive miniaturization and capacity increases take place with computer chips; portable computing comes into its own with PCs
1990s	Convergence continues to a practical level with telephones, PCs, and hand-held units all in one

electricity. By 1940 at Harvard University, Howard Aiken and his students progressed on another class of large calculators, later called the Harvard Mark machines. The one important exception involved Bell Labs, where engineers had searched constantly for new ways to handle switching of ever-increasing volumes of telephone calls, beginning their hunt in the science of electricity in the 1930s. This work led directly to their development of the transistor, about which we had much to say earlier. In the early 1940s, the U.S. government supported development of machines to calculate firing tables, decipher enemy military messages, and train pilots with simulators. That commitment of resources led to a variety of projects involving U.S. companies (e.g., NCR, IBM, and GE) and universities (e.g., MIT, Harvard, and the University of Pennsylvania), collaborating and creating a critical mass of skills and experiences in the development of what became known as the modern digital computer.[23] Simultaneously at Bell Labs, work on machines to switch calls had the collateral effect of encouraging basic scientific research on electronics, and, more specifically, semiconductors of electrical impulses. This led to development of the transistor in 1946—at the exact same moment when the digital computer had its coming-out party with the public unveiling of the ENIAC at the University of Pennsylvania.[24]

In the period immediately prior to World War II, the number of information-processing—related projects underway just in the United States became impressive. More than two dozen computers were under construction, while fewer than a half dozen existed in Western Europe (Britain, Germany, and France). These U.S. projects exposed a growing number of engineers to the concepts of electrically performed computation. As a consequence, by the end of the 1930s they had built a variety of analog computational devices, in the process creating a base of knowledge that would be applied in the 1940s to construction of digital computers.

In the 1940s, the digital computer finally came into its own.[25] Engineers who had worked on analog and mechanical/electronic calculators evolved into builders of digital machines. Wartime government funding and university-based resources, supplemented with manufacturing and engineering skills of electronics and office equipment vendors, made construction of the digital computer possible. Because of the large number of organizations participating in this work during World War II, engineers increased their knowledge of computing machines along with advanced concepts in electronics. By the end of World War II, one could see a new technology appearing on the American scene. Beginning with the ENIAC in 1946, over the next half dozen years more than a score of digital computers were built in the United States, funded by the U.S. government, all for federal use, constructed at U.S. universities, and often relying on components from American manufacturers, leading to machines that were be used for scientific and military applications.

Over the first half dozen years after the end of World War II, engineers figured out how to make these more reliable, smaller, less expensive, and practical to use. Speed and capacity improved sufficiently to encourage start–up computer manufacturers (e.g., ERA and Eckert-Mauchly), established office equipment suppliers (e.g., Remington Rand, which acquired the first computer in 1952, and the second two years earlier) and consumer electronics manufacturers (e.g., RCA in 1959) to begin thinking about producing commercial versions of these machines (see table 6.3).[26] One of the steps that facilitated this progress was rapid acceptance of an approach to the design of equipment, an architecture that came to dominate the "look–and–feel" of computers for the next half century.

A distinguished mathematician working in the United States, John von Neumann, had been involved with the government's support of the ENIAC project during World War II. Seeing that subsequent work on computers was imminent, he wrote a paper, "First Draft of a Report on EDVAC," released in mimeographed form in June 1945, in which he described the concept of a stored program and its possible implementation in a computer. Because it proved so influential with com-

Table 6.3 Early U.S.
Computers, 1946–1954

Machine	
ENIAC	1946
IBM SSEC	1948
UNIVAC I	1951
IBM 701	1953
UNIVAC 1103	1953
IBM 704	1954

puter designers, it became the conceptual rallying point for the design of this new thing called the digital computer. In short, an American approach to standardization of a computer's architecture rapidly predominated. Subsequently, von Neumann and others built machines that implemented the essential ideas of this paper.[27]

The primary source for the increased reliability, speed, and capacity of these machines came from underlying technologies embedded in them. Table 6.4 documents some of the more important technologies; all centered around development of technologies (some would say components) that could store electronic impulses (data) and permit reliable calculation of data (initially numbers, later analysis of information). The key to these machines—as it would be for many users of PCs in the 1990s—became the adequate supply of cost-effective and reliable memories in which to store data. While this chapter is not the place to discuss these early technologies, it is important to recognize that Amer-

Table 6.4 Technologies of U.S. Computers, 1940s–1950s

Machine	Year	Technology
ENIAC	1946	Vacuum tubes
IBM SSEC	1948	Electromechanical and electronic components
UNIVAC I	1951	Mercury delay lines
EDVAC	1952	Mercury delay lines & drum
Whirlwind	1950s	Magnetic core
IAS Computer	1952	Flip-flop switching circuits and CRTS
IBM 701	1953	Williams tubes and plastic tape
IBM 650	1953	Drum
IBM 704	1954	Ferrite cores
IBM NORC	1955	Williams tubes

ican engineers explored various technologies, such as relays, mechanical delay lines, and static magnetics, in their hunt for the right platform. They shared their findings at conferences, similar to AT&T's; as technologies began to perform, the engineers began to patent, license, and market their findings to each other.[28]

Concurrently, others developed something new that today we call software, ranging from operating systems (to direct all the activities in a machine) to programming languages (to feed systems specific commands).[29] In the 1940s and 1950s most of the basic concepts applied to software design in the 1960s–1980s were uncovered. As table 6.5 suggests, much went on in this period. While Europeans also worked on software, American operating systems, programming languages, and database tools became standards of the day. Easier to use software tools, when coupled to more reliable cost-effective computer systems, made it possible in the early 1950s for companies to begin introducing commercial versions of these high-tech devices. The speed with which software and hardware developments came in the first generation after World War II proved nothing less than phenomenal. In 1946, the total number of developments worldwide was no more than ten; by 1960, some 6,000 systems were installed around the world, mostly in the United States.[30]

Between the early 1950s and the introduction of IBM's System 360 (or S/360) (involving more than 150 products) in 1964, electronics firms (e.g., GE), start-up computer manufacturers (e.g., ERA), and office appliance vendors (e.g., Remington Rand, IBM, and Burroughs) built several dozen systems, each consisting of a computer, peripheral

Table 6.5 Major Events in the Early History of Software, 1940s–1950s

Event	Year	Comments
Flowchart developed	1946–1947	By several Americans
Plankalkul	1940s	Zuse and others describe in Europe
General-purpose subroutines	1945–1950	Machine-level instructions
SHORT CODE	1950	First high-level programming language
Bohm's Compiler	1950–1951	Early pseudocompiler
AUTOCODE	1952	An early compiler
System Control Program	1955	One of the first SCPs, ran on IBM 701
MATH-MATIC UNIVAC	1956	Widely used high-level language
FORTRAN developed	1956	Most widely used scientific language
COBOL	1959–1960s	Most widely used business language

equipment (e.g., such as printers and card readers), and software tools (e.g., operating systems, programming languages, and a few application packages to do primarily accounting). They were expensive, could only be leased to large organizations that could afford to spend millions of dollars on them (such as the *Fortune* 500 firms or government agencies), and required large staffs to maintain. Moving from one size of machine to another required a total rewrite of software, an experience no data processing manager was willing to go through more than once.

Demand for this technology, however, continued to grow and by the end of the 1950s a small computer industry had been born. Competitive rivalry among computer vendors, and growing interest by the business community, led each of the half-dozen major suppliers to bring out new machines every year in the late 1950s and early 1960s. Then, in 1964, a fundamental change came when IBM introduced the S/360 family of computers. For the first time, a vendor offered a group of different-sized machines in which software running in one could operate in another. Compatible peripheral equipment, and eventually operating systems and software tools, gave corporations a growth path as they built up their inventory of application software and increased volume of work and users. It would be difficult to overestimate the significance of this change in how computers were subsequently designed and built. IBM's innovation proved so popular that the old tabulating equipment supplier doubled its revenues by the end of the decade. Every major supplier had to introduce compatible lines of computers. Now no large organization had an excuse—all expected to operate with computers.[31]

A great deal of credit must be given to the underlying technologies involved (computer chips) and to the marketing of early computers. Yet American managers focused on computers' overall increased reliability and performance. For example, if we take the highly popular IBM 650 system of 1953 and give it a relative speed to price ratio of 1, IBM's machine for the same market in 1979 (the IBM 4341) had a relative speed to price ratio of 1,143,000. That order of magnitude improvement in price performance continued all through the 1980s and 1990s with both large systems and, by then, the personal computer (PC). While we speak of dozens of American machines in the 1940s, managers welcomed the improvements, installing tens of thousands in the 1970s.[32] By the end of the 1990s, managers and consumers around the world had acquired some 200 million PCs. The technology became smaller, had more capacity, and permeated most large organizations by the end of the 1960s. In every year from the beginning to the end of the 1990s, U.S. production and installation of computers normally outpaced manufactures in Europe and Asia by two to one.

Another important consequence of the S/360 was rapid standardization of the technologies that went into computers, peripheral equipment, and software. Standardization made it possible, for instance, to upgrade from one system to another if the new system came from the same or a compatible vendor. Standards made it possible for computer vendors to develop products that could compete against each other, thereby creating a very large computer industry in the 1960s and 1970s. The issue of standardization is an important one, most fully developed by U.S. manufacturers of computers, because with acceptance of basic formats for design and construction one had the ability to offer add-on products, rivals could compete, and a broad understanding of how to use a technology made hiring operators and programmers easier. A fundamental reason for the success of Microsoft in the 1980s and 1990s came from standardization. More than 90 percent of all PC users "standardized" on Microsoft's Windows operating system; some 150 computer vendors, and several thousand software developers, introduced products that customers understood and used. Thus, standardization of computing technology facilitated rapid expansion in deployment of new tools, startup of suppliers, and recruitment of users. Just as JoAnne Yates emphasized the consequence of standardization of such things as 3 in. $\times$ 5 in. cards, file cabinets, and punch-card equipment, so too we see with the S/360 and Windows the same process at work. Paper-based and electrically based technologies were subject to this common economic consequence of standardization.

Since the PC is the only computer most Americans have ever seen, it has conditioned their view of this technology, thereby making it imperative that we take this machine seriously, occupying center stage in any discussion of new computing technologies. The PC (also called the desktop computer) is a uniquely American development. While smaller machines were continuously built in the 1950s and 1960s (leading to the minicomputer, also an American original), it was not until the 1970s that one could take off-the-shelf electronic components and build a desktop-sized machine.[33] By 1977 several were commercially available, the most memorable being the Osborne and Apple's early models. By the end of the 1970s, these were being sold in the tens of thousands per year. Their costs continued to drop, while reliability, speed, and capacity grew—following the same pattern of evolutionary improvements evident with large mainframes since the 1940s—with the result that sales expanded. Simultaneously, as these computers became easier to use, many users new to computing met the technology for the first time. In 1981, in the United States, most sales went to noncomputer professionals (e.g., accountants and engineers), approaching levels of over 300,000 units. Yet, given the enormous progress made with these machines in the 1980s and 1990s, we have to emphasize that developments in the late 1970s were very primitive because this new class of machines was very much in its infancy. As we argue in chapter 1, computers emerged as part of an ongoing process of the chip penetrating many corners of the economy.

In August 1981, IBM introduced its machine, called the Personal Computer. That introduction legitimated desktop computing across the U.S. economy by recognizing that this technology had a place in the busines world.[34] Corporate and government sales grew, reaching out beyond the hobbyist and the nascent professional buyers. In the United States, customers bought 1.5 million PCs from several dozen vendors in 1983; by 1985 they had doubled their purchases each year. All through the 1990s Americans continued to buy these machines by the millions each quarter. The U.S. government estimated that by the end of 1994, more than 70 million units were installed in North America; with 31 million just in U.S. households. To provide a global perspective, in 1994, approximately 35 million PCs existed in Europe. By 1988, more than 200 million microcomputers had been built all over the world since the mid-1970s.

How can we account for the reaction of the American public to these new machines? From the beginning of the computer's existence, and continuing to the present, the largest quantity of publications on the subject—which we can use to gauge public interest—appeared in the United States. If, for example, we look at the index of articles in *Reader's Guide to Periodical Literature*, we see a steady increase in the number of articles appearing about computers from the 1940s to the late 1990s.[35] While we could count the number of articles in the 1940s and 1950s, it is easier to count the number of pages in the index listing individual articles for the later decades because so many articles were published. Beginning in the early 1960s, we see on average a range of three to six pages of citations on the subject, continuing until the widespread deployment of personal computers. Then we see the numbers jump to ten to twenty-eight pages per year in the 1980s and 1990s.

This huge jump is almost entirely attributable to the PC. The number of books on the topic also increased. By the late 1990s, one could not go into a general bookstore in the United States without seeing hundreds of titles on how to operate personal computers. On average, a Barnes & Noble bookstore will carry some 4,500 different titles on computers.[36] Ten years ago, the list was only several hundred. The overwhelming number of American articles and books on computing focus on how to use computers. Attention to the practical has characterized the majority of publications on the topic of computers since the early 1950s.[37]

A combination of technological innovations, increased capacity and reliability relative to cost, new uses identified by users of the technology, and a free flow of information about these machines made it possible for the United States to become not only the source of much innovation, but also home to the largest collection of users per capita in the world. Large corporations could build on their earlier experiences with tabulating and accounting equipment, which led them to understand quickly when and where to use these new machines, and what to demand of vendors of this technology.[38] Their needs, as much as what the engineers created; drove product innovation. For example, all through the 1950s and 1960s, demand for inexpensive memory (where information is stored and acted upon) provided economic incentive to expand use of ever more reliable computer chips. In the 1960s and 1970s, direct access to data from terminals became another compelling incentive for innovation. Speed and capacity intensified as a result of attempting to satisfy this demand for access. Faster chips, larger memories, more reliable software tools, and easier-to-maintain machines became the order of the day. In the 1970s and 1980s, it was not uncommon for an American data center to replace its computer with a larger one every twelve to eighteen months, or to modify its installed system by adding memory or peripherals almost on a monthly basis. That pattern has not yet ended. A similar process applied to PCs. For instance, as early as 1984, IBM had discovered that on average a purchaser of a personal computer spent an additional 40 percent of the original purchase price in the following year on components and PC-related supplies.[39] These subsequent transactions, like those involving large mainframes, required additional memory, upgrading printers, more application software, and supplies such as diskettes and paper.

History of the Computer Industry

The earliest and most continuously important channel for distributing chips and, therefore, building this invisible American digital information infrastructure, was and is the computer industry. Like the world of semiconductors, it came into being rapidly and dominated the computer business around the world, but it was in the United States that all the product development, manufacturing, distribution, marketing, and selling processes necessary were worked out to make this technology attractive to potential customers and users. Much like the semiconductor community, it enjoyed critical mass and a receptive base of customers. Critical mass came from both electronics and office supply firms which knew how to build precision equipment, employed engineers, and had strong links to the very universities and laboratories that had people who could invent new products. The same government agencies that supported scientific research and development (R&D) also funded projects that led to commercially viable computers, peripherals, and software. The one major exception, the PC, had almost no government support, although one could argue that many of its components, such as the integrated circuit, were earlier funded through R&D grants.

Second, this is an industry that could build on earlier experiences with office appliances. Since the 1870s, thousands of organizations had come to rely on a vast array of mechanical aids to calculation, from the simple adding machine to complex tabulating systems from IBM and Remington Rand. Early customers of the commercial computer in the United States all had previously been users of either IBM or Remington Rand punch card equipment. Most first-time users of computers in the 1950s and 1960s also had experience with complex machines for accounting, such as Burroughs's billing machines. Sales volumes for predecessor devices to the computer indicates that this base of experience acted as fertile encouragement for the next step to the computer, and the base was broad and massive across the U.S. economy. All the evidence confirms the pattern.[40]

We also have surrogate confirming evidence beyond numbers of calculating and adding machines sold by one vendor or another (although this is excellent testimonial). Economists, sociologists, and historians have quietly documented the rise and expansion in the population of office workers in the U.S. economy. Fashionably called the "knowledge worker," this community of clerks, lawyers, accountants, managers, consultants, teachers, engineers, and so forth, were always the ideal market for office appliances. In time, they became prime users of mainframes and even more so of personal computers. A quick look at this population suggests where the demand for computing came from, making possible rise of the computer industry into one that (depending on who's numbers are believed) today supplies slightly more than 5 percent of the U.S. gross national product (GNP), and helps support knowledge work that can account for between 55 and 85 percent of the economic activity of the nations.[41]

Knowledge Workers and the Professions

Knowledge workers are generally thought of as individuals who work with information—or with their brains rather than their brawn. While all workers gather, use, and reflect on knowledge, the definition is gravitating more toward those who rely on gathering and using information as their primary activity, like a professor or consultant. Complicating the history of this class of workers is the fact that they are varied and have always existed; we simply have not recognized them as a class of workers. What we had recognized were individual professions that had knowledge work as their content. These included accountants, lawyers, teachers, ministers and other religious professionals, government staff, and librarians, to mention a few. We always thought of them independently of each other, never as sharing any common practices. By viewing knowledge work as the intellectual infrastructure of their work, we see patterns of their activities in new ways; hence the growing interest among scholars in studying knowledge work.

Economic considerations also played a major role. As the economy grew in size all through the nineteenth and twentieth centuries, it could support more people in the same profession (e.g., increasing numbers of lawyers or engineers), and a variety of disciplines and subfields (e.g., teachers in elementary schools versus high schools, professors of modern history, versus ancient history, or workers in such new fields as engineering and later computer science). The phenomenon occurred in government, in nonprofit organizations, and in business, both large and small. New industries led to new knowledge workers.

Expanded reliance on science and technology, which began to influence American and European economic activity after 1865, created not only whole new knowledge professions, but also new fields. New professions included engineering (both civil and mechanical, later electrical in the 1900s) and a variety of others, such as mining and chemical, along with specialties in medicine and the law. The most dramatic examples include more than one million information processing (e.g., computer) workers who were employed by the 1990s just in the United States alone.[42] Add to this atomic energy scientists, the modern medical profession, and even the twentieth-century warrior (e.g., fighter pilots and submarine commanders), and we see additional waves of diversity and volume.

The latest research on the question of who made up the knowledge workforce suggests that this class of workers came into being as an important, if unidentified, element of the U.S. economy, at the same time that we saw a dramatic expansion in the use of office equipment and, later, the computer. Jorge Reina and Terry Curtis have conducted the most recent work on the size and dimensions of knowledge workers in the United States. They concluded that information activities were being broadly incorporated into ever-wider sets of jobs than had previously been thought. For instance, supervisors were doing more data handling and reporting than similar workers in their parents' generation. Equally interesting, they demonstrated that information workers began outnumbering agricultural workers as early as the mid-1920s, overshadowing industrial workers by the start of the 1930s. They concluded that by the end of the 1980s, more than 50 percent of the U.S. workforce could be called knowledge workers. Their statistics are dramatic: "The numbers of professional, technical and kindred workers increased by nearly 270% from 1900 to 1930; between 1930 and 1960, their numbers increased by 220%."[43] The census takers have simply expanded that population. Today, we are told that nearly 100 percent of the U.S. workforce is affected at least indirectly in their work by knowledge activities, and that the percent of the workforce in the knowledge worker arena is even larger than earlier thought.[44]

That is the broad picture of the workforce briefly stated. But what about the industry that supplied them with knowledge tools or what historians Aspry and Campbell-Kelly called the Information Machine? How did this new business come into being, and why so fast?

In many ways, it came together like as so many other businesses in North America. A new technology called for factories to make products, a sales force to sell them, and technical knowledge to know how to use them. But the extent of the investment requirement was not clear in the beginning. Companies that had gained experience during World War II building proto-computers for the government were encouraged through postwar federal funding to continue developing additional machines. By the end of the 1940s a few start-up computer vendors, composed primarily of engineers, were attempting to build commercial versions of these machines. Electrical appliance companies and the old office appliance firms were dabbling as well. In the early 1950s, awareness of commercial opportunities became obvious. The old Remington Rand company bought two computer start-up firms

(Eckert-Mauchly and ERA) and in 1951 introduced the UNIVAC I. Other companies quickly took note; within a few years, more than a dozen were offering computers, peripherals, operating systems, and nascent programming languages.[45]

By the early years of the 1960s, IBM dominated the new industry because it had realized more thoroughly than its competitors the enormous significance of the new technology and had moved quickly and most aggressively to stake out its position, building on one success after another in rapid fashion. But what did dominance mean? More than simply gaining the highest market share, there was the issue of commitment and focus. In his memoirs, Thomas J. Watson Jr., IBM's CEO in the 1950s, put it clearly: "demand for those products was accelerating, and it seemed clear the market wasn't going to wait. If IBM didn't grab the business, somebody else would, and we would never have this kind of opportunity again."[46] The foot race for market share was on. All through the 1960s more than a dozen vendors vied for this market, organized vertically for efficiency and marketing strength. That is to say, the major players offered everything: mainframes, peripherals, software, technical standards, training, and maintenance. The companies known in the industry as "Snow White and the Seven Dwarfs" soon became household names: Honeywell, Burroughs, GE, RCA, Sperry Rand, Control Data, DEC, and IBM (Snow White). Some also participated as leaders in other markets, such as GE and Westinghouse electrical devices and electrical utility industry hardware. American suppliers operated overseas as well, although European firms slowly came into the market (e.g., ICL, based on a former subsidiary of IBM and Remington Rand in Britain; Machines Bull in France; Olivetti for a while in Italy) but it was clearly an American show. The construction of this industry—vertical and manufacturing-centric—remained essentially the same through the 1960s and 1970s, built on incremental improvements of base technologies through thousands of product introductions. Very quickly, and certainly by the early 1960s, those companies that had sold office appliances prior to the computer dominated the nascent industry because they had the base of customers who were ideal for the computer. They bought start-up computer firms while electrical appliance companies went back to what they were better suited to do— selling consumer products, like television sets, or electronics to the military.[47]

Because of IBM's continuous acquisition of information about advanced electronics in the late 1940s and early 1950s (which it applied to various military computing projects), and then its subsequent and rapid commitment to the commercial computer market begun in the mid-1950s, the firm in effect, acquired, first entrant advantages. Thus, prior to its announcement of the industry-changing S/360 products in 1964, IBM had an enormous amount of practical experience with computers. This insight consisted of expertise on how to design, manufacture, distribute (sell and market), and support these systems in a profitable way. IBM figured out how to mass produce machines earlier than its rivals, to dedicate trained sales teams to persuade customers to acquire these machines, and to start the process of applying standardization from design through actual delivery of integrated products. In short, by the early 1960s, IBM knew more about the business of designing and marketing computers than any other firm in the world. It even had extensive experience in dealing with the U.S. Department of Justice's Antitrust Division, growing out of a variety of skirmishes and consent decrees over market dominance (in the 1930s, 1950s, and 1960s). IBM had the broad array of experience that made it possible for the company to dominate not only the U.S. computer business but also the global computer industry for so many years.[48]

Americans are a tribal society and no industry of theirs would be complete without its associations. In addition to giving members of any organization an opportunity to identify with a particular profession and industry, there is the issue of sharing information about computers. Hundreds of conferences were held across the nation in the first twenty years of the computer's existence, thousands since then; most are hosted by universities and associations, some by vendors such as IBM. The venerable management club of this industry, the Data Processing Management Association (DPMA) came into existence in 1949; two years later the IEEE Computer Society was founded. Users of specific vendors' equipment banded together to share experiences and maintain an organized dialogue with their suppliers: SHARE (IBM users) in 1955, USE (Univac users) in 1955, GUIDE (IBM users) in 1956, and the supra-organization above them all, the International Federation for Information Processing (IFIP) in 1960. Dozens of others appeared during the 1960s and 1970s.[49] As soon as desktop computers came into existence so did user clubs, then their associations as well. At the same time, magazines and journals appeared which also provided for sharing and community. Almost all the major publications around the world were of U.S. origin: *Computers and Automation* (1951), *Datamation* (1957), *IBM Journal of Research and Development* (1957), and the industry's most widely read weekly newspaper, *Computerworld* (1968). Jump ahead to the late 1990s and one finds move than 150 publications devoted to the PC, most with their home base in the United States.[50]

Technology created cracks in the newly forming computer industry by the end of the 1960s when it became possible to configure smaller systems—called minicomputers—which led to creation of a niche market populated by new suppliers with names such as Hewlett-Packard (often called H-P, established in 1939 as a supplier of electronics), Digital Equipment Corporation (DEC), Data General, Prime, and Wang. DEC was the innovator followed by the others. By the end of the 1970s, massive machines called super computers added yet another dimension, supplied by two additional American firms, CDC and Cray. Then came the microprocessor and the personal computer.[51]

Given the huge number of these machines in use today, it is difficult to imagine a time when people did not have PCs. PCs have now been around for more than a quarter of a century, enough time to change fundamentally how the computer industry operated. In the pre-PC era companies were vertical, leased their machines, and set standards. With the personal computer new entrants came into the computer market, appearing first in the United States. When IBM introduced its own machine in 1981, it opened the firm's standards, shared its architecture, and invited any other company to supply software, components, and other technologies. The result was nothing less than exhilarating. This step was taken to encourage software writers to offer applications, which in turn would stimulate sales of IBM's machines (not to ward off anti-trust risks). It not only accomplished this, but it also emboldened dozens (then hundreds) of vendors to offer look-alike machines and add-on parts and supplies (such as additional memory) to compete against IBM's machines.[52] Already on the market was the Apple, an innovation of the late 1970s complete with its own proprietary operating system and software (naturally modeling its strategy on the old mainframe approaches of the 1950s–1970s), and products from other pioneers. IBM, after being turned down by Gary Kildall, the leading maker of personal computer operating systems, went to a little programming company run by Bill Gates—barely an adult at the time— for an operating system, approached other vendors for off-the-shelf components, and farmed out much of the manufacture of such parts as the PC's metal shell and later fabrication of mother boards (which had commercially available ICs). By the early 1980s, Americans had bought millions of these machines. By the early 1990s, the pool of key providers stabilized into a handful, just as had occurred with mainframes and minicomputers, and in about the same amount of time: IBM, Compaq, Dell, Gateway 2000, AST Research, and Apple—all U.S. firms. The top ten providers owned between 50 and 60 percent of the market in the 1990s, while minicomputer vendors now began to go out of business (e.g., Wang) or painfully converted into workstation vendors (e.g., H-P and DEC), and even later into providers of PCs.[53]

The industry became horizontally organized during the 1980s. Once the PC had transformed into a machine used by individuals within and without corporations and other institutions, vendors, as IBM did with its PC, stopped attempting to provide everything themselves, as in earlier years. Thus a hardware manufacturer would contract for operating systems and other software from various companies; manufacturers would buy their microprocessors or license manufacturing rights from others; alliances with application developers proved essential to success. Many vendors quickly dotted the American landscape, providing tens of thousands of individual innovations in components and products, ranging from microprocessors and printer cables to parts for screens and metal frames for the PC. In the late 1990s, the cluttered market gained new entrants that competed with existing suppliers: for example, companies that sold laptops, electronic notebooks, handheld computers, and cellular phones that also doubled as PCs.[54]

Another section of the computer industry began forming in the 1960s to sell software products. Software consisted of operating systems to coordinate the activities of computers, tools that facilitated these (e.g., file managers), programming languages, and applications (e.g., spreadsheet and word-processing packages). Up to 1969, most hardware vendors provided such tools to their customers. In June 1969 IBM announced that it would begin to price software and services separate from computers, thereby "unbundling" hardware and software sales; this was done more to optimize sales and profits of existing hardware products than to placate the U.S. Department of Justice, which had started to pressure IBM over antitrust issues. While software firms had existed before 1969, IBM's action had the same effect on the software business as would its open-architecture announcement in 1981, when it introduced the IBM Personal Computer complete with the memorable Charlie Chaplin ads for "A Machine for Modern Times." By unbundling, IBM in effect caused the packaged software business to come into existence as a major element in the information processing world.

Operating in an economy in which copyright and patents laws gave protection to software developers, this new line of products exploded with growth far in excess of anything seen in Europe, where a nascent software industry also was emerging. In 1968, software revenues in the United States were approximately $400 million; by the end of 1976, annual volumes reached $1.1 billion, and doubled again within four years. Most software firms were small and highly specialized with one or two products.

The introduction of the PC provided yet another dramatic opportunity to develop and sell software for millions of users. Here is where the start-ups thrive. Again, the United States dominated, owning about 75 percent of this market in the 1980s and early 1990s. But unlike in the 1950s and 1960s, European and Japanese vendors, using U.S. software, were also active, such as Siemens Nixdorf (German) and Fujitsu and NEC (Japanese). Key U.S. vendors included IBM, Microsoft, Computer Associates, Novell, Lotus, and DEC. By the 1990s, the primary business came from PCs. In 1993 alone, for example, Americans bought $6 billion in software for their desktop computers. No wonder Microsoft, whose Window products owned upward of 95 percent of the market for PC tools, had become more valuable than General Motors, making Bill Gates the richest man in the world.[55]

How did people use all this evolving software and hardware infrastructure? Mainframe systems generally have been used to perform business applications such as in accounting, manufacturing, and distribution (often all simultaneously). The users of minicomputers (and their microcomputer successors, workstations) needed the power of a large machine but often dedicated their system to single or highly related applications, such as in manufacturing, engineering, data collection, or to operate point-of-sale terminals in stores. They were also very popular with engineers who frequently felt they could not get adequate time, attention, or horsepower from their corporate data-processing centers. PC applications overwhelmingly concentrated on word processing, accounting, spreadsheets, graphics, and, increasingly in the 1990s, communications (e.g., the Internet and e-mail).[56] Once again, as Americans found practical uses for a new technology they embraced them quickly.[57] It would not be until the mid-1990s, for example, that significant sales of PCs occurred in Europe and, as of the end of the 1990s, Japan remained one of the lowest per capita users of PCs in the industrialized world. Half of all software sales around the world came from U.S. suppliers.

But why the United States? There were some economic environmental factors at work, as had been the case in earlier decades, facilitating adoption of earlier technologies. The first and most obvious was the fact that the United States consisted of a very large, healthy, technologically advanced economy throughout the period of the computer. In 1950 (using 1972 dollars) the GNP hovered at $300 billion, and by 1980, $3 trillion. No other single-nation market of that size existed in the industrialized world. Growth remained impressive as well. Between 1950 and 1960, the GNP grew by 38 percent, 48 percent in the next decade, 32 percent in the 1970s, and another 22 percent in the 1980s.[58] So there was money to invest in product innovations and acquisitions by customers. As both vendors and customers learned how to use this technology, they could work jointly on its evolution, making subsequent products more useful. In the 1950s, for instance, clerks did data entry using punch cards and stored information on cards or magnetic tape.

With demand increasing for access to information in computer systems, vendors developed direct access devices which in turn made it possible in the 1960s to go on-line with terminals—the perhaps the greatest spurt to new applications in the period—followed by telecommunications facilitating sharing of data across enterprises in the 1970s and 1980s. The decision to make the government-sponsored telecommunications network for suppliers and scientists open to the public— the Internet—is causing the same kind of expansion in use of computing that was seen with the arrival of direct access and on-line processing in the 1960s.[59]

Already mentioned was the ongoing support for basic research funded by the U.S. government all through the cold war period,[60] with the government allowing vendors adopt a technology when it became commercially viable. Throughout most of the half century following World War II, nearly 85 percent of all the "R" in R&D expenses came out of Uncle Sam's Treasury, made affordable by the expanded economy that made tax dollars available. This government support was most critical in the 1950s, when dollars were poured into the development of computers for military purposes, causing an enormous increase in the body of knowledge about computing devices—which, during the 1960s, was commercialized with a declining participation of federal funding. U.S. government support for computing R&D continued in different ways in the 1960s and 1970s—primarily in networking technologies ultimately leading to the Internet—and hardly any for the development of the microcomputer. But for the entire period, as a general statement, nothing close to this kind of public support for computing R&D existed elsewhere, even in the old Soviet Union, the Common Market nations in Europe (later the European Community), or in Japan. The sheer raw number of dollars invested was massive.[61]

We have already discussed knowledge workers as the perfect users of computers, a by-product of an advanced industrial market economy. But just as important was the absolute size of the U.S. workforce, one that increasingly became dependent on computers as decades passed. In 1950 there were 63.8 million workers in the United States, 86 million by 1970, and more than 130 million in 1998.[62]

An important change also occurred in the mix of workers. Throughout the period of the computer the percent of workers moving into service sector industries—such as banking, finance, retail, and so forth—kept rising, and all these industries were crucial users of information processing technologies since the late nineteenth century. By 1970, some 60 percent of all workers were now in the services sector, at the continued long-term expense of the agriculture and manufacturing sectors. And as a percent of the economy, services continued to expand in the 1980s and 1990s, with almost all additional jobs in the postwar economy going into the services sector—prime territory for any computer salesperson.[63]

The huge economy also made it possible to have large organizations and companies. These institutions provided markets for even the early development of the computer because of their high prices paid by large enterprises. In the 1950s about one out of every four business employees in the United States worked for one of the largest 200 corporations in the nation—the core of the Industrial Age. That concentration continued in subsequent years; the top 200 corporations affected over half of the U.S. economy.[64]

Another environmental condition concerned the growth in the complexity of work which occurred during the Second Industrial Revolution in the United States. The many technologies emerging across the U.S. economy over the past century meant more application of science and scientific principles, the rise of engineering as an important profession, and the creation of the large American corporation previously mentioned.[65] That last development stimulated creation of many new specialized professions.[66] Each led to greater reliance on data, numerical and descriptive, thereby encouraging analysis and fact-based decision-making. Add in specialization and increasing rates of change, and one has the making of a more complex and evolving economy in which reliance on machinery to do more of the work became inevitable. The computer was perfect for this kind of a world.[67]

One other consideration was the protection given to inventors and entrepreneurs through patent and copyright laws, a protection that proved essential. Historically, U.S. courts and officials have vigorously safeguarded these rights, and this public policy remained intact during the first half century of the computer's existence. Computers were protected by patent law, and software came increasingly under the sheltering umbrella of copyright laws. From the 1950s to the 1980s, court cases and new federal laws reinforced the notion that software developers should have the opportunity to enjoy economic benefits from their work. By the 1980s, a whole new body of copyright law concerning software had grown up in the United States, encouraging the enormous expansion in this very new sector, by then called the Software Industry by its members. It would be difficult to underestimate the importance of copyright protection in facilitating the creation and expansion of this new industry in the United States.[68] Two economists looking at the international software industry, Stephen E. Siwek and Harold W. Furchtgott-Roth, stated the situation in clear language:

> Government policy has also benefited the software industry in the United States. Intellectual property law and its enforcement enable U.S. software firms to develop and manage software products with an understanding that intellectual property will be protected, whereas it is afforded relatively little protection in much of the world. In most countries, most software in use is pirated, and the financial losses from pirated software are in the billions of dollars annually.[69]

Closely paralleling patent and copyright protection came a coterie of federal regulations and laws designed to stimulate competition. Antitrust laws had been enacted in the 1890s, and when an information-processing company gained so much market share as to worry public officials, those firms faced the lawyers of the Antitrust Division of the U.S. Justice Department. Legal skirmishes, wars, and consent decrees littered the history of this industry: NCR (1914), IBM (1930s, 1950s, 1960s, and the largest antitrust suit in U.S. history in the 1970s and early 1980s); AT&T (1950s, 1970s, and the breakup of "Ma Bell" in 1982); Burroughs (1930s, 1950s), and Microsoft and Intel (late 1990s). Federal regulators also influenced, expanded, and constrained information processing over the majority of the twentieth century. Radio, television, and telephone were particularly subject to regulations, despite cries of foul from First Amendment proponents. The fairly consistent impulse of the regulators always remained the same: to provide a variety of perspectives and to foster competition, not censure expression of thought. And the process continues. In 1996, for example, the U.S. Congress passed a major new telecommunications law; in 1997 and 1998, Microsoft and the U.S. Justice Department argued over the company's Internet software marketing practices.[70]

In addition to these various consideration was an ideological component characteristic of American society at large. Each of the previous authors in this book have alluded to it. Belief in continuous progress,

the need for constant improvement, faith in the value of technology—
all these play out as common themes in the acquisition of computers
in the United States. So besides the economic and technological reasons
presented in this chapter are ideological considerations. What sociologists have noted is the constant action of Americans to link together
through associations (e.g., their company or political allies within a
firm) and their professions (e.g., computer experts) to put forth what
we can characterize as ideologies of adoption. Studies on the nature of
adoption clearly point out the collectivist quality of this activity.[71] In
particular, well-documented studies on an industry-by-industry basis,
and others covering specific clusters of computing activities—such as
the use of artificial intelligence, computer-based education, office automation, and personal computing—all point to the existence of some
common core ideological patterns. These patterns can briefly be summarized as:

- Computers are central to a reformed world or society
- Improved computers can help reform society even more
- More computers are better than fewer; there are no limits to
  how much is good
- Nobody loses, everyone wins; in the worst case, it is neutral or
  apolitical
- Those who resist computerization are hostile to social reforms.[72]

To be sure, counter-computerization movements always existed, re-
plete with their ideologies, and with those who pointed out the negative
aspects of computing, but such movements always seemed less organized or vociferous than those in favor of the use of computing.[73]

Extent of Deployment

One of the central themes of this book is that Americans have enthusiastically embraced every new information technology that came
along—indeed so much so that they unintentionally laid the groundwork and built the infrastructure for a new economic age that may well
be characterized as an Information Age. Pundits have argued for a
generation over what to call it. Part of the problem is that the technology and its uses keep changing, leading to dialogue over names; this is
most intense in the United States.[74] While it is too early to conclude
whether in the 1970s Daniel Bell was correct in heralding the arrival
of the Post-Industrial Society,[75] clearly an early indicator would be

data on the extent of deployment of computers across the U.S. economy. We have already established the changing nature of work and workers, suggested how many machines were being built and bought, but can we sense to what extent they were being used? And where?

Begin with U.S. consumption of computer chips. In 1978, after more than a dozen years of experiences, 56 percent of all integrated circuits were going into U.S. built computers; another 9 percent went into telecommunications equipment; 11 percent went into industrial and test equipment. Five years later, in 1983, only 48 percent of chips were going into computers, but now 13 percent were being embedded in telecommunications gear, and 9 percent in industrial and test equipment. In both periods the government used the same proportion—13 percent—but consumer goods went from 9 percent of consumption to 11 percent, suggesting that the major uptick in proportion came before the real impact of the PC became evident. Another indicator of the spread of this technology into other corners of the economy is what happened with automobiles. In 1978, auto manufacturers used only 2 percent of all computer chips, but 6 percent in 1983. So we see a broadening in the dispersion of computer chips in these early years prior to the main deployment of PCs. What makes the percentages so dramatic, however, is the fact that the sheer number of chips also continued to rise. In 1983, annual consumption was nearly triple that in 1978.[76] For comparative purposes, in 1983 North America consumed 38.1 percent of the world's supply of computer chips. Japan came in at 27 percent, all of Western Europe combined was 26.3 percent, and the rest of the world shared the remaining 8.5 percent.[77] Clearly Americans had the greatest appetite for these components. After the arrival of the PC—the most extensive users of chips by the end of the 1990s—Americans continued to be the largest class of consumers of this new information technology.

What about computing and accounting equipment? Manufacturing industries, historically the largest user of precomputer information-processing equipment, continued to enjoy a healthy appetite. In 1950 they absorbed about 48 percent of all computing and accounting equipment sales but lost purchasing share to other industries and sectors as different parts of the economy began to acquire this same equipment. Thus, by the end of 1980, manufacturing firms were only buying a third of all equipment and software, and in 1990, their share had dropped to 21 percent.

Now look at what happened to service sector industries. In 1950 retailers had acquired 3.7 percent of the total, and they remained more or less at that buying level until the late 1970s and early 1980s when industry-specific technologies, such as point-of-sale terminals; became available. In 1990 that industry had acquired 5.5 percent of the total and just a few short years later (1993) had 7.8 percent. Banks, insurance, and real estate—all information-intensive industries—acquired 16 percent of the total in 1950, slightly more than doubled by 1980 (34.1 percent), and essentially stayed at that level through most of the 1990s. The service sector as a whole went from roughly 6 percent of all acquisitions in 1950 to a continuous growth in share to 16–17 percent in the middle years of the 1990s.[78] In short, its share went up as manufacturing's share went down. In the same half century the manufacturing sector's share of the total U.S. economy went down, the services sector went up but, as indicated earlier, the overall economy expanded at 20 to 30 percent in each decade. Not only did Americans acquire more machines and software, but they also did it at a faster rate than the overall growth of the economy, clear evidence that the amount of work being shifted to computers continued unceasingly through the past half century. That was a sea change!

Along the way, specific applications encouraged one industry here, another there, to acquire more or less computing technology. Industry-specific technologies were crucial, and most of these were invented in the United States. Take point-of-sale (POS) terminals that we see today in most supermarkets and retail stores. These are computers that capture information about a sale made to an individual, notifying a computer's store that inventory just went down, collecting accounting information, and feeding data to the marketing and purchasing departments about what just happened. That technology came into the market first in the United States in the 1960s. Within a quarter century one would have been hard pressed to find an old-fashioned cash register. The world's largest cash register manufacturer was NCR—(originally National Cash Register)—U.S. firm—and by the end of the 1970s it had become the world's largest supplier of POS terminals.[79]

Closely related to acquisition of computers in all periods was inventory control. In theory, as the logic goes, if one could manage to have only the bare essentials in a warehouse or store, savings in costs of inventory and parts would be extraordinary. Computers offered the potential of keeping costs of inventory down through careful record keeping and forecasting demand. Everyone seemed to buy the logic. For example, Harold C. Plant, administrator of computer applications at RCA, in 1963 reported results of a survey he had done in which corporations expected savings in inventory from using computers, ranging from 5 to 75 percent.[80] From the earliest days of the computer, inventory applications drove massive sales of equipment. As new technologies came on stream, they were applied to inventory control; most of these were American innovations, and all of the most important were. The bar code (UPC, the Universal Price Code)—those little stripes on products of all kinds that can be read by a computer—is a U.S. creation that made it possible to track parts and inventory from factory to home. Today, Federal Express—another U.S. original— can track and deliver packages because of the bar code. Supermarkets monitor inventory and know what to charge customers because of the bar code. As Alfred Chandler noted about the UPC, it was an important innovation that "transformed the process of distribution and production."[81]

Like other industry-specific technologies, it spread out like a wave, beginning first in the grocery sector then moving into retailing and warehousing. Today no major industry ignores the UPC; it is not just for manufacturers, but for any firm or organization with inventory— even publishers and schools. Part of the UPC code is assigned to a specific enterprise, thus knowing who had, in effect, a license to use a particular UPC is yet another indicator of deployment of information technology. Until the late 1980s, after a decade of availability, the number of U.S. organizations using the technology amounted to fewer than 50,000, although that number included almost every *Fortune* 1000 enterprise and the largest U.S. government agencies (like the Armed Services). By 1994, that number had climbed to more than 110,000 enterprises, and for the latest year for which we have data (1997), 177,000.[82]

Banking is another industry useful to look at. This is an industry whose only inventory is information about money, since the amount of cash they keep is small in comparison to the amounts cataloged in accounts. It has a history of working collectively to establish technical standards and to exploit technology. It was the American banking industry, for example, that standardized the look of every check with machine-readable account numbers; that created the network permitting electronic transfer of funds; and that deployed automated teller machines (ATMs)—which are nothing more than a variant of the point-of-sale technology with the capability of dispensing cash.[83]

Another effective information technology, adopted first by the banking industry then by retail, and now used as identification across all industries, is the credit card. Deployment of credit cards began in the 1950s, exceeding per capita that of any country in the world then (and now). The convenience, credit, cash float, and liberty it gives to U.S. consumers and others interested in tracking data and security (e.g., a student identification badge or a security pass into a military installation) made this technology widely deployed. On average today, an American adult has ten cards, on average three times more than people in other industrialized nations.

In summary then, deployment of computers began with large manufacturing, insurance, banking, and government agencies in the 1950s and early 1960s. As new technologies came on stream (such as on-line processing, POS, ATM, UPC) and equipment and software became less expensive in the 1960s and 1970s, computing spread both to smaller organizations and to almost all industries. Applications in the 1940s and early 1950s overwhelmingly fell into the categories of engineering, science, and military uses; they became predominantly business and engineering in the late 1950s through the 1980s. One could easily argue that this remains so in the 1990s but the jury is not in yet—because not all PC applications are fully understood, despite the early evidence surrounding the use of spreadsheets, word processing, and games, and, more recently, Internet activity and e-mail. But more on these issues is presented in the next two chapters.

The explosive growth in computing came with the personal computer. With that one development we could begin to speak about ubiquitous computing, although by 1999 only a third of U.S. homes had personal computers. Keep in mind that two-thirds of American workers had access to these machines. The personal computer has rightfully been identified as a historic break point between computing in the past and what it is becoming in the present. However, it also shares some common features with the broader history of computing in the United States. First, it was invented in America, relying on preexisting American technology often initially acquired "off the shelf." That meant it did not require a complex organization, like Bell Labs, to pull it together but it did need people familiar with electronic components and computing to accomplish the initial work. Second, it spread through an economy that could afford to by it because the standard of living of customers of such machines proved sufficient, just as the economy had to have provided corporations and other organizations with the economic muscle and size to justify mainframes and minicomputers in an earlier period. The period from the late 1950s onward was one of rapidly expanding corporate demand for all manner of computing. Third, while most users of PCs met computers for the first time (often through their initial purchase of the PC itself, many had been exposed to computers at work, where the earliest users of personal computers had been professionals in programming, accounting, marketing, and finance. In short, there existed a prepared audience for this ubiquitous technology.

1. Learning and Reading

From the earliest days of the nation, Americans placed an emphasis on learning to read. In this early picture (circa 1800), young children are shown reading with the guidance of a young woman. Female teachers were often seen in early American society, instructing very small groups of children, as this illustration suggests. *From the private collection of Richard D. Brown.*

2. "This is a Precious Book"

Books were always cherished in America. Children were frequently exposed to them, particularly in middle- and upper-class homes in the eighteenth and nineteenth century and, by the twentieth, across all sectors of American society. This early nineteenth-century picture shows the close tie between religious instruction and books. Religious themes were among the most popular topics with book publishers in the 1700s and early 1800s. *From the private collection of Richard D. Brown.*

3. "The Young Traders"

Painted by William Page, this picture appeared in *The Gift: A Christmas and New Year's Present* (Philadelphia, 1844) to illustrate a moralistic story of the same name. The newspaper boy is supporting his family due to his father's drinking and irresponsible behavior, while the girl comes from a family of declining fortunes. Newspapers were so widely available by the 1840s, and so appealing to all classes of Americans, that even people far removed from politics and commerce found them interesting. *From the private collection of Richard D. Brown.*

4. The Newspaper Boy

This engraving illustrates a primary way that newspapers were made available to the American public throughout the 1800s and during the first half of the twentieth century. This picture dates from the mid-1800s when inexpensive, widely available printed materials were available, particularly in urban areas. Illustrators frequently depicted poor, young boys selling newspapers to "get ahead in life." *From the private collection of Richard D. Brown.*

5. THE TELEGRAPH

The telegraph was the first electronic means of transmitting information in the United States. In this illustration we see Western Union's telegraph operating center in New York City in 1873. By this time, commercial use of the telgraph was widespread, just as the telephone was about to come onto the scene to replace it as the technology of choice in business. Western Union missed the opportunity to become the AT&T of the U. S. economy. *Courtesy of the Library of Congress.*

6. THE WORD PROCESSING CENTER

Word processing centers are not an invention of the late twentieth century. In this photograph from the 1890s, we see an early American typing pool. Notice that all the typists are women, the supervisors and other clerks are men, and the workflow is set up almost like a production operation. Scenes like these could still be seen in government agencies and companies in the United States a century later, with Wang word processors and, later, with personal computers. *Courtesy of the IBM Archives.*

7. The Burroughs Adding Machine

Our Deepest Gratitude, Little One — You Brought Us Here

One of America's most successful office appliance vendors, Burroughs, built its core business around a line of small desktop adding machines, selling millions of them during the first half of the twentieth century. In this illustration from a 1926 issue of the company's magazine, *Burroughs Journal*, the firm acknowledges the popularity of this simple, practical device. The men are salesmen attending the 1926 recognition event to honor the achievements of the best of their peers. *Courtesy of the Charles Babbage Institute, University of Minnesota.*

8. A Corporate Accounting Office

In this product publicity photograph, we see the Burroughs Automatic Bookkeeping Machines in 1933, in a fairly typical office arrangement of the period. Burroughs was the largest supplier of American desktop adding machines in the decades just prior to World War II. Here we can see that women were making inroads into the lower levels of the accounting profession. *Courtesy of the Charles Babbage Institute, University of Minnesota.*

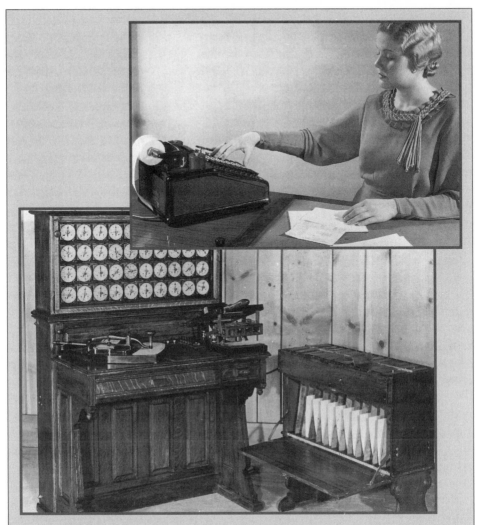

9. AN ACCOUNTING CLERK AT WORK *(top photo)*

This photograph from the Burroughs Archives was taken around 1932–1933 and demonstrates the ease of use and portability of a desktop calculator. The picture shows how fashionable it was to use such modern conveniences by having an attractive accounting clerk, fashionably dressed and coiffed, promoting its use. By the early decades of the twentieth century, branding and merchandising of information-processing tools included the use of attractive women to sell the line, just as other manufacturing firms did with their products. *Courtesy of the Charles Babbage Institute, University of Minnesota.*

10. HOLLERITH TABULATOR AND SORTERBOX *(bottom photo)*

Herman Hollerith developed the first widely used punch-card tabulating equipment in the United States. This is a picture of the 1890 model, used in the U. S. Census of that year (and now in the possession of IBM). On the tabulator's desk surface are two other early devices used to punch holes in cards. Already one can see the notion of "system" at work, with the two large pieces of equipment linked by a cable so that "instructions" from the machine on the left would guide the work of the "box" on the right. *Courtesy of the IBM Archives.*

11. OFFICE APPLIANCES IN SCIENTIFIC RESEARCH

IBM and Columbia University collaborated in the use of punch-card equipment in the 1920s and 1930s to develop new applications. In this photograph we see Dr. Ben Wood's laboratory in 1935 at Columbia, where he developed the first automated test scoring equipment. The picture is rich in detail, illustrating more than a half dozen different types of information-processing equipment in actual use. Wood is in the center of the photograph and is the senior of the two men shown. *Courtesy of the IBM Archives.*

12. AN EARLY DATA PROCESSING SYSTEM

During the early to mid-1900s, users of data processing equipment sought ways to link many machines together so that one machine could feed data to other devices for further processing. In this 1935 photograph, we see a tabulator and a summary punch from IBM wired together so that the calculating results from the device on the left were fed to the machine on the right. In the 1930s and 1940s, many corporations came to IBM to cobble systems together, thereby creating the notion of integrated systems. In time, this notion characterized how machines "talked" to each other during the age of computers. *Courtesy of the IBM Archives.*

13. Douglas Aircraft's Data Processing Center

Large U. S. companies were the most enthusiastic users of complex information-processing equipment. Aircraft manufacturers had extensive requirements for calculating and engineering applications. This photograph shows tabulating equipment from Remington Rand, probably in the early 1940s. Notice the large amounts of punch-cards used in this data center (see the cart with cards to the right, toward the background). Note on the far left the drawers of cards, called for many years "tub files" since in the beginning special furniture for cards did not exist; people used boxes and tubs to store them. *Courtesy of the Hagley Museum and Library.*

14. Dancing with Radio Music

In this 1910s photograph we see an early use of radio—for entertainment—with couples in a living room filled with musical technologies. In the far back is the piano, the home entertainment instrument of choice in many homes of the nineteenth century. Just behind the couple on the left is a phonograph player, which became the next source of musical entertainment after the piano by the early 1900s; finally, on the far left, is a radio. Notice the batteries to operate all the equipment; many homes were not yet wired for electricity. The ceiling lights were gas lamps. *Courtesy of the Smithsonian Institution.*

15. LISTENING TO THE RADIO AT HOME

During the 1920s, many middle- and upper-class Americans acquired radios, listening to them in the evening the way people would, decades later, sit down to watch television. In this illustration, probably a product promotional shot, we see a "typical American family" enjoying music on a relatively small radio. Unlike the telephone, which had to be wired to a house, a radio only needed electricity, so radios cost less to install. They spread across the nation very rapidly. By the end of the 1920s most middle- and upper-class American homes in urban centers had electricity, making acquisition of electrical appliances easier than before World War I. Demand drove down the cost of such devices as the radio, making them even more affordable to ever-increasing numbers of Americans. The square in front of the man is an antenna. *Courtesy of the Smithsonian Institution.*

16. Television, A Statement of Fashion

In this 1930s promotional picture, we see television positioned as an elegant fashion statement. The man is wearing evening clothes, as is the lady in white. Notice the fashionable setting in which this highly stylized, very early television set is presented. At the time, television was a rich person's toy. Also note the "tube" of the television at the upper end of the machine, framed in white. It is showing a baseball game, which in time became one of the most popular types of programs for Americans to watch on television. *Courtesy of the Smithsonian Institution.*

17. Sarnoff Sounds off on Radio and Television

In the 1920s, David Sarnoff made RCA a major U. S. communications and entertainment company. He also created NBC. In this photograph we see Sarnoff using both technologies

for which he is remembered. He is talking on an NBC radio program while also transmitting on television, using equipment developed and sold by RCA. Sarnoff did for radio and television what Theodore Vail did for the telephone nearly a half century earlier—he developed organizations and systems for national delivery of services. *Courtesy of the Smithsonian Institution.*

18. THE TECHNOLOGICAL BUILDING BLOCKS OF THE INFORMATION AGE *(top photo)*

On the left is the vacuum tube which made radio, television, and early computing possible. It was the first major building block of modern information technology. On the right is a very early transistor, which

evolved into the chip. Notice how the second technology was dramatically smaller; miniaturization has continued with electronic devices down to the present. The transistor used less electricity than the vacuum tube, enjoyed greater reliability, and offered more functions. This picture dates from the 1950s. *Courtesy of the IBM Archives.*

19. THE COMPUTER CHIP *(bottom photo)*

This picture dramatically emphasizes the relentless process of miniaturization that characterized the evolution of information technology throughout the second half of the twentieth century. Behind the picture of the chip is a sewing needle to suggest the size of this microprocessor. The printed circuits (in white on the chip) contained the instructions that made the chip perform its operations. This picture dates from the 1970s; by the standards of the year 2000, this chip will be considered by engineers to be a primitive, bulky chip. IBM is now working with computer chips at the Watson Labs which can only be seen with the use of a powerful microscope. *Courtesy of the IBM Archives.*

20. A POPULAR BUSINESS COMPUTER: IBM 650

In the mid-1950s, IBM introduced the 650 (in the center of the photograph), aimed at both mid-sized and large corporate customers for commercial applications. It was a huge success, with more than 1,000 delivered in a period when success with earlier systems was measured in the dozens. The UNIVAC of the early 1950s, for example, only went to a few dozen customers. The success of the 650 finally convinced IBM's senior executives that they needed to get into the computer business in a big way. *Courtesy of the IBM Archives.*

21. IBM System 360

The IBM System 360 was arguably one of the most successful, if not *the* most successful, product introduction in American history. IBM brought out a family of five computers and some 150 software and related hardware products in 1964. The S/360 revolutionized how systems were built, maintained and used, standardizing many practices in product development and use that are still in effect today. This photograph was widely used by IBM at the time of the system's announcement to depict the "360° capability" of the entire configuration to take care of a customer's

computing needs. The computer is the tall machine in the lower half of the photograph. Notice the tape drives in the back, which became so symbolic of what computer systems looked like in the 1950s and 1960s. (The computer itself hardly looked like a computer!) *Courtesy of the IBM Archives.*

22. The Personal Computer

While several thousand models of microcomputers (usually called personal computers or just PCs) have been introduced since the mid-1970s, it was IBM's initial product, introducing the phrase "Personal Computer" to the world, that brought desktop computing into the mainstream of U. S. business. This photograph is a formal product illustration of IBM's first personal computer, the IBM PC1, introduced in autumn 1981. Stylish and well-appointed with software and a practical matrix printer, its first widely

used application involved spreadsheets. Note that this is the application chosen to be shown on the screen. The keyboard, the best available on any PC of the period, emerged out of IBM's many decades of experience in developing keyboards for typewriters, such as its Selectric, the most popular typewriter among American secretaries. *Courtesy of the IBM Archives.*

That prepared audience is at work again with yet another wave of deployment of computer-based machines. Cellular phones, electronic games, and digitally controlled home entertainment centers are enjoying fast acceptance within the U.S. economy for the same reasons as favored the earlier technologies. In an important study done in the late 1990s on the computational skills and attitudes of American youth, Don Tapscott documented how they were comfortable with all manner of computing. He suggested that one could expect this latest generation to embrace the technology even more than earlier ones.[84] Then there is the Internet, another story for a future historian.

Conclusions

What can we make of the computer in the U.S. economy? Perhaps the most evident observation is that its introduction and adoption mimicked the pattern evident with other "high tech" gear, such as rockets, motor vehicles, airplanes, medical devices, nuclear energy, and a host of previous information technologies, such as the telegraph, telephone, adding machines, and even earlier print-and paper-based technologies, such as newspapers and books. Second, American faith and enthusiasm in new information technologies was grounded in long-standing economic realities. These included copyright and patent protection offered by a government committed to fostering competition and innovation. Americans operated in an economy that rewarded technical innovation with wealth; Bill Gates was not the first, nor will he be the last, to make a fortune through information technology. Third, Americans are a nation of tinkers who learn from using and doing, but who also became professional at it over time. The man inventing an adding machine in the 1870s on his kitchen table was replaced in the 1920s by brigades of scientists and engineers at MIT and at Bell Labs. Software amateurs working out of dorm rooms in universities in the 1970s gave way to whole campuses of software engineers at such places as Microsoft and Oracle in the 1980s.

It seemed that there always was effective and impatient exploitation of science and knowledge. In the case of science, information constantly moved about the economy with almost no hindrance. In the twentieth century, computer experts constantly met at conferences to share their findings and to publish tens of thousands of articles and thousands of books on this new form of information handling. The nation allocated large sums of its national treasury to invest in universities, industrial research labs, and government-run R&D facilities. Success fostered more success. Corollary to this has long been the role of government. Just as the U.S. government invested in the creation of an effective postal system in the early years of the Republic, so too did it invest in developing new forms of communications and computing in the middle decades of the twentieth century. The Internet is only the latest of a spectacular list of achievements, which must include deployment of electricity, construction of a national highway system, and continuous expansion of the nation's wire and wireless telephone networks.

From the time when the Founding Fathers wrote constitutional clauses protecting intellectual capital and product innovations, on the one hand, to freedom of information flows on the other, to the twentieth century and such legislation as the Telecommunications Act of 1996, this has been a government bent on creating three realities: an environment where new products and ideas could be created, tried out, and exploited; where competition would not be overly restricted through vagaries of the economy or by actions of the national government; and where technology would constantly be studied and improved even if the nation had to pay the bill for this. Creating universities where science and technology could be studied remains a hallmark of public and governmental policy and wish. In the depths of the American Civil War, the U.S. Congress found the time and energy to pass the Land Grant Act (1862), making it possible to establish technical institutions of higher education and a large collection of state universities. Some of those, like MIT, Penn State, Iowa State, and California's collection of universities, later built some of the earliest computers and telecommunications networks in the world.

America's economy hunts constantly for productivity. While the question of whether or not computers have made the economy productive is currently the subject of an extensive debate,[85] the fact remains that no nation would invest more than 5 percent of its GNP year after year in a technology that it did not perceive made economic sense. The ability to take acquired insight about a technology and apply it rapidly, usually faster than any other nation, characterized every major information technology development in the United States in the past century and a half. The computer is simply the latest example of the process at work. Emphasis on the practical, always with a sense of urgency driven either by the opportunity for personal economic benefit or out of fear of competition, appeared constantly as a feature of American computing.

Finally, we have the issue of the technology itself. Transistors, integrated circuits (chips), computers, and telecommunications are symbiotic technologies. That is to say, they mutually reinforce and augment the capabilities of one with the other. All were either invented in the United States or were commercialized there. As our earlier quote about everybody knowing everyone in the semiconductor industry suggests, one could gain access to information and people to work on the next innovation. We could have provided similar quotes about mainframe engineers, software and programming developers, and, of course, creators of the personal computer, all of whom knew and competed with each other.[86]

Other contributors to this book have written about the American propensity to learn, to apply technologies to reduce labor content of work, and to accept the intrinsic value of technology. The story of the chip and the computer is thus very much an American experience. What is never clear until after the fact, however, are the consequences of America's faith in new information technologies. But two are now very evident, at least as a result of the computer.

First, over the past half century a nearly invisible information infrastructure has been under construction across the U.S. economy that is digital and reliable. It began with electricity, and today more than 98 percent of all buildings have it. It then expanded to include radio, telephone, then television, and now the personal computer. In each instance, the rate and extent of deployment continued to be the highest in the world. While the nation's attention focused more on personal computers and cellular phones during the 1990s, electrical utilities, telephone companies, and cable providers have been quietly installing thousands of miles of fiber-optic cable. Since fiber optics can carry orders of magnitude more data on a line than metal wire, the capability to move far greater amounts of information through the economy is there.

Second, we now have a half century of experience with the computer. Tapscott's study of the next generation's comfort and reliance on computing is the tip of the iceberg. Armed with technology, and the technological infrastructure to move data, we may have, in fact, created the makings of the next turn of the knob on the nature of capitalism. Not only will we see computing being used in more novel ways and for higher percentages of the nation's work and play, but we face the prospect of building fortunes in equally innovative forms. IBM's own studies suggest that the stock (market) value of information-creating organizations—plus the hard assets of the firms themselves—exceeds that of many manufacturing companies.[87]

As representatives of three dozen firms sat in the audience in 1952 listening to descriptions of the transistor given by AT&T engineers, who among them could have known what they collectively would unleash on the world? To understand the true impact of this issue we must recognize that at the heart of its significance is the marriage of the new electronics and computers, and at the heart of hearts is deployment and that takes us squarely into corporate America. It is in the business arena that the benefits of computing had to be realized for this technology to be so widely adopted. How that happened—and why—is the subject of the next chapter, written by one of the leading students of the issue.

The present chapter has emphasized the supply side of the story—creation of the technology and getting it into the hands of users—so to continue the story we must now turn to the demand side, to the users. In chapters 7 and 8 we look at the role of computing in business and home. It is in the use of all these technologies, from the transistor to the chip, where the Information Age began to flower. Understanding how people used these technologies, and their effects, is the necessary next step toward our full understanding of how the Information Age came into being.

7

Information Technology Management Since 1960

Richard L. Nolan

Evolving from the earlier periods of electromechanical automated data processing (ADP) technologies described in chapter 6, the modern digital computer came into its own form of information technology during the period from 1960 to 2000. Heralded by the advances of the digital computer, Europeans are thought to have introduced the acronym IT, short for information technology.[1] This term, which Americans rapidly adopted, signified digital convergence in data, voice, and video. Also during this time the organization continuously reinvented and assigned new functions to the computer as dictated by improved economics and organizational learning. Eventually these changes accumulated so as to become an information revolution that changed the way companies structured and managed themselves.

Stages Theory of IT Management

The Stages Theory, first proposed in 1973,[2] has been widely used as a normative theory for the management of IT. The theory is based on the notion that the complicated nature of computer technology would produce a body of knowledge on the effective management of IT within an organization. As a result, the assimilation of computer technologies, and more broadly, information technologies, required bold experimentation, out of which emerged four stages of organizational learning.

These four distinct stages of organizational learning formed an "S-shaped" curve. Initially limited investment and contained experimentation for proving the value of the technology in the organization characterized Stage I: Initiation. Following initiation, the steep part of the S-shaped curve (Stage II: Contagion) represented a period of high learning in the organization, whereby the technology proliferated in a relatively uncontrolled manner. Uncontrolled growth eventually led to inefficiency, which created a demand for controls that slowed the growth to a more manageable rate—Stage III: Control. In Stage IV: Integration, the curve flattened, and ultimately the accumulated learning led to a balance of managed controls and growth. At Stage IV, organizations mastered the dominant design of the technology, providing a foundation for the next order of magnitude of progress (i.e., the next S-curve era) to be introduced through a major improvement in the dominant design.

The main dominant designs[3] experienced include mainframes, minicomputers, microcomputers, and networked client/servers. Figure 7.1 illustrates the three eras, described as the Sshaped organizational learning curves, in which the three dominant designs of IT have been and are being assimilated into organizations. The Data Processing (DP) Era dated from 1960 to 1980; the Microcomputer (Micro) Era dated from 1980 to 1995; and the Network Era, which had begun around 1995, is expected to continue until 2010. History shows that each industry, and each organization within an industry, experienced a few years' lead or lag in their learning of associated technologies. The senior level and IT management in each organization within an industry directly influenced the pace.[4]

The S-shaped curves of the eras overlapped during a period of "technological discontinuity."[5] During this period in the organization, further growth of the mature dominant design of the old technology directly conflicted with the vigorous growth of the emerging dominant design of the new technology. Management and IT workers who had mastered the old dominant design struggled to retain their knowledge power in the organization against those who were proposing to replace it with the new. This struggle was a familiar one in history, and one where (with few exceptions) the new technology won. Ironically, those who won the struggle in one round would lose it in the next. And, with the rapid growth of the IT industry, most management and IT workers faced "a diet of continual change."[6]

Relationship between Organizational Structure and IT Architecture

The dominant designs of IT related to the dominant designs of organizations.[7] The dominant form of organizational structures at the period of rapid commercialization of the digital computer during the 1960s

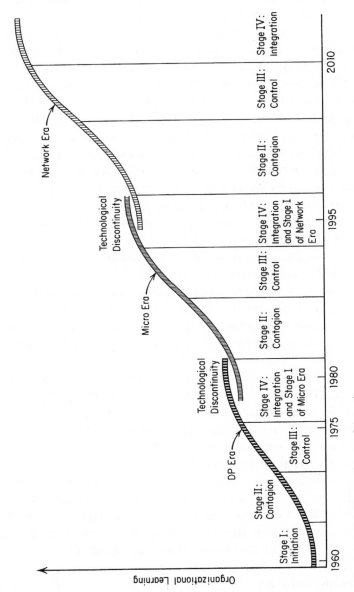

Figure 7.1 The Stages Theory of Growth

and 1970s was the familiar multidivisional (M-form) functional hierarchy.[8] M-form corporations were centrally administered industrial groups where corporate offices administered autonomous integrated operating enterprises that produced for different markets. Each divisional operating unit (e.g., plastics or chemicals) would include a hierarchy of line (e.g., manufacturing or, marketing) and staff (e.g., accounting or purchasing) functions. The first mainframe computers, with their hierarchically structured database systems—such as, IBM's IMS (Information Management System)—reflected this organizational hierarchy. The advent of the Micro Era introduced a "chicken and egg" proposition whereby lower costs enabled wide dispersal of computers in the organization, and organizations simultaneously became more networked, thereby breaking down barriers between middle management and upper management. This process continued to evolve as the networked infrastructures of the now familiar Internet and intranets linked consumers, vendors, and suppliers—at times blurring the boundaries not only between various functions within a single company, but also between one company and the next.

There have always been two types of customers for computers in the organization: (1) engineers and scientists (scientific computing), and (2) managers and administrators (commercial computing). Scientists and engineers wanted computers to help them conduct product research and solve problems associated with the design and manufacture of products. Their needs generally required collaboration and intensive computation to solve mathematical problems.

Managers and administrators wanted computers to help them run their large, hierarchical organizations more efficiently. Their needs involved massive amounts of data processing of sequential files such as paying payrolls and keeping track of payments by customers. Commercial data processing had lots of input and output data, and rather simple arithmetical calculations.

In the early history of computers (before the mid-1950s), scientists and engineers were the dominant customers of computers. With the decision by IBM to get into computers and its market dominance from the mid-1950s through the 1970s, dominant commercial customers became the dominant customers. However, Digital Equipment Corporation (DEC) was founded to meet scientific and engineering customer needs, and it grew to be the second largest computer company in the 1970s.

Table 7.1 shows the evolution of scientific and commercial computing through the eras of IT management, along with key product introductions by the major industry players. One can see that, over time,

Table 7.1 The Two Paths of Computing

Era	Scientific Computing	Shared Technologies	Commercial Computing
The Data processing Era 1960–1979			**1953:** IBM shipped 701, its first electronic computer.
			1954: IBM's 650 quickly takes over the commercial market. It leases for $3,250 a month.
	1957: Ken Olsen and Harlan Anderson found Digital Equipment Corporation.		
		1959: IBM's 7000 series mainframes are the company's first transistorized computers.	
			1960: A team drawn from several computer manufacturers and the Pentagon develops COBOL (Common Business Oriented Language).
	1963: DEC introduces the PDP-8, the first major, mass-produced mini computer; it is sold for $18,000.		
		1963: Finalization of the ASCII (American Standard Code for Information Interchange) code permits machines from different manufacturers to exchange data.	
	1965: DEC introduces the PDP-5, the fifth model in its line of minicomputers.		
			1964: IBM announces System/360, a family of six mutually compatible computers and 40 peripherals that can work together.
	1969: Data General introduces its minicomputer, the NOVA.		
	1969: AT&T Bell Laboratories programmers Kenneth Thompson and Dennis Ritchie develop the UNIX operating system on a spare DEC minicomputer.		

(continued)

The Data processing Era 1960–1979

1969: ARPANET, the precursor to the Internet, starts.

1970: Amdahl Corporation founded to produce clones to IBM's 370.

1972: HP branches into business computing with the HP 3000 minicomputer.

1973: Robert Metcalfe devises the Ethernet method of network connection at the Xerox Palo Alto Research Center.

1974: University of California at Berkeley obtains a UNIX tape. The system is soon running on several PDP-11s; Bill Joy arrives at UC Berkeley and begins working on UNIX.

1974: Researchers at the Xerox Palo Alto Research Center design the Alto—the first workstation with a built-in mouse for input. It is used for local networks and is not commercialized.

1974: The Altair personal computer kit is introduced. It is built by hobbyists for hobbyists.

1975: Amdahl installs its first mainframe produced by Fujitsu in Japan.

1976: Bill Gates and Paul Allen found Microsoft.

1975: Telnet, the first commercial packet-switching network and civilian equivalent of ARPANET, is born.

1977: DEC introduces a new product line, the VAX 11/780, to compete with the larger IBM 3031 and 3032. This enhanced minicomputer quickly makes impressive inroads in the low end of IBM's mainframe markets.

1977: Radio Shack (Tandy), Commodore, and Apple introduce microcomputers. The Apple II becomes an instant success.

1977: TCP/IP is used by other networks to link to ARPANET.

1979: 3Com Corp. is incorporated by Robert Metcalfe.

1979: DEC, Intel, and Xerox join to establish the Ethernet as a standard, with DEC using it for the VAX.

1980: RISC (Reduced Instruction Set Computer) architecture is introduced by John Cocke of IBM. It greatly boosted computer speed by using simplified machine instructions for frequently used functions.

1980: CompuServe, financed by H&R Block, begins aggressively to develop online technology.

1980: ARPA throws its support behind Berkeley UNIX as a common system the agency could recommend for all its clients. It also adopts the TCP/IP protocol.

1981: Apollo Computer unveils the first workstation, its DN100, offering more power than some minicomputers at a fraction of the price.

1981: IBM introduces its PC, making possible a computer on every desktop. The new PC includes MS-DOS (Microsoft Disk Operating System) and the Intel 8-bit chip. Its open standards allow a flood of new PC clones. It reveals a multi billion dollar market.

1981: 3Com makes and ships its first transceivers.

1982: Sun Microsystems is founded by Andreas Bechtoishelm, Bill Joy, Vinod Kholsa, and Scott McNealy. By May of this year, it introduces its workstation combining UNIX, a Motorola chip, and the Ethernet, making Sun the industry leader.

1982: Mitch Kapor develops the spreadsheet program Lotus 1-2-3, greatly stimulating sales of the IBM PC and its clones.

1982: Hewlett-Packard introduces the HP 9000 technical workstation with 32-bit "superchip" technology—its first "desktop mainframe"—as powerful as room-sized computers of the 1950s.

1982: DEC introduces three personal computers. They were incompatible with the VAX machines and not fully compatible with the IBM PC.

1982: Compaq is founded by Rod Canlon.

The Microcomputer Era 1980–1994

(continued)

1983: Ray Noorda takes over Novell and focuses on producing local area networking software (network operating systems). In October, Novell introduces its Sharenet X (eventually renamed NetWare) network operating system.

1983: Apple introduces its Lisa. The first personal computer with a graphical user interface, its development is central in the move to such systems for personal computer.

1983: Compaq Computer Corp. introduces the first successfully commercialized IBM-PC clone.

1984: Cisco is founded.

1984: DEC introduces the VAXstation I, the company's first 32-bit single-user workstation.

1984: IBM, Sears, and CBS form Prodigy. Originally called Trintex, the venture is conceived as a home banking and shopping service.

1984: MIPS Computer Systems, Inc., is founded in order to market the RISC chip it has developed.

1984: Michael Dell begins his computer business, which is based on his innovative marketing techniques.

1984: Microsoft enters the LAN networking software arena with its MS-NET product.

1985: The modern Internet gains support when the National Science foundation forms the NSFNET, linking five supercomputer centers at Princeton University, Pittsburgh, University of California at San Diego, University of Illinois at Urbana-Champaign, and Cornell University.

1986: IBM devises token-ring technology to control LAN traffic (between printers, workstations and servers) more effectively.

1986: Microsoft announces the retail shipment of Microsoft Windows, an operating system that extends the features of the DOS operating system.

1986: Cisco ships its first product, the AGS router.

1986: IBM, with MIPS, releases the first RISC-based workstations, the PC/RT and R2000-based systems. They are commercial failures.

1986: HP introduces broad new family of computer systems based on the RISC architecture.

1987: Sun launches "The network is the computer" campaign. It also introduces a workstation with a RISC chip called SPARC.

1987: The National Science Foundation (NSF) begins to manage the backbone of the Net (taking over from the government).

1988: Microsoft and Ashton-Tate announce the Microsoft SQL Server, a relational database server software product for LANs.

1988: IBM introduces the AS/400, a mid-range system.

1989: Sun's new SPARCstation 1 has more power and functionality than any other desktop computer in the world: 12.5 mips, RISC-based, and less than $9,000.

1989: America Online (AOL) is formed.

1989: Novell introduces a "multithread" SMP system that works with major operating systems, including IBM's OS/2, UNIX, and Apple's Macintosh, to run different tasks or applications simultaneously

1990: IBM introduces the RS/6000, its first successful exploitation of the RISC technology.

1990: The World Wide Web is born when Tim Berners-Lee, a researcher at CERN, the high-energy physics laboratory in Geneva, develops HyperText Markup Language (HTML).

(continued)

1990/1991: Programmers at the University of Minnesota create Gopher, which allows students and faculty to query campus computers for information.

1991: DEC moves into to the production of mainframes with the VAX 9000.

1991: Apple and IBM join forces with Motorola to produce a RISC microprocessor called PowerPC, which they hope will topple the Intel 8086 family. It becomes the processor for Apple's Macintosh computers.

1993: Microsoft formally launches Microsoft Windows NT.

1993: Early versions of the Mosaic Web browser written by Marc Andreesen and Eric Bina (at the University of Illinois) are available over the Internet. It is first written for UNIX, with versions for the MAC and PC platforms following.

1994: Andreesen's Netscape introduces its version of the Web browser.

1995: The NSF backbone becomes commercially supported and business by the thousands begin active work to move their IT architectures to the new network architecture.

1995: Sun introduces Java, the first universal software designed from the ground up for Internet and corporate intranet developers to write applications that run on any computer, regardless of the processor or operating system.

Sources: 3Com's Timeline of Successful Innovation (http://www.3com.com/inside/investor/timeline.html); Amdahl Corporate History (http://www.amdahl.com/about/timeline.htm); Cisco Systems corporate timeline (http://www.cisco.com/warp/public/750/minor_invest6.pdf); The Computer Museum timeline (http://www.tcm.org/html/history/timeline/); Data General (http://www.dg.com/about/html/generations.html); Dell Computer Corporation corporate history (http://www.dell.com/

what started out as two streams of computing serving different customers in the organization has converged by 1995 to network computing. The descriptions in the middle of the table are key events influencing the convergence.

The Data Processing Era

By 1960, M-form large businesses with revenues ranging from $100 million to multi-billions of dollars dominated the U.S. economy. Sophisticated information and communication systems supported the management of these larger organizations. For example, essential modern accounting and budgeting systems controlled the resource allocation process necessary for these organizations to sustain steady annual revenue and earnings per share (EPS) growth.

Early information resource leadership was conceptualized within the context of the functional hierarchy of the operating divisions of a multidivisional enterprise. Early computer systems were large and had significant electromechanical components, including peripheral devices for input, output, and storage. As a result, organizations generally viewed technology as "machine-oriented" because these early computer systems both looked like large machines and were used like the mechanically driven business machines of the Industrial Age whose evolution is described in chapter 4.

In 1952, John Diebold coined the term "automation"[9] as it applied to computer technology. This new computer technology "based on a mathematical formulation of a basic theory of communication and control, made possible the construction of self-regulating and self-programming machines." These new machines could automatically

corporate/access/dellstory/index.htm); Digital Equipment Corporation corporate history (http://www.digital.com/timeline/); Hewlett-Packard corporate history (http://www.hp.com/abouthp/history.html); IBM corporate history (http://www.ibm.com/IBM/history/timeline.nsf/); Microsoft corporate history (http://library.microsoft.com/mshist.1985.htm); MIPS corporate overview (http://www.mips.com/whoWeAre/index.html); Anonymous, "IBM PC XT Local-Network Scheme," *Byte* (October 1983): 593; Paul E. Ceruzzi, *A History of Modern Computing* (Cambridge, Mass.: MIT Press, 1998); Sun Microsystems corporate history (http://www.sun.com/corporateoverview/who/html_history.html); Alfred D. Chandler, "The Computer Industry: The First Half-Century," in *Competing in the Age of Digital Convergence*, ed. David B. Yoffie (Boston: Harvard Business School Press, 1997); 37–122; Kenneth Flamm, *Creating the Computer: Government, Industry, and High Technology* (Washington, D.C.: The Brookings Institution, 1998); Matt Kramer, "MS-Net Paves the Wave for LAN Applications," *PC Week* (November 13, 1984): 1; Bruce Sterling, "Short History of the Internet," *Fantasy and Science Fiction* (February 1993).

perform a sequence of logical operations, correct errors that occurred in the course of their own operation, and choose between several predetermined plans of action according to built-in criteria. Significantly, automation allowed such advances as a single machine being used for more than one process by the simple switching of a magnetic taped program. Each taped program contained a different series of instructions that the machine would follow, allowing for slightly different products to be produced—the innovation of the stored program. The end result was not only fewer personnel, but also fewer machines required to do the multiple tasks in organizations. A year later, Diebold published an article in the *Harvard Business Review*, which widely publicized this concept of the computer to managers.[10]

Early Scientific Computing Influenced Commercial Computing

The first applications of computers were in the scientific domain for national defense purposes, where they have a robust history of their own.[11] Scientific and engineering departments in large organizations such as Boeing had a long history of computer use, and in the 1960s used both analog as well as digital computers for simulation and calculations.[12] During the 1960s it even looked like hybrid computers, which integrated both analog and digital computer components (by interconnection of digital to analog converters and vice versa), might evolve into a major type of technology in scientific computing.[13] Hybrid computers combined the advantages of a digital computer's data storage, time-sharing, and logic capabilities with an analog computer's speed, lower cost, and easier programming.[14] However the more complex hybrid computers died out with the arrival of the IBM System 360 in the mid-1960s, which bridged scientific computing and commercial computing.[15]

IBM's introduction of the 360 computer series in 1964[16] spurred the major growth in commercial computing, which had begun to emerge in the mid- to late 1950s and early 1960s. IBM became the primary supplier of IT and the data processing manager became the major buyer—a common adage among these managers in that era was "you never get fired for buying IBM." Although IBM dominated the market during the 1970s with an average market share of 68 percent,[17] serving geographically dispersed operating units with centralized computing was expensive and provided a market environment for new entrants. Digital Equipment Corporation innovated the minicomputer and became the second largest computer company in the 1970s by successfully concentrating on serving the engineering-oriented factory and laboratory markets.

Minicomputers were medium-scale computers, which functioned as multiuser systems for up to several hundred users. The minicomputer industry began in 1960 after Digital introduced its PDP-1. However it wasn't until DEC's introduction of the PDP-5 in 1963 and the PDP-8 in 1965 that minicomputers entered the market in strength. Following Digital's successful launch, Hewlett-Packard, Data General, Wang, Tandem, Datapoint, and Prime all introduced similar successful systems.

It was while working on a spare DEC minicomputer that AT&T Bell Laboratories programmers Kenneth Thompson and Dennis Ritchie developed UNIX.[18] UNIX was not a complete operating system. Rather, it was a set of basic tools that allowed users to manipulate files in a simple and straightforward manner. One of the major benefits of UNIX was that although it was developed on DEC computers, it could run on any machine that had a C compiler. This was one of the first steps toward open standards and contrasted sharply with the traditional computer vendor's strategy of keeping its code secret. In version 4.2 of Berkeley UNIX (named as such because Bill Joy refined UNIX while at the University of California at Berkeley before becoming one of the founders of Sun Microsystems), support for the networking protocol TCP/IP[19] was added. As Paul Ceruzzi noted, "this protocol, and its bundling with Berkeley UNIX, forever linked UNIX and the Internet."[20]

Another important development in the initial stages of networking also occurred during the Data Processing Era. In 1973 Robert Metcalfe devised the Ethernet method of network connection at the Xerox Palo Alto Research Center; based on Hawaii's ALOHAnet, the Ethernet used cheap coaxial cable that allowed computers to send and listen for radio signals. These signals would then be gathered back together and delivered to the appropriate computer. The Ethernet, with its speed of three million bits per second, was unheard of at the time. As Ceruzzi notes:

> Those speeds fundamentally altered the relationship between small and large computers. Clusters of small computers now, finally, provided an alternative to the classic model of a large central system that was time-shared and accessed through dumb terminals.[21]

Ethernet's first big success came in 1979 when Digital, Intel, and Xerox joined to establish it as a standard, with Digital using it for its VAX computer.

First Commercial Applications in Vertically
Integrated Hierarchies

Responsibility for these early computers was grafted onto the functional organization within the M-form enterprise, and a sharp distinction between commercial computing and scientific computing remained. Commercial computing was usually grafted onto the accounting function, and scientific computing (if it existed in the firm) was grafted onto the engineering or research function. The information resource manager in the firm typically used the title of EDP (electronic data processing) or DP (data processing) manager.

The DP manager—often referred to as a "benevolent dictator"—became a relatively powerful manager of a centralized function because command and control were central to the management of multiproduct functional hierarchies during the DP Era.[22] The mantra for these managers during the DP Era was "manage DP as a business within a business."[23] General managers of single product companies and of divisions in multiproduct companies viewed the computer as a technology that supported an established way of doing business. These general managers ordered DP managers to support the business, and to apply the tenets of how the organization traditionally managed its business to managing the computers—not to use computers to innovate in new ways of running businesses.

A major source of competitive viability was the large-scale, efficient factory—regardless of whether that factory was a traditional car manufacturing plant, or a paper-processing factory, or an insurance company or bank. Vertically integrated corporations facilitated control by owning suppliers to ensure sources of supplies (e.g., car manufacturers owning steel mills), or owning distribution channels to ensure that customers would continue to buy at the rate of production (e.g., oil companies owning gas stations).

As a result, the first commercial applications generally included accounting, with automated tasks such as payroll processing and general ledger. As James Cortada explained in chapter 6, these applications were often coded in low-level assembler programming languages, although COBOL (short for Common Business Oriented Language) a higher level language, rapidly became the preferred programming language for commercial applications during the 1960s. Remarkably, in the late 1990s, COBOL remained the most used language in software and development.[24]

Figure 7.2 illustrates a typical applications portfolio for a functionally organized manufacturing company or a product division of a multidi-

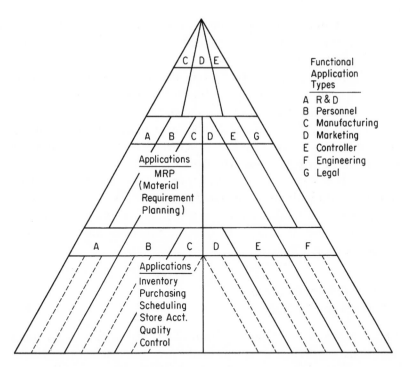

Figure 7.2 Applications Portfolio of a Functionally Organized Manufacturing Company

visional company. Here, the familiar pyramid icon has three hierarchical levels. Each level has functional application groupings such as manufacturing and accounting. Finally, within each functional application at each level, there are individual applications representing opportunities for use of the computer.

The applications portfolio evolved by first automating low-level operational support tasks within a function such as inventory control, shop floor control, and scheduling in manufacturing; or plant, cost, and general accounting in the controller operation. After sufficient automation of low-level operational support tasks within a function, the organization integrated automated tasks within a functional department (i.e., research and development, or engineering) by automating management control activities such as production operations management, accounting management, and human resources management. Accomplishing the more difficult cross-functional automation to support management–control activities within the firm laid the groundwork for the third and most difficult level of automation. At this level, automation supported strategic five-year plans through the integration of department profit plans and corporatewide human resource planning. Throughout this process, the organization moved up the S-shaped curve as managers learned more and more about how to apply IT and tap into its potential.

As illustrated in figure 7.2, given a computer technology and its associated economics, parts of the business functions or processes could not feasibly be automated at any point in time. Research conducted by Nolan, Norton & Co. during the 1980s determined that an organization could automate approximately 50 percent of all operational support functions and 47 percent of management control functions. Because of an overall lack of structure, the higher level strategic planning functions were more difficult to automate than either operational support or management control functions. Nevertheless, continued improvements in the technology increased the overall number of business functions that could be automated.

Corporate-level Financial and Management Accounting

While the product divisions of multidivisional organizations focused on automating tasks from the ground up, the corporate offices focused on tying their divisions together. Indeed, accounting applications of the computer contributed to managing efficiently the complexity of M-form command and control organizations. In this structure, two main types of accounting control tools played major roles: annual budgeting and capital budgeting. The first controlled expenditures aimed at generating revenue during the calendar year; the second controlled expenditures that generated multiple-year revenues.

Annual budgeting. The annual budgeting process for a large M-form hierarchical organization usually based itself upon an incremental growth model of 10 to 15 percent growth per year. Once the company became large, the planning process intended to maintain consistent year-to-year incremental growth in revenue and profit. The line-item general ledger and the codified hierarchical organization chart formed the foundation of the accounting model. The line-item general ledger typically consisted of thousands of objects of expenditures. The organizational chart typically consisted of hundreds of boxes, each associated with a similar group of general ledger accounts. For example, most of the boxes on the organization chart included types of overhead expenses such as paper and office equipment. Before the computer, summarized profit-center accounting was done at a high level (and done infrequently during the year). After the computer, which largely enabled the process, complex divisional and profit-center accountability evolved.

Accountants categorized the assets and equities of the firm into general ledger accounts and then structured these accounts into a balance sheet, which defined the financial position of a company at a point in time. Another set of accounts referred to as "temporary" accounts recorded the inflows (revenue) and outflows (expenditures) of assets intended to generate annual profit. At the end of the year accountants closed out the revenue and expenditure accounts to their respective general ledger permanent asset and equity accounts, resulting in a profit and loss (P&L) statement, and a new end-of-the-year balance sheet. Comparing the beginning balance sheet with the ending balance sheet determined the profit or loss for the company's operations during the year.

Information technology, first in the form of electromechanical data processing devices and later in the form of computers, allowed companies to drive this very powerful accounting process down to the divisional "lines of business" of the organization for decentralized P&L accountability, as well as accountability for return on investment (ROI). By assigning each box on the hierarchical organization chart a number code, managers could conduct the annual budgeting process at the lower levels of the organization. With a group of expense accounts and revenue accounts assigned to the boxes, Managers then could budget revenues and expenses for activities during the calendar year. Then at any level of the organization chart, management could summarize the planned revenues and expenses and compare them with the actual revenues and expenses at a point in time. Furthermore, managers of the departments, lines of business, regions, and other such combinations could receive budget responsibility, budget performance, could be summarized by the computer, and managers could be rewarded or penalized for financial performance. During the electromechanical period, most large firms struggled to conduct the annual budgeting process and the closing of the books efficiently. However, the computer made it easy to do the process monthly or weekly, and in some financial institutions (e.g., Morgan Stanley Dean Witter) in the 1990s the "closing of the books" was done around the world on a daily basis—almost in real time. With efficiently managed computers, organizations routinely produced multitudes of P&L statements by levels in the organization, regions, and even to the detailed level of individual customer profitability.

Capital budgeting. The capital budgeting process was as important as the annual budgeting process in enabling the M-form company to achieve consistent financial performance. The capital budgeting process was a methodology for analyzing the financial returns and risks of capital expenditures that spanned multiple annual accounting periods, such as construction of a new building or acquiring a new machine. Organizations used this methodology to calculate the inflows and outflows of cash for the life of an expected multiyear expenditure. Then managers applied a variable discount factor that would discount the net value of the flows to the present to equal zero. The discount factor that did this was equal to the expected ROI. Companies used various "hurdle rate"[25] discount factors (typically 15 to 20 percent) to account for risk and to screen potential investments to ensure that they used their scarce capital resources most effectively.

Organizations found the computations for capital budgeting during the electromechanical period long, tedious, and expensive, but the computer made these computations trivial, and by the 1990s virtually all companies routinely used sophisticated capital budgeting techniques at almost zero cost.[26] Firms extended command and control accountability from divisional P&L responsibility to divisional ROI responsibility. In many ways, just as farmers and engineers of the Industrial Age applied steam engine technology to mechanize the farm and make the farm more efficient, engineers and computer programmers applied computer technology to the traditional command and control, M-form functional hierarchy to make it more efficient.

This sophisticated use of accounting in the M-form hierarchy enabled managers to control complex operations and support their goal of consistently increasing revenues and earnings per share (EPS). As a result, shareholders regularly saw annual bar charts in the first or second pages of company annual reports showing unbroken 10 percent to 15 percent growth rates in revenues or EPS for periods of 10 to 15 years. People termed this phenomenon the "march to the northeast corner," because the sequence of bars for each year seemed to march to the upper right corner of the graph. This "march" is illustrated in figure 7.3.

IBM and AT&T, two companies considered to be widely successful in the 1970s, had 13.2 percent and 11.6 percent compound annual growth rates, respectively, for the 1970s.[27] EPS growth, which was also reflected by the march to the northeast corner, generally represented the increasing return that an investor realized from investing in the stock. In the case of IBM and AT&T, the average EPS rates for the 1970s were $1.70 per year and $5.65 per year, respectively.[28]

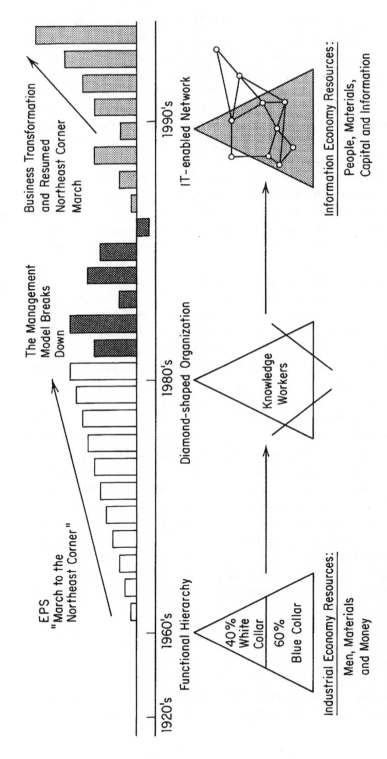

Figure 7.3 Business Transformation Summary

Figure 7.3 also illustrates that the DP Era and the march to the northeast corner corresponded with a period when organizations did not usually challenge either the M-form functional hierarchy or the Industrial Age management model of managers managing scarce resources of "men, materials, and money." However, as the computer penetrated deeper and deeper into organizations, learning transpired to the point that organizations understood the role of the computer to be much broader than its use to support the efficient transaction processing in organizations. Many manual and clerical functions became totally automated, eliminating the need for blue-collar and clerical human resources. As illustrated in figure 7.3, layoffs and downsizing began to mutate the symmetrical pyramid organization structure. This major mutation of the functional organization challenged management in many ways, and often led to disruption in the march to the northeast corner.

Batch processing on standalone mainframe computers was extended through communication lines to input devices such as punch-card readers. Then card readers were refined to permit direct keyboard input to computers through the use of "dumb terminals."[29] The next refinement was the timesharing of a mainframe computer by a number of users. And, because the mainframe computer could carry out computations so much faster than the manual keyboarding of a user, the illusion was that each user had the exclusive use of a computer.

After the initial automation, managers began to realize that they could network computers together, permitting a greater sharing of the data contained in the various computers used by the company. As a result, the ability of workers to obtain and manipulate figures rapidly, previously available to only select individuals in the firm, increased the knowledge of the firm as a whole and further blurred the lines between the various levels of management. In chapter 6, Cortada described the recasting of professionals such as engineers, lawyers, and accountants into knowledge workers. Businesses transformed themselves as well, and with the help of their new information resource, namely the microcomputer, many businesses began their march to the northeast corner once again.

Transition to the Micro Era

By 1980, just before the IBM PC and its clones began to transform the industry, most of the administrative functional tasks of the organization had been automated. The minicomputer had also largely completed its automation of factory tasks such as bill of materials, inventory control, and production scheduling. The Database emerged as an important technology for managing the data used in integrated applications, and data administration also evolved to identify the activities necessary for rudimentary information resource management.

In October 1981, IBM introduced its personal computer, and industry pundits began to predict that soon everyone in a business would be able to have a "mainframe" on their desktop.[30] In order to develop its radically new and different product in an expedient manner, IBM had to turn from the policy it used in the production of its existing mainframes and minicomputers—namely, of developing and manufacturing all the necessary components. Instead it set up a standalone microcomputer business, and gave the management team freedom to go outside to Intel to develop the central processing unit (CPU), to Microsoft to develop the operating system, to Tandon to develop the internal disk storage unit, to Matsushita to develop the monitor, and to Epson to develop the printer.[31] IBM units made the board assembler and keyboards. In addition, in order to market its mass-produced consumer product, IBM began to sell its first PC through Sears's new business machine stores and through Computerland.[32]

As pointed out in chapter 1, IBM's introduction of its PC profoundly transformed the computer industry in five years. The result was a new horizontally integrated IT industry with many competitors in each tier, great levels of innovation, and severe price competition. Within two years, Compaq (which had been founded in 1982) introduced the first commercially successful PC clone and others soon followed.

Novell, which was taken over by Ray Noorda in 1983, was quick to realize that companies would need help and software, in the form of local area networks (LAN) and network operating systems (NOS), to permit a number of personal computers within an office or business unit to share the same peripheral devices such as printers and disk drives. In October 1983 Novell introduced its Sharenet X (later renamed NetWare), which allowed as many as 255 IBM PC XTs to share up to 320 megabytes of storage.[33] In response to Novell's success, other corporations also entered the LAN market. 3Com Corporation, formed in 1979 by Robert Metcalfe (the inventor of the Ethernet), began to compete in 1981 using Metcalfe's new technology. 3Com became one of Novell's major competitors. In 1984, Microsoft entered the market when it introduced its MS-NET. The server portion of MS-NET ran general file servers and controlled the use of printers, plotters, and other shared network resources.[34] But both IBM and Microsoft had little success in challenging the two pioneers until the appearance of Microsoft's Windows NT in 1993.[35]

While PCs were proliferating among the general corporations in the commercial market, many computer makers were developing a microprocessor-based product, the workstation, for their scientific and engineering markets. From the start, workstations were networked systems in which high-powered "servers" stored information and transmitted to "client" desktop computers within a department or other operating unit. Workstations were typically powered by RISC-based[36] microprocessors, ran on UNIX operating systems, and were often linked together using Ethernet technology.[37]

The workstation industry got its start when William Poduska and much of the top management of the minicomputer maker Prime Computer left the company to start Apollo in 1981.[38] That year, Apollo unveiled the industry's first workstation, its DN100. Once again, others soon followed and Sun Microsystems, which was incorporated at the beginning of 1982, became the industry's technological innovator. Sun was founded by four 27-year-olds, three Stanford University graduates and Bill Joy, Berkeley's UNIX expert. It became the industry's progenitor by connecting a Motorola chip to Joy's version 4.2 of Berkeley UNIX and the TCP/IP protocol.

In 1984, a group of Stanford students who had been further refining the RISC chip formed MIPS Computer Systems to market their product.[39] In 1986 Hewlett-Packard and IBM both introduced RISC chip-based lines developed by MIPS. Hewlett-Packard's line was a great success, while IBM's line was a failure. The next workstation was Sun's powerful SPARC system, introduced in 1987. In 1989, DEC made its shift to the RISC microprocessor, while in 1990 IBM began to market its RS/6000 computer.[40]

PC Adoption in Firms in the Commercial Market

Although the workstation client-server technology came to play a central role in the development of corporate, university, and institutional intranets—and their connection to the larger Internet—the scientific engineering market was much smaller in terms of revenue than the commercial markets. During the early years of the Micro Era, the PC dominated. However, like many new technologies, not all employees readily adapted the PC. Moreover, the switch from the mainframe to the microcomputer did not occur overnight. Many DP managers felt (correctly) that PCs threatened their positions; just as JoAnne Yates' described how the decentralization of vertical files altered the work of filing managers (chapter 4), microcomputers directly challenged the conventional centralized management approach of IT activity. DP managers feared PCs threatened their effective control of the computer in the organization. First, because PCs cost relatively little (IBM suggested that the typical system used for business—including color graphics and a printer—would cost about $4,500),[41] many departments in the business had the budgetary authority to purchase them directly. Second, the proliferation of many computers throughout the company resulted in the replication of accounting and reporting functions carried out on large mainframe computers, threatening a loss of data integrity control. Furthermore, the organization lost a great deal of time in confusing arguments about whose numbers were the "right" ones. Finally, wide dispersion of desktop microcomputers presented a major risk of breakdowns in the security of corporate data and computer applications.

Control efforts by DP managers tended to constrain the movement (and use) of computers in the organization, to the point that PCs went underground. Users began dealing directly with PC vendors and introducing PCs into the various parts of the organization without the knowledge of—or in direct defiance of—the DP manager. Vendors specialized in selling to end users who used microcomputers for word processing, graphics (desktop publishing), and computer-aided design (CAD). The success of their tactics were such that penetration of PCs in the organization became ubiquitous. The end result was a fragmented organization in terms of IT; centralized mainframes and minicomputers coexisted with multiple pockets of decentralized user-managed PCs.

In order to get their information systems back under control, senior management of organizations realized that more emphasis had to be put on the importance of IT. During the Micro Era, Bill Synnott, then Vice President of information systems at Bank of Boston (now BankBoston), coined the term Chief Information Officer (CIO). The term, which Synnott defined as the "senior executive responsible for establishing corporate information policy, standards, and management control over all corporate information resources,"[42] was intended to reflect the expanded role of IT leadership and focus on "information" as the key resource to be managed.

Once DP managers had accepted the ubiquitous nature of PCs within organizations, the use of PCs set off new levels of organizational learning and experimentation. There were challenges to Industrial Age organizational structures and management principles, in part because command and control was so institutionalized in the management of the M-form functional hierarchy that it was difficult to move beyond to risk management and flexible response—skills required for effective competition in the Information Age. The Total Quality Management movement (TQM) demonstrated that the sharing of information among workers led to higher efficiency and fewer product defects. Downsizing occurred when owners realized that with computers a company could accomplish the same amount of work with significantly fewer workers. As shown in figure 7.3, by the mid-1980s, organizations were beginning to treat information as a resource, hierarchical structures were undergoing creative destruction, knowledge workers were emerging, and the hoped-for consistency of the march to the Northeast corner was breaking down.[43]

As a result of these technological changes, organizational learning reached a level in which it viewed the computer as more than a machine to automate low-level tasks within a function. It viewed the computer as a technology that could make managers and workers more productive. Shoshana Zuboff conducted a seminal study during this period and introduced the term informate (instead of automate) as a more appropriate term to describe the potential of computers in the firm.[44] The idea was not simply to replace workers with computers, but also to leverage workers with computers. Through time, the idea formed into thinking about workers as "caseworkers" where the computer facilitated work.[45]

The Beginnings of the Internet

While organizations learned about and utilized mainframes, minicomputers, and eventually microcomputers, the U.S. Department of Defense and universities quietly developed another technology. In 1969, ARPANET,[46] the precursor to the Internet, started.[47] As part of the ARPANET project, in 1971 computer scientists linked four university supercomputers enabling scientists to share information with one another. Throughout the 1970s, the Internet continued to evolve as new languages and technical enhancements emerged. By 1984, the term Internet emerged, although few outside the community of scientists, educational institutions, the military and computer hobbyists knew of its existence. In 1997, Andrew Zimmerman, chairman of the telecom and media industry group at Coopers & Lybrand, noted:

this procedural change—this great renaming—marked an evolution-ary turning point: one from a straight back-and-forth communications network to a new form of media, one with content and context and seemingly unlimited possibilities. Expanded addressing technology enabled thousands of "broadcasters" to take to the Net. The Net began to resemble a complex and highly adaptive life form, with a personality composed of many different interests and motivations. With each advance in technology and each new use that was found for the Net, the whole of the thing adapted and grew.[48]

Throughout the late 1980s and early 1990s a series of events laid the foundation for the now familiar Internet: in 1987, the National Science Foundation (NSF) began to manage the backbone of the Net; in 1990 the World Wide Web was introduced as a system in which vast amounts of information could be linked; in 1991, scientists introduced HyperText Markup Language (HTML), which made it possible to switch relatively rapidly among all the files and directories of the Internet. And in 1993, the introduction by the University of Illinois of the first widely used browser, NCSA Mosaic, made accessing the Internet both easier and faster. Individuals, organizations, and govern-ments began to build Web sites offering information, files, and pro-grams that could be downloaded. Zimmerman noted that "the Web was growing at 340 percent annually. The number of host computers on the Internet rose from 80,000 in 1989 to 1.3 million in 1993 to 2.2 million in 1994." This number continued to soar. A survey by Bellcore indicated 14.7 million host computers in September 1996 and 26 mil-lion in September 1997.[49]

Transition to the Network Era

The uncoordinated management of the exploding numbers of PCs by user groups in the organization rapidly led to inefficiencies and costly situations, leading senior management to intervene and trigger searches for better solutions. The natural and obvious solution integrated cen-tralized mainframe/minicomputer applications and databases with de-centralized PCs. Unfortunately, the way in which mainframe/mini-computer applications had evolved over time, along with the vast number of PCs and their myriad of software approaches and vendors, made the integration easier said than done. Nevertheless, client-server concepts and implementation, which had begun to appear in the Micro

Era, emerged in full force as the new dominant design—in which the client was designed for direct user access to computing (similar to the PC), and the server provided direct access to databases and other facilities required by the user. Thus, the notion of network-centric computing evolved and was embraced by the IT industry.

Makers of workstations such as Sun Microsystems,[50] Hewlett-Packard, IBM, Digital, and Microsoft (with its Windows NT) provided specialized server capabilities to thousands of workers in companies who were hooked up to networks of hundreds of thousands of computers. The complexity of interconnected networks reached a point that necessitated simplification and led to renewed interest in "open standards." The Internet had proven itself to be a reliable network of thousands of interconnected computers, and its IT architecture (UNIX, HTML) and protocols (TCP/IP) were quickly seized upon as internal client-server standards for companies. The term "intranet" emerged to describe the adoption of Internet architecture standards for internal networks. Once intranets were developed inside companies, it was an easy step to hook them directly to the outside by hooking into the Internet. These intranets hooked to the Internet vastly increased the capability of companies to communicate with outside suppliers, customers, and even competitors.

Internet Phenomenon

A number of authors have reflected on the nature of the Internet, its attributes of self-management, and the role of open standards versus a "control-oriented" development philosophy.[51] In a similar manner, the development of intranets required more coordination and promulgation of open standards than the traditional use of controls and fixed long-range plans. Organizations also maintained focus by rationalizing key IT decisions that were based on delivering value to customers.

The CIO now faced an environment of building an IT architecture that consisted of many partners, strategic alliances, and outsourcers. It was a much different environment than that of the 1960s and 1970s, when the IS manager could get most of their products and services from one or two vendors. In the Network Era, there was a constantly changing, large number of vendors that the CIO had to manage.

By 1998, Information Age companies in the IT industry had become exemplars for companies in other industries. Cisco, just fourteen years old, had become the fastest company ever to reach a market value exceeding $100 billion.[52] All of its manufacturing of the physical routers was outsourced to strategic partners, and coordinated through its computer network: its intranet. Cisco's gross margins, which exceeded 70 percent, were primarily the result of building and selling intangible knowledge assets.[53]

Cisco, and Information Age companies like it, had adopted open Internet standards (TCP/IP and HTML), which provided workers access to the company's databases. Companies like Cisco realized internal efficiencies by making their benefits information directly accessible to their employees through client computers and the use of Web browsers (i.e., Netscape's Navigator and Microsoft's Internet Explorer). Sometimes leading and sometimes following, a company integrated its external Web site with its internal intranet, which enabled its customers to "self-serve" themselves through their own computers within their organizations. In 1998, 70 percent of Cisco's $800 million of service revenue was provided over the Internet by connecting customers to their intranet. In addition, more than 50 percent of Cisco's product revenue of $8 billion was shipped over the Internet directly to customers.[54] The cost advantage, as well as the robust customer service, enabled by IT set a new competitive standard in Cisco's industry. Similar IT leveraging of networks began in other industries as well, and in turn established new competitive standards.

The Internet demonstrated that a network architecture was scalable to the point that large organizations could operate their thousands of PCs in a robust network environment (TCP/IP) and transfer information among the networked computers in an efficient and timely manner. In response, when the NSF backbone became commercially supported in 1995, businesses by the thousands began active work on moving their IT architectures to the new network architecture, which proved that e-mail and multimedia documents could be easily sent around the world over the existing telecommunications infrastructure. In 1995 *The Economist* suggested that "the Internet will almost certainly have a stronger impact than the PC . . . a reasonable guess might put it ahead of the telephone and television but behind the printing press."[55] At the end of 1995, there were approximately 90,000 sites on the Web, about half of which were commercial.[56] As of July 1998, approximately 36.7 million sites (every on-line host and individual machine connected to the Internet) existed on the Web, about one-third of which were commercial.[57]

George Gilder proposed "Metcalfe's[58] law of the telecosm"; this law is based on the idea that interconnecting *n* number of computers results in a potential value of *n* squared.[59] For example, the network of roads for *n* number of cars results in a potential value of *n* squared. The idea applies to telephones, fax machines, and computers. The explosion of the Internet in business can be attributed to its potential value as projected by Metcalfe's law of the telecosm. The Internet is the fastest technology ever to achieve 50 million connected users; as of July 1998, approximately 130 million people used the Internet; about 70 million were in the United States and Canada.[60] IntelliQuest, a provider of information services to technology companies, suggests that the number of U.S. users online has doubled between 1996 and 1998.[61]

Similar to Moore's Law,[62] Gilder ordained that: "the total bandwidth[63] of communications systems will triple every year for the next 25 years." He went on to predict that within the first decade of the twenty-first century, the all-optical network would be thousands of times more cost effective than electronic networks.[64]

Not only was the bandwidth expanding, the underlying economics of computers and telecommunications had made it possible to process and transmit massive amounts of information around the world more cheaply the next year, the year after that, and so on for as long as we could foresee. Starting with the processing of binary coded alphanumeric data on the computer, and proceeding through fax, voice, graphics, and video digital coding, protocols and standards had emerged, enabling the power and declining cost of information technologies to be applied to organizational activities. The overall phenomenon became known as "digital convergence."

The fusion of computers and telecommunications led to deregulation of telecommunications in the United States and the 1984 breakup of AT&T.[65] The introduction of competition produced a deluge of new products and created the environment for the rise of the Internet. The ultimate result was a huge, vibrant IT industry that drove the U.S. economy through the 1990s and into the 2000s. In the spring of 1998, Ira Magaziner, senior advisor to President Clinton for policy development noted that "over the past three years over one third of the real growth of the economy has been accounted for by information technology industry growth and that has been primarily driven by the building out of the Internet."[66] Familiar examples included the following:

- Wal-Mart used store level point-of-sale data to drive supplier replenishment more efficiently.[67]
- Amazon.com efficiently sold books over the Internet, cutting out the physical need to house all the books that they sold. Amazon's average inventory holding periods of five to six days, plus accounts payable terms of up to 180 days, reduced working capital levels.[68]

- Edmunds and Microsoft's CarPoint provided buyers with automobile dealer invoice information, thus equalizing the power of the car dealer and the customer for more efficient car purchasing transactions.[68]

Digital convergence was playing a role in the restructuring of all industries. The IT industry in general enabled businesses to manage information resources more efficiently, to the extent that new economies of organization resulted (e.g., virtual organizations and vast reductions in the use of expensive paper communications),[70] and information was incorporated into products and services to create more value for customers (e.g., automatic diagnostics and call-back to repair facilities from elevators around the world greatly reduced elevator breakdowns in buildings).[71] The more that corporations reengineered the business processes to take advantage of information technologies, the greater their opportunities to improve the economics of the business and value to the customer.[72]

Challenge of System Management in the Network Era

During the three eras, information resource leadership continued to evolve in response to the changing dominant design of IT, and through the increased influence of IT on the economics and strategy of the organization. Just as the Industrial Age IT architectures of the 1960s and 1970s mirrored the functional hierarchical organization structures, the Information Age IT architectures of the 1990s and beyond mirrored the highly organic, flexible network organization structures that emerged in the Information Age.[73]

These flexible network structures challenged all organizations in the Network Era to coordinate the thousands of computers that made up the their internal networks, as well as the tens of thousands of computers with which the organizations communicated through the various connections with other intranets[74] of suppliers and customers and the overall Internet. This challenge was one of coordination rather than control, and it required new, emerging approaches to management. Not surprisingly, both senior management of the organization as well as the leaders responsible for IT throughout the eras struggled with this new model for information resource leadership. John Sifonis and Beverly Goldberg noted that "the technology leader of tomorrow must be a business leader with all the management skills of any other senior executive. The CIO has gone from being a corporate god in the 1980s to the chief blame taker in the 1990s, when IT initiatives often have failed to deliver their promised productivity gains."[75]

Indeed, it appeared that the importance of the CIO's role had diminished in the early 1990s. A survey of 300 CIOs conducted by Heidrick and Struggles Inc. in 1997 found that only 2 percent of those CIOs surveyed were on their corporate boards, just 7.7 percent reported directly to the CEO and/or the president of the corporation, and just 40 percent were on one or more senior management committees.[76] In contrast, in 1974, Robert J. Greene looked at some 300 firms and found that 10 percent of the DP managers reported directly to the president, 2 percent reported directly to the chairman of the board, and 7 percent reported to the executive vice president. A full 14 percent of the DP managers in Greene's study reported to the controllers.[77]

This struggle has been reflected through high turnover rates: in their study, Gomez Advisors found that 34 percent of the CIOs interviewed reported having less than 10 percent of their IT employees leave each year, 42 percent said that 10 to 20 percent left annually, and the remaining 24 percent reported that 20 to 30 percent of their IT staff left the firm each year.[78] Further, Deloitte & Touche found that in 1991 the CIO turnover rate was 14 percent, it peaked in 1993 at 18.8 percent, and in 1996 (latest available data) the rate was 17.7 percent.[79]

Information Resource Management

The fundamental difference between Industrial Age companies and Information Age companies was the formal recognition of information as an important resource, and the incorporation of new management principles to manage information effectively and explicitly as a resource.[80] Furthermore, management viewed IT as the underlying technology of the information resource. Management used IT to exploit information directly as a resource to add value to the product or service; as a result, management attention shifted from the technology itself to what the technology could produce through the extraction of value from information resources.

Impact on "Work"

The recognition of information as a resource had a dramatic impact on managing "work"—that is, the activities that people did to create value in the firm. In the Industrial Age, organizations divided work into its smallest elements and then assigned the work to small groups that repetitively and consistently carried out their tasks. Organizations coordinated successive modules of the output of tasks across functions and integrated the components into a finished product. Each product was the same as the other—this was mass production. Therefore, employees accessed codified and consistent information for producing a product. The management principle of "need to know" governed the distribution of information in the organization.

In contrast, the Information Age organization moved from mass production to highly tailored products or services for the customer. The concept of using a static system to produce a static product was replaced by a dynamic, interactive system utilized to produce rapidly changing products. Also, the ability to continue to coordinate activities and sort out how to produce a product or service better (or more efficiently) led to a continuously changing production process. The concept of work and the role of information shifted from a "need to know" environment to one where information generation, flows, and use were incorporated into the concept of work itself. For example, in the Network Era, workers use knowledge gained from networked computers to leverage the creation of customer value. Concepts such as the "shadow partner" arose to describe the emerging IT network architectures whereby the dominant role of the knowledge worker was leveraged through easy-to-use but highly robust computers facilitating access of information.[81]

Real-time Resource Allocation and Management

An important tenet of management in the precomputer period was the annual budget cycle for major resource allocation, described earlier. In the M-form functional hierarchy, upper management completed change and resource allocation once a year, and then for the rest of the year the organization focused on execution and actions to correct deviations from the plan. This cycle time seemed long by the 1980s, but it facilitated the coordination of many workers doing many tasks required to mass-produce products and services in an economical manner.

The computer enabled companies to obtain performance information rapidly that before was difficult to obtain and took a long time to process. As noted earlier, first firms completed monthly "closings" to summarize performance and take corrective action, then weekly summaries appeared, and finally daily closings emerged in some industries like financial services. Accordingly, real-time resource allocation—using real-time messaging IT architectures—was possible, permitting organizations to be extremely responsive to changing market conditions, to pursue newly discovered opportunities swiftly, and to allocate the resources of the firm dynamically.

An integral component of these real-time resource allocation systems was relational shared databases, which permitted knowledge workers to obtain current information on the results of operations, and to take actions necessary to correct variances from objectives. For example, State Street Corporation developed a global architecture system that was designed to deliver information and investment services to their customers on a near real-time basis.[82] The phenomenal growth of enterprise resource planning (ERP), systems[83] was likewise fueled by the strategic advantages of information transparency among customer and supplier organizations.

From "Make and Sell" to "Sense and Respond"

IT-enabled network organizational structures facilitated the adoption of more sophisticated competitive strategies that extended beyond "making and selling" products and services to "sensing and responding" to individual customer needs in real time.[84]

One of the ways that corporations sensed customers needs was to use information technology to connect to their customers electronically. Examples in the early 1990s included:

- Use of scanning data in retail stores—Levi Strauss & Co. used consumer database information and regional market-demand characteristics revealed by geodemographic data to match supply and demand in each store.[85]
- Use of geographical information systems (GIS)—Isuzu used GIS applications to identify the optimal locations for new dealerships.[86]
- Use of network computers in an automobile—Intel designed a high-performance, highly integrated microchip for engine- and transmission-control systems that monitored and continually adjusted engine performance.[87]
- Use of wireless in the automotive industry—Siemens Automotive released a wireless Traveler Information System (TIS™) that used cellular communication to retrieve information related to traffic conditions along a specific route.[88]

- Use of search agents in electronic commerce—Excite's Jango 2.0 agent searched the Web and returned a consolidated list of prices and availability for the item the user had requested.[89]

Not only did corporations use IT to strategically sense customer needs, but they also strategically used IT to respond electronically to fulfill customer needs. Examples included:

- Use of knowledge management software—Corporations such as Fidelity Investments, AT&T, and Allied Signal used BackWeb technology to push items such as software updates, company directories, news from the Net, and data from corporate data-bases to their employees' desktops.[90]
- Virtual manufacturing—By the time Netscape Navigator was officially released in August 1996, it had been through six beta versions. Each of these beta versions had gradually and syste-matically improved the end product by incorporating user feed-back about features and bugs.[91]
- Supermarket replenishment—H. E. Butt Grocery Company (HEB) first teamed up with Procter & Gamble (P&G) to employ Continuous Replenishment (CRP) in 1989. CRP allowed P&G to supply HEB with products based directly upon warehouse shipment and inventory data rather than upon receipt of HEB-generated purchase orders. This reduced order cycle time by six to ten days and dramatically reduced inventory levels in the store. By mid-1997, 65 percent of warehouse cubic volume was on CRP.[92]

By the late 1990s IT-enabled "sense and respond" strategies had made a strategic impact on most if not all industries. IT innovation became an integral part of almost every company's strategy formulation pro-cess. More often than not, however, a particular IT breakthrough surprised companies, and they found themselves in a position of stra-tegic jeopardy—that is, the breakthrough forced a company to match a competitor's IT initiative just to keep their customers. Furthermore, by the late 1990s, horizontally integrated structures had already weak-ened and replaced more vertically integrated structures in most indus-tries. IT had facilitated these changes by lessening coordination costs and permitting more efficient, but more complex, outsourcing and strategic alliance relationships.[93] Thus, it was easier for specialists to penetrate various parts of the value chain of industries. Product and service development cycles continued to shorten, and innovative ways were developed to sense and respond to customers' needs. The strategic role of the computer, in turn, brought line management directly into the management of IT through both capital and annual budgeting processes.

Impact on Product and Services

Much of an ongoing controversy about the value of IT investments resided in the inherent robustness of IT. IT could be applied to increase efficiency in order to reduce the price of products and services, and IT could be used to add unique features to products and services. But, unless organizations directly managed the investments in IT so that the investments increased profits in the firm, the measurements of investments were elusive and hard to quantify.

Halving the cost. The economics of information as a declining cost resource relative to the increasing costs of scarce resources resulted in a gradual phenomenon in which organizations increasingly substituted information for scarce resources in the production of goods and services. As the mix of resources continued toward information and away from scarce resources, the cost of the product or service declined— firms eventually passed these savings onto the consumer. Once senior managers recognized the strategic importance of the substitution, they often rallied their organizations with goals to halve the cost of the product or service over time without reducing its quality.

Doubling the quality. The information resource was much more robust than just affecting the cost of the product or service of the organization; organizations also used it to increase the quality. Similarly, once senior management realized how information could be used to increase the value to the customer through increased levels of service (e.g., easy-to-use information on how to use the product or service more effectively) or increased levels of performance of the product (e.g., substituting electronic fuel systems for mechanical fuel systems in automobiles to improve the overall performance and reliability of the vehicle), goals were often set to double the "quality" of the product or service while holding cost constant.

Adding previously impossible features. Closely aligned with increasing the quality was using IT to add features to the products or services that had not before been possible. For example, car manufacturers incorporated (computer-based antilock braking systems (ABS) into vehicles. The way that ABS worked to sense and respond electronically to the friction of the wheel on the road incorporated unique features of computer technology not previously available in other technologies.

By the late 1990s, the application of computer chips that cost only dollars per chip had made the computer ubiquitous. More than a trillion chips were embedded in millions of products. An automobile had as many as 150 embedded computer chips doing everything from the aforementioned ABS based upon road conditions to communicating the location of the vehicle to the driver through accessing the Global Positioning System (GPS). Networking of computers through the Internet had come of age, and it set off a new wave of computer applications promising new IT-enabled benefits for customers.

Rise of the Caseworker

In the Industrial Age, companies divided work into work done by two classes of workers. Companies differentiated classes by the amount of their education: white-collar workers usually were college educated and were managers and professionals such as accountants and engineers; blue-collar workers usually had graduated from high school. The overall business model was such that white-collar workers designed the way that work would be carried out as codified through task definitions, job responsibilities, and policies. White-collar workers also supervised blue-collar workers to ensure that they carried out the work properly. When firms detected variances in a plan, the white-collar workers "managed" by taking corrective actions.

In the Information Age, the line between white-collar and blue-collar workers broke down as the sharp distinction between designing work and carrying out that work blurred. Also contributing to the breakdown was that serving customers with "sense and respond" strategies required workers to operate as caseworkers and cope with a much more complex work environment. Consumers further complicated the new work environment with their new demands for faster product cycles and service times, which in turn required access to more knowledge faster than ever before. The combination of these factors is illustrated in figure 7.4.

Also illustrated in figure 7.4 is the barrier that workers encountered as complexity and access to knowledge reached a point where the workers could not perform without effectively leveraging IT. As noted previously, the role of IT in leveraging the capabilities of a worker had been conceptualized as providing a "shadow-partner" to a caseworker,

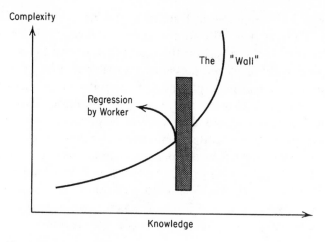

Figure 7.4 The Caseworker Paradox

enabling the caseworker to quickly access databases and networks that contained the knowledge necessary for the worker to carry out value-added activities.[94]

The IT-enabled caseworker promoted the paradigm of client–server computing. The caseworker used a "client" computer interact directly in real time to other computers (servers) to access customer information and product databases. Rapidly, the interaction began to expand to networked computers of suppliers, outsourcers, and others that might provide information to enhance the service to the customer.

New Benchmarks of Organizational Performance

During the latter part of the DP Era the broader role that computers could play in the organization began to emerge, but the impact of the Micro Era made apparent that computers were much more than transaction-processing machines. New benchmarks began to emerge, pioneered by the innovative, high-growth companies in the Information Age which aggressively led the way in applying computers. As shown in table 7.2, IBM ranked number one in market value [95] during the DP Era and most of the Micro Era. However, by 1997 both Microsoft's and Intel's market values were greater than IBM's. And in July 1998, Cisco, a company that started by making switches and routers.[96] for networks, also surpassed $100 billion in market value.[97] Cisco not only pioneered the use of the intranet in its own business,

Table 7.2 Market Value and Sales per Employee

Market Value Rank				Sales per Employee		
1978	1986	1997	Company Name	1978	1986	1997
5	3	1	General Electric	$49,012	$98,081	$320,797
16	16	2	Coca-Cola	120,164	309,259	639,593
NA	577	3	Microsoft	NA	171,304	510,885
3	2	4	Exxon	464,112	685,176	1,503,490
17	9	5	Merck	69,040	134,492	439,348
273	216	6	Intel	36,690	69,506	393,564
27	8	7	Philip Morris	82,814	186,315	369,171
1	1	8	IBM	64,747	127,011	291,348
2	4	9	AT&T	50,969	169,391	401,557
54	39	10	Pfizer	58,038	111,900	254,146
11	18	11	Procter & Gamble	147,267	208,635	337,396
53	26	12	Bristol-Myers Squibb	75,167	138,564	311,586
467	17	13	Wal-Mart Stores	51,446	84,461	142,979
25	30	14	Johnson & Johnson	52,199	90,829	250,044
70	41	15	American International Group	11,026	315,842	762,217

Source: Standard & Poor's Compustat. Market value ranks and SPE reflect calendar year-end values.

thus demonstrating the strategic value of networking, but they also built the hardware/software products required by other companies to move toward an integrated network and strategic intranets.

Sales per Employee (SPE). Before computers became ubiquitous, SPE remained around $50,000 to $100,000. Employers considered labor fungible and measured it in hours. When sales increased, planning factors automatically proportionately increased all other resources required to produce the increment in sales, thus maintaining the "march to the northeast corner." As noted, during the Micro Era overall organizational learning about how to use and exploit the potential of IT expanded tremendously. SPE became a variable, and leading companies achieved SPE that grew to levels between $250,000 and more than $1,000,000. Table 7.2 illustrates the top fifteen U.S. companies in terms of market value at the end of 1997 and their respective SPE. Five of these leading companies had SPE that were more than one and a half times that of their industry's average, and all but two companies had SPE that were higher than the industry average.[98] While not conclusive, these numbers provide evidence that SPE correlated with computer-leveraged revenue-generation activities in the firm—as companies transformed from DP Era practices (1978) to Micro Era practices (1986) to Network Era practices (1997) their SPE increased at rates of 1.5 times to close to 29 times their previous era's SPE.[99] Organizations who paid more attention to mining customer databases, building intellectual assets, and knowledge management, appeared to have higher SPE.

Market value.   Market value of companies went a long way toward replacing sales as a benchmark of successful companies. In the Industrial Age, sales generally correlated with market share, and companies with a large market share could more easily control prices and protect margins. Market value of companies was a rough measure of what investors expected would be the long-term return for their investments in a company. The suspicion was that market value also reflected the overall capacity of the company to innovate in maintaining their competitive position.

In table 7.2, the 1978 and 1986 ranks of the market values for the top fifteen companies in 1997 are also shown. As noted earlier, both Microsoft's and Intel's market value in 1997 exceeded that of IBM. Both Microsoft and Intel, however, had vastly smaller sales (IBM, Microsoft, and Intel had 1997 sales of $78.5 billion, $11.4 billion, and $25.1 billion, respectively).[100]

Summary

The management of IT has passed through three eras during which long periods of organizational learning have transpired. Management of the computer as an Industrial Age machine characterized the DP Era. Engineers installed massive computers that consisted of room-sized cabinets and whirling tape drives, with the entire computer enclosed in specially designed machine rooms. Technicians were recruited to tend to the machines. People associated the large size of mainframe computers with the power of the machine to do work. It is amusing to know that as computers were miniaturized into minicomputers, some DP managers placed the smaller minicomputers into larger cabinets because they feared senior managers would not think that the smaller computers were powerful enough to do the work of the larger ones.

But with the cumulative experience of applying computers, DP managers began to discover that computers were much more than the electric mechanical machines of the Industrial Era. They discovered that not only could paper-based transactions be automated, but the paper-based processes could also be redesigned to be much more efficient through the electronic processing. Furthermore, they discovered that transaction processing could be integrated across the traditional functions: simultaneously, an order could be taken from a customer, inventory reserved, the order scheduled for production in the factory, and an invoice sent. Attempting to implement these types of applications put the DP managers on the fulcrum of complex, hard-to-do organizational changes. Failures to consummate the required organizational changes effectively resulted in less than optimal use of computers, and, in turn, the turnover of DP managers increased to 30 to 40 percent during the mid-1970s[101] and remained high through the 1980s and 1990s. Nevertheless, the opportunity to continuously change and improve business operations and customer service through IT became the hallmark of managing Information Age organizations.

The Micro Era formally began with IBM's introduction of the Personal Computer (PC). The term connoted that the computer was not necessarily a large, high-cost machine, but something that could be used by individual workers to do more work efficiently. The innovation of the desktop PC was so radical in its time that most centralized DP or IS departments either ignored it or attempted to rid the organization of the machines. But the PC makers went around the DP departments and sold PCs directly to users in the various functional areas: spreadsheets to financial and accounting departments, word processing to secretaries, and graphic systems to graphic arts departments. The result was a bifurcation in the management of IT in the firm: the central DP department used its centrally managed mainframes for transaction processing, and the users managed their PCs individually.

While IBM introduced the low-cost PC to the commercial organization, Apollo Computer invented a more expensive microcomputer to appeal to the scientific customer; it called this computer the workstation. Sun Microsystems followed close behind and became the industry's innovator, by introducing a workstation that included the UNIX operating system, the Ethernet, and the TCP/IP protocol for networking computers efficiently.

The first shifts toward the convergence of scientific and commercial computers could be seen during the Micro Era. In 1986, Cisco shipped its first product, the AGS router that facilitated the integration of computers in the organization into networks. And corporations such as Novell and Microsoft were developing software that would help corporations to link their microcomputers with workstations that acted as servers.

By the 1990s, the fragmentation resulting from the proliferation of computers in the organization reached a point where many began to question the overall return from IT investments, and the impetus for networking clients and servers was greater than ever.[102] Then, in the mid-1990s, many businesses discovered the Internet. The dawn of the Network Era once again changed the paradigm from managing individual computers to managing networks of computers. Broadening the management paradigm to networks shifted the focus from managing technology to managing information resources enabled by IT. Accordingly, refinements such as knowledge management, creating and maintaining intellectual assets, providing self-service to customers over the Internet, and even directly distributing products over the Internet have become emerging areas of study. A major shift has occurred in the organizational concept of a computer—from a machine to automate work to an enabler of a new information resource that could be leveraged by workers to create value.

8

Computers in U.S. Households Since 1977

Lee S. Sproull

By the concluding years of the twentieth century, the information age was no stranger in the home or the office. By this time the American household was extraordinarily well-equipped with information and communication technologies. By 1995, 99 percent of U.S. households had at least one radio; 98 percent had at least one television; 94 percent had at least one telephone; 81 percent had at least one VCR; 63 percent had cable service. In 1995, people over the age of eighteen spent about 3,400 hours watching television and videos, listening to the radio and recorded music, playing home video games, and reading newspapers, magazines, and books.[1]

The newest and potentially most powerful information technology to enter the U.S. household is the personal microcomputer. In naming the personal computer "Machine of the Year" for 1982, *Time* magazine proclaimed, "The 'information revolution' that futurists have long predicted has arrived, bringing with it the promise of dramatic changes in the way people live and work, perhaps even in the way they think" (see figure 8.1). America will never be the same." By 1997, twenty years after the introduction of the personal computer (PC) 37 percent of U.S. households owned one.

This chapter offers a sociological perspective on the spread, use, and effects of computing technology in the U.S. home from 1977 to 1997.[2] It extends the focus of the two previous chapters on the development of computer technology and its role in business. In comparison with literature on other information technologies in the home, little has been written about the use and effects of the household computer. This has occurred for at least two reasons. One is that the diffusion of computers into the home is still in progress; therefore, documenting its spread requires tracking a moving target.[3] A second reason is that

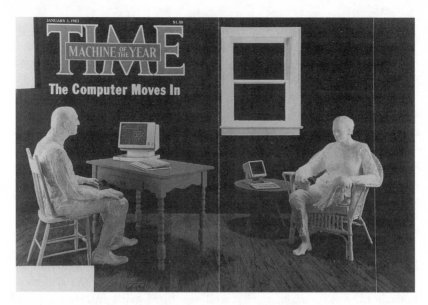

Figure 8.1 Machine of the Year. Each year, *Time* magazine normally selects one person who made the greatest difference in events of the prior year around the world. In 1983, for the first time in its history, *Time* selected something other than a person—the personal computer. As the article accompanying the selection explained, this information-handling appliance had quickly and powerfully effected a profound influence on how Americans worked and played. In 1982, more than a million personal computers were sold. Reprinted with permission from Time, Inc., © 1983 All Rights Reserved.

the basic functionality of the home computer changed radically during this twenty-year period. Consequently the computer's uses and effects also changed, and theories or explanations based on one set of uses (such as efficient word processing or numerical calculation) are not especially helpful in understanding another set of uses (such as online chatrooms.)

Home computers merge attributes of what were previously three distinct realms of information technology found in the home: stand-alone tools like typewriters and calculators; printed media like mail, newspapers, and magazines that are delivered by physical transport; and signal media like telephone, radio, and television that are delivered by beams, wires, or cables. Information in printed media could be archived in the home, manipulated to at least some extent, and shared or accessed asynchronously. Information in signal media was more difficult to archive and manipulate in the home and, with the exception of prerecorded music and video, could be experienced only in real time. Home computers connected to the Internet can access, store, and manipulate information; they can also be used to participate in synchronous or asynchronous communication. Ultimately satisfying explanations for the spread, use, and effects of household computing must acknowledge how merging attributes of these previously separate realms changes peoples' relationship to information and their world.

The "information revolution" claimed by *Time* in 1983 is still underway in 1997. The technology continues to evolve: machines become more powerful; software becomes more complex. The industry structure for providing hardware, software, communications, and content is in a state of flux. The political and regulatory environment for such issues as privacy, free speech, and intellectual property is at least as uncertain. In the meantime, computers in the home have become the new focus for some enduring themes in the history of information technology and media.

First, acquisition of information technology is associated with social privilege. The presence of a home computer is associated with markers of social privilege such as family income, education level, race, and gender. To the extent that the use of home computers confers advantage in knowledge, skills, or outlook, differential access to home computers will reinforce distinctions based on social privilege.

Second, children are particularly susceptible to the potential consequences of information technology, both positive and negative. Public officials and at least some parents see great educational potential in home (and school) computers. At the same time, they worry that children can easily be exposed to inappropriate content and people and behavior.

Third, information technology has affected family dynamics. In many cases, the networked household computer brought together family members residing outside the household, just as the telephone helped people stay in touch with local or distant relatives. And it also reduced family interaction within some households as the television has done.

Fourth, all information technologies change the boundaries between the household and the larger world. This may become the most important and enduring effect of the computer on the household. Sociability boundaries were changed by the telephone, which was used to reinforce patterns of face-to-face communication and reduce rural isolation. While the telephone extended the boundaries of face-to-face relationships, networked computers allowed people to communicate with others whom they had never met and join groups of people that will never meet face-to-face.

This chapter explores each of these themes in turn, after describing how the home computer changed and diffused over the first twenty years of the PC era. (see table 8.1).

Three Eras of Household Computing

During the twenty-year period covered by this chapter, household computers increased and changed in functionality and were acquired for different reasons for different family members. In the first era of home computing (1977–1984), stand-alone machines were acquired for entertainment and self-improvement. In the second era (1984–1994), household machines began to be connected to on-line databases and to people in distant areas. In the third era (1994–1997), household machines were connected to the Internet and the World Wide Web. The era boundaries are approximations that characterize a difference in emphasis, rather than delineating discrete periods.

Stand-alone Machines

The personal computer first entered the U.S. household by way of the garage and the workbench in 1975 with the introduction of a machine for electronics hobbyists. The January 1975 cover story of *Popular Electronics* introduced the Altair 8800—"a full-blown computer that can hold its own against sophisticated minicomputers," a machine that could be put to uses such as "an automated control for a ham [radio] station, a digital clock with time zone conversion, an autopilot for planes and boats, navigation computer, and a brain for a robot."[4] The Altair came "complete" with a 256 bytes of memory (expandable for an additional cost), but no keyboard, monitor, or storage device; it cost $395 in kit form or $495 "fully assembled." The Altair and its brethren thrilled electronics hobbyists and tinkerers, many of whom worked with larger computers in their day jobs but craved a machine of their own.

One of those hobbyists, who had been a video arcade game designer for Atari, built a machine in 1977 that propelled the home computer out of the garage and into the living quarters. The hobbyist was Steve Wozniak; the machine was the Apple II.[5] Its color graphics, sound, and control paddles referenced the video game arcade more than the electronics shop, but its sleek case looked more at home in the family room than on the workbench.[6] Hobbyists and gamers bought most of the earliest Apples, enchanted by their interactivity and controllability.

Table 8.1 Timeline for Computers in the U.S. Household, 1977–1997.

1975	Altair 8800 launched
1977	Apple II introduced; generates $2 million in revenue
	24,000 home computers sell this year
1979	Apple enters education market
	VisiCalc introduced
	Usenet News introduced
1980	H&R Block acquires and funds CompuServe
	VisiCalc is top-selling program
	52,000 home computers sell this year
1981	Apple revenue is $335 million
	IBM introduces PC in August
1982	*Time* named computer "Machine of the Year" for 1982, in January 3, 1983, issue
1983	Microsoft launches Word, a word processing program
	IBM announces PC Jr. (in November)
	2 million home computers sell this year
	90 percent of software sales are games
1984	IBM, Sears, and CBS found Prodigy
	6.98 million households have computers
	50 percent of software sales are games; 50 percent are self-improvement (educational software or home management)
1985	The 'WELL founded
	Q-Link, precursor of America Online, founded
	Intuit founded
1989	13.68 million households have computers
	2 million subscribers to on-line services
	AOL nationwide service launched
1993	First Internet mail message sent by a U.S. president, 2 March 1993
	22.6 million households have computers
	1 million households subscribe to Prodigy; 1.2 million households subscribe to CompuServe
	150 Web sites (July)
1994	Estimated number of subscribers to on-line services: 3.8 million
	Estimated number of Usenet sites: 180,000
1995	Netscape goes public
	Estimated number of subscribers to on-line services: 12 million
1996	Four NetDays held in 1996 and 1997
1997	AOL: 10 million household subscribers
	Compuserve: 2 million household subscribers
	2.4 million Web sites (December)

Early software vendors targeted these users, mostly young males; through 1983, 90 percent of all home software sold was game software.[7]

A second early route into the home was motivated by self-improvement, or vicarious self-improvement for one's children, rather than hobbies and entertainment. In this route the home computer was viewed as an information-processing tool that could be employed in the service of improving one's performance at work or school. Before corporations began providing their employees with PCs, some managers and professionals purchased home computers expressly for work-related purposes. They brought work home from the office to run on their home machines in the evening and amazed their co-workers the next day with the speed and complexity of their analyses. VisiCalc, the first commercially available spreadsheet program, was the most popularly used software for this purpose. Indeed, VisiCalc, introduced in 1979 for the Apple II, became the home computer industry's first "killer application"—an application so important that it alone justified the computer purchase. Beginning in 1979, customers would apparently go to a computer retail store to purchase VisiCalc, and then "ask for something to run it on."[8]

In 1979 educational software for the Apple II began to appear. School districts bought thousands of machines in the early 1980s and parents began buying home computers and educational software for their children. Whether or not children actually learned any more or any differently as a result of using computers (at home or at school), educational improvement for children was another important motivation for acquiring a home computer. Indeed by 1984 when 7 million households (8 percent of all U.S. households) had a personal computer, software sales for games had dropped from 90 percent to 50 percent of total sales; self-improvement software (educational and home office) represented the other 50 percent.[9]

The number of households with a home computer had tripled from 7 million in 1984 to 22.6 million at the end of 1993 (24 percent of households), with most of those machines running more powerful and varied descendents of the entertainment and self-improvement software introduced in the first decade of home computers. The early days of the home computer, whether as toy or tool, emphasized personal control and independence from the rest of the world—people using a home machine did not have to share it with anyone else. They could write programs, play games, run educational software, do numerical calculations and word processing in their own home and on their own schedule. There was no need to stand in line at the video arcade, schedule time at the school computer lab, or "borrow" computing resources from an employer.

On-line Services

The early home computers could not store much data in a permanent form. The data required to store a book, an encyclopedia, or a map database was too bulky for these machines. Kitchen databases for recipes, menu planning, and grocery lists seemed more trouble than they were worth. The same home users who bought VisiCalc for spreadsheet analysis would probably have been very interested in databases of financial information, news, and flight schedules. But these databases were too big to be stored on a home machine, needed to be updated frequently, and were owned and maintained by commercial interests whose business models were based on providing access to commercial mainframe customers.

During the 1980s, businesses such as Compuserve, Prodigy, and America Online began providing households with on-line access to commercial databases.[10] Each on-line service provided an interface to a variety of different commercial databases such as airline schedules, newswires, and financial information. A customer, using a modem, made a telephone call to connect the home computer to the on-line service's mainframe computer. Once the call connected the two machines, the home customer could see information from any of the provided databases displayed on the screen of the home machine. By 1994 an estimated 3.8 million households subscribed to on-line services, representing about 17 percent of all households with computers.

Internet and the Web By 1987, ten years after the introduction of the Apple II, all the elements of the home information revolution seemed to be in place. Home computer hardware had continued to increase in power. Large disks and CD-ROMS supplied bulk data and storage. Entertainment and self-improvement were supported by extensive software. The most compelling ten-year forecast at that time would simply extend these elements directly into 1997. Children and teenagers would use more powerful home machines for ever-more engaging games and learning. Adults would use the machines for more home information management and analysis. Everyone would do more word processing and document preparation. And, via commercial services, people would access more databases. While all of these trends did indeed continue as forecasted through 1997, there were two big surprises.

The first surprise—electronic mail—echoed an earlier surprise experienced by the computer science research community in the early 1970s. In order to share scarce research computing resources at that time, the U.S. Department of Defense Advanced Research Projects Agency (ARPA) sponsored the development of networking technologies to link remote computers together. Using this technology, researchers at any computer "on the Net" could remotely log-in to any other computer on the net and run jobs or exchange files.[11] To people's surprise the most popular and extensively used feature of the ARPANET was electronic mail (e-mail), a way for people to send text-based messages rapidly and conveniently to other people or groups.[12]

On-line services companies defined their business as providing database access to household customers hungry for information. Like the ARPANET developers, they did not realize that people were also eager to talk with one another.[13] Most of the on-line services viewed e-mail as a necessary but unprofitable and technically uninteresting feature. They imposed strict limits on the size of people's mailboxes, shut down service during high-volume periods, censored people's messages to groups, and terminated service to customers who complained about unsatisfactory e-mail performance.[14]

Only one on-line services company, America Online (AOL, established in 1989), actively courted households whose members wanted to communicate with one another (via e-mail, electronic discussion forums, and electronic chat rooms) as well as acquire information via databases. After Netscape introduced its browser in 1994, AOL grew to more than 10 million subscribers by 1997, representing more than half of the 19 million households with on-line services in that year. AOL sales rose from $40 million in 1993 to $105 million in 1994, and to $394 million in 1995. In 1997 the average subscriber spent 51 minutes a day logged in to AOL; 43 percent of that time was spent for sociability (e-mail and chat), 57 percent was spent for information and entertainment (content sites and "surfing" the web).[15]

The second surprise was the introduction of the World Wide Web in 1990 and that of the browser in 1994; both innovations together provided an easy way to find and publish information on the Internet. The Web created a positive information feedback loop for its users. Because it was easy to find information, more people "surfed the Web" looking for information. Because more people were looking for information, more people and organizations published information on the Web for them to find. In 1993 there were 150 web sites, and by the end of 1997. There were 2.45 million Web sites.[16] People could use their home computer and a Web browser to order a book, download a form from the IRS, submit a college application, follow a sports team, read a presidential proclamation, or "publish" their wedding pictures. The stand-alone home computer gave household members personal control in their pursuit of entertainment and self-improvement. On-line services gave them access to large databases and electronic sociability. The World Wide Web gave them personal control of on-line information-based transactions.

Access to Household Computing Varies by Social Status

Although access to home computers continued to increase by the end of the twentieth century, access and the increase in access were not homogenous across social categories. Like access to printed materials in the eighteenth and nineteenth centuries and access to household telephones in the first half of the twentieth century, social status influenced access to home computers and how they were used. Because using a home computer is perceived to lead to such socially desirable consequences as better-educated children and a more-informed citizenry, inequality in access is viewed as a public policy problem.

Gender Inequality

The two earliest routes for computers into the homes—electronics tinkering and video arcade games—were unfamiliar and unappealing territory for females. By the early 1980s boys outnumbered girls in programming courses and computer camps by eight to one, and boys monopolized computers at school. Game software for home machines offered "an array of land battles, space wars, and other forms of destruction."[17] And even educational software relied heavily on sports or battle metaphors. By the late 1980s, girls were still less likely than boys to have a computer in the home. And even when they did have a computer at home, girls did not derive as much educational benefit from it as did boys, based on standardized test scores and school grades.[18]

After 1989 the gender gap in access to home computing closed, so that by 1995 males and females were equally likely to have a computer in the home. Men still made more frequent use of it than did women, however, both for stand-alone activities and for on-line activities.[19] But girls nineteen years old and younger used it as frequently as boys, leading observers to conclude that the gender gap in home computing could disappear entirely with the next generation. Usage styles and preferences continued to differ, however, which may lead to a continuation of differences in educational outcomes.[20]

Income Equality

During the 1980s and 1990s, when tens of millions of computers were bought by households, their acquisition varied greatly by household income level in the United States (see table 8.2). By 1993 only 7 percent of the lowest income-quartile households (annual income of $15,000 a year or less) had a computer while about 55 percent of the highest income-quartile households (annual income of $50,000 or more) had a computer.[21] By 1997, although more households at all income levels had a computer, the "digital divide" had actually increased: about 13 percent of households with an annual income of $15,000 a year or less had a computer in 1997, whereas about 68 percent of households with an annual income of $50,000 or greater had a computer.[22]

Racial and Ethnic Inequality

Home computers were also unequally distributed across households of different racial or ethnic status in the United States. In 1993 more than 30 percent of whites and 37 percent of Asians lived in a household with a computer, whereas only 13 percent of Hispanics, Blacks, and Native Americans lived in a household with a computer. Statistically controlling for other factors—such as income and level of education—that are also associated with racial or ethnic status reduces the disparity attributable exclusively to racial or ethnic status. Net of other factors, about 29 percent of whites and 31 percent of Asians lived in households with computers in 1993; between 17 percent and 19 percent of Hispanics, Blacks, and Native Americans did so.[23]

In 1997 white households were still more than twice as likely (40.8 percent) to own a computer as black (19.3 percent) or Hispanic (19.4 percent) households. As with income, the digital divide between racial groups in household computers had increased since 1994. Even at income levels above $75,000, white households are more likely to have computers (76.3 percent) than are black households (64.1 percent).[24]

That vicarious self-improvement (i.e., improvement for one's children) is a motivation for home computer ownership is signaled by the fact that by 1997 almost twice as many households with children owned a personal computer as did households without children.[25] And in those families with children, the children spent more time using the computer than did their parents.[26] To be sure, children more often used the computer for entertainment rather than for learning.[27] But parents believed that computer use would also improve children's school performance and help prepare them for twenty-first-century careers. This belief was probably fueled partly by vendor advertising campaigns targeted to parents that delivered precisely those messages, and partly by schools embracing first stand-alone computers, then the Internet, as important learning technologies.

The only large-scale research on the effects of home computers on children's educational performance, conducted midway through the twenty-year history of home computers, did document positive educational effects, thus validating parental optimism. However after statistically controlling for other household variables (such as economic status) that are also associated with children's educational performance, the net effect of household computers was found to be rather small, an increase of about 3 percent to 5 percent in standardized test scores.[28]

In the 1990s household and school Internet access impelled two apparently contradictory public policy orientations toward children being on-line. One was that children and teens should be encouraged to use the Internet for self-improvement. In 1996 and 1997, "NetDay" programs saw volunteers from high-technology companies and politicians, including Vice President Al Gore, wiring public school buildings for Internet access. Approximately 50,000 schools, 10,000 business sponsors, and 100,000 volunteers participated to wire an average of six classrooms per school in four NetDays.[29] Also various governmental subsidies have been authorized to reduce economic disparities in household (and school) Internet access. But while encouraging Internet access, public figures also believe they must protect children and teens from unsavory people and content they could encounter on-line. The federal Communications Decency Act was passed in 1996, making it illegal to provide "indecent" or "patently offensive" material to minors via the Internet. While this legislation was ruled unconstitutional in the same year, officials continued to press for protection through requiring that publicly funded programs use filtering software to block

Table 8.2 Level of Access and Use of Computers in U.S. Households, 1984–1997

Access, use, and age	Number				Percent			
	1984	1989	1993	1997	1984	1989	1993	1997
Households with computer	6,980	13,683	22,605	38,748	8.2	15.0	22.8	36.6
A. All races								
3 to 17 years (14 years in 1997)	51,482	52,667	55,827	47,961				
Access to a computer at home	7,697	12,082	17,829	27,750	15.3	24.2	31.9	46.6
Use home computer	5,679	8,547	12,527	18,774	74.2	71.1	74.7	80.7
Use computer at school	12,284	20,664	28,848	30,839	28.0	46.0	60.6	70.7
Use computer any place	15,542	24,216	32,659	34,800	30.2	46.0	58.5	72.5
18 and over (15 in 1997)	169,786	180,123	187,405	207,730				
Access to a computer at home	14,999	29,615	47,988	85,730	9.1	17.3	25.6	41.3
Use home computer	7,757	16,758	30,165	62,240	53.3	58.4	65.6	72.9
Use computer at school	3,839	5,564	7,439	18,730	30.8	43.6	53.8	65.9
Use computer at work	24,172	40,245	51,106	64,330	24.6	36.8	45.8	49.0
Use computer any place	31,099	50,668	67,397	n.a.	18.3	28.1	36.0	n.a.
B. White								
3 to 17 years (14 years in 1997)	41,915	42,262	44,242	37,600				
Access to a computer at home	7,048	10,773	15,821	19,980	17.1	26.7	35.8	53.0
Use home computer	5,186	7,685	11,248	16,310	74.0	71.7	75.3	81.6
Use computer at school	10,827	17,463	23,799	24,710	30.3	48.2	62.7	72.5

Use computer any place	13,782	20,662	27,178	n.a.	32.9	48.9	61.4	n.a.
18 and over (15 and over in 1997)	146,693	154,236	158,927	173,500				
Access to a computer at home	13,782	26,902	42,814	77,500	9.6	18.3	26.9	43.9
Use home computer	7,151	15,462	27,417	55,590	53.4	59.2	66.7	73.5
Use computer at school	3,269	4,709	5,980	14,708	31.0	43.6	53.1	65
Use computer at work	21,795	35,977	45,326	55,899	25.3	37.8	47.1	50.3
Use computer any place	27,940	45,264	59,532	n.a.	19.0	29.4	37.5	n.a.
C. Black								
3 to 17 years (14 years in 1997)	7,721	8,212	8,836	7,793				
Access to a computer at home	461	806	1,152	1,880	6.1	10.6	13.0	24.4
Use home computer	350	518	721	1,382	75.9	65.0	67.3	73.5
Use computer at school	1,032	2,416	3,786	4,583	15.9	35.1	50.9	63.9
Use computer any place	1,254	2,622	4,031	n.a.	16.2	31.9	45.6	n.a.
18 and over (15 and over in 1997)	18,403	20,007	21,361	24,750				
Access to a computer at home	780	1,573	2,949	5,407	4.4	8.4	13.8	21.8
Use home computer	406	733	1582	3,618	54.0	50.6	56.8	67.9
Use computer at school	367	506	909	2,843	26.1	38.9	54.8	69.4
Use computer at work	1,724	2,990	4,072	5,647	18.3	27.6	36.1	39.5
Use computer any place	2,259	3,673	5,335	n.a.	12.3	18.4	25.0	n.a.

The 1997 data were collected in October 1997 in the Current Population Survey (CPS), which is an ongoing monthly survey of approximately 55,000 households. The 1993 data were collected in the October 1993 CPS. The 1993 and 1997 data are consistent with Current Population Reports (CPR), Series P-23 No. 171, "Computer Use in the United States: 1989" and No. 155, "Computer Use in the United States: 1984." The 1997 data were derived from the U.S. Census Department on-line database; the 1993, 1989, and 1984 data are based on Census reports. As with all sample surveys, the CPS estimates may differ from the figure that would have been obtained if a complete census had been taken on the same date using the same schedules, instructions, and enumerators.

access to objectionable sites. The tension between the potential for information technology to uplift and improve and the potential for it to corrupt and degrade has been a persistent theme in U.S. society since the nineteenth century. Children's use of the home computer and the Internet provide just the most recent variation of the theme.

Another tension played out in the family household is that between the potential for the home computer to strengthen family ties by bringing the family closer together and the potential to weaken those ties by encouraging family members to pursue independent interests. By the mid-nineteenth century, information abundance allowed people to express their individuality in their choice of what to read. Family members could choose different newspapers, tracts, and books, depending on their interest.[30] In the first half of the twentieth century, family members gathered around their one family radio to listen together to the same programs. All family members listened to the same program at the same time.[31] By the late 1990s, when the average U.S. household had 5.6 radios, listening together had become exceedingly uncommon. After World War II television replaced radio as the household information technology with the potential to alter family dynamics. Although television was marketed as a way to bring household members together, research has consistently documented that an increase in television viewing has resulted in a decrease in family communication.[32]

In 1982 the Family Opportunity Act was introduced in the U.S. House of Representatives; the act was to provide a $500 tax credit to U.S. households purchasing home computer hardware and software, in order "to keep families together more often and to strengthen loosening family ties."[33] Although the legislation did not pass, the vision behind its rhetoric evoked the same hope as that held for the earlier household technologies of radio and television. Unlike those earlier technologies, whose design at least afforded the opportunity for shared experience, the household computer was intentionally designed to be used by only one person at a time. Indeed in its 1983 "Computer of the Year" issue, *Time* characterized the family computer as "kind of like the bathroom. If someone is using it, you wait your turn."[34]

If family members do not share the household computer at the same time, a simple time-displacement argument suggests that a family member who spends more hours at the computer would have fewer hours available for other activities, including family interaction. Newspaper accounts and letters to advice columnists describe the agony of "computer widows" whose husbands disappeared from the family to spend all their time in front of the home-computer screen. Although such stories are colorful, they are not unique to home computers. The "football widow" was deserted by her television-engrossed spouse; the "baseball widow," by her radio-engrossed one.

Systematic research suggests that the time spent using a home computer in part displaces television viewing but not reading books, newspapers, and magazines.[35] To the extent that television viewing is an individual activity rather than one embedded in family interaction, increased computer use would not diminish family interaction. But increased computer and Internet use can also directly diminish family interaction. Both self-report surveys and longitudinal studies using logs of computer time show that family members who spend more time using the home computer are likely to spend less time interacting with other household family members.[36]

Changing Boundaries between the Household and the Larger World

The Office–Home Boundary

Before home computers, the primary technology for bringing office work into the home was the briefcase. In the 1960s and 1970s, many white-collar workers and professionals worked at home in the evenings at least occasionally, usually reading or writing.[37] In the earliest days of the home computer, before corporations began providing PCs in offices, small numbers of managers and professionals purchased home computers expressly for work-related purposes and brought work home from the office to run on their home machines. As previously discussed, VisiCalc was probably the most popular software for this activity.

Beginning in the late 1970s, commentators expected that household computers would allow large numbers of workers to telecommute from home.[38] Using a home computer connected to an employer's mainframe by a dial-up telephone line, employees could do their information work just as productively at home as in the office. Policy-makers and corporations saw telecommuting as a mechanism for energy conservation (through reducing the consumption of gasoline) and financial savings (through reducing office overhead). They believed employees would benefit through reduced expenses for commuting, clothing, and meals, and increased availability to other household members.

While all these benefits could possibly accrue as a result of telecommuting, by the mid-1990s the number of employees using their home computer for full-time telecommuting was still quite small. Energy consumption had become less important as gasoline prices returned to relatively low levels. Employers and employees both came to recognize the value of "face-time," the time spent in the office engaged with co-workers and managers. And being available to other household members during the day was considered a mixed blessing. While the numbers of full-time telecommuters remained small, in the late 1990s the laptop computer joined (or replaced) the briefcase as a technology for bringing work home. Workers also used the laptop as a way to stay in touch with the office, via e-mail.

Employees have used their employers' computing resources for extracurricular activities since at least the late 1960s, when computer science researchers began playing "Space Wars" on university computers. In the mid-1970s, "swarms" of people used university machines to play "Adventure"—a fantasy, questing game, which later spawned an entire industry of adventure games.[39] In the 1980s several popular game programs for personal computers came with a "disguise" feature, which could be used to mask the game screen swiftly with a spreadsheet screen if the boss walked into the office.

Whenever people gained network access at work, they used the net for extracurricular reasons as well as for work-related ones. Scientists who were members of the early ARPANET community used research machines to send personal e-mail, play games, and participate in non-technical electronic discussions.[40] An early study of corporate e-mail categorized 40 percent of email messages as having a "non work" topic. Moreover, most of the "non work" messages were not one-to-one messages but were from electronic groups devoted to such topics as movie reviews, wine tasting, and social clubs.[41] Most corporations have policies forbidding or regulating non work-related use of corporate computing resources, but small violations are usually undetected or unremarked.

The Home–Commerce Boundary

Beginning in 1994 with the availability of "browser" software for the Web, households could use their home computers to connect directly to retail stores and services. Because household access to the Web was available for only the final two years in the period of this chapter, good data on its uses and effects are not yet available. Many commentators assert that the Web will both encourage more households to buy computers and change patterns of use. If so, there are likely to be three major ways in which household behavior will change with respect to commerce.

The first is that people will be able to access information about products and services at their convenience, independent of time and geography. Many consumer goods and services companies are posting information for potential customers on their Web sites. Households can find out about houses for sale in a particular area, with mortgage terms and rates; books or records available at the nearest relevant store; and price and product information for sewing machines or power tools, and the address of the nearest distributor. When comparable information for different retailers is easily available on-line, comparison shopping becomes easier. And customers can become better informed consumers.[42]

The second major way in which household behavior may change is that people may engage in on-line purchase transactions, bypassing or eliminating some face-to-face transactions entirely. The telephone and postal service have long supported some kinds of home shopping. The difference here is twofold: a much broader scope of goods and services is likely to be offered via the Web, with more up-to-date and complex product information; and intermediaries between the customers and the product are likely to be Reduced. Thus, for example, a household member may use an on-line brokerage service to buy or sell securities with less delay—and paying a lower commission—than trying to reach a human broker on the phone. On-line customers accounted for about 17 percent of all retail stock trades in 1997.[43] Or a family member might use an on-line bookstore to purchase a book at any hour of the day or night. The technology underlying the Web makes it easy to search and display the bookseller's wares in many different ways. In addition to the common categories found in physical bookstores and paper-based catalogues such as genre, author, customer popularity, and topic, customers can also see such categories as "other books purchased by people who bought the book I'm considering," "books similar to ones I've purchased from this site previously," "books favorably reviewed by specified reviewers, publications, or prize committees."

Changing the ease with which a family member buys a product or service is not by itself sociologically interesting. More interesting—and the third major behavioral change anticipated—is the possibility that extensive use of home-computer–based commerce could change some of the asymmetries between household consumers and businesses. Families whose rural or inner-city location gives them relatively limited access to goods and services (because merchants choose not to locate nearby) may enjoy increased purchasing power. Families in any location may have increased opportunity to talk with other consumers about their experiences, advice, or warnings. By 1997, some commercial Web sites had begun to support chat rooms or discussions forums where potential customers could communicate electronically with sales personnel or other customers. Self-organizing electronic interest groups not affiliated with any particular vendor afford an opportunity for people to trade advice or experiences about purchases relevant to members of the particular interest group. Merchants may also benefit by using these groups as a form of unobtrusive market research.

The Home–Government Boundary

Households can also use their home computers to connect to local, state, and federal government agencies with the same three types of potential effects as is the case for commerce. Beginning in 1995 many government agencies began providing on-line information about their operations. Citizens could see up-to-date information about such matters as schedules for local transit, refuse collection, city council meetings, congressional or agency hearings. They could also see minutes or reports of meetings, press releases, and other public documents. Although the government sector has no direct analogy to comparison shopping in the commercial sector, commentators hope that the easy availability of government information on-line could lead to a better informed citizenry just as people could become better informed consumers. Such outcomes are purely speculative at this point, however.

Analogous to on-line purchase transactions for commerce, households can or will be able to engage in on-line governmental transactions. In a small number of municipalities residents can already pay utility bills on-line (for example, in Blacksburg, Virginia) or apply for a building permit (for example, in Cleveland, Ohio). At the federal level, citizens can download tax forms. The Internal Revenue Service (IRS) home page, displayed in figure 8.2, illustrates two ways in which computer-mediated interaction with government agencies can differ from other mediated forms of interaction with those agencies. First, if a citizen has access to Web technology, time and space are no longer constraints to the interaction. All forms are accessible twenty-four hours a day. Second, the "voice" with which the agency interacts with citizens can be modified relatively easily. This may lead to some confusion on the part of citizens. Note the strangely informal tone of the IRS site. Although this will surely be modified, it seems more than slightly disconcerting to have the federal revenue service display such a jocular, "aw shucks" tone.

Again, as with the case of commerce, merely moving transactions on-line is not likely to cause a noticeable change in the relationship between households and government. What it may do is increase opportunities for citizens to connect with one another electronically about civic or governmental issues Again, a small number of municipalities have established electronic discussion groups or forums where residents or citizens can discuss issues of mutual concern such as affordable housing or local pollution. Special interest nongovernmental organizations also offer opportunities for people to connect electronically. The Civic Practices Network, for example, lets people share ideas about grassroots projects throughout the United States.

Electronic Sociability and Affiliation

Household members with a network connection can access not only information on-line, they can also access other people. Some people use e-mail to stay in touch with distant family members and friends. When most colleges and universities provided their students with e-mail accounts by the early 1990s, household e-mail became a popular way for parents to stay in touch with their college-attending children. In one national survey conducted in 1995, more than one-third of respondents who had used the Internet for at least a year reported using it several times every month to contact family members.[44] Unlike the telephone, which helps sustain only preexisting relationships, the networked household computer also lets people initiate new relationships—even with previously unknown relatives. Some people use Internet search programs to find others who share their (presumably uncommon) last name, then send an e-mail query to introduce themselves and discover if they are related. Although "meeting" previously unknown family members via the Internet does occur, more common is the case of a first encounter with a stranger in an electronic forum or discussion group and, over time, developing a private e-mail relationship with that person. In the same national survey conducted in 1995, 14 percent of Internet users report that they had friends whom they knew only through the Internet. A majority of these respondents (60 percent) also reported meeting at least one of these friends face to face.[45]

Electronic mail lets household members communicate with friends and family members, but electronic bulletin boards, distribution lists, chats, and forums let people participate in discussions, arguments, or

PRINTED DAILY AND IT'S FREE! | DEPARTMENT OF THE TREASURY *Presenting The Fastest, Easiest* | INTERNAL REVENUE SERVICE *Tax Publication On The Planet* | AND YOU DON'T HAVE TO RECYCLE!

THE DIGITAL DAILY

FASTER THAN A SPEEDING 1040-EZ . . . OCT 29, 1998 (168 DAYS UNTIL APRIL 15TH).

[Text Only Version]

IN TODAY'S ISSUE

Local News Net

E-Mail News Service

1998 Tax Products CD-ROM

IRS Problem Solving Day
Relief From The Symptoms Of Long Standing Tax Problems.

TAX*interactive*

Learn More About How Federal, State, And Local Taxes Work For You.

BACK ISSUES

IRS
Department of the Treasury
Internal Revenue Service

Veteran Recruiter Recruited On-Line By IRS Recruiters

The IRS Wants You, Too!

QUANTICO, VA.   Marine recruiter Sgt. Sam Fidelis enlisted his last raw recruit today. Next week civilian Sam Fidelis signs on for a new career, with the IRS.

"I give the Corps a full day, everyday", explained the short timer, "so I didn't have a lot of time left over to research the job market." Sam put his recruiting experience and computer skills to use searching the internet for a new career. "I was surprised to learn that the IRS is not just about taxes.", Sam continued, "They had positions for Y2K programmers, engineers, economists, and one just right for me!"

Sam learned that the Internal Revenue Service is striving to make *service* more than just a name; and to get there they need motivated, skilled, innovative employees - like Sam ... and you. "Be all that you can be - and more.", Says Sam,

"Check out the IRS *Employment Opportunities* today!"

At ease Sam.

Tax Stats Tax Info For You Tax Info For Business
Electronic Services
Taxpayer Help & Ed   Tax Regs In English IRS Newsstand
Forms & Pubs
What's Hot Meet The Commissioner Comments & Help
Site Tree

Previous   Next   Home   Search   Help!   Email

Sunday, 27-Sep-1998 15:33:00 EDT

debates with hundreds or thousands of other people whom they could never meet face to face. Commercial services support proprietary groups that are open only to their subscribers. Beginning in the 1990s they also offered access to Internet groups, sometimes called Usenet groups. Usenet groups were first created on the ARPANET in 1979 and, at that time, were accessible only via university computer accounts. In 1980 there were fifteen ARPANET groups and ten posts a day; in 1987, 5,000 groups saw 2.5 million bytes of posts a day; in 1992, 2.5 million people read Usenet groups totaling 35 million bytes a day.[46] Commercial services such as The Source began offering dial-up access to electronic communication in 1979, although in the early 1980s few households participated relative to the number of people on Usenet. The WELL, an active electronic community begun in 1985, was characterized by one of its members as like a "family of invisible friends."

By 1995 more than 100,000 electronic discussion groups were available to anyone with Internet access.[47] Groups were self-organized around technical topics (for example, hardware, software, or languages); hobbies and entertainment (for example, soap operas, sports teams, bicycle racing, or dog breeding); social, cultural, and religious orientations (for example, Lebanese culture, Catholicism, or gay and lesbian groups); civic and political causes (for example, neo–Nazism, marine pollution, or home schooling); and physical, mental, or emotional ailments (for example, traumatic brain injury, diabetes, or depression). Although people could use their home computer to access databases of information about such topics, on-line groups flourished because people like to talk to and hear from other people with opinions, experiences, and information relevant to topics they care about. For many household members, when determining whether to continue paying for an on-line service, having an electronic connection to other people was a more important decision factor than access to information.[48]

Figure 8.2 A "Cool" IRS. Following extensive criticisms of its treatment of U.S. taxpayers by both the press and the U.S. Congress, the Internal Revenue Service began an extensive public relations campaign in the late 1990s to improve its image. One of the first things it did was to develop a friendly Web site on the Internet that presented a far different image of the IRS than the agency had ever had before. Like many other organizations of the time, it used the Internet to reach out to the American public. This figure illustrates the IRS home page as of October 29, 1998. Address: www.irs.ustreas.gov/prod/cover.html.

Some local government electronic sites offered discussion forums as well as access to the kinds of local government information described in the previous section, thereby giving residents the opportunity to participate in local community discussions from the convenience of their home. As of 1997, however, most electronic groups were composed of people who did not share a common geographic location. Indeed the only attribute they necessarily shared in common, other than network access, was an interest in the topic of the particular group. In fact, the text-based nature of electronic communication eliminated or attenuated most information about the people communicating— other than the words they typed. At its best, this meant that people could be judged solely by their words and not by other personal characteristics such as race, gender, age, or appearance. At its worst, this meant that people could forget that other human beings were reading their words, leading to thoughtless remarks and inflammatory behavior. The absence of personal information in electronic communication was aptly characterized in a 1993 *New Yorker* cartoon, which noted that, "On the Internet, nobody knows you're a dog" (see figure 8.3).

Electronic groups are typically characterized by egalitarian, free-wheeling discussion. Anyone may post a message to a group; anyone may respond, with the response visible to the entire group. Active groups often have more than 100 new messages posted each day. The energetic give and take in these groups led one on-line political activist to characterize the role of on-line discussion in home computing in this way:

> Ben Franklin would have been the first owner of an Apple Computer. Thomas Jefferson would have written the Declaration of Independence on an IBM PC. But Tom Paine would have published *Common Sense* on a computer bulletin board.[49]

Many on-line groups are characterized by lively, sometimes aggressive, sometimes inane posts. But some are also characterized by deep personal intimacy and support. Hundreds of groups, lists, and forums are explicitly devoted to offering support to people with medical or psychological ailments or afflictions. In these groups people ask and answer questions about pharmaceutical dosages and side effects, alternative treatment protocols, likely or unlikely complications. Whereas the topics of these posts could be found in medical databases, the

"On the Internet, nobody knows you're a dog."

Figure 8.3 Dog on the Internet. In 1993, cartoonist Peter Steiner pointed out an obvious reality about the Internet, that any person (or apparently any animal) could publish on the Internet without identifying themselves the way one normally did in publishing an article or book, or in signing a letter. This anonymity was a new feature of information exchange in the United States, raising concerns for accuracy and accountability at the same time that Americans were enthusiastically embracing the new medium. Courtesy *The New Yorker Collection* © 1993 Peter Steiner from www.cartoonbank.com. All Rights Reserved.

information is conveyed through personal experience and feelings.[50] Participants report deriving great psychological comfort from feeling that they are "not alone" when they participate in these groups. Because anyone can participate, there is no guarantee that information is accurate or advice is appropriate. Yet for people who might be homebound or isolated, the home computer with a network connection can offer solace and affiliation as well as entertainment, self-improvement, and information–based transactions.

Conclusion

The personal computer was not invented as a business machine; indeed, even the IBM PC was initially introduced as the "IBM home computer."[51] Yet the personal computer diffused much more rapidly and extensively into the business world than into the household. One plausible reason for the difference in diffusion rates is that the need for the information-processing tools provided by the personal computer was not as great in households as in business. A related reason is that the infrastructure for supporting computer users was also not as developed in households as in business. Observation of home computer users even as recently as 1996 documented that installing and using a home computer was a seriously daunting task for many people.[52] For those households that were early adopters, the twin motives of entertainment and self-improvement were clearly central.

The Web provided information-processing tools more attractive than those provided by stand-alone machines. The ability to access up-to-date information independent of time and geography across a wide variety of domains is likely to become attractive to large numbers of households. This may lead to changes in the current mix of information coming into the home via newspapers, television, magazines, catalogs, and other mass mailings. The ability to execute on-line information and commercial transactions may also become attractive.

Although some commentators speculate that on-line "content" will be completely taken over by large corporations, to this point one of the most amazing features of the "information revolution" has been its character as a "people's revolution" once the household computer went on-line. Although large, formal organizations controlled many Web sites by 1997, anyone with a home computer and a network connection could publish his or her personal Web site, complete with family pictures, favorite jokes, and advice of the day. Anyone could create a Web site about an obscure topic and be visited by the only 3, 30, or 300 other people in the on-line world who shared an interest in that topic. Hundreds of thousands of self-organizing electronic groups supported by chats, forums, distribution lists, and bulletin boards give people the opportunity to make connections with other human beings. Finding, building, and sustaining connections among groups of people via electronic communication reminds us that affiliation and sociability can be significant goals for information technology, just as important as efficiency and productivity.

9

The Information Age
Continuities and Differences

Alfred D. Chandler Jr. & James W. Cortada

This concluding chapter focuses, as did the introductory one, on the evolving infrastructure for the transmission of information in today's Information Age. Here we do not attempt to summarize or evaluate how the recipients used the information transmitted by the evolving broader information infrastructure. Those responses, the primary subjects in the preceding chapters, reflect the ever-changing economic, political, social, and cultural changes experienced in the United States. They will continue to do this in the future. Speculating on the future is really outside the scope of this book. However, a reader interested in the future should take notice of the patterns of the ebb and flow of information-handling in America's past and present.

There is a striking continuity in the infrastructural evolution that began with the postal system in the eighteenth century, then moved to the railway and the telegraph, the telephone, radio and television, and then computers both big and small. That continuity will probably have a significant impact on the ongoing evolution of the infrastructure of the Information Age for reasons that will be made clear later.

As we also describe in this chapter, just as there were continuities, simultaneously there were differences. The most obvious, dramatic, and important difference was software. This aspect of the history of information—the story of how software came into being and was deployed throughout the economy—represents the first major discontinuity with the past because it is very new in three ways:

- In what it is
- In how it came into the economy
- In how it was sold

The software exception is significant because it provides a body of evidence of the change we are entering at the start of the twenty-first century, the migration underway from the Industrial Age to the emerging Information Age. Just as the Conestoga wagon of the 1800s carried pioneers and goods into new territories, so too software and the Internet carry us into a different economy. Yet in balance, the continuities in the larger story—the role of the American people in adopting and using information—outweigh the discontinuities, and therefore it is to the continuities that we first turn our attention.

Continuities from Theodore Vail to Digital Convergence

These continuities sharply differentiate the coming of the Information Age from the evolution of the basic infrastructure for the Industrial Age. The foundations of the Industrial Age, based on the energy of fossil fuel, almost completely replaced the infrastructure of the Commercial Age, which was based on wind, water, and muscle power. The foundations of the Information Age, resting on electrical and electronic power, did not replace those of the Industrial Age, but instead built on them. The underlying difference in their evolution was that the technological innovations that built the infrastructure for the Industrial Age were commercialized by a large number and a wide variety of business and government enterprises, whereas the innovations of the Information Age were commercialized by a very small number of enterprises, mostly all private.

The creation and application of the electrical and electronic-based infrastructure evolved in terms of innovative organizational as well as technological concepts, and the resulting technical and organizational systems of the Information Age evolved from the telephone rather than the telegraph. The telegraph proved critical in the development of the Industrial Age; the telephone did not.

The telegraph quickly became an essential handmaiden to the operation and management of railroads. In fact, by the 1870s three-fourths of Western Union's operating activities were carried out by railroads. But in 1882 Western Union sold its manufacturing facilities to Bell Telephone and so had no learning base on which to develop and improve new operating technology and new organizational systems. In contrast, within a decade of its initial operation the Bell Telephone Company had already become the learning base on which much of the infrastructure of today's Information Age rests.

Nevertheless, the nation's telephone network evolved from the basic information infrastructure of the Industrial Age—from the U.S. postal system, its Railway Mail Service, and Western Union. The creative entrepreneur most responsible for this evolution was Theodore Newton Vail. His story vividly illustrates how technologies, people, and organizations—and their collective learnings and experiences—evolved consecutively over time, how the technological infrastructures and resulting organizational system (and those involved creating these infrastructures and the resulting systems) became the building blocks of the emerging Information Age. From Vail to today, a clear line of events suggests the nature of continuity at work. That is why the story is worth reviewing.

BEFORE VAIL BEGAN his short and most impressive career in the U.S. Mail Service, his occupation was that of a telegrapher. As a boy he had grown up in Morristown, New Jersey, a neighbor of his cousin Alfred Vail. Alfred had been Samuel F. B. Morse's co-worker and patent holder in the invention of the telegraph, and in fact Alfred was at the receiving end of Morse's famous first message, "What God hath wrought!" which in 1846 opened the nation's first telegraph line between Baltimore and Washington.

Twenty years later after graduating from Morristown Academy, Theodore Vail became a telegraph operator at Western Union's New York office. When his parents moved to Iowa in 1866, Vail went with them and became a telegraph operator on the Union Pacific Railroad. In 1886 Theodore moved to the U.S. Mail Service. His success in improving mail operations and routing in the trans-Mississippi west led in 1873 to his call to the Mail Service's Washington headquarters. Three years later his outstanding performance improving that service led to his appointment as its general superintendent.

In that same year, 1876, Vail came to know Gardner Greene Hubbard, who was running the newly formed Bell Telephone Company, and whom President Ulysses S. Grant had just appointed chairman of a committee to recommend to Congress improvements in the mail service. That appointment reflected Hubbard's broad knowledge of both the telegraph and the railway mail service, expressed in widely read articles he had published in 1873 and 1875.

When Vail arrived in Boston early in 1878, Hubbard's telephone enterprise was little more than a paper company. At that moment it was being challenged by the electric telegraph giant Western Union. It had almost no funds to meet the challenge nor to raise capital needed to assist in financing of the franchised local exchanges. During that spring Vail began his campaign to protect the Bell patents from Western Union. In July he incorporated the Bell Telephone Company, selling the new securities to local investors. Nevertheless, by January Bell Telephone faced bankruptcy.

Vail and the company's investors then turned to the Forbes financial group for support. Vail and the new investors replaced Hubbard with William Forbes as president. The powerful financial group provided funding initially to carry on the litigation that validated Bell's patents (and led to the withdrawal of Western Union from the telegraph business) and then for financing of local telephone exchanges throughout the nation.

From 1879 on Vail, as general manager, defined and executed the Bell Enterprises' initial strategy of growth. First, Bell's patents were vigorously enforced. The lawyers who had won the case against Western Union over the following years handled 600 legal suits and never lost one. Next came the building of a national telephone system. Here Vail's underlying plan was to finance the local franchised operating exchanges to assure their more rapid and systematic expansion than if these operating exchanges had to be funded locally. At the same time this method would provide a measure of control over them. The market on which Vail focused were offices of business enterprises and homes of businessmen, because those subscribers had the strongest need for local personal voice communication and could afford to pay the relatively high rates. Finally, in order to provide the telephones and switching equipment on a national scale, in 1881 Vail purchased Western Electric, a Chicago company that had since 1871 made electrical and telegraph equipment for Western Union.[1]

As the network expanded, Vail proposed that nearby existing operating exchanges be connected by linking them through long-distance lines. By extending these lines the Bell Company would have the competitive advantages of being the first to provide telephone services in a given area. Forbes, backed by the investors, protested that the costs would reduce dividends and threaten loss of control.

Frustrated, Vail submitted a letter of resignation in May 1885. After much discussion, Forbes and the board were able to get him to stay on to head a specialized new subsidiary, American Telephone & Telegraph Company (AT&T) to build the long-distance lines. When in 1887 he had completed the lines from New York to Albany and to Boston, he resigned.

Twenty years later in 1907, as described in chapter 3, a consortium of bankers headed by J. P. Morgan called Vail back to AT&T, which by then had become the parent company of the Bell System. After the basic Bell patents had expired in the 1890s, many local companies had entered the market. By 1907, AT&T was floundering financially and was unable to sell its bonds. The consortium of bankers gave Vail carte blanche to revive the company.

During the following decade Vail fashioned the modern Bell Telephone System that dominated telephone communications in the United States until the 1980s. By concentrating on the development of its long-distance technology his company created a "natural monopoly" to unify its several regional operating companies through Vail's slogan of "One Policy, One ystem, Universal Service." At his retirement in 1919, the Bell System was a giant enterprise. Its revenues were $1.2 billion, substantially larger than those of the Standard Oil Company of New Jersey and topped only by those of the United States Steel Corporation. Central to the system's successful operations was its manufacturing arm. By 1919 Western Electric had made AT&T, in the words of the historian Louis Galambos, "an innovative business, certainly one of the most technically advanced firms in the United States."[2]

AT&T's powerful technical capabilities lay in its own engineering department, which concentrated on long-term planning and research, and the Western Electric engineering department, which focused on the commercializing of new products and processes. In 1925 the two were consolidated into the Bell Telephone Laboratories. In the 1910s Western Electric's department had played a critical role in commercializing the audion invented by Lee de Forest, a device Margaret Graham (chapter 5) calls "the ancestor of all later vacuum devices." In 1946 the Bell Laboratories invented and in 1952 licensed the transistor, the power source for computer technology worldwide.

As Western Electric was developing its electronic equipment for long-distance telephones at the time of World War I, the work of Irving Langmuir and his associates at the General Electric Research Laboratory (formed in 1900) was turning the incandescent lamp into the vacuum tube. Westinghouse, the third leader in the U.S. electrical equipment industry, which had invested less in research than AT&T or General Electric, entered the race to perfect the vacuum tube by acquiring a patent from Edwin Armstrong for a crucial feedback circuit. In 1920 the three corporations—AT&T, GE, and Westinghouse—became the owners of the joint venture Radio Corporation of America (RCA).

With the sudden appearance of the new radio broadcasting and receiving technology, the three companies agreed in 1926 that AT&T was to concentrate on vacuum-tube technology for the telephone, and GE and Westinghouse would concentrate on that technology for radio broadcasting and receiving. In 1930 the latter two turned their radio and television involvement over to RCA. As noted in chapter 1, the evolving development of today's consumer-electronic industry worldwide can be told within the framework of the histories of RCA; one European company, Philips; and, after the collapse of RCA, the successful Japanese competitors led by Matsushita and Sony. In much the same way the evolution of the electronic developments in the telephone industry can be encompassed in the history of AT&T in the United States, its two competitors in Europe—Siemens and L. M. Ericsson—and Japan's Nippon Electric Company (NEC), which had been Western Electric's initial outpost in Asia (established in 1899).

In the creation of the digital computer industry, IBM played an even greater role than RCA did in consumer electronics. It set the standard worldwide in large mainframe computers and again for the personal computer (PC), both of which played a critical part in building the infrastructure of today's Information Age. As table 1.1 in chapter 1 shows, IBM remained in the 1990s the leader in revenues—or very close to the leader—in all seven of the industry's major sectors.

The Coming of Digital Convergence

In the 1990s these electronic-based industries were beginning to converge. As the computer infrastructure base was evolving during the 1970s and 1980s, as told in chapters 6, 7, and 8, so were the infrastructures in both the transistor-based telephone and the vacuum-tube–based radio and television. In the 1950s the introduction of coaxial cable was critical, because it provided an alternative to airwave frequencies to reach the television viewers. The cable-television industry began by providing radio and television communications in areas where local conditions prevented clear reception. Soon local cable stations, funded by local advertising, came into being.

Newspapers quickly began to play a significant role in the growth of cable television. Even before World War II, newspapers had expanded their advertising revenue base by acquiring local radio stations. In the 1950s they began to buy or build local television stations using airwave frequencies and then acquired them in more distant areas. Then they entered coaxial-cable television in much the same manner, often on a national scale. In addition, the newspaper-owned and independent cable companies began to develop and sell nationwide specialized channels via satellite that provided sports, weather, entertainment, and other programs.

In the telephone industry such changes came a little later. Here the heir of Theodore Vail's AT&T continued to enjoy its "natural monopoly" well into the 1970s. But in 1984 the Justice Department broke off the operating companies from AT&T's long-distance enterprise and made them independent entities. At the same time much smaller competitors, most notably MCI Communications and Sprint, moved aggressively into the long-distance market.

The U.S. Federal Communications Commission (FCC) further enhanced competition by opening a new array of bands for wireless communication, particularly through the use of cellular telephones. Easily mass produced, the new cellular telephones began to flood the market much in the manner of PC clones. In addition, the modem and other peripheral equipment permitted the flow of information provided by a microprocessor to be transmitted directly from computers through telephone wires.

The coming together of the products of the different players in the information infrastructure has been termed "digital convergence." As David B. Yoffie writes in the introduction to *Competing in the Age of Digital Convergence*, a collection of essays by a team of experts: "We define convergence as the unification of functions—the coming together of previously distinct products that employed digital technologies. The telephone and computer, for example, utilize digital technologies, but historically they have served completely different markets with entirely different functions. The process of digital convergence implies that a computer begins to incorporate the functionality of a communicating device, and the telephone takes on the functionality of a computer." Or, as noted in a later chapter of that book, such digital convergence enables "the same infrastructure to accommodate manipulation and transmission . . . of voice, video, and data."

The lesson learned from computers, Yoffie continues, has been "that success is more likely to emerge from *creative combinations* that build on complementary technologies." The enterprises "best positioned to influence this emerging global standard may be the existing incumbents, not start-ups who are pioneering these efforts. Today's dominant firms have the advantage of *scale economies* and the ability to bundle complementary technologies." Indeed, Yoffie adds, such convergence is already underway. A partial study of investments and acquisitions indicates that from January 1993 to June 1995 "$96 billion had been committed to projects in anticipation of convergence."[3]

In the spring of 1998 American Telephone & Telegraph made one such commitment by paying $31.8 billion to acquire TeleCommunications, Inc. (TCI), the nation's second largest cable television company. AT&T's chairman, Michael Armstrong, explained to its stockholders about this merger: "We plan to create an advanced broadband network that can deliver an array of communications, entertainment and information services directly to a million U.S. households. We consider this a critical step toward our goal of becoming the total communication source for our customers—supplying complete packages of local telephone, long distance, wireless, Internet, entertainment and next-generation digital services."[4]

Thus well over a century after Vail laid the foundation of the national telephone system, the company he established, American Telephone & Telegraph, is bundling the several basic technologies together in a single enterprise and a single piece of informational infrastructure. That bundling includes the information technology that has been the subject of much of this book—the evolution over the past century of the telephone (local and long distance), radio and television, the computer for data processing in the office and for messages and entertainment in the home—information that can converge through the Internet.

How then to account for this continuity in the creation of the infrastructure for the flows of information for well over a century? The key explanatory word is *system*—the U.S. Postal System, the Bell Telephone System, RCA's National Broadcasting System and its competitor Columbia Broadcasting System, IBM's System 360 and 370 and their clones. In microcomputers Bill Gates's operating system permitted Microsoft to move beyond the production of sets of major software applications—spreadsheets, databases, networking and the like—and reach what it terms the marketing of whole "business systems" and "personal systems."

These systems fit the Oxford English Dictionary's definition of *system*: "an organized or connected group of objects, a set of assemblage of things connected, associated, or interdependent, so as to form a complex unity; a whole composed of parts in an orderly arrangement according to some scheme or plan; rarely applied to a simple or small assemblage of things."[5]

These information systems, these complex unities, were created to assure a high-volume flow of information among millions of senders and receivers by means of written words, voice, and images. The systems, in turn, were embedded in large business enterprises: the Railway Mail Service in the Postal System; Bell's regional operating companies within the Bell Telephone System; one of the two national broadcasting systems that were created within RCA; the compatible mainframe systems within IBM and its competitors; and Gates' systems within Microsoft. In recent years the size of those enterprises that build and operate systems has grown through merger and acquisition and, above all, through digital convergence. The convergence has concentrated their technology and their operating know-how into a very small number of very large corporate enterprises.

It is this continuity and convergence that marks the contrast between the Industrial Age and the Information Age in the evolution of their broad underpinnings. The Industrial Age arrived after the railroad, telegraph, and steamship, and cable provided transportation and communication in historically unprecedented speed, volume, and regularity. These tools made mass production and mass distribution possible and therefore provided the initial opportunities to develop a multitude of the new capital-intensive technologies. The successful exploitation of these new technologies, in turn, led entrepreneurs to create modern enterprises that integrated production, marketing, and product development in a wide variety of industries which remained at the industrial core of the U.S. economy. Only in very few cases were those industries dominated by a single company in the manner of RCA and IBM.

In the electronic-based industries on which the Information Age rests, opportunities for individual entrepreneurs to build long-term competitive enterprises also came primarily with the introduction of a new technology. But these opportunities only occurred three times. The first was in the early 1920s with the coming of broadcasting. The second opportunity occurred in the late 1960s and early 1970s, after the introduction of IBM's System 360 and Digital's PDP series greatly expanded computerized data processing for commercial activities. The third took place in the first half of the 1980s with the sudden and unexpected coming of the multi-billion-dollar microcomputer industry. Since the mid-1980s, opportunities for entrepreneurial start-ups in hardware arose primarily in the production of specialized niche products or for providers of supplies and services to the large established core companies. So if history is any guide, a small number of large complex enterprises, particularly those experienced in building systems, will continue to lead in commercializing the hardware for today's Information Age.

On the other hand, the processes of producing and transmitting electronic-based information differ from those of producing and marketing industrial products because electronic information requires software. Radio and television receiving sets are useless until they make contact with the broadcasting media. So too a computing device is useless if it is not guided by an operating system which in turn serves a variety of information applications. It is precisely these differences in the industry's products that have differentiated, and will continue to differentiate, the evolution of the infrastructure of the Information Age from that of the Industrial Age. In fact, just as the multitude of Industrial Age industries could not operate without fossil fuel, so the much smaller number of those on which the Information Age rests could not operate without software. Therefore, software has provided—and will continue to provide on an even greater scale—entrepreneurial opportunities, much more than did any of the many new technologies that evolved during the Industrial Age. The variety of uses for different types of information becomes almost unlimited.

The Case of Software

In the history of information, one thing led to another so directly and intimately as to produce clear patterns of continuity. As we have demonstrated throughout this book, patterns of continuity remain. Yet there are also insights to be gained by looking for discontinuities—differences—when they exist. Software presents us with such a case because it is unique and has many points of departure from prior experience. It now also makes up an important component of U.S. business activity, serving as the symbol of the new information economy that so many commentators like to write about out. As one of the least capital-intensive and most knowledge-intensive of all information technologies ever to emerge, the software industry has from the start created wide and continuing opportunities for entrepreneurial start-ups. Given the size of this industry at the dawn of the twenty-first century, and the speed with which it has generated wealth and fundamentally changed how work is performed, understanding its pattern of evolution within U.S. society is crucial to any appreciation of this nation's economic future.

The most basic and fundamental observation one can make about software is that computers cannot operate without it. It is the fuel that drives computers, just as coal made trains operate, and gasoline ran motor vehicles. But unlike coal and gasoline, software represents instructions transmitted electronically through computers, making it difficult for many people to understand exactly what it is. But no understanding of software makes sense without some appreciation of what it is.

We have the admittedly difficult problem faced by all new industries of providing an architecture, or description of what that new industry is. The software industry, and its historians, still struggle with the issue.[6] At a superficial level, however, we can speak of three types of software. The first type is operating systems and their utilities. This is software that allows a computer to "talk" with all the parts of the machine and any equipment linked to it, from information-storage devices to telephone networks. No computer works without this software "traffic police." A second body of software consists of "programming languages" which, like human languages, allows one to command a computer to do something. In the United States more than 1,000 programming languages have been invented since the early 1950s, including all those that have been most widely used around the world. In this group one can also include tools that, like a human language, help users to use a programming language (e.g., dictionaries, translators, and so forth). The third group of software, and the one most visible to users of computers, consist of software tools called "application software." These tools, also called "packages," enable users to do data processing. An example is word processing for desktop computers. Another example would be major billing systems, resident on large mainframe computers that generate monthly credit-card bills.

Software evolved in all three categories over the entire half century for which this class of technology has existed. Operating systems emerged first and continued to evolve down to the present. By the end of the 1950s, a "golden age" of programming languages and related tools began to flow through the U.S. organizations that used large mainframe systems. Originally, applications were "written" by and for the user, but by the early 1960s applications began to appear as products that other firms could acquire. By the time the microcomputer became available in the late 1970s and early 1980s, application software for these small machines was being purchased as products, such as Microsoft's Windows (operating system) and Word (word processing). The variety of products from independent providers grew rapidly, and included such well-received software as WordStar (another word processing package); large software firms provided infrastructure software tools and application packages, such as Lotus Notes, with its e-mail and word processing products, in the 1990s.

The historical evolution of software was a four-phase process, occurring over the period from roughly 1950 to the present. In the first phase, lasting into the 1960s, most software was written to order by individual companies for their own use. Most of it was for accounting or manufacturing and process control, and it relied on the few tools developed primarily by computer manufacturers (e.g., operating systems and programming languages). There was no true software industry at that time. All these early software developments were tied to the machines of the day, often to the specific, one-of-a-kind computer in a user's organization.

The second phase began after IBM's System 360 family of computers appeared in the early 1960s and led the way to rapid technological standardization of both hardware and software in the computer industry. The System 360 deployed across the U.S. economy in the middle and late 1960s, picked up additional momentum in the early 1970s, and was joined by an emerging family of minicomputers, most notably the PDP series from Digital Equipment (DEC). The PDP series partially encouraged standardization for minicomputers much as the IBM systems did for large mainframes.

IBM's unbundling software from its hardware offerings in June 1969, together with DEC's reliance on customers to provide software, brought about a rapid rise in the availability of standardized software packages. A team of programmers could write a program for billing, for example, and know that there were thousands of firms that might buy the software because they all shared common technical standards. In other words, these systems were compatible, so a billing package running on one machine could also run on another—because the machines were becoming standardized and compatible. In this period a great deal of software was still homegrown, or available in versions delivered by hardware vendors and limited to products that ran only on specific classes of machines. And only a handful of firms specialized in the development and sale of software. But that specialization represented an important distinction from the past.

The availability of compatible systems led to the emergence of what we now call the software industry, then small but continuously expanding. It was composed of firms populated with former programmers from companies that had early experience in software development, or data processing hardware vendors who had gone out on their own. During the 1970s in particular, and continuing through the 1980s, a growing collection of software products became available for all sizes and types of computers. Thus occurred the historic shift from custom-written software to the installation of software packages.

Then, in the third phase of software evolution, there was a profound, historic explosion in the number of software vendors. This phase, beginning around 1982, was dominated by the arrival of the PC. In the new circumstances, the vast majority of software did not originate from the hardware vendors (Apple, IBM, Compaq, and others), but rather from independent producers that had no ties to any of the preexisting vendors of information technology in the United States. Developers came from preexisting computer centers or were even college students, like Bill Gates. Later, as they formed companies to market their products, what little capital they needed to get launched came from outside the computer industry, either from personal resources or venture capitalists. As table 1.1 in chapter 1 suggests, a huge new market for individual users materialized rapidly with a burst of new application producers.

Included in this list of new suppliers (nearly all American by the way) were Microsoft, Lotus, WordPerfect, and Borland, to mention just a few out of the many hundreds that by the early 1990s turned out thousands of software application products. In time, these companies provided products that mimicked the types available on mainframes: operating systems (e.g., Windows), programming languages (e.g., BASIC), applications (e.g., word processing and spreadsheet tools), and computer games. During the 1990s these products were expanded to include the capability of sharing data among multiple machines and then to become highly interactive network-based tools,[7] which, by the end of the 1990s, made PCs the entry and exit points on the Internet. More than a third of all U.S.-installed machines were equipped with both hardware and software tools with which to participate in on-line computing. The dominance of two operating systems in this period came, however, from the Microsoft/Intel combination for PCs and the combination of UNIX systems and RISC chips for workstations.

The expansion in function of software from the 1950s to the present is always closely linked to the availability of chip and memory capacities. In the world of computers, capacity has always meant the amount of data that could be processed in a computer within a period of time or the speed with which a piece of data could be processed. Chips provided processing speed, while memory and related components increased the volume of data that could be moved through a system. As the "horsepower" and memory of a computer expanded, so did the amount of software that could be run within the machine, and thus the more sophisticated the software could be, enriched with an increased functions or ability to process simultaneously greater volumes of data. In time, particularly with regard to PCs, the ability of software suppliers to expand their own work came to depend on some new basic technological platforms, primarily from Microsoft and Intel; this dependency explains to a large degree the importance these two firms achieved within the U.S. economy in the last two decades of the twentieth century.

To be sure, there were always those who challenged the emerging standards and the leading providers. The most obvious was UNIX, originally a combination of components of an operating system and collection of application tools, developed mainly by universities and by engineers at Bell Labs with the purpose of providing an open architecture. That is, UNIX was to offer tools that could work on any type of computer, freeing a user from dependence on any one supplier, such as IBM or DEC, while optimizing the freedom to perform innovative computing. In time, hardware components came in support of this approach, most notably RISC chips (discussed in chapter 6). Although UNIX had a large following, particularly within universities, the commercial success of Microsoft and Intel was what came to dominate the vast majority of desktop computing products and software tools used around the world.

The fourth phase in the evolution of software blossomed in the 1990s. It was characterized by the integration of nearly independent trends that were first evident during the third phase. Although we are very close to those events, and thus not yet aware of all the consequences that may be revealed by the passage of time, a few of the period's features are evident. The most obvious feature is networking. Software, and hence computing, evolved toward greater use of networks. Firms and government agencies in the mid-1990s had been creating PC-based internal networks—what came to be called intranets—which built on earlier experiences with private networks. During the second half of the 1990s, companies used the Internet to link intranets and private networks to each other, or to link companies together. The Internet grew out of the U.S. government's development of ARPANET in the 1960s to 1980s. The Internet thus became a public conduit for the flow of various types of information, from text and video to graphics and sound. The software to make all of that happen came either from government-sponsored projects like ARPANET or from independent software producers (e.g., Novell, Oracle, and Lotus).[8]

So the first major difference between software and its predecessor technologies is that most of the software emerged from new firms and from people who had not worked in companies that had supplied products such as computers. A second difference is the software itself. It is not metal, wood, or plastic, but rather an intellectual product. However, its features that best distinguish it from earlier information technologies are economic ones. All the other information technologies and products discussed in this book emerged from some previously existing industry, product, or firm. IBM's tabulating equipment later became IBM computers. Radio firms later became television companies. Television firms owned other channels of distribution of information (such as newspapers,) or formed partnerships with print media (e.g., Ted Turner's CNN with *Sports Illustrated*). But software was different.

Buried in the four phases of software's evolution were events that had the consequence of defining how the software industry would take shape. Let us summarize these events. First, in 1969, IBM stopped giving away software with its mainframes, thereby creating an environment—an opportunity—for others to compete against the mainframe manufacturers in the sale of all manner of software, from operating systems and programming languages to tools and applications. Hence the enormous growth in new entrants into what we would eventually call the software industry. At the same time, however, as desktop computers came into the marketplace, a new breed of software developers (including Bill Gates) showed up to supply these machines with tools.

But it was not until IBM made a second fateful decision that the software business for desktop machines exploded with growth. During 1980 and 1981, IBM developed its PC without use of proprietary software of its own design. In 1981 it publicly encouraged "the industry" (which at that time meant anybody in the economy who could program) to write software that would work in a PC, thereby driving up sales of IBM's desktop machines. That encouragement led to the development of software for these devices by small groups of individuals with few or no ties to the traditional computer industry or even to existing mainframe software developers. Their tools required little or no capital to develop; one just needed an inexpensive personal computer, some knowledge of programming, and a certain amount of time. Thousands of little start-ups began and, in time, factories built to duplicate copies of software for distribution. By the end of the 1990s, these companies were generating over a $100 billion a year in sales.

How software products are manufactured and sold differs from more conventional models for handling hardware. As with books, investment costs lie in the development of the first copy and, like books, all subsequent copies cost less to manufacture. But unlike books, software can be distributed at almost no cost; one can simply and quickly transmit it over a telephone line, that is to say, deliver it over the Internet. True, one can still buy a software package in a "cardboard box" from Microsoft in a computer software store in an American shopping mall—a throwback to pre-Internet distribution methods. But at the century's end, these old methods were coming under siege as people discovered the convenience of electronic distribution, which is new and different.

The arrival of the PC led to both enormous variety and volume of software packages as the number of machines sold each year proliferated into the millions around the world. Strategies borrowed initially from publishing, when combined with the ability to distribute inexpensively, kept the costs of the software products relatively low. By the late 1990s, hardware manufacturers were designing machines that met the needs of these software tools. This was the complete reverse of the practice during the Data Processing Era of the 1950s to the late 1980s, when software was written to conform to the specifications of machines—a practice, by the way, that was the cause of the "Y2K problem" in connection with the year 2000.

The wide acceptance of the Internet provided yet another clue that software represented a profound discontinuity with prior information-technology patterns of behavior. It points out, for example, as noted by both Cortada (chapter 6) and Nolan (chapter 7) that software, and data, often can be given away for free in exchange for some other sale of products or services. Software can be acquired and then copied or modified—in violation of conventional copyright laws—far easier than, for example a book.

We have alluded to the fact that capital requirements to enter into the software business are virtually nonexistent for PCs. One needs a machine, electricity, a desk and chair, and then a venture capitalist to get into business. That is largely why so many people could enter the software industry in its early years, particularly into the PC market. More and more, however, we are observing that important software tools, such as operating systems and increasingly sophisticated word processors, do require large development staffs and facilities (as Microsoft learned). But the principle still holds that capital requirements are not the barriers to entry into the market that they always were for computer hardware or complex radio and TV transmission equipment.

Although software development is very much a knowledge business, the personal commitment required to learn enough to write software is far less than is needed by a computer scientist who is developing either hardware or the next generation of computer chips. The teenager or college student who writes software and ultimately finds a distributor has far less training in the field than the engineer working on Intel's future product line. Yet both arrive at the same point: they create a marketable product. Thus, in economic terms, software so far has required less intellectual capital, hence offering fewer knowledge barriers to new entrants. Will that change? Perhaps, but what occurred in the 1980s and 1990s is that the barriers to entry remained far lower than for any previous form of information technology and products.

The one exception we are witnessing to this pattern of software development—and it may be only momentary—is Microsoft's dominance in the PC operating system segment of the software market. However, with alternative operating systems and architectures emerging (as of this writing, mostly driven by Java and Linux mostly driven by Java[9]), and a tendency of software firms to support adoption of technical standards to drive down costs and complexity, Microsoft faces the possibility of challenges to its dominance. This possibility exists because software historically does not long tolerate technical or economic barriers of the type one could identify for earlier information-processing technologies and products.

Because of all these various features of software, we conclude that it is a new element in the business and technological landscape of American information history, especially when linked to the emergence of the Internet. It would be easy, because we are so close to the events that led to the acceptance of the Internet, to overstate the discontinuity that software has with earlier patterns of information technology. But the laws of economic behavior have not been suspended in the case of software or the Internet, just as they were not suspended for the telegraph, railroad, telephone, radio, television, or even earlier knowledge tools such as newspapers and books. Copyright laws in the United States still pose barriers to infringement while simultaneously encouraging novelty and entrepreneurship on the part of software developers. Government policy of encouraging and supporting high-risk technological innovation remains a bedrock of federal policy. Software sales are still the most profitable when there is massive scale. Consolidations of software providers are leading to enhanced scale and scope that parallel what manufacturing and service-sector firms have experienced for decades. But of all the new high-technology businesses to emerge in the past half century, the one that seems to have the least number of economic or technological ancestors is software. It finds its origins in the new information-based sector of the American economy, in electrons and intellect, not in the wood and metal of earlier products.

The key historical observation to be made, even after our argument that software represented an important shift from earlier experiences (particularly in the third and fourth phases of evolution), is that the software industry became possible because of the constant flow of new technological developments that occurred. During the second, third, and fourth phases—and especially during the third and fourth—these technologies created almost all the entrepreneurial opportunities for the development of new applications and other software products. The American press often emphasizes the role of operating systems (e.g., Microsoft's Windows), but the new story coming from software is the development of applications.

An American Story

Information has always played a profound role in American society. It is essential for conducting the nation's politics and government, the national economy's activities, and the business of information-handling and communications. Information has been and remains an almost invisible part of the economic infrastructure of the nation—almost invisible because it is so ubiquitous, from the skills and knowledge people acquire to the visible newspaper on the kitchen table, the book of prayers by the nightstand, the telephone and PC on the desk at work.

As economists increasingly recognize, a great percentage of the nation's economic activity has involved the creation, transfer, and use of information. The authors of this book have told the story of how information technologies and their providers made it possible for information to play such a crucial role in U.S. society. This is not to say that such was not the case in other countries—these experiences have yet to be fully described by historians—but in the case of information in the United States we at least know of its importance. That importance grew as we moved through the twentieth century.

Now, as we enter a new century, we can view the Internet and its related technologies (e.g., telephony and computing) as a historical extension of much that has gone on in this nation for some 300 years. The dynamic input to the process that sped it along was the harnessing of electricity for the transmittal of information, more than 150 years ago. We can conclude that when a television journalist or some economist speaks about the Age of Information, historical experience suggests that he or she may be correct.

Historical evidence demonstrates that Americans have found information technology crucial to many of their business and personal activities. They have demonstrated a clear penchant to develop, exploit, distribute, and profit from a large array of information technologies—and Americans often to do this quicker than citizens in other economies. To a large extent the reason for this has been the economic adaptation that this nation historically has followed from its earliest days.

This is a nation that enjoys the taste of information. This is more more than just an appetite needed to sustain economic life. Across almost all aspects of their economic and political life, Americans have reached out to technology and built the business infrastructure necessary to deliver it to the economy, with which to solve problems or to define how things are done. It is no accident that the United States led in the exploration of space, not just for altruistic reasons, but for practical purposes. America's love affair with the automobile is as much an infatuation with how it works as it is with the freedom of movement it promises all drivers.

Patterns of the past and predictions of the future all come together in one inescapable reality, namely, that information and its technology have a long history in this country. Therefore, to a large extent, an appreciation of the Information Age in its historical perspective is crucial to our understanding of information's in the role of the transformation of the United States from the Colonial Period to the present.

Notes

Chapter 1

1. Maury Klein, *The Life and Legend of Jay Gould* (Baltimore, Md.: John Hopkins University Press, 1987), 196–197.
2. Menahem Blondheim, *News over the Wires: The Telegraph and the Flow of Public Information in America, 1944–1997* (Cambridge, Mass.: Harvard University Press, 1997), 117.
3. Thomas C. Cochran, *Railroad Leaders: The Business Mind in Action*, (Cambridge, Mass.: Harvard University Press, 1953), 35. The information on Vail's role in the beginnings of the Bell Telephone enterprise is from Robert V. Bruce's excellent biography of Alexander Graham Bell, *Bell: Alexander Graham Bell and the Conquest of Solitude* (Boston: Little, Brown, 1973): 228–231, 241–247, 258–260, 270–271, 281–283; and Arthur S. Pier, *Forbes: Telephone Pioneer* (New York: Dodd, Mead & Co., 1953), 117–121.
4. Edward C. Kirkland, *Men, Cities, and Transportation: A Study in New England History* (Cambridge, Mass: Harvard University Press, 1948), 1: 338.
5. Hugh G. H. Aitken, *The Continuous Wave: Technology and American Radio 1900–1932* (Princeton, N.J.: Princeton University Press, 1985), 480–482. The quotation that follows is from page 485. The remaining 3.9 percent went to individuals, mostly stockholders of American Marconi, which GE had acquired from the British wireless pioneer in 1919. The U.S. government had no financial or managerial presence in this corporate joint venture.
6. Mark Mason, *American Multinationals on Japan: The Political Economy of Japanese Capital Controls, 1899–1980* (Cambridge, Mass.: Harvard University Press, 1992), 37, 93–95.
7. Kenneth Bilby, *The General: David Sarnoff and the Rise of the Communications Industry* (New York: Harper & Row, 1986), 173–175.

8. In 1996 *Datamation* changed its classification of the industry's sectors. Workstations were reclassified as Server Suppliers and PCs as Table Tops. That year IBM was the number one revenue producer in all six sectors.

9. Marie Anchordoguy, *Computers Inc.: Japan's Challenge to IBM* (Cambridge, Mass.: Council on East Asian Studies, Harvard University, 1989), 111.

10. Mason, *American Multinationals in Japan*, 176–178.

11. Gordon E. Moore, "Intel—Memories and the Microprocessor," in *The Power of Boldness: Ten Master Builders of American Industry Tell Their Success Story*, ed. Elkin Blout (Washington, D.C.: Joseph Henry Press, 1996), 81.

12. "The PC Wars: IBM vs. the Clones," *Business Week* (July 28, 1986): 62, 69.

Chapter 2

1. David D. Hall and Hugh Amory, eds., *The Colonial Book in the Atlantic World* (Cambridge University Press: Cambridge, 2000), chap. 1–10.

2. Ibid., chap. 3, 8.

3. Ibid., chapt 10. Richard D. Brown, "Shifting Freedoms of the Press in the Eighteenth Century," in *Colonial Book*, ed. Hall and Amory, pp. 366–76, 592–94.

4. Richard D. Brown, *Knowledge Is Power: The Diffusion of Information in Early America, 1700–1865* (New York: Oxford University Press, 1989), chap. 1, 2.

5. Charles E. Clark, "Early American Journalism: News and Opinion in the Popular Press," in *Colonial Book*, ed. Hall and Amory, chapt. 10. Charles E. Clark, "Early American Journalism: News and Opinion in the Popular Press," 347–66, and Brown, "Shifting Freedoms," 366–76, 592–94. (Brown, "Free Speech in Colonial America").

6. Lawrence A. Cremin, *American Education: The Colonial Experience, 1607–1783* (New York: Harper & Row, 1970), 330–32, 404–06, 460–68, 499–516.

7. Harvey J. Graff, *The Legacies of Literacy: Continuities and Contradictions in Western Culture and Society* (Bloomington: Indiana University Press, 1987), 246–257; R. A. Houston, *Scottish Literacy and Scottish Identity: Illiteracy and Society in Northern England, 1600–1800* (Cambridge: Cambridge University Press, 1985), 162–92; Carl F. Kaestle et al., *Literacy in the United States: Readers and Reading since 1880* (New Haven, Conn.: Yale University Press, 1991), 3–32.

8. Philip G. Davidson, *Propaganda and the American Revolution, 1763–1783* (Chapel Hill: University of North Carolina Press, 1941); John C. Miller, *Sam Adams: Pioneer in Propaganda* (Boston: Little, Brown, 1936); Richard D. Brown, *Revolutionary Politics in Massachusetts: The Boston Committee*

of Correspondence and the Towns, 1772–1774 (Cambridge, Mass.: Harvard University Press, 1970).

9. Richard D. Brown, *The Strength of a People: The Idea of an Informed Citizenry in America, 1650–1870* (Chapel Hill: University of North Carolina Press, 1996), 8–9.

10. Lois G. Schwoerer, "Liberty of the Press and Public Opinion, 1660–1695," in *Liberty Secured?: Britain before and after 1688*, ed. J. R. Jones (Stanford Calif.: Stanford University Press, 1992), 202–230; Frederick Seaton Siebert, *Freedom of the Press in England, 1476–1776: The Rise and Decline of Government Controls* (Urbana: University of Illinois Press, 1952), chapters 14–17.

11. Brown, *Strength of a People*, 53.

12. Edmund S. Morgan and Helen M. Morgan, *The Stamp Act Crisis: Prologue to Revolution*, rev. ed. (New York: Macmillan, 1963).

13. Peter D. G. Thomas, *John Wilkes: A Friend to Liberty* (Oxford: Oxford University Press, 1996), chap. 10; Pauline Maier, "John Wilkes and American Disillusionment with Britain," *William and Mary Quarterly*, 3d Ser., 20 (1963): 373–395.

14. Carl F. Kaestle, "The Public Reaction to John Dickinson's *Farmer's Letters*," *Proceedings of the American Society* 78, pt. 2 (1963): 325–338; Brown, *Strength of a People*, 58–60.

15. Brown, *Revolutionary Politics in Massachusetts*, 95.

16. Brown, *Strength of a People*, 64.

17. Ibid., chap. 3.

18. Ibid., 66.

19. Ibid.,

20. Richard R. John, *Spreading the News: The American Postal System from Franklin to Morse* (Cambridge, Mass.: Harvard University Press, 1995), 25.

21. Brown, *Strength of a people*, 80–81.

22. John, *Spreading the News*, 48.

23. Brown, *Knowledge is Power*, 268–296; Donald M. Scott, "The Popular Lecture and the Creation of a Public in Mid-Nineteenth Century America," *Journal of American History* 66 (March 1980): 791–809; Scott, "Print and the Public Lecture System, 1840–1860," in William L. Joyce, et al., *Printing and Society in Early America* (Worcester, Mass.: American Antiquarian Society, 1983), 278–299; David Paul Nord, "The Evangelical Origins of Mass Media in America, 1815–1835," *Journalism Monographs*, no. 88 (May 1984); Nord, "Systematic Benevolence: Religious Publishing and the Marketplace in Early Nineteenth-Century America," in *Communications and Change in American Religious History*, ed. Leonard I. Sweet (Grand Rapids, Mich.: Eerdmans, 1994); Lawrence Thompson, "The Printing and Publishing Activities of the American Tract Society from 1825 to 1850," *Papers of the Bibliographical Society of American*, 35 (1941): 81–114; Karl Eric Valois, "To Revolutionize the World: The

American Tract Society and the Regeneration of the Republic, 1825–1877," Ph.D. diss., University of Connecticut, 1994; Peter J. Wosh, *Spreading the Word: The Bible Business in Nineteenth-Century America* (Ithaca, N.Y.: Cornell University Press, 1994); John, *Spreading the News*, 3–7.

24. Nord, "Evangelical Origins of Mass Media"; Wosh, *Spreading the Word*; Rosalind Remer, *Printers and Men of Capital: Philadelphia Book Publishers in the New Republic* (Philadelphia: University of Pennsylvania Press, 1996).

25. Richard D. Brown, "The Disenchantment of a Radical Whig: John Adams Reckons with Free Speech," in *John Adams and the New Republic*, ed. Richard Alan Ryerson (Boston: Massachusetts Historical Society, forthcoming).

26. John, *Spreading the News*, 269–272.

27. Leonard L. Richards, *The Life and Times of Congressman John Quincy Adams* (New York: Oxford University Press, 1986): 130.

28. Richard D. Brown, "The Emergence of Urban Society in Rural Massachusetts, 1760–1820," *Journal of American History* 61 (1974): 29–51.

29. Brown, *Strength of a People*, 133–153.

30. Alexis de Tocqueville, *Democracy in America*, ed. J. P. Meyer and Max Lerner, trans. George Lawrence (New York: Harper & Row, 1966), 174, 175, 495.

31. Brown, *Strength of a People*, 170–179, 183–187.

32. Nord, "Evangelical Origins of Mass Media"; Thompson, "The Printing and Publishing Activities"; Valois, "To Revolutionize the World"; Wosh, *Spreading the Word*.

33. John, *Spreading the News*, 5, 27; Brown, *Knowledge is Power*, p. 218; Richard D. Brown, *Modernization: The Transformation of American Life, 1600–1865* (New York: Hill & Wang, 1976), 166.

Chapter 3

For suggestions and advice, I am grateful to David Hochfelder, Alfred D. Chandler Jr., and James W. Cortada. None of these individuals should be held accountable for the ideas expressed in this essay, which are mine alone.

1. On the informational ancien régime, see Ian Steele, *The English Atlantic, 1675–1740: An Exploration of Communication and Community* (New York: Oxford University Press, 1986); and Richard D. Brown, *Knowledge is Power: The Diffusion of Information in Early America, 1700–1865* (New York: Oxford University Press, 1989). For a brief overview, see Richard R. John, "Communications and Information Processing," in *Encyclopedia of American Social History*, ed. Mary Kupiec Cayton, Elliott J. Gorn, and Peter W. Williams (New York: Scribner, 1993), 2351–2353.

2. Richard R. John, *Spreading the News: The American Postal System from Franklin to Morse* (Cambridge, Mass.: Harvard University Press, 1995), 27.

3. Richard D. Brown, *The Strength of a People: The Idea of an Informed Citizenry in America, 1650–1870* (Chapel Hill: University of North Carolina Press, 1996), chap. 4. See also J. R. Pole, *The Gift of Government: Political Responsibility from the English Restoration to American Independence* (Athens: University of Georgia Press, 1983).

4. Benjamin Rush, "Address to the People of the United States," *American Museum*, 1 (1787): 8.

5. James Madison, "Public Opinion," *National Gazette* (December 19, 1791), in *Papers of James Madison*, ed. William T. (Charlottesville: University Press of Virginia, 1962–), 14:170. Italics are in the original.

6. John, *Spreading the News*, chap. 2.

7. *National Intelligencer* (Washington), November 22, 1826.

8. John, *Spreading the News*, 5. The United States total excludes Indians and slaves; the British total includes Ireland.

9. For totals on settled area, see Carville Earle and Changyong Cao, "Frontier Closure and the Involution of American Society, 1840–1880," *Journal of the Early Republic*, 13 (summer 1993): 164.

10. Thomas C. Leonard, *News for All: America's Coming-of-Age with the Press* (New York: Oxford University Press, 1995).

11. John, *Spreading the News*, 38.

12. *Annals of Congress*, 4th Cong., 2d sess., February 1, 1797, 2057–2058.

13. John F. Stover, "Canals and Turnpikes: America's Early Nineteenth-Century Transportation Network," in *An Emerging Independent American Economy, 1815–1875*, ed. Joseph R. Frese and Jacob Judd (Tarrytown, N.Y.: Sleepy Hollow Restorations, 1980), 75.

14. McLean to John Quincy Adams, November 17, 1828, in *American State Papers: Post Office* (Washington: Gales and Seaton, 1834): 183.

15. Pliny Miles, "Post-Office Improvements," *New-York Quarterly* 4 (1855): 24.

16. John Lambert, *Travels through Canada, and the United States of North America in the Years 1806, 1807, and 1808*, 2d ed. (London: C. Cradock and W. Joy, 1814), 2:498–500.

17. Richard R. John and Thomas C. Leonard, "The Illusion of the Ordinary: John Lewis Krimmel's *Village Tavern* and the Democratization of Public Life in the Early Republic," *Pennsylvania History* 65 (winter 1998): 87–96.

18. *Congressional Globe* (January 24, 1842): 978.

19. Amos Kendall, "Report from the Postmaster General," Sen. Doc. 1 26th Cong., 1st sess., November 30, 1839, (serial 354), 616. See also *History of the Railway Mail Service: A Chapter in the History of Postal Affairs in the United States* (Washington, D.C.: Government Printing Office, 1885), 39–40.

20. Amos Kendall, "Report of the Postmaster General," Sen. Doc. 1, 24th Cong., 2d sess., December 1, 1835, (serial 279), 405–406.

21. William D. Merrick, *Speech of Mr. Merrick, of Maryland, on the Bill to Reduce the Rates of Postage* . . . (Washington, D.C.: Gales and Seaton, 1845), 13.

22. James W. Hale, "History of Cheap Postage," *American Odd Fellow* 10 (1871): 183.

23. Daniel P. Carpenter, "The Corporate Metaphor and Executive Department Centralization in the United States, 1888–1928," *Studies in American Political Development* 12 (spring 1998): 162–203.

24. Theodore N. Vail to Thomas J. Brady, November 1, 1877, in *Annual Report of the Postmaster General* (Washington: Government Printing Office, 1877), 151.

25. Alexander J. Field, "French Optical Telegraphy, 1793–1855: Hardware, Software, Administration," *Technology and Culture* 35 (April 1994): 315–347; Gerard J. Holzmann and Bjorn Pehrson, *The Early History of Data Networks* (Los Alamitos, Calif.: IEEE Computer Press, 1995), chap. 2.

26. Geoffrey Wilson, *The Old Telegraphs* (London: Phillimore, 1976), 210–217.

27. Cited in John R. Parker, *A Treatise upon the Telegraphic Science* (Boston: Dutton Wentworth, 1835).

28. Printed memorial from John R. Parker to the Senate and House, January 1837, copy addressed to Amos Kendall, Incoming Correspondence, RG 28, Post Office Department, National Archives, Washington, D.C.

29. Samuel F. B. Morse to Levi Woodbury, in House Report 753, 25th Cong., 2d sess., September 27, 1837, (serial 335), 9.

30. Cave Johnson, "Report of the Postmaster General," in Sen. Doc. 2, 29th Cong., December 1, 1845, 1st sess. (serial 470), 861.

31. James D. Reid, *The Telegraph in America: Its Founders, Promoters, and Noted Men* (New York: Derby Brothers, 1879), 530. Reid issued a second (much expanded) edition of this work in 1886. Unless noted, all references are to the 1879 edition. The phrase "methodless enthusiasm" was later popularized by telegraph historian Robert Luther Thompson; see his *Wiring a Continent: The History of the Telegraph Industry in the United States, 1832–1866* (Princeton: Princeton University Press, 1947), vii.

32. Thompson, *Wiring a Continent*, 241.

33. David Homer Bates, *Lincoln in the Telegraph Office* [1907]. (Lincoln: University of Nebraska Press, 1995), 3.

34. Reid, *Telegraph in America* (1886 ed.), p. 531. For a related discussion and some additional citations, see Richard R. John, "Elaborations, Revisions, Dissents: Alfred D. Chandler's *The Visible Hand* after Twenty Years," *Business History Review* 71 (summer 1997): 186–187.

35. Joel A. Tarr, Thomas Finholt, and David Goodman, "The City and the Telegraph: Urban Telecommunications in the Pre-Telephone Era," *Journal of Urban History* 14 (November 1987): 49–52, 57.

36. Richard R. John, "The Politics of Innovation," *Daedalus* 127 (fall 1998): 198–203; Paul Israel, *From Machine Shop to Industrial Laboratory: Telegraphy and the Changing Context of American Invention, 1830–1920* (Baltimore, Md.: Johns Hopkins University Press, 1992), 135–138.

37. Gardiner G. Hubbard, "Government Control of the Telegraph," *North American Review* 325 (December 1883): 522.

38. Norvin Green to Henry H. Bingham, December 11, 1890, president's letterbooks, Western Union Records, Archives Center, Smithsonian Institution, Washington, D.C. (hereafter WUR-SI).

39. See, for example, William Orton to Anson Stager, January 24, 1871, and Orton to T. H. Willson, January 2, 1889; both in president's letterbooks, WUR-SI.

40. Francis O. J. Smith, "The Post-Office Department," *Merchant's Magazine* 12 (February 1845): 151.

41. Alonzo B. Cornell, *"True and Firm": Biography of Ezra Cornell* (New York: A. S. Barnes, 1884), 104.

42. James Rees, *Foot-Prints of a Letter Carrier: Or, A History of the World's Correspondence* (Philadelphia: J. B. Lippincott, 1866), 248.

43. Cited in George L. Anderson, "Banks, Mails, and Rails, 1880–1915," in *The Frontier Challenge: Responses to the Trans-Mississippi West*, ed. John G. Clark (Lawrence: University Press of Kansas, 1971), 277.

44. Richard B. Kielbowicz, *News in the Mail: The Press, Post Office, and Public Information, 1700–1860s* (Westport, Conn.: Greenwood Press, 1989), 155.

45. U.S. Bureau of the Census, *Historical Statistics of the United States, Colonial Times to 1970* (Washington D.C.: Government Printing Office, 1976), 2:790.

46. Green to William F. Vilas, November 17, 1887, president's letterbooks, WUR-SI.

47. Ibid. "Another large class of customers," Green added, "are the patrons of the race course, and the pool rooms connected therein by wires; where chances are bought and sold in all the cities, some of which are a thousand miles from the scene of contest."

48. "The Telegraph," *De Bow's Review* 16 (February 1854): 168.

49. Alfred D. Chandler Jr., *The Visible Hand: The Managerial Revolution in American Business* (Cambridge, Mass.: Harvard University Press, 1977), 211.

50. Kenneth Lipartito, "The New York Cotton Exchange and the Development of the Cotton Futures Market," *Business History Review* 57 (spring 1983): 50–72.

51. William Cronon, *Nature's Metropolis: Chicago and the Great West* (New York: W. W. Norton, 1991), 120–132.

52. Menahem Blondheim, *News Over the Wires: The Telegraph and the Flow of Public Information in America, 1844–1897* (Cambridge, Mass, Harvard University Press, 1994); Richard A. Schwarzlose, *The Nation's News-*

brokers, 2 vols. (Evanston Ill.: Northwestern University Press, 1989, 1990).

53. Cited in Thompson, *Wiring a Continent*, 204.

54. Reid, *Telegraph* (1886 ed.), 585.

55. *Quarterly Review* (London) 95 (June 1854): 161.

56. Edward Harold Mott, *Between the Ocean and the Lakes: The Story of Erie* (New York: Ticker Publishing, 1908), 415–423.

57. Daniel C. McCallum, "Superintendent's Report," 1856, in Alfred D. Chandler, Jr., comp. and ed., *The Railroads: The Nation's First Big Business: Sources and Readings* (New York: Harcourt, Brace & World, 1965), 104.

58. Ibid., p. 105.

59. Alvin F. Harlow, *Old Wires and New Waves* (New York: Appleton, 1936), 212. It was during the 1860s, Harlow added, that the "welding" of the telegraph and the railroad took place (p. 213).

60. JoAnne Yates, *Control through Communication: The Rise of System in American Management* (Baltimore, Md.: Johns Hopkins University Press, 1989), 118.

61. Reid, *Telegraph*, 482, 488.

62. Ibid., 479.

63. James H. Madison, "The Evolution of Commercial Credit Reporting Agencies in Nineteenth-Century America," *Business History Review* 48 (summer 1974): 176.

64. Alexander James Field, "The Magnetic Telegraph, Price and Quantity Data, and the New Management of Capital," *Journal of Economic History* 52 (June 1992): 401–413.

65. Chandler, *Visible Hand*, 396.

66. Cited in ibid., 396.

67. Burton J. Hendrick, "Telephones for the Millions," *McClure's* 44 (November 1914): 45.

68. Louis Galambos, "Theodore N. Vail and the Role of Innovation in the Modern Bell System," *Business History Review* 66 (spring 1992): 123.

69. Cited in Robert V. Bruce, *Alexander Graham Bell and the Conquest of Solitude* (Boston: Little, Brown, 1973), 210.

70. Thomas A. Watson, *Exploring Life: The Autobiography of Thomas A. Watson* (New York: Appleton, 1926), 107.

71. Charles A. Tinker to Thomas Eckert, April 17, 1890, president's letterbooks, WUC-SI.

72. For a related discussion, see Bernard Carlson, "Entrepreneurship in the Early Development of the Telephone: How Did William Orton and Gardiner Greene Hubbard Conceptualize this New Technology?" *Business and Economic History* 23 (winter 1994): 161–192.

73. Alexander Graham Bell, "To the Capitalists of the Electric Telephone Company," 25 March 25, 1878, in J. E. Kingsbury, *The Telephone and*

Telephone Exchanges: Their Invention and Development (London: Longmans, Green, 1915), 89–92.

74. Reid, *Telegraph*, 629–632.

75. Robert W. Garnet, *The Telephone Enterprise: The Evolution of the Bell System's Horizontal Structure, 1876–1909* (Baltimore, Md.: Johns Hopkins University Press, 1985).

76. Arthur S. Pier, *Forbes: Telephone Pioneer* (New York: Dodd, Mead, 1953), 123.

77. Pier, *Forbes*, 118–120; Bruce, *Bell*, 281.

78. Theodore N. Vail, *Views on Public Questions* (n.p.:n.p., 1917), 308.

79. Norvin Green to William H. Forbes, September 3, 1879, president's letterbooks, WUR-SI.

80. William H. Forbes, *Report of the Directors of the American Bell Telephone Co.* (Boston: A. Mudge & Son, 1881), 2.

81. Frederick Leland Rhodes, *Beginnings of Telephony* (New York: Harper, 1929), 53.

82. Stephen B. Adams and Orville R. Butler, *Manufacturing the Future: A History of Western Electric* (New York: Cambridge University Press, 1999), chap. 1. See also George David Smith, *The Anatomy of a Business Strategy: Bell, Western Electric, and the Origins of the American Telephone Industry* (Baltimore, Md. Johns Hopkins University Press, 1985).

83. For a related yet somewhat different assessment of Vail's contribution, see Galambos, "Vail and the Role of Innovation." Galambos downplays the centrality of Vail's efforts prior to 1887, and concentrates on his role in shaping the "expectational horizons" of AT&T in the years of following his return to the presidency in 1907.

84. Milton Mueller, "The Switchboard Problem: Scale, Signaling, and Organization in Manual Telephone Switching, 1877–1897," *Technology and Culture* 30 (July 1989): 534–560.

85. Kenneth Lipartito, "System Building at the Margin: The Problem of Public Choice in the Telephone Industry," *Journal of Economic History* 49 (June 1989): 330.

86. Kenneth Lipartito, *The Bell System and Regional Business: The Telephone in the South* (Baltimore, Md.: Johns Hopkins University Press, 1985); Milton L. Mueller, Jr., *Universal Service: Competition, Interconnection, and Monopoly in the Making of the American Telephone System* (Cambridge, Mass.: MIT Press, 1997), chap. 9.

87. Roland Marchand, *Creating the Corporate Soul: The Rise of Public Relations and Corporate Imagery in American Big Business* (Berkeley: University of California Press, 1998), chap. 2.

88. Lipartito, "System Building," 336.

89. Theodore S. Vail to Arthur Brisbane, June 25, 1915, president's letterbooks, AT&T Archives, Warren, N.J.

90. Venus Green, "Goodbye Central: Automation and the Decline of 'Personal Service' in the Bell System, 1878–1921," *Technology and Culture*

36 (October 1995): 912–949. See also Kenneth Lipartito, "When Women Were Switches: Technology, Work, and Gender in the Telephone Industry, 1890–1920," *American Historical Review* 99 (October 1994): 1075–1111.

91. Lipartito, *Bell System*, 225.

92. Hendrick, "Telephones for the Millions," 45.

93. Francis X. Welch, *Sixty Years of the Independent Telephone Movement* (n.p.: n.p., [1957]), 17.

94. For a different conclusion, see Claude S. Fischer, *America Calling: Social History of the Telephone to 1940* (Berkeley: University of California Press, 1992), esp. p. 83.

95. Arnold Bennett, "Your United States," *Harper's Monthly Magazine* 125 (July 1912): 191.

96. John Brooks, *Telephone: The First Hundred Years* (New York: Harper & Row, 1976), 94.

97. Ithiel de Sola Pool, ed. *The Social Impact of the Telephone* (Cambridge, Mass.: MIT Press, 1977), 30.

98. Quoted in John Kimberly Mumford, "This Land of Opportunity: The Nerve Center of Business," *Harper's Weekly* 52 (August 1, 1908): 23.

99. Olivier Zunz, *Making America Corporate, 1870–1920* (Chicago: University of Chicago Press, 1990), 117.

100. Cited in Yates, *Control through Communication*, 185.

101. Claude S. Fischer, " 'Touch Someone': The Telephone Industry Discovers Sociability," *Technology and Culture* 29 (January 1988): 34.

102. U.S. Bureau of the Census, *Historical Statistics*, 2: 784.

103. Mueller, *Universal Service*, 6.

104. Claude S. Fischer, "The Revolution in Rural Telephony, 1900–1920," *Journal of Social History* 21 (fall 1987): 8; Roy Alden Atwood, "Telephony and its Cultural Meanings in Southeastern Iowa, 1900–1917," Ph. D. diss., University of Iowa, 1984.

105. Cited in "Editors' Comment," in Pool, *Social Impact*, 300.

106. Claude S. Fischer, "Technology's Retreat: The Decline of Rural Telephony in the United States, 1920–1940," *Social Science History* 11 (fall 1987): 295–327.

Chapter 4

1. One measure of this shift is the percentage distribution of national income or aggregate payments; see U.S. Bureau of the Census, *Historical Statistics of the United States, Colonial Times to 1957* (Washington, D.C.: Government Printing Office, 1960). In the 1879–1889 period, the manufacturing sector edged out the previously dominant agricultural sector, 16.6 percent to 16.1 percent, respectively; subsequently, manufacturing accounted for an increasing percentage while agriculture stagnated and then gradually fell in percentage (Series F34 and 43, p. 140).

2. JoAnne Yates, *Control through Communication: The Rise of System in American Management* (Baltimore, Md.: Johns Hopkins University Press, 1989); see also James R. Beniger, *The Control Revolution: Technological and Economic Origins of the Information Society* (Cambridge, Mass.: Harvard University Press, 1986).

3. Daniel Nelson, *Managers and Workers: Origins of the New Factory System in the United States, 1880–1920* (Madison: University of Wisconsin Press, 1975), 3–4; Alfred D. Chandler Jr., *The Visible Hand: The Managerial Revolution in American Business* (Cambridge, Mass.: Harvard University Press, 1977), 50–64; Yates, *Control through Communication*, chap. 1.

4. Yates, *Control through Communication*, 5–6, 101–158; Chandler, *The Visible Hand*, 109–127.

5. Chandler, *Visible Hand*, 109–127; Gary John Previts and Barbara Merino, *A History of Accounting in America: An Historical Interpretation of the Cultural Significance of Accounting* (New York: Wiley, 1979): 55–62.

6. Chandler, *Visible Hand*, 104, 109.

7. U.S. Bureau of the Census, *Historical Statistics*, Series P250–306, pp. 420–422. See also James W. Cortada, *Before the Computer: IBM, NCR, Burroughs, and Remington Rand and the Industry They Created, 1865–1956* (Princeton, N.J.: Princeton University Press, 1993), 6–8, for other indices of growth.

8. Chandler, *The Visible Hand*; Philip Scranton, *Endless Novelty: Specialty Production and American Industrialization, 1865–1925* (Princeton, N.J.: Princeton University Press, 1997).

9. H. M. Norris, "Shop System," *Iron Age* 54 (November 1, 1894); 746, as quoted in Joseph A. Litterer, "Systematic Management: The Search for Order and Integration," *Business History Review* 35 (winter 1961): 472.

10. In his dissertation and subsequent articles, Joseph Litterer has explored this phenomenon in most detail. Joseph A. Litterer, "The Emergence of Systematic Management as Indicated by the Literature of Management from 1870–1900," Ph.D. diss., University of Illinois, Champaign, 1959; "Systematic Management," 461–476; "Alexander Hamilton Church and the Development of Modern Management," *Business History Review* 35 (summer 1961): 211–225; and "Systematic Management: Design for Organizational Recoupling in American Manufacturing Firms," *Business History Review* 37 (winter 1963): 369–391.

11. Robert H. Wiebe, *Search for Order, 1877–1920* (New York: Hill & Wang, 1967). Here and elsewhere, I use the term "ideology" interchangeably with philosophy to refer to a system of beliefs.

12. Litterer, "Design for Organizational Decoupling," 389; Yates, *Control through Communication*, pp. 10–15.

13. Horace Lucian Arnold, *The Complete Cost-Keeper* (New York, 1901), 9, quoted in Litterer, "Search for Order and Integration," 471.

14. Henry Metcalfe, "The Shop-Order System of Accounts," *Transactions of the American Society of Mechanical Engineers* 7 (May 1886 meeting): 440.

15. Scranton, *Endless Novelty*, pp. 18–19. While flexible or specialty manufacturers did not seek standardization of production of labor, articles in *System* magazine indicate that, for example, even smaller firms with custom products sought standard office products. Moreover, systems aimed at creating order out of variety and systems striving for efficiency and standardization in mass production required large amounts of information (see, for example, Yates, *Control through Communication*, pp. 159–200).

16. For more detailed discussion of the developments in cost accounting, see H. Thomas Johnson and Robert S. Kaplan, *Relevance Lost: The Rise and Fall of Management Accounting* (Boston, Mass.: Harvard Business School Press, 1987), especially pp. 47–58; Chandler, *Visible Hand*, pp. 272–274; Scranton, *Endless Novelty*, pp. 99–103; Previts and Merino, *History of Accounting*, p. 116.

17. Johnson and Kaplan, *Relevance Lost*; Theodore M. Porter, *Trust in Numbers: The Pursuit of Objectivity in Science and Public Life* (Princeton, N.J.: Princeton University Press, 1995).

18. For example, the "Salesman's Manual" for the Schwab Safe Company of Lafayette, Indiana, also provides detailed guidance in the sales process, including a list of "Objections Raised by the Prospective Buyer and Arguments Overcoming Them"; The Schwab Safe Company, "Salesman's Manual" (Lafayette, Indiana, 1922), in Imprints Department, Hagley Museum and Library. Similarly (though for a very different product, sales force, and target customer), the 1899 "Manual of Instruction" prepared by Avon for all the women who sold their products door to door—independent agents referred to as "Depot Managers"—provides guidelines on "How to Canvass," "When to Canvass," "When to Make First Delivery," how to fill out the form provided for "Weekly Reports," "How to Order Goods on Credit," and a section on how to use the catalogues that could also be distributed to buying customers, called "Regarding Catalogues" ("Manual of Instruction," Acc. 2155, Avon Historical Collection, Box 4, Hagley Museum and Library).

19. As Scranton notes in *Endless Novelty*, however, systematization in specialty manufacturing did not follow this path (pp. 18–19).

20. JoAnne Yates, "Evolving Information Use in Firms, 1850–1920," in *Information Acumen: The Understanding and Use of Knowledge in Modern Business*, ed. Lisa Bud-Frierman (New York: Routledge, 1994), 26–50.

21. One of many examples of adoptions by smaller firms is provided by E. A. Clark, "How We Keep Costs in our 75-Man Plant: A Boiled-down System that Can be Worked by Two Clerks in the Average Small

Factory," *Factory* 17 (October 1916): 405–408. The spread of systematic management to nonmanufacturing businesses may also be seen in *System* magazine. As early as 1901, for example, we find a column entitled "Published About System," which notes articles in other publications relevant to systematizing. It includes sections for manufacturers, mail order businesses, professional offices, and hotels; see *System* 1: 8 (July 1901): n.p. We find articles in *System* itself covering everything from the real estate business: Thomas G. Wade, "Cards that Help Sell Real Estate," *System* 29 (April 1916): 428–430; to retailing: Charles A. Whelan, "How I Watch the Sales of a Chain of 1,000 Stores," *System* 29 (May 1916): 481–487.

22. See for example, William Henry Leffingwell, *Office Management: Principles and Practice* (New York: A. W. Shaw, 1927).

23. Angel Kwolek-Folland, *Engendering Business: Men and Women in the Corporate Office, 1870–1930* (Baltimore, Md.: Johns Hopkins University Press, 1994), 4.

24. For discussion of the office appliance industry as a precursor to the data processing industry, as well as of the definitional problems facing those studying precursors to the computer, see Cortada, *Before the Computer*, pp. 3–5 and elsewhere.

25. Calculated from U.S. Bureau of the Census, *Historical Statistics*, 411.

26. William Henry Leffingwell, ed., *The Office Appliance Manual* (Chicago: National Association of Office Appliance Manufacturers, 1926), 18.

27. Yates, "Evolving Information Use in Firms," 44–45.

28. Of course, as business increased, the quantity of communication *between* firms and external parties such as customers and suppliers, increased at least in proportion to the increased business. This chapter, however, focuses on internal business uses of communication and information, where dramatic changes in the proportion, types, and quantity of documentation occurred.

29. Richard N. Current, *The Typewriter and the Men Who Made It* (Champaign, Ill.: University of Illinois Press, 1954), 59–73; Yates, *Control through Communication*, 39–42.

30. Cortada, *Before the Computer*, 17; *Scientific American* estimate quoted in Current, *Typewriter*, 110.

31. Harry E. Barbour, "Typewriters," 4, in U.S. Bureau of the Census, Twelfth Census, Bulletin no. 239 (July 28, 1902).

32. See also Cortada, *Before the Computer*, 17, for a slightly different, but not incompatible, interpretation of the typewriter business's rapid takeoff.

33. From *Typewriter Magazine*, as quoted by Bruce Bliven Jr., *The Wonderful Writing Machine* (New York: Random House, 1954), 34.

34. In early twentieth-century Japan, for example, new management methods that depended more on face-to-face contact and less on documentation evolved, even as production grew.

35. Kwolek-Folland, *Engendering Business*, 3–6; see also Elyze Rotella, *From Home to Office: U.S. Women at Work 1870–1930* (Ann Arbor, Mich.: UMI Research Press, 1981).

36. Leffingwell, *Office Appliance Manual*, 510–540.

37. Cortada, *Before the Computer*, 66–68; quote from p. 68.

38. Yates, *Control through Communication*, 26–28.

39. W. B. Proudfoot, *The Origin of Stencil Duplicating* (London: Hutchinson, 1972), 25, 32–33. Before this time, double-sided carbon paper was used with a stylus, or single-sided with a pencil. Carbon paper was not used for internal or external business correspondence, however, because the pens of the day tore the paper if a writer applied adequate pressure to make carbon copies.

40. Yates, "Evolving Information Use in Firms," 32–33.

41. Yates, *Control through Communication*, 56–63.

42. Scovill Manufacturing Company, a brass manufacturer, provides a nice example of this problem (Yates, *Control through Communication*, 181).

43. At around the same time, the rolling copier, a press copying device that resulted in unbound press copies, also appeared on the market and was adopted by many firms, allowing similar reorganization of storage systems.

44. A. Chaffee, *How to File Business Papers and Records* (New York: McGraw-Hill, 1938), 4. For more detail, see Yates, *Control through Communication*, 56–63.

45. See Gerri Lynn Flanzraich, "The Role of the Library Bureau and Gaylord Brothers in the Development of Library Technology, 1876–1930," Ph.D. diss., Columbia University, 1990, for a fuller story of Dewey's business ventures.

46. For example, see C. E. Wilson, "Filing Correspondence," *System* 1 (July 1901), n.p.; E. R. Hudders, *Indexing and Filing: A Manual of Standard Practice* (New York: Ronald Press, 1916).

47. Yates, *Control through Communication*, 62–63.

48. See, for example, Henry Metcalfe, *The Cost of Manufactures and the Administration of Workshops, Public and Private*, 3d ed. (New York: Wiley, 1885, 1894); F. C. Morse, "Keeping Accounts without Books," *System* 1 (September 1900), n.p.; William Henry Leffingwell, *Scientific Office Management* (New York: A. W. Shaw, 1917).

49. Metcalfe, *Cost of Manufactures*, 22.

50. Charles W. Wootton and Carel Wolk, "The Evolution and Acceptance of the Loose Leaf Accounting System, 1885–1935," unpublished manuscript, 1998; Leffingwell, *Office Appliance Manual*, 754–802.

51. Martin Campbell-Kelly and William Aspray, *Computer: A History of the Information Machine*, (New York: Basic Books, 1996), 34–36.

52. The material in this paragraph comes from and is documented in Yates, *Control through Communication*, 268–269.

53. Campbell-Kelly and Aspray, *Computer*, 36–37; Cortada, *Before the Computer*, 25–31.

54. Campbell-Kelly and Aspray, *Computer*, 38–39. On the relationship between the demand and the innovations, see Cortada, *Before the Computer*, 29; and Leffingwell, *Office Appliance Manual*, 18.

55. See Cortada, *Before the Computer*, 162–170, for more details on the evolution of this technology and on the markets they served.

56. See Leffingwell, *Office Appliance Manual*, 55–163; Cortada, *Before the Computer*, 158–162.

57. Campbell-Kelly and Aspray, *Computer*, 39.

58. For example, see Henry W. Belfield, "InterHouse Correspondence," *System* 5 (February 1904): 113–114; see also Yates, *Control through Communication*, 15, 95–98.

59. Leffingwell, *Office Appliance Manual*, 574–578.

60. Yates, *Control through Communication*, 24–25.

61. Information on the early history of the telephone may be found in Frederick L. Rhodes, *Beginnings of Telephony* (New York: Harper, 1929); J. E. Kingsbury, *The Telephone and Telephone Exchanges: Their Invention and Development* (London: Longmans, Green, 1915); Rosario Jeseph Tosiello, *The Birth and Early Years of the Bell Telephone System: 1876–1880* (New York: Arno Press, 1979).

62. Carbon paper could only be used to make up to ten copies, and then only when the paper was thin and the typist strong.

63. Proudfoot, *The Origin of Stencil Duplicating*, 34–36 (on hectograph) and throughout; Yates, *Control through Communication*, 50–54.

64. The 1946 copy of Avon's sales manual, for example, was copiously illustrated to show the sale agents how to dress, how to sit, what to say, and so on (Acc. 2155, Avon Historical Collection, Box 11, File Rep. Instruction, 1941–1946). Unlike such manuals, which were intended only for the sales staff, catalogues were sometimes meant for both— such as, the "Salesmen's Catalogue" of the Tabulating Machnine Company, which showed illustrations of various devices and provided their specifications, potential uses, and prices, and was clearly meant for showing to potential customers, as well as for use by the sales staff ("Salesmen's Catalogue," The Tabulating Machine Company, ca. early 1920s, IBM Archives).

65. "Getting More Out of Shop Conferences," *Factory* 17 (October 1916): 490–494.

66. Yates, *Control through Communication*, 235–238.

67. Howard Gray Funkhouser, "Historical Development of the Graphical Representation of Statistical Data," *Osiris* 3 (November 1937): 281, 337–342.

68. See, for example, J. Bismer, "Graphs: Charts that Illustrate the Comparative Value of Figures; How They are Made Up and How They are Used as Time-savers and Danger Signals," *System* 20 (1911): 270–276;

Willard C. Brinton, *Graphic Methods for Presenting Facts* (New York: Engineering Magazine, 1914).

69. Yates, "Graphs as a Managerial Tool: A Case Study of Du Pont's Use of Graphs in the Early Twentieth Century," *The Journal of Business Communication* 22 (winter 1985): 5–33.

70. Yates, *Control through Communication,* 91–98.

71. In Du Pont, for example, the Efficiency Division of the High Explosives Operating Department undertook as one of its first activities a thorough study of internal correspondence that attempted to make it more efficient (Yates, *Control through Communication,* 250–253).

72. For discussions of the welfare movement, see, for example, Stuart D. Brandes, *American Welfare Capitalism, 1880–1940* (Chicago: University of Chicago Press, 1976); Henry Eilbirt, "The Development of Personnel Management in the United States," *Business History Review* 33 (1959): 348–352; Sanford M. Jacoby, *Employing Bureaucracy: Managers, Unions, and the Transformation of Work in American Industry, 1900–1945* (New York: Columbia University Press, 1985), 49–67; Daniel Wren, *The Evolution of Management Thought,* 2d ed. (New York: Wiley, 1979), 202–203.

73. Richard Gillespie, *Manufacturing Knowledge: A History of the Hawthorne Experiments* (New York: Cambridge University Press, 1991), 29–34; Mauro F. Guillen, *Models of Management: Work, Authority, and Organization in a Comparative Perspective* (Chicago: University of Chicago Press, 1994), 60–65.

74. Gillespie, *Manufacturing Knowledge,* 29–30; Jacoby, *Employing Bureaucracy,* 126–129.

75. David Noble, *American by Design: Science, Technology, and the Rise of Corporate Capitalism* (New York: Oxford University Press, 1977) 265.

76. Lawrence B. Glickman. *A Living Wage: American Workers and the Making of Consumer Society* (Ithaca, N.Y.: Cornell University Press, 1997).

77. Jacoby, *Employing Bureaucracy,* 7; Gillespie, *Manufacturing Knowledge,* 30.

78. The data in this paragraph come from Guillen, *Models of Management,* 74–75. Guillen derives his data from published surveys conducted by the National Industrial Conference Board.

79. Carter A. Daniel, *MBA: The First Century* (Lewisburg, Va.: Bucknell University Press, 1998), 98, 141–142.

80. Jacoby, *Employing Bureaucracy,* 118, 120–126, 148–150.

81. Cortada, *Before the Computer,* 161–162.

82. JoAnne Yates, "Coevolution of Information Processing Technology and use: Interaction between Life Insurance and Tabulating Industries," *Business History Review,* no. 1 (1993): 1–51, especially pp. 14–16; Cortada, *Before the Computer,* 50.

83. The Illinois Central Railroad, for example, did not gather all the required data, and its new company president, Stuyvesant Fish, used the

act as a way of forcing added system on his organization (Yates, *Control through Communication*, 133–137).

84. Chandler, *The Visible Hand*, 145–187.

85. For example, the railroads adopted the Edison Electric Pen, an example of technological overkill in the area of stencil duplicating that was soon replaced by lower-tech and more reliable methods of making stencil masters (Yates, *Control through Communication*, 50–52, 122).

86. Yates, "Coevolution of Information Processing Technology and Use."

87. Martin Campbell-Kelly, "Large-Scale Data Processing in the Prudential, 1850–1930," *Accounting, Business, and Financial History* 2: 2 (1992): 117–139.

88. The best source on the Armstrong Hearings and the fallout from those hearings is Morton Keller, *The Life Insurance Enterprise, 1885–1910: A Study in the Limits of Corporate Power* (Cambridge, Mass.: Harvard University Press, 1963). On the ideologies of insurance, see Viviana A. Rotman Zelizer, *Morals and Markets: The Development of Life Insurance in the United States* (New York: Columbia University Press, 1979).

89. See Geoffrey D. Austrian, *Herman Hollerith: Forgotten Giant of Information Processing* (New York: Columbia University Press, 1982), for details of the development and early use of tabulating technology in the Census. Other accounts of the technology and its early use include Arthur L. Norberg, "High Technology Calculation in the Early 20th Century: Punched Card Machinery in Business and Government," *Technology and Culture* 31 (1990): 753–779; Martin Campbell-Kelly, "Punched-Card Machinery," in *Computing before Computers* ed. William Aspray (Ames: Iowa State University Press, 1990), 122–155; Cortada, *Before the Computer*, 44–63. Much of this discussion is drawn from my discussion of these developments, particularly in regard to the life insurance industry's use of this technology, in Yates, "Co-evolution of Information Processing Technology and Use."

90. Austrian, *Herman Hollerith*, 238; Norberg, "High Technology Calculation," 764.

91. Norberg, "High Technology Calculation," 762; Yates, "Co-evolution of Information Processing Technology and Use," 12.

92. Yates, "Co-evolution of Information Processing Technology and Use," 14–16.

93. Cortada, *Before the Computer*, 50; W. E. Freeman, "Automatic Mechanical Punching, Counting, Sorting, Tabulating, and Printing Machines Adaptable to Various Lines of Accounting and Statistical Work Essential for Public Service Corporations with Particular Reference to Improvements in the Art of Mechanical Accounting," paper presented at the annual convention of the National Electric Light Association, San Francisco, June 7–11, 1915; reprinted by the Accounting and Tabulating Corporation of Great Britain, (London: n.d.), 13–14.

94. See Yates, "Co-evolution of Information Processing Technology and Use," for details and full documentation.
95. Cortada, *Before the Computer*, 102, 108.
96. The two terms, accounting machines and tabulating machines, both came to be used for the same equipment, the latter because of the extensive use of the technology for accounting applications.
97. Leffingwell, *Office Appliance Manual*, 176.
98. Calculated from figures in Cortada, *Before the Computer*, 158. The upper limit, 13 percent, is the percentage accounted for by IBM's sales and Powers's sales. Because the IBM sales figures include all products, not just tabulating products, and Cortada's use of "Powers" rather than Remington Rand suggests that that figure includes only tabulating machines, we can compute a more likely figure of 10 percent by assuming the eight to one ratio of IBM over Powers, which would mean that only about $16 million of IBM's $20.3 million total sales in 1930 were attributable to the tabulating segment.
99. JoAnne Yates, "The Structuring of Early Computer Use in Life Insurance," *Journal of Design History* 12, no. 1 (1999: 5–24).
100. Ibid.
101. Cortada, *Before the Computer*, 102.
102. Campbell-Kelly and Aspray, *Computer*, 49.

Chapter 5

1. Electronics, originally referred to as "the radio art," is defined as "a branch of physics that deals with the emission, behavior, and effects of electrons in vacuums and gases and with the use of electron's devices," *Webster's Seventh Dictionary* (Springfield, Mass.: G.8C. Merriam, 1963): 267. Vacuum-tube–based technologies were known as "radio-related" technologies, or the "applications" of electron devices involving electrons flowing in gas or in a vacuum—radio and television, radar and other aids to navigation, control systems and computers. The field of electricity, by comparison, included power generation, lighting, directly driven machinery, and other equipment, in which the flow of electrons is usually confined to metallic conductors.
2. Michael Riordan and Lillian Hoddeson, *Crystal Fire: The Birth of the Information Age* (New York: W. W. Norton, 1997).
3. Brian Winston, *Media Technology and Society: A History From the Telegraph to the Internet* (London: Routledge, 1998), 75–81; Ithiel de Sola Pool, *Technologies of Freedom* (Cambridge, Mass.: 1983 Harvard University Press, 1983 p. 121–129.
4. James R. Beniger, *The Control Revolution: Technological and Economic Origins of the Information Society* (Cambridge, Mass.: Harvard University Press, 1986). To Beniger, "control" means purposive influence toward a predetermined goal, including the influence of an agent over

another. In this last phase of the Industrial Revolution, the revolution involved not material or energy (as with previous major revolutions) but information processing, an attempt to organize the material world.

5. Philip Marchand, *Marshall McLuhan: The Medium and the Messenger* (Cambridge, Mass.: MIT Press, 1989), chap. 5.

6. Winston, *Media Technology, and Society*, 3–8, makes a point of this, stating that most histories of mass communications have focused misleadingly on the technologies and not the social forces that served as the "supervening necessities" that shaped them.

7. Hugh G. J. Aitken, *The Continuous Wave: Technology and American Radio, 1900–1932* (Princeton, N.J.: Princeton University Press, 1985), 195–249. Aitken's book is the most detailed source for this history—business and technical—in print. Most other authoritative sources date from the 1950s or earlier. The next section relies on Aitken unless otherwise noted. Two older invaluable accounts, long out of print, are W. Rupert MacLaurin, *Invention and Innovation in the Radio Industry* (New York: Macmillan, 1949) and Gleason Leonard Archer, *History of Radio*, 2 vols. (New York: American Historical Society, 1939).

8. Margaret B. W. Graham, *RCA and the VideoDisc: The Business of Research* (New York: Cambridge University Press, 1986); Aitken, *Continuous Wave*.

9. Aitken, *Continuous Wave*. A point of considerable controversy was whether deForest's invention could in fact have been reduced to practice for the purpose AT&T had in mind when it purchased the rights in 1912. Many engineers claimed that deForest did not recognize that his tube was capable of generating radio waves at all; he only recognized the amplification. In terms popularized in the history of technology by Wiebe Bijker, it took those with a different "technological frame" than deForest's to tease out the audion's broader potential. "The Social Construction of Bakelite: Toward a Theory of Invention," in Wiebe Bijker, Thomas P. Hughes, and Trevor Pinch, *The Social Construction of Technological Systems: New Directions in the Sociology and History of Technology* (Cambridge, Mass.: MIT Press, 1987). 159–187.

10. Leonard Reich, "Research, Patents, and the Struggle to Control Radio," *Business History Review* 51 (summer 1977): 230–235.

11. Michael Schiffer, *The Portable Radio in American Life* (Tucson: University of Arizona Press, 1991), 30.

12. Aitken, *Continuous Wave*.

13. Winston, *Media Technology and Society*, 112.

14. "The Glass Heart of a Major Weapon," *The Gaffer* [Corning (N.Y.) Glass Works in-house newspaper], December 1945.

15. "Note on Radio Receiving Tubes," Corning Glass Works (hereinafter CGW) Archives, Television Folder ARV 27, notes that the T16 tube was a standard lightbulb enclosure used for a receiving tube.

16. Schiffer, *Portable Radio*, 56–67, uses his fascinating and detailed account of radio as artifact to demonstrate the evolution of the society around it.

17. Philips, C. J., "Glass in Electrical Transmission and Communication," in *Glass the Miracle Maker*, 298–313. Philips lists the following glass properties that make it an effective insulator: durability, very high volume and surface resistivity, and high dielectric strength. Some formulations of glass could insulate against electric surges, others could reduce static, or reduce resistance for maximum transmission.

18. Schiffer, *Portable Radio*, 28.

19. Internal note labeled "Television," no author, dated 1983, CGW Archives, Television Folder ARV 27.

20. Jeffrey L. Meikle, *Twentieth Century Limited: Industrial Design in America, 1925–1939* (Philadelphia Temple University Press, 1979), 97.

21. Ibid., 98.

22. Robert Buderi, *The Invention that Changed the World* (Cambridge, Mass: MIT Press, 1997), provides a detailed account of the MIT Radiation Laboratory and its achievements.

23. Graham, *RCA and the VideoDisc*; John Sheldon, "101 Years of Television," CGW Archives, Television Folder ARV 27.

24. Graham, *RCA and the VideoDisc*; William Boddy, "The Beginnings of American Television," in *Television: An International History*, ed. Anthony Smith, 2d ed., (New York: Oxford University Press, 1998): 23–37.

25. Robert Kargon, Stuart W. Leslie, and Erica Schoenberger, "Far Beyond Big Science: Science Regions and the Organization of Research and Development," in *Big Science: The Growth of Large-Scale Research* ed. Peter Galison and Bruce Hevly (Stanford, Calif. : Stanford University Press, 1992), 345–347.

26. Schiffer, *Portable Radio*, 28–30. These portable sets of World War I were the first U.S. radios manufactured on a large scale. Their manufacture gave General Electric the capability to move into manufacturing consumer radios after the war.

27. Aitken, *Continuous Wave*; Graham, *RCA and the VideoDisc*, 36.

28. David Sarnoff, "The Development of Radio and the Radio Industry," speech delivered at Harvard Graduate School of Business Administration, 1928.

29. Susan Douglas, *The Invention of American Broadcasting, 1899–1922* (Baltimore, Md.: Johns Hopkins University Press, 1987), 174–210. Also discussed in Michele Hilmes, *Radio Voices: American Broadcasting, 1922–1952* (Minneapolis: University of Minnesota Press, 1997); on the shift from distance listening to entertainment radio; see pp. 36–45.

30. Douglas, *Invention of American Broadcasting*; Hilmes, *Radio Voices*.

31. Graham, *RCA and the VideoDisc*, 38–39.

32. Susan Smulyan, *Selling Radio: The Commercialization of American Broadcasting, 1920–1934* (Washington, D.C. : Smithsonian Institution Press, 1994), 20–24.

33. Hilmes, *Radio Voices*, 51.

34. *Ibid.*, 50–51.

35. Boddy, "Beginnings of American Television," 24.

36. Smulyan, "The Rise of the Network System," in Smulyan, *Selling Radio*, chap. 2, 37–64.

37. Hilmes, *Radio Voices*, 35, describes this as a service that began with the amateurs who would relay the latest information via code to a centrally located amateur who in turn would translate and spread the news.

38. Douglas, *Invention of American Broadcasting*, 16.

39. Graham, *RCA and the VideoDisc*, 38–39; MacLaurin, *Invention and Innovation*, 135.

40. As described in detail by Steven J. Ross, *Working Class Hollywood: Silent Film and the Shaping of Class in America* (Princeton, N.J.: Princeton University Press, 1998).

41. Ross, *Working Class Hollywood*, 179.

42. Anthony Slide, *The American Film Industry: A Historical Dictionary* (New York: Greenwood, 1986), 381.

43. Winston, *Media Technology and Society*, 115.

44. Robert Sklar, *Movie-Made America: A Cultural History of American Movies*, rev. ed. (New York: Random, House, 1994), 156. Sklar's book is the principle source for the material here on the movie industry unless otherwise indicated.

45. *Ibid.*, 157.

46. Winston, *Media Technology and Society*, 110–114.

47. Smulyan, *Selling Radio*.

48. Hilmes, *Radio Voices*.

49. Douglas, *Invention of American Broadcasting*, 306–307.

50. Hilmes, *Radio Voices*, p. 10, quotes the NBC mission statement to make this point.

51. *Ibid.*, pp. 10–13; and Sklar, *Movie-Made America*, 75–96 and 130–150.

52. Robert Skidelsky, "New Deals," in *John Maynard Keynes, A Biography*, vol. 2, *The Economist as Savior, 1920–1937* (New York: Macmillan, 1983–), 483.

53. Roland Marchand, *Advertising the American Dream: Making Way for Modernity, 1920–1940* (Berkeley: University of California Press, 1985), 88–94. Unless otherwise indicated Marchand's work is the prime source for this discussion of radio advertising.

54. Hilmes, *Radio Voices*, 68–69.

55. Marchand, *Advertising the American Dream*.

56. Hilmes, *Radio Voices*, 92–95.

57. "Dark and Disorderly: The Backlash Against Broadcast Advertising," in Smulyan, *Selling Radio*, 125–153.

58. Sklar, *Movie-Made America*, 80–91.
59. *Ibid.*
60. Doris Kearns Goodwin, *No Ordinary Time* (New York: Simon and Schuster, 1994), 57–59.
61. Daniel Boorstin, *The Americans: The Democratic Experience* (New York: Random House, 1979). Boorstin stresses that radio made an intimate one-to-one connection with the audience, changing the relationship. It was not, he pointed out, possible for dictators to use radio in the same way—they had to rely instead on mass rallies.
62. David A. Cook, *A History of Narrative Film, 3rd ed.* (New York: W. W. Norton, 1996).
63. Quoted in Smulyan, *Selling Radio*, 132–138, quotation taken from Rorty, "The Impending Radio War."
64. Marchand, *Advertising the American Dream*.
65. *Ibid.*
66. Ibid., 89.
67. Smulyan, *Selling Radio*, 85.
68. Ibid., 88.
69. Ibid., 91. The following section on the effectiveness and profitability of early radio advertising draws on Smulyan's work.
70. Ibid., 63.
71. Marchand, *Advertising the American Dream*, 217.
72. "On the Home Front, Fighting to be Heard," in Hilmes, *Radio Voices*, chap. 8. Unless otherwise noted, the account of the role of radio in World War II draws on Hilmes.
73. Schiffer, *Portable Radio*, 121.
74. Hilmes, *Radio Voices*, 240.
75. "Hollywood at War with America and at War with Itself," chap. 15 of Sklar, *Movie-Made America*, is devoted to the movies and the war effort.
76. "Motion Picture," *Encyclopedia Americana*, (New York: Grolier Educational Corp.), 1998.
77. Hilmes, *Radio Voices*, 243.
78. Buderi, *Invention*; Larry Owens, "The Counterproductive Management of Science in the Second World War: Vannevar Bush and the Office of Scientific Research and Development," *Business History Review* 68, no. 4: (1994): 515–576.
79. Albert Abramson, "The Invention of Television," in *Television: An International History*, ed. Anthony Smith, 2d ed. (Oxford: Oxford University Press, 1998).
80. Kargon et al., "Far Beyond Big Science."
81. Sheldon, *Ibid.*
82. Boddy, "Beginnings of American Television."
83. Buderi, *Invention*.
84. "The Glass Heart of a Major Weapon."
85. Boddy, "Beginnings of American Television."

86. Quoted in Winston, *Media Technology and Society*.

87. Boddy, "Beginnings of American Television," 31.

88. Schiffer, *Portable Radio*, 133–134.

89. Hilmes, *Radio Voices*, 277. Although NBC's Robert Weaver is credited with inventing the successful television formats that distinguished television programming in the United States for decades, Hilmes shows that much of his programming was in fact derivative of earlier radio.

90. Andy Meisler, "HEADLINE: How the Earlier Media Achieved Critical Mass: Television; Lucy Sure Didn't Start It, But She Has Stuck to It," *New York Times*, November 20, 1995.

91. Boddy, "Beginnings of American Television," 30.

92. Marchand, *Marshall McLuhan*, 147. Unless otherwise indicated, this discussion of McLuhan draws on the Marchand biography.

93. *Ibid.*, 150.

94. *Ibid.*

95. *Ibid.*

96. *Ibid.*

97. Sklar, *Movie-Made America*, 259–263.

98. Michael Tracey, "Non-Fiction Television," in Smith, ed., *Television*, 73.

99. Boddy, "Beginnings of American Television," 31.

100. Tracey, "Non-Fiction Television," 73.

101. The earlier judgment against the G.E. and Westinghouse, RCA's parents, in 1930, had benefited RCA, by making it an independent company with continued control over the radio-related patents.

102. Graham, *RCA and the VideoDisc*, 66.

103. *Ibid.*, 63–66. RCA had further angered the industry by public announcements claiming complete victory with the second NTSC settlement and not acknowledging the contribution of any other companies.

104. *Ibid.*, 81–84.

105. *Ibid.* The denouement of the RCA story goes beyond the scope of this chapter. RCA did make one more effort to lead the industry through a major innovation. By this time most of the companies in the industry were overseas, many in Japan. The company's bet on the VideoDisc, and its ultimate failure, was a primary factor in weakening RCA to such an extent that it was absorbed back into its parent company, General Electric, in 1984.

Chapter 6

1. A. Tradup, T. N. Pope, and H. A. Affel, "Memorandum: Transistor Symposium," April 27, 1951, File 11-04-02-02, AT&T Archives. In the same memo, it states, "No information will be given out on the methods of producing transistors" (p. 3); the question of sharing had not yet been resolved.

2. Cynthia F. Morgan to J. Millstein, October 13, 1982, File 11-04-02-01, AT&T Archives.

3. Martin Campbell-Kelly and William Aspray, *Computer: A History of the Information Machine* (New York: Basic Books, 1996) made this one of their central points about the role of the computer.

4. John Diebold, "Bad Decisions on Computer Use," *Harvard Business Review* 47 (January 1969): 14.

5. L. Fred Boyce Jr., "Installing a Medium-Sized Computer," *The Journal of Accountancy* 110 (July 1960): 48.

6. *Dictionary of Computing* (White Plains, N.Y.: IBM Corporation, 1987); 443. This dictionary has been published in various editions since the 1950s and continues to appear in new editions approximately every two years.

7. Ibid., 220–221.

8. Stan Augarten, *Bit by Bit: An Illustrated History of Computers* (New York: Ticknor and Fields, 1984), 225–251.

9. Ernest Braun and Stuart Macdonald, *Revolution in Miniature: The History and Impact of Semiconductor Electronics* (Cambridge: Cambridge University Press, 1982); 33–44.

10. The notion that a society had to be wealthy enough to afford such institutions of higher learning, and that they gave a nation a competitive leg-up over other countries, was noted by historians when discussing Western Europe versus the rest of the world in the Middle Ages and later. In that earlier case, the benefits were similar to those enjoyed by the United States in the late twentieth century. See David S. Landes, *The Wealth and Poverty of Nations* (New York: W. W. Norton, 1997); 276–291.

11. The best study of the physical proximity of this industry is by sociologist Manuel Castells, *The Informational City* (Oxford: Blackwell, 1989); 33–125.

12. Ibid.

13. Quoted in Braun and Macdonald, *Revolution in Miniature*, 137.

14. Ibid., 148. Because ICs prior to the mid-1990s overwhelmingly went into capital goods, and capital goods (such as computers) only sold well when the nation was not experiencing a recession, down years coincided with poor economic performance across the United States. As use of ICs in smaller products not sensitive to capital markets increased (e.g., as in children's games and kitchen appliances), the new digital infrastructure's sales, and future prognosis, became less dependent on U.S. economic health.

15. The latest survey of the industry is by Daniel E. Sichel, *The Computer Revolution: An Economic Perspective* (Washington, D.C.: Brookings Institution Press, 1997).

16. Joseph Badaracco, *The Knowledge Link: How Firms Compete through Strategic Alliances* (Boston: Harvard Business School Press, 1991); 107–128.

17. *Technology Forecast: 1996* (Menlo Park, Calif. : Price Waterhouse World Technology Centre, 1995); 6–7.

18. Ibid., 7, 17–18.

19. *Time*, December 29, 1997, p. 8.

20. Yates explains in detail in *Control through Communication: The Rise of System in American Management* (Baltimore, Md.: John Hopkins University Press, 1989): 1–64.

21. Paul E. Ceruzzi, *Reckoners: The Prehistory of the Digital Computer, From Relays to the Stored Program Concept, 1935–1945* (Westport Conn.: Greenwood, 1983), gives the background; Campbell-Kelly and Aspray, *Computer*, 79–104.

22. An Wang, *Lessons: An Autobiography* (Reading, Mass.: Addison-Wesley, 1986): 46.

23. Michael R. Williams, *A History of Computing Technology* (Englewood Cliffs, N.J.: Prentice-Hall, 1985): 271–378.

24. F. M. Smits, ed., *A History of Engineering and Science in the Bell System: Electronics Technology (1925–1975)* (Indianapolis: AT&T Bell Laboratories, 1985); 30–32; Michael Riordan and Lillian Hoddeson, *Crystal Fire: The Birth of the Information Age* (New York: W. W. Norton, 1997), 146–147, 195–224.

25. There are essentially two types of computers: analog and digital. An analog device is one that gives a continuous stream of information; a wristwatch with hands continuously moving gives data on what time it is. A digital device provides specific pieces of information. A clock radio that shows that it is exactly 11:59 A.M. is an example of a digital device. The overwhelming majority of computers are digital because they provide specific pieces of information, such as the answer to the question what is 2 × 2? The answer: Four. An analog computer would answer that it is in the range of four. PCs are digital computers, so are the machines that produce paychecks and bills. *Dictionary of Computing* (New York: Oxford University Press, 1983): provides a formal definition of the digital computer: "A computer that operates on discrete quantities. All computation is done within a finite number system and with limited precision, associated with the number of digits in the discrete numbers. The numerical information is most often represented by the use of two-state electrical phenomenomena (on/off)" (p. 106).

26. James W. Cortada, *The Computer in the United States: From Laboratory to Market, 1930 to 1960* (Armonk, N.Y. : M. E. Sharpe, 1993); 30–63.

27. William Aspray, *John von Neumann and the Origins of Modern Computing* (Cambridge, Mass: MIT Press, 1990); 34–48. For von Neumann's papers from the period, see William Aspray and Arthur Burks, eds., *Papers of John von Neumann on Computing and Computing Theory* (Cambridge, Mass: MIT Press, 1987); for the report, see pp. 17–82.

28. William Aspray, "International Diffusion of Computer Technology,

1945–1955," *Annals of the History of Computing* 8, no. 3 (1986): 351–360; Cortada, *The Computer in the United States*, 54– 60.

29. Software is a difficult word to define. But we can begin with the idea that it includes programs, rules, any procedures, and related documentation on the operation of a computer. In practice, it refers to programs written to instruct a computer what to do.

30. On the early years, see Franklin M. Fisher, James W. McKie, and Richard B. Mancke, *IBM and the U.S. Data Processing Industry: An Economic History* (New York: Praeger, 1983); 3–26.

31. Alfred D. Chandler Jr., "The Computer Industry: The First-Half Century," in *Competing in the Age of Digital Convergence*, ed. David B. Yoffie (Boston: Harvard Business School Press, 1997), 52–68.

32. Montgomery Phister Jr., "Computer Industry," in *Encyclopedia of Computer Science and Engineering*, ed. Anthony Ralston and Edwin D. Reilly, Jr. (New York: Van Nostrand Reinhold, 1983); 337. In 1955 a million instructions in a computer cost $40, only $2 in 1961, and, by 1985, 0.004 cents; see James W. Cortada, *Information Technology as Business History* (Westport, Conn.: Greenwood, 1996); 57.

33. In fact, how to do that was the subject of one of the most famous articles written about computers. In July 1974, *Radio-Electronics*, a magazine for electronic hobbyists, published a four-page "how-to-build" article by Jonathan Titus, "Build the Mark-8 Your Personal Minicomputer," the first "how to" on PCs. For the story behind this story, see Augarten, *Bit by Bit*, 269–270.

34. Two leading authorities on the early history of the IBM PC quoted the reaction of the *Wall Street Journal* the day after the PC was announced: "Now that IBM has jumped in, nobody expects the personal computer industry to stay the same"; James Chposky and Ted Leonsis, *Blue Magic: The People, Power, and Politics Behind the IBM Personal Computer* (New York: Facts on File, 1988); 112; Campbell-Kelly and Aspray commented on the significance of the new product: "IBM had legitimated the personal computer" (*Computer*, 25).

35. Cortada, *The Computer in the United States*, 104–107.

36. Conversation with Rachel McCloud of Barnes & Noble, March 31, 1998.

37. This same focus on the practical was evident with all publications on computational equipment written in the United States since the 1870s. This literature is vast and very similar to PC manuals of the 1990s. For an exposure to this earlier literature, see James W. Cortada, *Before the Computer: IBM, NCR, Burroughs, and Remington Rand and the Industry They Created, 1865–1956* (Princeton, N.Y.: Princeton University Press, 1993). A quick search of the online version of *Books in Print* (March 29, 1998) flagged 37,834 books in English on the topic.

38. This ability to learn how to apply a technology also was a primary reason that the British led in the creation and exploitation of technology during the First Industrial Revolution of the 1700s–1800s; David S. Lanes, *The*

Wealth and Poverty of Nations: Why Some Are So Rich and Some So Poor (New York: W. W. Norton, 1998); 276–285.

39. Comment to the author by Bill Lowe, president of the IBM division manufacturing and selling PCs, March 19, 1988.

40. Cortada, *Before the Computer*, 83–87, 182–186, 247–263.

41. Samplings of the growing body of literature on the subject is reprinted in James W. Cortada, ed., *Rise of the Knowledge Worker* (Boston: Butterworth-Heinemann, 1998).

42. For a table listing the number of U.S. workers in general, and then the number of workers in information processing (1800–1993), see Daniel E. Sichel, *The Computer Revolution: An Economic Perspective* (Washington, D.C. : Brookings Institution, 1997), 115.

43. Jorge Reina Schement and Terry Curtis, *Tendencies and Tensions of the Information Age: The Production and Distribution of Information in the United States* (New Brunswick, N.J.: Transaction, 1995), 86.

44. For a major study of the nature of work in the United States, see Peter Cappelli et al., *Change at Work* (New York: Oxford University Press, 1997).

45. Fisher, McKie, and Mancke, *IBM and the U.S. Data Processing Industry*, 65–100.

46. Thomas J. Watson Jr. and Peter Petre, *Father, Son & Co.: My Life at IBM and Beyond* (New York: Bantam, 1990), 253.

47. Robert Sobel, *RCA* (New York: Stein and Day, 1986), 171–176; Homer R. Oldfield, *King of the Seven Dwarfs: General Electric's Ambiguous Challenge to the Computer Industry* (Los Alamitos, Calif.: IEEE Computer Society Press, 1996), 233–236; Fisher, McKie, and Mancke, *IBM and the U.S. Processing Industry*, 180–228.

48. IBM's technical capabilities has been thoroughly studied in a series of well-researched histories. Charles J. Bashe et al., *IBM's Early Computers* (Cambridge, Mass.: MIT Press, 1986); Emerson W. Pugh, Lyle R. Johnson, and John H. Palmer, *IBM's 360 and Early 370 Systems* (Cambridge, Mass.: MIT Press, 1991); Emerson W. Pugh, *Memories that Shaped an Industry: Decisions Leading to IBM System/360* (Cambridge, Mass.: MIT Press, 1984); Emerson W. Pugh, *Building IBM: Shaping an Industry and Its Technology* (Cambridge, Mass: MIT Press, 1995).

49. Cortada, *The Computer in the United States*, 103–107.

50. The infrastructure of that portion of the information processing industry devoted to the PC has not yet been studied by historians: however, for a sampling of what awaits those scholars, see Jay Ranade and Alan Nash, eds., *The Best of BYTE: Two Decades on the Leading Edge* (New York: McGraw-Hill, 1994).

51. Chuck House, "Hewlett-Packard and Personal Computing Systems," in *A History of Personal Workstations*, in ed. Adele Goldberg (New York: ACM Press, 1988), 403–437; Amar Gupta and Hoo-min D. Toong, "Microprocessors: The First Twelve Years," in *Insights into Personal*

Computers, ed. Amar Gupta and Hoo-min D. Toong (New York: IEEE Press, 1985), 167–200.

52. Charles H. Ferguson and Charles R. Morris, *Computer Wars* (New York: Times Books, 1993), 51–65.

53. The issue is so painful for these firms that official publications hardly mention them. For example, David Packard, *The HP Way: How Bill Hewlett and I Built Our Company* (New York: HarperBusiness, 1995). There have been more than two dozen studies done in the mid- to late 1990s on U.S. firms in the information processing industry; almost all have documented dislocations caused by rapidly changing technologies. One of the first view of the problems published in modern times is Clayton M. Christensen, *The Innovator's Dilemma: When New Technologies Cause Great Firms to Fail* (Boston: Harvard Business School Press, 1997); many of Christensen's case studies are from the information processing industry.

54. Listed and described in *Technology Forecast: 1996, passim.*

55. Ibid.

56. *USA Today*, June 16, 1985, p. 2 reports a study by Dunn & Bradstreet Corporation.

57. By the late 1990s, U.S. managers recognized that yet another phase in the evolution of computing was emerging—a network-based phase, symbolized by the Internet. This new phase in computing is the subject of Richard Nolan's essay (chapter 7). He correctly emphasizes changes caused by networking and productivity of machines, software, and telecommunications rather than adopting the more traditional focus on the PC itself.

58. I have explored these issues in some detail in "Economic Preconditions that Made Possible Application of Commercial Computing in the United States," *Annals of the History of Computing* 19, no. 3 (1997): 27–40.

59. Ibid.

60. Alan Stone, *How America Got On-Line* (Armonk: M. E. Sharpe, 1997), 191–212.

61. Government motivation was political, linking R&D to the needs of the Cold War; see Paul Edwards, *The Closed World: Computers and the Politics of Discourse in Cold War America* (Cambridge, Mass: MIT Press, 1996), 1–41; it was also part of a broader pattern of national commitment to science and technology, Carroll Pursell, *The Machine in America: A Social History of Technology* (Baltimore, Md:. Johns Hopkins University Press, 1995); 299–319; Kenneth Flamm, *Targeting the Computer: Government Support and International Competition* (Washington, D.C.: Brookings Institution Press, 1987), 42–92.

62. S. Ratner, J. H. Sollow, and R. Sylla, *The Evolution of the American Economy: Growth, Welfare, and Decision Making* (New York: Basic Books, 1979), 403; Cappelli, *Change at Work*, 23–65.

63. Schement and Curtis, *Tendencies and Tensions of the Information Age*, 21–46.

64. Alfred D. Chandler, Jr., *The Visible Hand: The Management Revolution in American Business* (Cambridge, Mass.: Harvard University Press, 1977), 482–483.

65. Pursell, *The Machine in America*, 203–228. a central theme of Chandler, *The Visible Hand*.

66. Accounting has been brilliantly studied by H. Thomas Johnson and Robert S. Kaplan, *Relevance Lost: The Rise and Fall of Management Accounting* (Boston: Harvard Business School Press, 1987).

67. Numeration increasingly became a feature of American scientific, technological, and business thinking, long predating the computer. This point is well made, for example, by Alfred W. Crosby, *The Measure of Reality: Quantification and Western Society, 1250–1600* (Cambridge: Cambridge University Press, 1997): "During the late Middle Ages and Renaissance a new model of reality emerged in Europe . . . a quantitative model" (xi); Stephen M. Stigler spoke of numbers as providing the basis for a "quantitative technology for empirical science," *The History of Statistics* (Cambridge, Mass: Harvard University Press, 1986), 1.

68. The leading expert on software's legal issues is Anthony Lawrence Clapes, who has written extensively on the U.S. experience, *Software, Copyright, and Competition* (Westport, Conn.: Quorum, 1989) and *Softwars: The Legal Battles for Control of the Global Software Industry* (Westport, Conn.: Quorum, 1993).

69. Stephen E. Siwek and Harold W. Furchtgott-Roth, *International Trade in Computer Software* (Westport, Conn.: Quorum, 1993), 115.

70. The other side of the policy question is the role of public investments in science and technology. Lewis M. Branscomb, "The National Technology Policy Debate," in *Empowering Technology: Implementing a U.S. Strategy*, ed. Lewis M. Branscomb (Cambridge, Mass.: MIT Press, 1993), 1–35.

71. For an excellent introduction to this notion, along with case studies and additional bibliography, see Rob Kling and Suzanne Iacono, "The Mobilization of Support for Computerization: The Role of Computerization Movements," *Social Problems* 35, no. 3 (June 1988): 226–243.

72. Ibid.

73. The two anti-computer works most cited in the United States are Joseph Weizenbaum, *Computer Power and Human Reason* (New York: W. H. Freeman, 1976) and Thomas K. Landauer, *The Trouble with Computers* (Cambridge, Mass.: MIT Press, 1995). The literature in favor is massive.

74. The Europeans, less sensitive to the rate of change, have settled for such terms as cybernetics and informatics, neutral terms that are less application- and technology-focused than the Americans would like, but still useful in covering a multitude of topics.

75. His point is that society was changing, driven as much by technological evolution as by any other consideration, leading to a new knowledge-based workforce and economy; Daniel Bell, *The Coming of Post-Industrial Society* (New York: Basic Books, 1973).

76. Gunther Rudenberg, *World Semiconductor Industry in Transistion: 1978–1983* (Cambridge, Mass.: Arthur D. Little, 1980), 11, 31.

77. *Dataquest*, various reports (1982–1983).

78. U.S. Department of Commerce data presented by Sichel, *The Computer Revolution*, 44.

79. Louis P. Bucklin, "Technological Change and Store Operations: The Supermarket Case," *Journal of Retailing* 56, no. 1 (spring 1980): 3–15; Brian L. Friedman, "Productivity Trends in Department Stores, 1967–86," *Monthly Labor Review* 111, no. 3 (March 1988): 17–21.

80. Harold C. Plant, "New Directions in Data Processing," *Data Processing Proceedings 1963* (Detroit: DPMA, 1963): 200.

81. Quoted on dust jacket of the only history available on the UPC, Stephen A. Brown, *Revolution at the Checkout Counter: The Explosion of the Bar Code* (Cambridge, Mass.: Harvard University Press, 1997).

82. Ibid., 3–5.

83. James L. McKenney, *Waves of Change: Business Evolution through Information Technology* (Boston: Harvard Business School Press, 1995): 41–96.

84. "What makes this generation different from all others before it? It is the first to grow up surrounded by digital media"; Don Tapscott, *Growing Up Digital: The Rise of the Net Generation* (New York: McGraw-Hill, 1998), 1.

85. Sichel, *The Computer Revolution*, 32–36, 75–112; Landauer, *The Trouble with Computers*, 1–46.

86. If you still have doubts that "everyone knows each other," see Ferguson and Morris, *Computer Wars*.

87. IBM internal marketing studies, 1995–1998; this kind of data, however, is also available in Karl Svelby, *The New Organizational Wealth* (San Francisco: Berrett-Koelher, 1997).

Chapter 7

1. Harry Newton, *Newton's Telecom Dictionary*, 13th ed. (New York: Flatiron, 1998), 378.

2. The Stages Theory was first published in Richard L. Nolan, "Managing the Computer Resource: A Stage Hypothesis," *Communications of the ACM* 16 (July 1973): 399–403. This original Stages Theory of computer growth was based on the learning curve reflected through the data processing budget. Subsequent publications focusing on the Stages Theory as applied to organizational learning include Cyrus F. Gibson and Richard L. Nolan, "Managing the Four Stages of EDP Growth," *Har-*

vard Business Review 52 (January–February 1974): 77–88; Richard L. Nolan, "Managing the Crises in Data Processing,"*Harvard Business Review* 57 (March–April 1979): 115–126.

3. For a discussion of the emergence of "dominant designs" in technology, see William J. Abernathy and James M. Utterback, "Patterns of Industrial Innovation," *Technology Review* 80 (June–July 1978): 40–47; James M. Utterback, *Mastering the Dynamics of Innovation* (Boston: Harvard Business School Press, 1994); 23–55.

4. Richard L. Nolan, "Managing the Advanced Stages of Computer Technology: Key Research Issues," in *The Information Systems Research Challenge: Proceedings*, ed. Warren F. McFarlan (Boston: Harvard Business School Press, 1984); 195–216, lists various corporations that have applied the stages theories to their information systems. Several Harvard Business School cases have applied the Stages Theory to a particular industry or company. These include: Linda M. Applegate, "Frito-Lay: The Early Years (A)," 9–193–154 *Harvard Business School Case* (1993); Linda M. Applegate and Donna B. Stoddard, "Xerox Corp.: Leadership of the Information Technology Function (A)," 9–188–113 *Harvard Business School Case* (1988); Linda M. Applegate, "Xerox Corp.: Leadership of the Information Technology Function (B)," 9–191–024 *Harvard Business School Case* (1990); Linda M. Applegate and Ramiro Montealegre, "Eastman Kodak Co.: Managing Information Systems through Strategic Alliances," 9–192–030 *Harvard Business School Case* (1991).

5. See Louis A. Girifalco, "The Dynamics of Technological Change," *The Wharton Magazine* 7 (fall 1982): 31–37. Also, Edwin Mansfield, *Economics of Technological Change* (New York: W. W. Norton, 1968); Richard N. Foster, *Innovation: The Attacker's Advantage* (New York: Summit Books, 1986); Clayton M. Christenson, *The Innovator's Dilemma: When New Technologies Cause Great Firms to Fail* (Management of Innovation and Change Series) (Boston: Harvard Business School Press, 1997); Philip Anderson and Michael L. Tushman, "Technological Discontinuities and Dominant Designs: A Cyclical Model of Technological Change," *Administrative Science Quarterly* 35 (1990): 604–633.

6. "Institutionalizing Change," *Crossborder Monitor* (April 1, 1998): 1.

7. James I. Cash, Robert G. Eccles, Nitin Nohria, and Richard L. Nolan, *Building the Information-Age Organization: Structure, Control, and Information Technologies* (Chicago: R. R. Donnelley, 1994).

8. Alfred D. Chandler Jr., "The M-Form: Industrial Groups, American Style." *European Economic Review* 19 (1982): 3–23; also refer to Alfred D. Chandler Jr., *The Visible Hand: The Managerial Revolution in American Business* (Cambridge, Mass.: Harvard University Press, 1977).

9. John Diebold, in his note on automation in *Automation: the Advent of the Automatic Factory* (New York: D. Van Nostrand, 1952), ix, mentions that D. S. Harder, vice president in charge of manufacturing of the Ford Motor Company, had used the word "automation"—previous to

Diebold's introduction of the term—to describe the automatic handling of materials and parts in and out of machines.

10. John Diebold, "Automation—The New Technology," *Harvard Business Review* 31 (November–December 1953): 63–71.

11. See for example, James W. Cortada, *The Computer in the United States: From Laboratory to Market, 1930 to 1960* (Armonk, N.Y.: M. E. Sharpe, 1993); 64–101; Kenneth Flamm, *Creating the Computer: Government, Industry, and High Technology* (Washington, D.C.: The Brookings Institution, 1988), 29–79.

12. George McDaniel, ed., *IBM Dictionary of Computing* 10th Edition (New York: McGraw-Hill, 1994) describes an analog computer as one whose operations are analogous to the behavior of another system and that accepts, processes, and produces analog data; this data is in the form of a physical quantity that is considered to be continuously variable and whose magnitude is made directly proportional to the data or to a suitable function of the data. A digital computer is a programmable functional unit that is controlled by internally stored programs and that uses common storage for all or part of a program and also for all or part of the data necessary for the execution of the programs. A digital computer operates on discrete data represented as strings of binary digits.

13. "More Hybrid Computers Become Available," *Chemical and Engineering News* 42 (May 4, 1964): 51–52.

14. "New Hybrid Computer System a Product of Joint Agreement," *Chemical and Engineering News* 41 (July 1, 1963): 43.

15. For a brief history of the IBM System 360, see James W. Cortada, *Historical Dictionary of Data Processing: Technology* (Westport, Conn.: Greenwood Press, 1987), 212–220.

16. Ibid.

17. Standard & Poor's Compustat.

18. The discussion on UNIX and Ethernet is summarized from Paul Ceruzzi, "Workstations, UNIX, and the Net, 1981–1955" in *A History of Modern Computing* (Cambridge, Mass.: MIT Press, 1998); 281–306.

19. TCP/IP stands for Transmission Control Protocol/Internet Protocol. Thomas G. W. Keen, Walid Mougayar, and Tracy Torregrossa, *The Business Internet and Intranets: A Manager's Guide to Key Terms and Concepts* (Boston: Harvard Business School Press, 1998); 253–255, explain that TCP/IP, the procedures and formats that create, transmit, and receive messages on the Net, is the Internet's core. TCP/IP allows any computer anywhere to talk to any other computer anywhere, even if the two computers are completely dissimilar in hardware, operating system, and applications software.

20. Ceruzzi, *History of Modern Computing*, 284.

21. Ibid. 292.

22. Richard L. Nolan, "Plight of the EDP Manager," *Harvard Business Review* (May–June 1973): 143–152.

23. Richard L. Nolan, "Business Needs a New Breed of EDP Manager," *Harvard Business Review* (March–April 1976): 123–133.

24. Robert L. Glass, "COBOL—A Contradiction and an Enigma," *Communications of the ACM* 40 (September 1997): 11.

25. A "hurdle rate" is the minimum return on investment that a proposed investment must yield in order to be considered for funding by the corporation. For further information about hurdle rates, see Clyde P. Stickney and Roman L. Weil, *Financial Accounting: An Introduction to Concepts, Methods, and Uses* (Philadelphia: Dryden Press, 1994). Stickney and Weil define hurdle rate as the required rate of return in a discounted cash flow (DCF) analysis (pp. G-32, G-47). A DCF uses either the net present value or the internal rate of return in an analysis to measure the value of future expected cash expenditures and receipts at a common date.

26. By the 1990s, every electronic calculator costing $10 or more embedded these complex present-value calculations into their logic, enabling the calculations to be done by entering some basic data and pressing a button.

27. Standard & Poor's Compustat.

28. Ibid.

29. "Dumb terminals" were input devices that did not have a central processing unit (CPU) that enabled the terminal to carry out computations in a stand-alone environment. Later on PCs were used for both stand-alone use, and for input to mainframes.

30. "A Mainframe on Three Chips." *Business Week (Industrial Edition)* (March 2, 1981): 116.

31. Foster, *Innovation*.

32. Ron Scherer, "IBM Unveils New Home Computer Line," *The Christian Science Monitor* (August 21, 1981): 5.

33. The Sharenet operating system provided the file server with support for multiple disk operating systems (DOS) sharing network and file space, a means for managing the functioning of multiple computers in the same directory simultaneously, file security, and support of spooled printers and station-to-station pipes. The network protocol was CSMA/CD (Carrier Sense Multiple Access) and the data-transfer rate was 1.43 megabits per second. For an additional fee, electronic mail could be incorporated into the network operating system. Source: "IBM PC XT Local-Network Scheme," *Byte* (October 1983): 593.

34. Matt Kramer, "MS-NET Paves the Wave for LAN Applications," *PC Week* (November 13, 1984): 1.

35. *International Directory*, vol. 6 (1992), 269; *Hoover's Guide to Computer Companies* (Austin, Tex.: Hoover's Business Press, 1996), 26–27, 164–165.

36. RISC (Reduced Instruction Set Computer) architecture was introduced in 1980 by John Cocke of IBM. It greatly boosted computer

speed by using simplified machine instructions for frequently used functions.

37. For a discussion of broader technological developments of the workstation, refer to "Workstations, UNIX, and the Net, 1981–1955" in Ceruzzi, *History of Modern Computing*, 281–306.

38. Alfred D. Chandler Jr., "The Computer Industry: The First Half-Century," in *Competing in the Age of Digital Convergence*, ed. David B. Yoffie (Cambridge, Mass.: Harvard Business School Press, 1997), 70, 89–94.

39. Ceruzzi, *History of Modern Computing*, 289.

40. Chandler, "The Computer Industry," 92–93.

41. Scherer, "IBM Unveils New Home Computer Line."

42. William R. Synnott and William H. Gruber, *Information Resource Management: Opportunities and Strategies for the 1980s* (New York: Wiley, 1981), 66.

43. In addition to the proliferation of computers, the march had broken down in the 1970s and 1980s for a wide variety of macroeconomic reasons—such as recession, oil crisis, breakdown of international financial arrangements, and foreign competition.

44. Shoshana Zuboff, *In the Age of the Smart Machine: The Future of Work and Power* (New York: Basic Books, 1988), 9–11.

45. See Maryam Alavi, "KPMG Peat Marwick U.S.: One Giant Brian," 9-397-108 *Harvard Business School Case* (1997); Robert G. Eccles and Julie Gladstone, "KPMG Peat Marwick: The Shadow Partner," 9-492-002 *Harvard Business School Case* (1995).

46. The ARPANET was named for and sponsored by the Defense Department's Advanced Research Project Agency.

47. The information about the history of the Internet, presented in the following paragraphs of this chapter, is taken from Andrew B. Zimmerman, "The Evolution of the Internet; Internet/Web/Online Service Information," *Telecommunications* 31 (June 1997): 39; Barry M. Lerner et al., "The Past and Future History of the Internet; The Next 50 Years: Our Hopes, Our Visions, Our Plans," *Communications of the ACM* 40 (February 1997): 102; Katie Hafner and Matthew Lyon, *Where Wizards Stay Up Late: The Origins of the Internet* (New York: Simon & Schuster, 1996). For a more detailed history of the Internet, refer to these sources.

48. Zimmerman, "The Evolution of the Internet."

49. "Host Computers Almost Double within the Year," *New Media Age* (October 9, 1997): 16. Bellcore's survey classified host computers as centralized server computers, workstations, and each modem in the modem back of Internet Service Providers.

50. For a further discussion of the simplification of corporate networks, see Mark Cotteleer and Robert D. Austin, "Network Computing at Sun Microsystems: A Strategic Deployment," 9-198-007 *Harvard Business School Case* (1997).

51. See various articles by Mary Cronin published in *Fortune* (February 2, 1998, p. 142; March 30, 1998, p. 158; May 11, 1998, p. 163); John Hagel III and Arthur G. Armstrong, *Net Gain: Expanding Markets through Virtual Communities* (Boston: Harvard Business School Press, 1997).

52. Lee Gomes, "Cisco Passes Significant Milestone, Topping $100 Billion in Market Value," *Wall Street Journal Interactive Edition* (July 20, 1998), http://interactive.wsj.com.

53. Richard L. Nolan and Kelley A. Porter, "Cisco Systems, Inc.," 9-398-127 *Harvard Business School Case* (1998).

54. Ibid.

55. "The Accidental Superhighway," *The Economist* (July 1, 1995): S3.

56. Zimmerman, "The Evolution of the Internet."

57. Values are based on "The Internet Domain Survey," *Network Wizards* (July 1998), http://www.nw.com/zone/WWW/dist-bynum.html. Commercial sites reflect the percentage of total domain names that end in .com. The survey methodology is described at http://www.nw.com/zone/WWW/new-survey.html.

58. Robert Metcalfe's idea of the Ethernet, was outlined in Metcalfe's Harvard Ph.D. dissertation in 1993; Ethernet is now used to network more than 100 million computers.

59. See George Gilder, "Metcalfe's Law and Legacy," *Forbes ASAP* (September 13, 1993), 158.

60. Numbers are from Nua Internet Surveys (http://www.nua.ie/surveys/howmanyonline/index.html). Each month, this firm looks at the many published surveys on Internet users and makes an educated guess of the best number of people who are online.

61. "Latest IntelliQuest Survey Reports 62 Million American Adults Access the Internet/Online Services," (February 5, 1998), http://www.intelliquest.com/press/release41.asp.

62. Gordon Moore, chairman emeritus of Intel Corporation, observed that the technology for cramming transistors on a fixed size silicon chip doubled approximately every 18 months. His theory was first published in Gordon E. Moore, "Cramming More Components onto Integrated Circuits," *Electronics* (April 19, 1965): 114–117.

63. The TechWeb Technology Encyclopedia defines bandwidth as the transmission capacity of an electronic line such as a communications network, computer bus, or computer channel. It is expressed in bits per second, bytes per second, or Hertz (cycles per second). Source: http://www.techweb.com/encyclopedia/defineterm?term=bandwidth.

64. George Gilder, "Fiber Keeps Its Promise," *Forbes ASAP* (April 7, 1997): 2.

65. Stephen P. Bradley and Jerry A. Hausman, *Future Competition in Telecommunications* (Boston: Harvard Business School Press, 1989); Peter Temin and Louis Galambos, *The Fall of the Bell System: A Study in Prices and Politics* (New York: Cambridge University Press, 1987).

66. Ira Magaziner, "Call to Action," *Second International Harvard Conference on Internet & Society* (May 29, 1998).

67. Stephen P. Bradley, Pankaj Ghemawat, and Sharon Foley, "Wal-Mart, Inc.," 9-794-024 *Harvard Business School Case* (1996).

68. Pankaj Ghemawat and Bret Baird, "Leadership Online: Barnes & Noble vs. Amazon.com (A)," N-798-063 *Harvard Business School Case* (1998).

69. John J. Sviokla, "Edmund's—www.edmunds.com," 9-397-016 *Harvard Business School Case* (1997).

70. Donna B. Stoddard, Anne Donnellon, and Richard L. Nolan, "VeriFone (1997)," 9-398-030 *Harvard Business School Case* (1997).

71. Warren F. McFarlan and Donna B. Stoddard, "Otisline (A)," 9-186-058 *Harvard Business School Case* (1990).

72. Michael Hammer and James Champy, *Reengineering the Corporation: A Manifesto for Business Revolution* (New York: HarperBusiness, 1993), was an important book in triggering the campaign to reengineer business processes rather than simply use computers to automate the existing business functions and tasks.

73. Nitin Nohria and Robert G. Eccles, ed., *Networks and Organizations: Structure, Form, and Action* (Boston: Harvard Business School Press, 1992).

74. Thomas G. W. Keen, Walid Mougayar, and Tracy Torregrossa, *The Business Internet and Intranets: A Manager's Guide to Key Terms and Concepts* (Boston: Harvard Business School Press, 1998), define intranets as networks built on Internet-based technology that limit access to people within the originating organization and others who have been granted permission to access the internal networks (p. 231). The intranet may or may not link to the external Internet.

75. John G. Sifonis and Beverly Goldberg, "Changing Role of the CIO," *Information Week* (March 24, 1997), 69–82.

76. Ibid., 79.

77. Robert J. Greene, "The DP Manager's Status," *Datamation* (June 1974): 66–67.

78. Ivy Schmerken, "Hail to the Chiefs," *Wall Street & Technology* 16 (January 1998): 40.

79. Chuck Nunamaker, "CIO Profile," *Leading Trends in Information Services: Ninth Annual Survey of North American Chief Information Executives—1997* (New York: Deloitte & Touche Consulting Group, 1997): 15.

80. For a more detailed discussion on the new management principles that evolved, refer to Richard L. Nolan and David C. Croson, *Creative Destruction: A Six-Stage Process for Transforming the Organization* (Boston: Harvard Business School Press, 1995), 14–17.

81. Eccles and Gladstone, "KPMG Peat Marwick: The Shadow Partner."

82. Chiara Francalanci and Donna Stoddard; "State Street Corporation:

Leading with Information Technology," 9-195-135 *Harvard Business School Case* (1994).

83. The TechWeb Technology Encyclopedia (http://www.techweb.com/encyclopedia/defineter?term=ERP) defines ERP as an information system that integrates all manufacturing and related applications for an entire enterprise. An ERP implies the use of advanced information technologies, including graphical user interfaces (GUI), CASE tools, 4GLs, client-server architecture, and open systems.

84. Stephen P. Bradley and Richard L. Nolan, ed., *Sense and Respond: Capturing Value in the Network Era* (Boston: Harvard Business School Press, 1998).

85. Ibid., 132.

86. Ibid., 129.

87. "New Intel Chip for Autos; Intel Corp. Introduces High-performance Microchip," *Ward's Auto World* (December 1995), 33.

88. "Siemens' Access to 'Real-time' Driver Information Can Help Reduce Symptoms of Road Rage," *PR Newswire* (May 6, 1998), n.p.

89. Megan Loncto, "Bots Search for Best Prices," *Computer Shopper* (April 1998), p. 79.

90. Rochelle Garner, "Barkat's Big Leap," *Upside* (March 1998) http://www.upside.com/texis/mvm/story3id=34c90ba90.

91. Bradley and L. Nolan, *Sense and Respond*, 184.

92. Theodore H. Clark, David C. Croson, James L. McKenney, and Richard L. Nolan, "H. E. Butt Grocery Company: A Leader in ECR Implementation (Abridged)," 9-196-061 *Harvard Business School Case* (1997); Robert D. Austin and F. Warren McFarlan, "H. E. Butt Grocery Company: A Leader in ECR Implementation (B) (Abridged)," 9-198-016 *Harvard Business School Case* (1997).

93. T. W. Malone, J. Yates, and R. I. Benjamin, "Electronic Markets and Electronic Hierarchies," *Communications of the ACM* 30 (1987): 484–497.

94. See Alavi, "KPMG Peat Marwick U.S.," for a discussion of the history of knowledge management at the firm and the facilitating role of the Internet and intranet technologies in executing the firm's knowledge management strategy; Robert H. Buckman, "Knowledge Sharing at Buckman Labs." *Journal of Business Strategy* (January–February 1998), for a discussion the implementation of a "knowledge management culture" at Buckman Laboratories; and Jeff Moad, "The Working Web," *PC Week* 14 (March 17, 1997): 125, for a discussion on the rollout of intranets to nontraditional knowledge workers at companies such as Delta, Levi Strauss, and Tektronic Inc.

95. Approximate market value is calculated by multiplying the value of a common share (as reported on a stock exchange) by the number of common shares outstanding.

96. Keen, Mougayar, and Torregrossa, *The Business Internet and Intranets*, define routers as a key component of all networks; as their name suggest, they handle the routing of traffic across a network, interpreting destination addresses and managing traffic jams among their many other communication, coordination, and management functions (p. 195).

97. Gomes, "Cisco Passes Significant Milestone."

98. Sales per employee numbers were compared with the industry averages presented in "1998 Fortune 500," *Fortune* (April 27, 1998). General Electric was the only company presented in Table 7.2 that had sales per employee more than double that of its industry average (2.09 times). At the other end of the spectrum, IBM had sales per employee that were only 0.85 times that of its industry's average and Johnson & Johnson had sales per employee that were 0.99 times that of its industry's average.

99. Rates of increase were based on the difference in SPE between each of the eras for the firms listed in table 7.2. The average rate of increase between 1978 and 1986 (not including International Group's 28.63 rate of increase) was 2.00; the average rate of increase between 1986 and 1997 was 2.60.

100. Standard & Poor's Compustat.

101. Richard L. Nolan, "Business Needs a New Breed of EDP Manager."

102. See Paul A. Strassman, *The Business Value of Computers* (New Canaan, Conn.: Information Economics, 1990).

Chapter 8

1. U.S. Department of Commerce, *Statistical Abstract of the United States* (Washington, D.C.: Government Printing Office, 1997), 565–566. Estimates for recorded music and video games include persons 12 years and older.

2. A complete sociological analysis will treat many topics omitted or only touched on here, such as the role of the mass media in creating rather than simply reporting "the computer revolution" and a comparison of the role of the household computer with that of the telephone and television.

3. Data on the acquisition of home computer hardware and software are generally sparse and of uneven quality. Sales figures are often proprietary; industry polls use sampling frames that produce upwardly biased estimates. Federal government surveys, which have minimal sampling bias, include few questions about household computers. See Donna L. Hoffman, William D. Kalsbeek, and Thomas P. Novak, "Internet and Web Use in the U.S.," *Communications of the ACM 39* (December 1996): 36–46, for an analysis of shortcomings in estimates of Internet use. While nationally representative data on the diffusion of home computers are sparse, national data on their use and effects are practically nonexistent.

Here the investigator must rely upon a combination of small-scale academic studies and consumer polls.

4. H. Edwards Roberts and William Yates, "Altair 8800 Minicomputer, Part 1," *Popular Electronics* (January 1975): 33, 38.

5. Wozniak built his first machine, the Apple I, in 1976 and sold about 250 of them for $666. The Apple II, which was introduced at the First West Coast Computer Fair in April 1977, sold for $1,298. It came with from 4K to 48K of memory, color graphics, sound, text screen display, and the BASIC program loaded in its read–only memory (ROM).

6. The Apple II was designed to appeal to people beyond the world of the electronics hobbyist. Wozniak explained:

   A lot of features of the Apple II went in because I had designed Breakout for Atari. I had designed it in hardware. I wanted to write it in software now. So that was the reason that color was added in first—so that games could be programmed. I sat down one night and tried to put it into BASIC. . . . I got this ball bouncing around, and I said, "Well it needs sound," and I had to add a speaker to the Apple II. It wasn't planned, it was just accidental. . . . Obviously you need paddles, so I had to scratch my head and design a simple minimum-chip paddle circuit, and put on some paddles. So a lot of these features that really made the Apple II stand out in its day came from a game.

   Jack Connick, ". . . And Then There Was Apple," *CALL-A.P.P.L.E.* (October 1986): 24.

7. Serious Software Helps the Home Computer Grow Up; *Business Week* (June 11, 1984): 114–118.

8. Robert X. Cringely, *Accidental Empires* (Reading, Mass.: Addison-Wesley, 1992), 64. VisiCalc is often given much of the credit for the enormous increase in Apple II sales, from $800,000 in 1977 to more than $47 million in 1979. James Chposky and Ted Leonsis, *Blue Magic: The People, Power, and Politics Behind the IBM Personal Computer* (New York: Facts on File Publications, 1988), 8. Even though most software sold was game software, by 1980 VisiCalc was the top-selling personal computer program in the United States.

9. *Business Week*, (June 11, 1984).

10. The earliest database services such as CompuServe and The Source were actually established in the late 1970s. No significant customer base, however, grew until after the mid-1980s.

11. Larry Roberts and Barry Wessler, "Computer Network Development to Achieve Resource Sharing," *AFIPS Spring Joint Computer Conference Proceedings 36* (1970): 543–549.

12. Katie Hafner and Matthew Lyon, *Where Wizards Stay Up Late: The Origins of the Internet* (New York: Simon and Schuster, 1996), 187–218; J. C. R. Licklider and Albert Vezza, "Applications of Information Networks," *IEEE Proceedings* 66 (1978): 1330–1346.

13. Overlooking or underestimating the importance of computer-based sociability via e-mail echoes the telephone industry's earlier overlooking the sociability uses of the telephone. Claude Fischer, *America Calling: A Social History of The Telephone to 1940* (Berkeley: University of California Press, 1992), 60–85.

14. Jonathan Zittrain, "The Rise and Fall of Sysopdom," *Harvard Journal of Law and Technology* (summer 1997): 495, describes how commercial services use sysops (from "system operators") to regulate on-line discussions.

15. Marc Gunther, "The Internet Is Mr. Case's Neighborhood," *Fortune* 137, no. 6 (March 30, 1998): 68.

16. Netscape's browser (introduced in 1994) had a distinct impact, making it easier for people to create and view Web sites. AOL's sales rose from $40 million in 1993 to $104 million in 1994, and $394 million in 1995. *Hoover's Guide to Computer Companies* (Austin, Tex: Hoover's Business Press 1996), 37.

17. Sara Kiesler, Lee Sproull, and Jacquelynne S. Eccles "Second-class Citizens?" *Psychology Today* 17 (1983): 40–48.

18. Paul Attewell and Juan Battle, "Home Computers and School Performance," *The Information Society* 15 (February, 1999): 1–10. Their analysis was based on data from the U.S. Department of Education's National Educational Longitudinal Study of 1988, which surveyed a stratified random sample of 18,000 U.S. schools and 8th grade students.

19. This disparity is not seen in male and female television viewing, radio listening, or newspaper reading. *Statistical Abstract*, 565–566.

20. In 1996 girls made up only 17 percent of those taking the high school advanced placement exam in computer science, see *Boston Globe*, October 15, 1998: A-28 Women were also less likely than men to major in computer science in college or pursue graduate work in computer science. In 1995 women represented 29 percent of students graduating from college with a major in computer science; they comprised 23 percent of students enrolled in graduate programs in computer science; see National Science Foundation, *Science and Engineering Degrees: 1966–95* (Washington D.C.: Government Printing Office,

21. Robert H. Anderson, Tora K. Bikson, Sally Ann Law, and Bridger M. Mitchell, *Universal Access to E-mail: Feasibility and Societal Implications* (Santa Monica, Calif.: The Rand Corporation, 1995). The authors based their estimates on U.S. Bureau of the Census Current Population Surveys conducted in 1993 on a random sample of 143,000 U.S. households.

22. National Telecommunications and Information Administration, *Falling through the Net II: New Data on the Digital Divide* (Washington D.C.: Government Printing Office, 1998). This report was based on data compiled by the U.S. Census Bureau through 48,000 door-to-door surveys in October 1997.

23. Anderson et al., *Universal Access to E-mail.*
24. National Telecommunications and Information Administration, *Falling through the Net.*
25. Computer Intelligence, *Consumer Technology Index* (1998). This industry survey of more than 50,000 households estimated that almost 60 percent of households with children own a computer, while 35 percent of households without children own a computer. Although, like most industry studies, this one overestimates the total extent of computer ownership, there is no reason to suspect any bias in the relative estimates of households with children versus households without children.
26. Robert Kraut, William Scerlis, Tridas Mukhopadlyay, Jane Manning, and Sara Kiesler. "The HomeNet Field Trial of Residential Internet Services," *Communications of the ACM* 39 (December 1996): 55–63.
27. See, for example, Joseph B. Giacquinta, JoAnne Bauer, and Jane E. Levin, *Beyond Technology's Promise: An Examination of Children's Educational Computing at Home* (Cambridge: Cambridge University Press, 1993).
28. Attewell and Battle, "Home Computers and School Performance." As the authors of this analysis noted, the average increase in student test scores associated with a home computer was comparable to that associated with taking an after-school art, music, or dance class or going to science or history museums with one's parents.
29. "The Internet Index": http://new-website.openmarket.com/intindex/index.cfm. NetDay wiring programs bore no resemblance to the rural telephony wiring parties of the early twentieth century. Farmers who wanted telephone service raised the money and supplied their own labor and materials to string wire and connect to switches. They were ignored by the phone industry, politicians, and the media; see Fischer, America Calling 94–98. As Fischer documents, farmers needed and used their telephone service. In the case of the schools, many of them have not yet figured out what to do with their Internet access.
30. Richard D. Brown, *Knowledge Is Power: The Diffusion of Information in Early America, 1700–1865* (New York: Oxford University Press, 1989), 270–286.
31. Families listened together to entertainment, self-improvement, and news programs. On May 16, 1923, one radio station's broadcast schedule included several musical programs, "things to tell the housewife about cooking meat," a short story, a lecture, and an adventure program; Tom Lewis, *Empire of the Air* (New York: HarperCollins, 1991), 163–164. On the evening after the attack on Pearl Harbor in December 1941, 80 percent of the country's 56 million radios were tuned to President Franklin D. Roosevelt's speech; see Lewis, *Empire of the Air,* 280. Popular accounts of the time and retrospective evocations emphasize families listening together. But because there is no body of systematic research on family radio listening behavior, we do not know the extent to which these portrayals overestimate base rates.

32. Eleanor Maccoby, "Television: Its Impact on School Children," *Public Opinion Quarterly* 15 (1951): 421–444; M. Jackson-Beeck and John P. Robinson, "Television Nonviewers: An Endangered Species?," *Journal of Consumer Research* 7 (1981): 356–359; G. H. Brody, "Effects of Television Viewing on Family Interactions: An Observational Study," *Family Relations* 29 (April 1980): 216–220. The research literature on the effects of television viewing on individuals is voluminous and not without controversy. The focus here is only on the effects of television viewing on time spent in family communication.

33. *Computerworld* (December 13, 1982): 15 Representative Newt Gingrich (R-Ga.) was the author of act.

34. *Time* (January 3, 1983): 17.

35. John P. Robinson, K. Barth, and A. Kohut, "Social Impact Research: Personal Computers, Mass Media, and Use of Time," *Social Science Computer Review* 15 (1997): 65–82.

36. Nick P. Vitalari, Alladi Venkatesh, and K. Gronhaug, "Computing in the Home: Shifts in the Time Allocation Patterns of Households," *Communications of the ACM* 28 (May 1985): 512–522; Robert Kraut, Michael Patterson, Vicki Lundmark, Sara Kiesler, Tridas Mukopadhyay, and William Scherlis, "Internet Paradox: A Social Technology that Reduces Social Involvement and Psychological Well-being?," *American Psychologist* 53 (September 1998,): 1017–1031. This analysis of data from seventy-three households shows a statistically significant negative effect of increased computer use on a person's family communication centrality, reducing that centrality by approximately 10 percent when controlling for other variables known to affect communication centrality such as family size.

37. A 1982 national probability sample of households found that 30 percent of those employed outside the household brought work home with them; those bringing work home were primarily white-collar workers. Robert E. Kraut, "Predicting the Use of Technology: The Case of Telework," in *Technology and the Transformation of White-Collar Work*, ed. Robert E. Kraut (Hillsdale, N.J.: Lawrence Erlbaum, 1987), 113–134.

38. Margarethe H. Olson, "Telework: Practical Experience and Future Prospects," in Robert E. Kraut, *Technology and the Transformation*, 135–154.

39. Hafner and Lyon, *Where Wizards Stay Up Late*, In fact, one version of "Adventure" was shipped on the original IBM PC in 1981. Chposky and Leonsis, *Blue Magic*, 110.

40. Hafner and Lyon, *Where Wizards Stay Up Late*, 205–21.

41. Lee Sproull and Sara Kiesler, "Reducing Social Context Cues: Electronic Mail in Organizational Communication," *Management Science* 32 (1986): 1492–1512; Thomas Finholt and Lee Sproull, "Electronic Groups at Work," *Organization Science* 1 (1990): 41–64.

42. On the supply side, businesses are striving to understand what it means

to have a "presence" on the Web, including how to display their product information in a way that will best reach their potential customers.

43. *Boston Globe*, May 5, 1978, C1.

44. James E. Katz and Philip Aspden, "A Nation of Strangers?," *Communications of the ACM* 40 (December 1997): 84. In addition, seventeen percent of respondents who had used the Internet for less than a year reported using it for family contact.

45. Ibid., 85.

46. Howard Rheingold, *The Virtual Community: Homesteading on the Electronic Frontier* (Reading, Mass: Addison-Wesley, 1993): 120.

47. About 18,000 Usenet groups and about 85,000 listservs or mailing lists.

48. Woo Young Chung, "Why Do People Use the Internet?" (Ph.D. dissertation, Boston University, 1998).

49. Dave Hughes, quoted in Rheingold, *The Virtual Community*, 241.

50. For an analysis of discourse strategies in electronic support groups, see Jolene Galegher, Lee Sproull, and Sara Kiesler, "Legitimacy, Authority, and Community in Electronic Support Groups," *Written Communication* 15 (1998): 493–530.

51. Chposky and Leonsis, *Blue Magic*, 65.

52. Kraut et al., "The HomeNet Field Trial," 57; Marita Franzke and Anne McClard, "Winona Gets Wired: Technical Difficulties in the Home," *Communications of the ACM* 39 (December 1996): 64–66. An analysis of reasons why people did not buy a home computer as rapidly as they did a home television could be the topic of a separate chapter. See Alladi Venkatesh, "Computers and Other Interactive Technologies for the Home," *Communications of the ACM* 39 (December 1996): 47–54, for some possible explanations. The twenty-year diffusion of the personal computer (36.6 percent of U.S. households by 1997) more resembles the diffusion of the telephone into households in the first twenty years of the twentieth century than it does the diffusion of the PC into organizations in the last twenty years of the century. The telephone also diffused much more rapidly into business markets than into households; Claude Fischer, *America Calling*, 42. One should not conclude from the telephone and the personal computer, however, that the household is always slow to adopt technology. As Margaret Graham reminded us in chapter 5, 90 percent of U.S. households acquired a television during the ten-year period of the 1950s.

Chapter 9

1. See Arthur T. Pier, *Forbes: Telephone Pioneer* (New York: Dodd, Mead, 1953), chap. 10, 11. J. Alan Moyer, "Urban Growth and the Development of the Telephone: Some Relationships at the Turn of the Century," in *The Social Impact of the Telephone*, ed. Ithiel de Sola Pool (Cambridge,

Mass. MIT Press, 1977); 347–361, has an excellent description of the beginning and continuing growth of a local telephone operating company, the New England Telephone Company.

2. Louis Galambos, "Theodore N. Vail and the Role of Innovation in the Modern Bell System," *Business History Review* 66 (spring 1992): 115–117.

3. David B. Yoffie, ed., *Competing in the Age of Digital Convergence* (Boston: Harvard Business School Press, 1997), "Introduction," 2–3, 9, also 160–161. Italics are Yoffie's.

4. *New York Times*, January 9, 1999, p. B-1.

5. A pioneering and outstanding work on the nature of evolution of technological systems is Thomas P. Hughes, *Networks of Power: Electrification in Western Society, 1880–1930* (Baltimore, Md.: Johns Hopkins University Press, 1983); chap. 1 is especially valuable.

6. Even by the autumn 1998, historians and experts on software could not come to agreement on the types and scope of software. The Charles Babbage Institute of the University of Minnesota, the world's largest center for the study of the history of computing, concluded a study on what initiatives the center should take to study the history of software. Though projects were identified and initiatives launched, no definition of the scope of software could be arrived at. The study, commissioned by James W. Cortada, was intended in part to lay out precisely a blueprint for the historical study of this important component of the Information Age.

7. These included client-server tools from such firms as Oracle and IBM and, later, Web browsers from such firms as Netscape, Lycos, and Microsoft.

8. For an excellent overview of the U.S. software experience, see W. Edward Steinmueller, "The U.S. Software Industry: An Analysis and Interpretive History," in *The International Computer Software Industry: A Comparative Study of Industry Evolution and Structure*, ed. David C. Mowery (New York: Oxford University Press, 1996), 15–52.

9. Java is a set of software tools that allows someone, to, for example, write and create an individualized web browser or to measure user behavior by collecting data on computer-based transactions. For an excellent discussion of the applications of Java, see Carl L. Shapiro and Hal Varian, *Information Rules: A Strategic Guide to the Network Economy* (Boston: Harvard Business School Press, 1999): 37, 72–73, 275–276. Java is a development of the late 1990s, a true child of the networking computing of the decade.

Bibliographic Essay on the Role of Information in the Transformation of the United States

The general topic of the role of information in the development of the American character and in influencing the course of events has long interested historians and, recently, economists. The work, however, has been piecemeal in nature: a study here on freedom of expression in the early days of the Republic, a study there about the role of information in the U.S. economy of the late twentieth century, another on communications and information flows in late nineteenth-century corporations, and so forth. In short, there has been a constant stream of studies on aspects of the role of information in American society. In the present book, we attempt to bring together the thinking of many historians, sociologists, and economists on the deployment of information, and information-handling technologies, in North America and about its role in the development of U.S. society, with a particular emphasis on business and economic issues. The closest to covering the topic as a whole was Steven Lubar of the Smithsonian Institution, who wrote *Infoculture: The Smithsonian Book of Information Age Inventions* (Boston: Houghton Mifflin, 1993); a lavishly illustrated history of various inventions from the printing press to the computer, including a lively narrative and a bibliography. Aimed at general readers is Wade Rowland's *Spirit of the Web: The Age of Information from Telegraph to Internet* (Toronto: Somerville House, 1994), and Brian Winston, *Media Technology and Society: A History from the Telegraph to the Internet* (London: Routledge, 1998). But the underlying work of many previous scholars enriches the whole topic of information in America. This bibliographic essay suggests some of the most obvious and readily accessible studies one can look at to gain a deeper knowledge of the themes explored in this book.

Early American Origins of the Information Age

For the earliest years of the North American experience there are two books. The first, David Cressy, *Coming Over: Migration and Communication between*

345

England and New England in the Seventeenth Century (Cambridge: Cambridge University Press, 1987), is a very solid piece of research. Also very useful is the volume by Ian K. Steele, *English Atlantic, 1675–1740: An Exploration of Communication and Community* (New York: Oxford University Press, 1986). On the eighteenth century, there are two important contributions by Richard D. Brown, *Knowledge Is Power: The Diffusion of Information in Early America, 1700–1865* (New York: Oxford University Press, 1989) and *The Strength of a People: The Idea of an Informed Citizenry in America, 1650–1870* (Chapel Hill: University of North Carolina Press, 1996). In the first book Brown demonstrates that there was a communications revolution in the United States, and he emphasizes cultural and ideological factors in explaining this development. In the second volume, Brown traces the development of the basic American notion that an informed citizenry makes for good democracy, documenting the role of the U.S. government from the earliest days in creating the infrastructure needed for the free flow of information.

One of the earliest vehicles for the transmission of information in America was the book. For a collection of essays on the role of this vehicle for books in communication, see David D. Hall and Hugh Amory, eds., *The Colonial Book in the Atlantic World* (Cambridge: Cambridge University Press, 1999). Early communication efforts are also treated in Steele, *The English Atlantic*, and Charles E. Clark, *The Public Prints: The Newspaper in Anglo-American Culture, 1665–1740* (New York: Oxford University Press, 1994). On the critical role of education, see Lawrence A. Cremin, *American Education: The Colonial Experience, 1607–1783* (New York: Harper & Row, 1970).

There is a large body of literature on the role of literacy in America. For two introductions to the subject, see Kenneth A. Lockridge, *Literacy in Colonial New England: An Enquiry into the Social Context of Literacy in the Early Modern West* (New York: W. W. Norton, 1974), and Harvey Graff, *The Labyrinths of Literacy: Reflections on Literacy Past and Present* (London: Falmes Press, 1987). For those who want to take the story closer to the present there is Carl Kaestle et al., *Literacy in the United States: Readers and Reading since 1880* (New Haven, Conn.: Yale University Press, 1991).

Much attention in the early years on the subject of information concerned politics, and the role of expression in formulating the practices and attitudes of the nation toward the significance and function of knowledge, data, and information. For a case study focusing on the highly influential colony of Massachusetts, see Richard D. Brown, *Revolutionary Politics in Massachusetts: The Boston Committee of Correspondence and the Towns, 1771–1774* (Cambridge, Mass.: Harvard University Press, 1970); it challenges earlier studies by John C. Miller, *Sam Adams: Pioneer in Propaganda* (Boston: Little, Brown, 1936) and Philip G. Davidson, *Propaganda and the American Revolution, 1763–1783* (Chapel Hill: University of North Carolina Press, 1941). But also look at the broader study by J. R. Pole, *The Gift of Government: Political Responsibility from the English Restoration to American Independence* (Athens: University of Georgia Press, 1986).

The literature on the impact of printing on public discourse and also on publishing in nineteenth-century America is massive. However, several recent publications help define many of the key issues. A good start is an article by Donald M. Scott, "The Popular Lecture and the Creation of a Public in Mid-Nineteenth Century America," *Journal of American History 66* (March 1980): 791–809, and the same author's "Print and the Public Lecture System, 1840–1860," in *Printing and Society in Early America*, ed. William L. Joyce, (Worcester Mass.: American Antiquarian Society, 1983); 278–299. Religious organizations were particularly active in communicating their views and distributing materials; for a useful overview, see Peter J. Wosh, *Spreading the Word: The Bible in Nineteenth-Century America* (Ithaca, N.Y.: Cornell University Press, 1994). The indispensable starting point, however, on the general theme of religious communications, and which also contains an excellent bibliography, is Leonard I. Sweet, ed., *Communication and Change in American Religious History* (Grand Rapids, Mich.: William B. Eerdmans, 1993). Also readable, and influential on historians, is an essay by David Paul Nord, "The Evangelical Origins of Mass Media in America, 1815–1835," *Journalism Monographs* 88 (May 1984): 1–31.

Printing and printing presses represented a crucial early technology. For a case study that illustrates the transition from printer to publisher in the early years of the Republic, see Rosalind Remer, *Printers and Men of Capital: Philadelphia Book Publishers in the New Republic* (Philadelphia: University of Pennsylvania Press, 1996). An older book that still reads beautifully and retains its reputation as a good place to begin is by Frank Luther Mott, *American Journalism: A History, 1690 to 1960*, 3d ed. (New York: Macmillan, 1962). On newspapers see Michael Schudson, *Discovering the News: A Social History of American Newspapers* (New York: Basic Books, 1978). Also very useful, theoretically wide-ranging, and even fun to read, is a book of essays by various contributors edited by John E. Hench, *Three Hundred Years of the American Newspaper* (Worcester Mass.: American Antiquarian Society, 1991).

Inasmuch as the postal system was vital to newspaper distribution, Richard R. John's *Spreading the News: The News: The American Postal System from Franklin to Morse* (Cambridge, Mass.: Harvard University Press, 1995; paperback ed., 1998) is crucial. See also his essay, "Expanding the Realm of Communications," in *An Extensive Republic: Print, Culture, and Society in the New Nation*, ed. Robert A. Gross and Mary Kelley (Cambridge: Cambridge University Press, forthcoming). The speed at which information traveled is treated in Allen R. Pred, *Urban Growth and the Circulation of Information: The United States System of Cities, 1790–1840* (Cambridge, Mass.: Harvard University Press, 1973). Many of Pred's ideas have found their way into the historical literature, particularly through the works of Thomas Cochran. See, in particular, the latter's very useful essay, "The Business Revolution," *American Historical Review* 76 (December 1974): 1449–1466, which for the purposes of this bibliography is the better of the two sources. For a study of the social penetration of printed goods a key work is William J. Gilmore, *Reading*

*Becomes a Necessity of Life: Material and Cultural Life in Rural New England,
1780–1835* (Knoxville: University of Tennessee Press, 1989). In a book intended for a general audience, Thomas C. Leonard looks at how newspapers
were read in the nineteenth century as mass spectacle and how they are read
today. *News for All: America's Coming-of-Age with the Press* (New York: Oxford University Press, 1995).

Recasting the Information Infrastructure for the Industrial Age

The history of the information infrastructure in the nineteenth century has
yet to find its historian, although significant work has been done on the general
subject. As in the case with the seventeenth and eighteenth centuries, most
scholarship has focused on specialized topics. Some general studies exist, as
do monographs on specific institutions.

One of the key infrastructures created for the dissemination of information
was the creation of the U.S. postal system. How and why that came about
presaged a long-standing role of the American government in facilitating the
distribution and access to information evident down through the past two
centuries. The critical study of the creation and early history of the U.S.
postal system is Richard R. John, *Spreading the News: The American Postal
System from Franklin to Morse* (Cambridge, Mass.: Harvard University Press,
1995). On postal policies see Richard B. Kielbowicz, *News in the Mail: The
Press, Post Office, and Public Information, 1700–1860s* (Westport, Conn. Greenwood, Press, 1989). See Wayne E. Fuller, *The American Mail: Enlarger of the
Common Mail* (Chicago: University of Chicago Press, 1972), the best overview
of American postal history. However, for greater attention to policy and
institutional dynamics, rely on Kielbowicz and John.

The physical ability of Americans to distribute paper-based information,
such as books and newspapers, depended on the development of transportation. For an introduction to the role of canals and railroads, see George R.
Taylor, *The Transportation Revolution, 1815–1860* (New York: Rinehart,
1951), and Ronald E. Shaw, *Canals for a Nation: The Canal Era in the United
States, 1790–1860* (Lexington: University Press of Kentucky, 1990), for a
current study. By the mid-1800s, railroads came into the own as a major
transporter of information, a role it continued to play through most of the
twentieth century. Classic studies on the creation of the railroad network are
Thomas C. Cochran, *Railroad Leaders: The Business Mind in Action* (Cambridge, Mass.: Harvard University Press, 1953), and Edward C. Kirkland,
Men, Cities, and Transportation: A Study of New England History, 2 vols.
(Cambridge, Mass.: Harvard University Press, 1948). For the origins of U.S.
railroads, Colleen A. Dunlavy, *Railroads and Industrialization: Early Railroads
in the United States and Prussia* (Princeton, N.J.: Princeton University Press,
1994), focuses on the railroad's beginnings in the 1830s and 1840s. On railroads and mail, see George L. Anderson, "Banks, Mails, and Rails, 1880–

1915," in *The Frontier Challenge: Responses to the Trans-Mississippi West*, ed. John G. Clark (Lawrence: University Press of Kansas, 1971), 277–278; we do not, however, have a modern history of railway mail, a major lacuna in the history of information handling in the nineteenth century. The critical study of the relationship of railroads, the communication of information, and the rise of the modern U.S. corporation is by Alfred D. Chandler Jr., *The Visible Hand: The Managerial Revolution in American Business* (Cambridge, Mass.: Harvard University Press, 1977).

A critical information technology originating in the nineteenth century is the telegraph. The number of studies on the subject is growing rapidly, although we lack institutional histories. Histories range from technical discussions about how the medium's devices worked and evolved, to studies on their use and significance. Several histories, however, suggest the key findings of historians over the past several decades. On the early years, see Robert Luther Thompson, *Wiring a Continent: The History of the Telegraph Industry in the United States, 1832–1866* (Princeton, N.J.: Princeton University Press, 1947). On early technological developments there is Paul Israel, *Machine Shop to Industrial Laboratory: Telegraphy and the Changing Context of American Invention, 1830–1920* (Baltimore, Md. Johns Hopkins University Press, 1992). Gerard J. Holzmann and Bjorn Pehrson, *The Early History of Data Networks* (Los Alamitos, Calif.: IEEE Computer Press, 1995), focuses on the optical telegraph with a somewhat antiquarian approach. There is also Geoffrey Wilson, *The Old Telegraphs* (London: Phillimore, 1976), a usable general study. A popular history of the telegraph is Tom Sandage, *The Victorian Internet: The Remarkable Story of the Telegraph and the Nineteenth Century's On-Line Pioneers* (New York: Walker, 1998). A very readable work on telegraphy is by Edwin Gabler, *The American Telegrapher: A Social History, 1860–1900* (New Brunswick, N.J.: Rutgers University Press, 1988).

On early wire services see Menahem Blondheim, *News over the Wires: The Telegraph and the Flow of Public Information in America, 1844–1897* (Cambridge, Mass.: Harvard University Press, 1994). For a more comprehensive history of the use of wire services and journalism, there is Richard A. Schwarzlose, *The Nation's Newsbrokers*, 2 vols. (Evanston, Ill.: Northwestern University Press, 1989).

A number of narrower studies focus on uses of the telegraph. Joel A. Tarr, Thomas Finholt, and David Goodman, in "The City and the Telegraph: Urban Telecommunications in the Pre-Telephone Era," *Journal of Urban History* 14 (November 1987): 30–80, remind us that before the telephone Americans were exploiting telegraphic technology for a variety of uses. On economic applications there is Richard B. DuBoff, "The Telegraph and the Structure of Markets in the United States, 1845–1890," *Research in Economic History* 8 (1982): 253–277, but also see Alexander James Field, "The Magnetic Telegraph, Price and Quantity Data, and the New Management of Capital," *Journal of Economic History* 52 (June 1992): 401–413. On the early use of telegraphs for commodity exchanges, there is Kenneth Lipartito, "The New

York Cotton Exchange and the Development of the Cotton Futures Market," *Business History Review* 57 (spring 1983): 50–72, but also see William Cronon, *Nature's Metropolis: Chicago and the Great West* (New York: W. W. Norton, 1991). On the complex issue of important continuities in nineteenth-century communications policies from the postal system down to the telephone, see Richard R. John, "The Politics of Innovation," *Daedalus* 127 (fall 1998): 187–214, which stresses the enduring significance of the Founders' commitment to universal access.

The telephone equally spawned a massive bibliography. On the inventor of the telephone we have the excellent biography by Robert V. Bruce, *Bell: Alexander Graham Bell and the Conquest of Solitude* (Boston: Little, Brown, 1973). Institutional histories abound. Some of the most useful include Rosario Joseph Tosiello, *The Birth and Early Years of the Bell Telephone System, 1876–1880* (New York: Arno, 1979); Robert W. Garnet, *The Telephone Enterprise* (Baltimore, Md.: Johns Hopkins University Press, 1985); Kenneth Lipartito, *The Bell System and Regional Business: The Telephone in the South, 1877–1920* (Baltimore, Md.: Johns Hopkins University Press, 1989); on Theodore N. Vail The creator of AT&T, see Louis Galambos, "Theodore N. Vail and the Role of Innovation in the Modern Bell System," *Business History Review* 66, no.1 (spring 1992), 95–126 although the article emphasizes Vail's innovations after 1907, not of the 1880s when the "system" was envisioned. For an overview of how telegraphy became its own industry there is Richard B. Du Boff, "The Telegraph and the Structure of Markets in the United States, 1845–1890," in *Research in Economic History*, ed. Paul Uselding vol. 8 (Greenwich, Conn.: JAI Press, 1982), 257–265. The first history of Western Electric has now been published, filling in a large gap in U.S. telephone history: Stephen B. Adams and Orville R. Butler, *Manufacturing the Future: A History of Western Electric* (Cambridge: Cambridge University Press, 1998).

The most useful history of AT&T for the middle years of the twentieth century is Peter Temin and Louis Galambos, *The Fall of the Bell System: A Study in Prices and Politics* (Cambridge: Cambridge University Press, 1987). On the effects of the telephone on U.S. society, see Claude S. Fischer, *America Calling: A Social History of the Telephone to 1940* (Berkeley: University of California Press, 1992), which also includes a massive bibliography. But because Fischer underestimates the effects of the telephone on cities, the reader should consult a key work on the telephone, Ithiel de Sola Pool, ed., *The Social Impact of the Telephone* (Cambridge, Mass.: MIT Press, 1977). Technological and organizational issues often intertwined and their effective coordination made technologies available in the U.S. economy. For an example of how such issues evolved in the United States, see the case study on the telephone: Milton Mueller, "The Switchboard Problem: Scale, Signaling, and Organization in Manual Telephone Switching, 1877–1897," *Technology and Culture* 30 (July 1989): 534–560. On the consequences of this technology, there is Venus Green, "Goodbye Central: Automation and the Decline of 'Personal Service' in the Bell System, 1878–1921," *Technology and Culture* 36

(October 1995): 912–949. Telephones created jobs for women just as did the simultaneous creation of the function of office secretary. See Kenneth Lipartito, "When Women Were Switches: Technology, Work, and Gender in the Telephone Industry, 1890–1920," *American Historical Review* 99 (October 1994): 1075–1111. On telephone policy of the United States, the primary source remains Robert Britt Horwitz, *The Irony of Regulatory Reform: The Deregulation of American Telecommunications* (New York: Oxford University Press, 1989).

A volume on telecommunications in the United States (telegraph, telephone, internet, etc.) and U.S. government regulatory practices is Alan Stone, *How America Got On-Line: Politics, Markets, and the Revolution in Telecommunications* (Armonk, N.Y. M. E. Sharpe, 1997). Historians tend to agree, however, that the best one-volume general history of the telephone is John Brooks, *Telephone: The First Hundred Years* (New York: Harper & Row, 1975).

Business Uses of Information Technology from 1880 to 1950

This was the period in which the U.S. corporation came into existence and evolved into essentially its present form. The primary history of that process is Chandler, *Visible Hand*, cited earlier. Chandler continued to explore the subject with a comparison to activities in other nations in *Scale and Scope: The Dynamics of Industrial Capitalism* (Cambridge, Mass.: Harvard University Press, 1990). The role of information in U.S. corporations is the subject of many studies. One that received much attention when it first came out is by James R. Beniger, *The Control Revolution: Technological and Economic Origins of the Information Society* (Cambridge, Mass.: Harvard University Press, 1986), which has not been superseded by others. For example, there is JoAnne Yates, who studied a number of firms of the late 1800s and early 1900s to demonstrate how communications took place in corporations, in *Control through Communication: The Rise of System in American Management* (Baltimore, Md.: Johns Hopkins University Press, 1989). For a general history of the information processing industry of this period, covering adding and calculating machines, typewriters, tabulators, and cash registers, there is James W. Cortada, *Before the Computer: IBM, NCR, Burroughs, and Remington Rand and the Industry They Created, 1865–1956* (Princeton, N.J.: Princeton University Press, 1993). On the development of punch card equipment, there is a biography of its inventor by Geoffrey D. Austrian, *Herman Hollerith: Forgotten Giant of Information Processing* (New York: Columbia University Press, 1982). For their applications in the early decades of the twentieth century, see Arthur L. Norberg, "High Technology Calculation in the Early 20th Century: Punched Card Machinery in Business and Government," *Technology and Culture* 31 (1990): 753–779, and William Aspray, ed., *Computing Before Computers* (Ames: Iowa State University Press, 1990).

Uses of various technologies proved crucial to the work of corporations and nowhere was this more evident than in accounting. For an introduction to the issues, see Gary John Previts and Barbara Merino, *A History of Accounting in America: An Historical Interpretation of the Cultural Significance of Accounting* (New York: John Wiley, 1979). For changes in the way manufacturing occurred, there is Philip Scranton, *Endless Novelty: Specialty Production and American Industrialization, 1865–1925* (Princeton, N.J.: Princeton University Press, 1997). On management practices there is Joseph A. Litterer, "Systematic Management: Design for Organizational Recoupling in American Manufacturing Firms," *Business History Review* 37 (winter 1963): 369–391. Also useful is Robert H. Wiebe, *Search for Order, 1877–1920* (New York: Hill & Wang, 1967), which views the issue of control (Chandler's theme) as a hunt for order. For a discussion of the effects of information technology on accounting both in the precomputer and postcomputer period for U.S. corporations, see H. Thomas Johnson and Robert S. Kaplan, *Relevance Lost: The Rise and Fall of Management Accounting* (Boston: Harvard Business School Press, 1987). But also see JoAnne Yates, "Evolving Information Use in Firms, 1850–1920," in *Information Acumen: The Understanding and Use of Knowledge in Modern Business*, ed. Lisa Bud-Frierman (London: Routledge, 1994), 26–50; and a study sponsored by the accounting profession, Richard L. Nolan, *Management Accounting and Control of Data Processing* (New York: National Association of Accountants, 1977). One of the most useful histories of the office (and thus of the use of information technology within it) is by Angel Kwolek-Folland, *Engendering Business: Men and Women in the Corporate Office, 1870–1930* (Baltimore, Md.: Johns Hopkins University Press, 1994). The role of women has recently drawn much attention. One of the most thorough studies on the subject was completed by Elyze Rotella, *From Home to Office: U.S. Women at Work, 1870–1930* (Ann Arbor, Mich.: UMI Research Press, 1981), while another study, Sharon Hartman Strom, *Beyond the Typewriter: Gender, Class, and the Origins of Modern American Office Work, 1900–1930* (Urbana: University of Illinois Press, 1992) places greater emphasis on the effects of information technologies on women's role. For a history of knowledge workers that includes samplings from economists and historians on the subject, there is James W. Cortada, ed., *Rise of the Knowledge Worker* (Boston: Butterworth-Heinemann, 1998).

Vacuum Tubes, Radios, and Television

For the first half of the twentieth century the most visible application of vacuum tube technology in the United States was the radio. An excellent, comprehensive study of the subject is Hugh G. J. Aitken, *The Continuous Wave: Technology and American Radio, 1900–1932* (Princeton, N.J.: Princeton University Press, 1985). An older, still useful account, is by W. Rupert MacLaurin, *Invention and Innovation in the Radio Industry* (New York: Macmillan, 1949). On some of the newer versions of the radio, see Michael

Schiffer, *The Portable Radio in American Life* (Tucson: University of Arizona Press, 1991). The early history of radio use can be found in Susan Douglas, *The Invention of American Broadcasting, 1899–1922* (Baltimore, Md.: Johns Hopkins University Press, 1987), but also see another study that carries the story forward: Michele Hilmes, *Radio Voices: American Broadcasting, 1922–1952* (Minneapolis: University of Minnesota Press, 1997). On the radio business there is Susan Smulyan, *Selling Radio: The Commercialization of American Broadcasting, 1920–1934* (Washington, D.C.: Smithsonian Press, 1994). But also see Thomas Streeter, *Selling the Air: A Critique of the Policy of Commercial Broadcasting in the United States* (Chicago: University of Chicago Press, 1996).

The technological transition from still pictures to television was the movie. On the early role of movies in American society, see Steven J. Ross, *Working Class Hollywood: Silent Film and the Shaping of Class in America* (Princeton, N.J.: Princeton University Press, 1998). An excellent reference on the general subject is Anthony Slide, *The New Historical Dictionary of the American Film Industry* (Lanham, Md.: Scarecrow Press, 1998). An essential history of the movie industry is Robert Sklar, *Movie-Made America: A Cultural History of American Movies* (New York: Random House, 1994). Another general history of American film and society is Richard Maltby, *Harmless Entertainment: Hollywood and the Ideology of Consensus* (Metuchen, N.J.: Scarecrow Press, 1983). On the introduction of sound technology and its effects on films there is Donald Crafton, *The Talkies: American Cinema's Transition to Sound, 1926–1931* (New York: Charles Scribner's Sons, 1997), which is vol. 4 of *History of the American Cinema*. But for a truly fascinating study of how the mode of production, film technology, and film style combined to create a standardized approach to filmmaking in Hollywood, see David Bordwell, Janet Staiger, and Kristin Thompson, *The Classical Hollywood Cinema: Film Style and Mode of Production to 1960* (New York: Columbia University Press, 1985).

The literature on television, particularly as it was developed and adopted in the United States, is extensive. A good place to start is with the anthology of articles on this theme in Anthony Smith, ed., *Television: An International History* (New York: Oxford University Press, 1998). A monumental study on many aspects of broadcasting is Erik Barnouw's *A History of Broadcasting in the United States* (3 vols.), which covers the period from the earliest years to 1953 (New York: Oxford University Press, 1966–1970). He also wrote on the rise of television in *The Tube of Plenty: The Evolution of American Television* (New York: Oxford University Press, 1975). The role of RCA proved critical throughout the majority of the twentieth century. A short useful history of the firm was written by Robert Sobel, *RCA* (New York: Stein and Day, 1986). A useful biography of David Sarnoff written by Carl Dreher, *Sarnoff: An American Success* (New York: Quadrangle, 1977), has been superseded by Kenneth Bilby, *The General: David Sarnoff and the Rise of the Communications Industry* (New York: Harper & Row, 1986). Margaret B. W. Graham has written a case study on the VideoDisc episode, *RCA and the VideoDisc: The Business of Research* (New York: Cambridge University Press, 1986). Two important studies began the process of documenting the effects of television on American society in a methodical manner. The first is a collection of studies by experts on the topic, George A. Comstock et al., *Television and Human Behavior* (New York: Columbia University Press, 1978), one of the earliest such projects. A more recent one is by Joshua Mayerowitz, *No Sense of Place: The Impact of Electronic Media on Social Behavior* (New York: Oxford University Press, 1985).

Development of Chips, Computers, and Their Industry

The story of how the transistor and the computer chip came into being has been told by many writers. A good introduction to the story about the transistor is by Michael Riordan and Lillian Hoddeson, *Crystal Fire: The Invention of the Transistor and the Birth of the Information Age* (New York: W. W. Norton, 1997). A minor classic on semiconductors is by Ernest Braun and Stuart Macdonald, *Revolution in Miniature: The History and Impact of Semiconductor Electronics*, 2d ed. (Cambridge: Cambridge University Press, 1982). A very readable book about the chip is T. R. Reid, *The Chip: How Two Americans Invented the Microchip and Launched a Revolution* (New York: Simon & Schuster, 1984). For a large collection of articles on all aspects of the chip, see Tom Forester, ed., *The Microelectronics Revolution* (Oxford: Basil Blackwell, 1980).

The best one-volume history of computers, particularly in the United States, is by Martin Campbell-Kelly and William Aspray, *Computer: A History of the Information Machine* (New York: Basic Books, 1996); while, there are now more than three dozen such histories, this one was written by two historians and includes a useful bibliography. On the period 1965–1995, see Paul Ceruzzi, *A History of Modern Computing* (Cambridge, Mass.: MIT Press, 1998), which emphasizes the technological side of the story in nontechnical language. For a short history that weaves customer needs and wants with the technical history of the early stages of computing, see James W. Cortada, *The Computer in the United States: From Laboratory to Market, 1930 to 1960* (Armonk, N.Y.: M. E. Sharpe, 1993).

The special role played by the U.S. government in fostering the development and use of computing has been the subject of several important studies. Kenneth Flamm led with *Targeting the Computer: Government Support and International Competition* (Washington, D.C.: Brookings Institution, 1987) and *Creating the Computer: Government, Industry, and High Technology* (Washington, D.C.: Brookings Institution, 1988). On the role of government in creating what we now call the Internet, see Arthur L. Norberg and Judy E. O'Neill, *Transforming Computer Technology: Information Processing for the Pentagon, 1962–1986* (Baltimore, Md.: Johns Hopkins University Press, 1996) and Janet Abbate, *Inventing the Internet* (Cambridge, Mass.: MIT Press, 1998). One of the best histories of computing during the Cold War, and about the role of the U.S. government, was written by Paul N. Edwards, *The Closed World: Computers and the Politics of Discourse in Cold War America* (Cambridge, Mass.: MIT Press, 1996). The subject of the role of the government continues to attract the attention of policy makers. During the second Clinton administration an important study was commissioned by the president on the future role of the government with computing; the resulting work has an excellent summary of lessons learned by policy makers of the past: *President's Information Technology Advisory Committee Interim Report to the President* (Arlington, Va.: National Coordination Office for Computing, Information, and Communications, 1998). Another study, addressing similar issues, is worth looking into as a companion project: Computer Science and Telecommunications Board National Research Council, *Funding a Revolution: Government Support for Computing Research* (Washington, D.C.: National Academy Press, 1999).

Studies of the U.S. computer industry are now beginning to proliferate, particularly studies of major corporations such as AOL, IBM, and Microsoft. For an introduction to the subject and its literature see James W. Cortada, *Information Technology as Business History: Issues in the History and Management of Computers* (Westport, Conn.: Greenwood, 1996). For a general overview of the 1970s to the early 1990s, see Charles H. Ferguson and Charles R. Morris, *Computer Wars: How the West Can Win in a Post-IBM World* (New York: Times Books, 1993). A thoughtful book on Microsoft is Michael A. Cusumano, *Microsoft Secrets: How the World's Most Powerful Software Company Creates Technology, Shapes Markets, and Manages People* (New York: Free Press, 1995). Of the more than one dozen histories of IBM, the most comprehensive is by Emerson W. Pugh, *Building IBM: Shaping an Industry and Its Technology* (Cambridge, Mass.: MIT Press, 1995). One of the best business memoirs ever published in the United States is by the head of IBM in the 1950s and 1960s, Thomas J. Watson Jr., and Peter Petre, *Father Son & Co.: My Life at IBM and Beyond* (New York:Bantam Books, 1990). The most thorough analysis of the computer industry in the United States prior to the impact of the PC on its structure is by Franklin M. Fisher, James W. McKie, and Richard B. Mancke, *IBM and the U.S. Data Processing Industry: An Economic History* (New York: Praeger, 1983), covering the period of the 1940s through the 1970s.

A more up-to-date history of the industry is needed; however, several studies fill in parts of the story. AnnaLee Saxenian looked at two parts of the United States that manufactured and sold computing technology, *Regional Advantage: Culture and Competition in Silicon Valley and Route 128* (Cambridge, Mass.: Harvard University Press, 1994). A massive sociological study of the industry and the society it is spawning is underway by Manuel Castells, with three volumes in print, *The Information Age: Economy, Society, and Culture*, 2 vols. to date (Cambridge, Mass.: Blackwell, 1996, 1997, 1998). Alfred D. Chandler Jr. has looked at the structure of this industry, "The Computer Industry: The First Half-Century," in *Competing in the Age of Digital Con-*

vergence, ed. David B. Yoffie (Boston: Harvard Business School Press, 1997), 37–122. The entire book is a collection of case studies of how various technologies are affecting business practices, mostly based on U.S. examples.

Closely linked by historians to computers has been knowledge work, which is the increasingly fashionable way to label the work of professions. Although we have attempted to demonstrate in this book that information technologies and knowledge-based work have a long history dating back to the 1600s, the majority of literature on the subject focuses on twentieth-century developments, primarily the by-product of economists. The first major studies on what constituted knowledge work in America and who did it were conducted by Fritz Machlup at Princeton University. His major work is *Knowledge: Its Creation, Distribution, and Economic Significance*, 3 vols. (Princeton, N.J.: Princeton University Press, 1980–1984). The next major study, one that expanded the number of workers in the United States relying on information technology to do their work—hence creation of the postindustrial economy so often heralded—was done by Michael Rogers Rubin and Mary Taylor Huber, *The Knowledge Industry in the United States* (Princeton, N.J.: Princeton University Press, 1986). The Information Economy was expanded further in a study by Marc Uri Porat, *The Information Economy: Definition and Measurement* (Washington, D.C.: U.S. Department of Commerce, May 1977). The latest study, one with extensive historical perspectives, is Jorge Reina Schement and Terry Curtis, *Tendencies and Tensions of the Information Age: The Production and Distribution of Information in the United States* (New Brunswick, N.J.: Transaction Publishers, 1995).

Information Technology Management

Nearly a third of the some 2,000 books published each year in the United States on business management topics discuss computers and telecommunications. Many of these books are also translated into more than a dozen languages and published around the world. For more than a half-century Americans have written on the subject of information technology management. A DP-era management study that well portrayed issues of the 1960s and 1970s is F. Warren McFarlan, Richard L. Nolan, and David P. Norton, *Information Systems Administration* (New York: Holt, Rinehart and Winston, 1973). A highly influential book on systems thinking and IS management of the DP era is Sherman Blumenthal, *Management Information Systems: A Framework for Planning and Development* (New York: Prentice-Hall, 1969). One of the best anthologies of articles on the general theme is Lynn M. Salerno, ed., *Catching Up with the Computer Revolution* (New York: John Wiley, 1983). The classic study on the role of innovation, facilitated in large part by the use of information technology, is Richard N. Foster, *Innovation: The Attacker's Advantage* (New York: Summit Books, 1986). But also see Clayton M. Christenson, *The Innovator's Dilemma: When New Technologies Cause Great Firms to Fail* (Boston: Harvard Business School Press, 1997).

Creating I/T-influenced organizational structures can be understood through James I. Cash, Robert G. Eccles, Nitin Nohria, and Richard L. Nolan, *Building the Information-Age Organization: Structure, Control, and Information Technologies* (Chicago: R. R. Donnelley, 1994); James L. McKenney, *Waves of Change: Business Evolution through Information Technology* (Boston: Harvard Business School Press, 1995); Michael S. Scott Morton, ed., *The Corporation of the 1990s: Information Technology and Organizational Transformation* (New York: Oxford University Press, 1991); and Thomas J. Allen and Michael S. Scott Morton, eds., *Information Technology and the Corporation of the 1990s: Research Studies* (New York: Oxford University Press, 1994). All have U.S. case studies on the business use and effects of I/T. One of the classic studies on the effects of computing on workers (and one of the most widely read) is Shoshana Zuboff, *In the Age of the Smart Machine: The Future of Work and Power* (New York: Basic Books, 1988). It is a sociological study, relying extensively on interviews with workers, particularly in the paper industry, examining the consequences of such technology on skills, work, and the role of people. The first important account of the effects of electronic communications as a whole on an organization was done by Lee Sproull and Sara Kiesler, *Connections: New Ways of Working in the Networked Organization* (Cambridge, Mass.: MIT Press, 1991).

The Internet is so new that histories of the network hardly exist. An early, useful introduction, however, is by Katie Hafner and Matthew Lyon, *Where Wizards Stay Up Late: The Origins of the Internet* (New York: Simon & Schuster, 1996). The best history of the Internet is Abbate, *Inventing the Internet* (previously cited). For contemporary thinking about how to use the Internet, see Thomas G. W. Keen, Walid Mougayar, and Tracy Torregrossa, *The Business Internet and Intranets: A Manager's Guide to Key Terms and Concepts* (Boston: Harvard Business School Press, 1998). But also see Nitin Nohria and Robert G. Eccles, ed., *Networks and Organizations: Structure, Form, and Action* (Boston: Harvard Business School Press, 1992). A highly influential book on middle managers in U.S. corporations, which argued processes needed to be designed that were more compatible with computer technology, is Thomas H. Davenport, *Process Innovation: Reengineering Work through Information Technology* (Boston: Harvard Business School Press, 1993). Applications and strategies is also the subject of Stephen P. Bradley and Richard L. Nolan, eds., *Sense and Respond: Capturing Value in the Network Era* (Boston: Harvard Business School Press, 1998). We are also beginning to see publications on the implications of the Internet on U.S. management practices. Perhaps the most useful is written by two economists, Carl Shapiro and Hal R. Varian, *Information Rules: A Strategic Guide to the Network Economy* (Boston: Harvard Business School Press, 1999); this book argues that the classical laws of economic behavior have not been abrogated by the Internet, but they are just applied in different ways. An analysis of how one competes in the I/T industry was prepared by Michael A. Cusumano and David B. Yoffie, two highly knowledgable experts on management issues and contemporary I/T industry issues: *Competing on Internet Time: Lessons from Netscape and Its Battle with Microsoft* (New York: Free Press, 1998). For an example of how the Internet affects an industry, see Bruce M. Owen, *the Internet challenge to Television* (Cambridge, Mass.:Harvard University Press, 1999).

The direct management of information processing departments and infra-structures has yet to be properly studied by historians. For a short introduction to the issues, see Cortada, *Information Technology as Business History* (cited previously). For a bibliography of all the key studies on American I/T management, see James W. Cortada, *Second Bibliographic Guide to the History of Computing, Computers, and the Information Processing Industry* (Westport, Conn.: Greenwood, 1996). We lack a comprehensive study of applications of information technology in business, although the contemporary literature on the U.S. experience is now massive. For a bibliography of this material, see James W. Cortada, *A Bibliographic Guide to the History of Computer Applications, 1950–1990* (Westport, Conn.: Greenwood, 1996).

Personal Computers and Their Use

The PC has now been around for more than a quarter of a century and is beginning to leave a trail of historical literature behind it. Lee Butcher wrote an early biography of the cofounder of Apple Computer, *Accidental Millionaire: The Rise and Fall of Steve Jobs at Apple Computer* (New York: Paragon House, 1987). On Apple's product development, written by an insider in the firm, there is Guy Kawasaki, *The Macintosh Way* (Glenview, Ill.: Scott, Foresman, 1989). For a history of the Macintosh itself, see Steven Levy, *Instantly Great: The Life and Times of Macintosh, The Computer That Changed Everything* (New York: Viking, 1994). The most complete account of Apple available today is by Jim Carlton, *Apple: The Inside Story of Intrigue, Egomania, and Business Blunders* (New York: Times Business, 1997).

On the early history of MITS and Altair, see the memoirs of Forrest M. Mims III, *Siliconnections: Coming of Age in the Electronic Era* (New York: McGraw-Hill, 1986). A massive anthology of contemporary articles on PCs that appeared in *BYTE* magazine (1975–1994) provides an excellent window into the period in the United States: Jay Ranade and Alan Nash, eds., *The Best of BYTE* (New York: McGraw-Hill, 1994).

On IBM's role with PCs, there is the early yet excellent account by James Chposky and Ted Leonsis, *Blue Magic: The People, Power, and Politics Behind the IBM Personal Computer* (New York: Facts on File, 1988). Charles H. Fergusson and Charles R. Morris, *Computer Wars: How the West Can Win in a Post-IBM World* (New York: Times Book, 1993), provides a hard attack on IBM, but along the way we learn a great deal about the PC business in the United States. See also Ceruzzi, *A History of Modern Computing* (cited previously).

Material is beginning to appear on the role of users of PCs in the United States. An early account, written by an expert on the U.S. I/T scene, is

Howard Rheingold, *The Virtual Community: Homesteading on the Electronic Frontier* (Reading, Mass.: Addison-Wesley, 1993). A recent important study on the use of PCs by young Americans is by Don Tapscott, *Growing Up Digital: The Rise of the Net Generation* (New York: McGraw-Hill, 1998).

America as a Information Society

A wonderful readable study is David Shenk, *Data Smog: Surviving the Information Age* (New York: HarperCollins, 1997). There are those who would argue that the notion of the "information age" is false; for that contrary view see Theodore Roszak, *The Cult of Information: A Neo-Luddite Treatise on High Tech, Artificial Intelligence, and the True Art of Thinking* (Berkeley: University of California Press, 1994); or Bill McKibben, *The Age of Missing Information* (New York: Plume, 1993). Three broad studies enrich our understanding of the role of technology in society: James C. Carey, *Communication as Culture: Essays on Media and Society* (Boston: Unwin Hyman, 1989); Carolyn Marvin, *When Old Technologies Were New: Thinking About Electric Communications in the Late Nineteenth Century* (New York: Oxford University Press, 1990); and Joshua Meyrowitz, *No Sense of Place: The Impact of Mass Media on Social Behavior* (New York: Oxford University Press, 1990). All of these works go beyond just the role of computers.

Sociological material and social/personal comments on computing and the internet is proliferating rapidly. A few publications have emerged that are crucial to our understanding of what is going on. An early study remains useful for its broad considerations: Starr Roxane Hiltz and Murray Turoff, *The Network Nation: Human Communication via Computer* (Reading, Mass.: Addison-Wesley, 1978). For a personal view and recounting of early activities with what eventually became known as the Internet, see the fascinating account by Howard Reingold, *The Virtual Community* (cited previously), which has become a "best seller." Sara Kiesler brought together a number of experts to explore the *Culture of the Internet* (Mahwah, N.J.: Lawrence Erlbaum, 1996), while similar issues were explored by William Mitchell, *City of Bits* (Cambridge, Mass.: MIT Press, 1995).

The broad subject of the effects of computing and telecommunications in the United States is not a new topic. In fact, scholars and consultants have discussed the subject for many years. The book that most dramatically brought the U.S. public's attention to the subject was Alvin Toffler, *Future Shock* (New York: Random House, 1970), in which the author described a world filled with computers and telecommunications. He continued this theme in *The Third Wave* (New York: Morrow, 1980) and in *Power Shift* (New York: Bantam, 1990). An even more influential early commentator on the general theme was Daniel Bell. His book, *The Coming of Post-Industrial Society: A Venture in Social Forecasting* (New York: Basic Books, 1973), argued that industrial society was evolving into a new, postindustrial phase characterized in part by the use of computing. This book defined for many scholars their research themes for the next two decades. For a short version of his ideas, see his "The Social Framework of the Information Society," in *The Computer Age: A Twenty-Year View*, ed. Michael L. Dertouzos and Joel Moses (Cambridge, Mass.: MIT Press, 1979), 163–211. The granddaddy of all these comments about the future effects of computing was John Diebold who, during the 1950s and 1960s, influenced the thinking of many business executives, sociologists, and government policy-makers, with his comments on automation. Of all his publications, the most useful is his *Automation: Its Impact on Business and Labor*, Planning Document No. 106, Special Committee Report (Washington, D.C.: National Planning Association, 1959). However, the book that made him famous was *Automation: The Advent of the Automatic Factory* (New York: Van Nostrand, 1952).

Tools for the Scholar of Information in the United States

It was probably inevitable that the first major guide to the use of the Internet by historians would have been published in the United States, with an overwhelming number of citations originating in the United States: Dennis A. Trinkle, Dorothy Auchter, Scott A. Merriman, and Todd E. Larson. *The History Highway: A Guide to Internet Resources* (Armonk, N.Y.: M. E. Sharpe, 1997), which includes a bibliography on the Internet. Prior to this book's publication, the most widely used reference to all information processing tools for historians was Daniel Greenstein's *A Historian's Guide to Computing* (New York: Oxford University Press, 1994).

Archival guides to the American experience with information are largely limited to the information processing industry. However, Arnita A. Jones and Philip L. Cantelon edited a small volume on archival management and in the process described many U.S. business and technical archives: *Corporate Archives and History: Making the Past Work* (Malabar, Fla.:Krieger Publishing Company, 1993). The most definitive book on the subject, aimed at archivists but describing many U.S. holdings, is James M. O'Toole, ed.,*The Records of American Business* (Chicago: The Society of American Archivists, 1997). On U.S. computer-related collections, see James W. Cortada, ed., *Archives of Data-Processing History: A Guide to Major U.S. Collections* (Westport, Conn.: Greenwood, 1990). For more current information, contact the Charles Babbage Institute (CBI) at the University of Minnesota. CBI is the largest center for the study of the history of computing anywhere in the world and it tends to focus primarily on the U.S. experience.

Two anthologies of documents in the history of telecommunications are by George Shiers, ed., *The Telegraph: An Historical Anthology* (New York: Arno, 1977) and *The Telephone: An Historical Anthology* (New York: Arno, 1977).

There are a number of useful guides to sources and archives on various information technologies. Donald G. Godfrey and Frederic A. Leigh, eds., *Historical Dictionary of American Radio* (Westport, Conn.: Greenwood, 1998) is an excellent tool. So is Anthony Slide, *The New Historical Dictionary of the American Film Industry* (Lanham, Md.: Scarecrow, 1998). On television, a good starting point is George Shiers, *Early Television: A Bibliographic Guide to 1940* (New York: Garland, 1997). Two other guides are crucial: ATAS/ UCLA Television Archives, *ATAS/UCLA Television Archives Catalog: Holdings in the Study Collection of the Academy of Television Arts & Sciences of the University of California, Los Angeles Television Archives* (Pleasantville, N.Y.: Redgrave, 1981) and *World Directory of Moving Image and Sound Archives* (New Providence, N.J.: K. G. Saur, 1993).

Historical dictionaries on information technology are just beginning to appear. The first was James W. Cortada, *Historical Dictionary of Data Processing*, 3 vols. (Westport, Conn.: Greenwood, 1987), which covers technology, biographies, and corporate histories. A massive biographical dictionary on computer scientists and engineers (primarily American) is now available: J. A. N. Lee, *Computer Pioneers* (Los Alamitos, Calif.: IEEE Computer Society Press, 1995). On the U.S. computer industry, see an annual publication by Egil Juliussen, Portia Isaacson, and Luanne Kruse, *Computer Industry Almanac* (Dallas: Computer Industry Almanac, 1987–).

Index

Deployment, extent for computers, 208–213; home PCs, 262; of Internet, 243–244; PCs in homes and businesses compared, 280

Dewey, Melvil, 118

Dewey Decimal System, 118

Dick, A., mimeograph and, 18

Dickens, Charles, 63

Dickinson, John, political argument of, 44–45, 46

Diebold, John, 228; coined terms "automation," 227; quoted on rationale for acquiring computers (1960s), 179

Diffusion, why rate different for PCs in homes and businesses, 280

Digital computer, 202; came into its own, 190–196

Digital convergence, 286–290; concept explained, 244; resulted in restructured industries, 245

Digital divide, increased (1990s), 266

Digital Equipment Corporation (DEC), 35, 200, 204; embraced RISC technology, 238; origins of, 30; PDP-1, 229; PDP-5, 229; PDP-8, 229 role of, 228–229; served scientific and engineering customers, 220; software role of, 292

Digitally controlled home entertainment centers, 213

Diode vacuum tube, 138

Discussion groups, number and role on Internet, 277–279

DN 100, workstation from Apollo, 238

Documents, volume of business versions increase, 117–118

Downsizing, made possible by computers, 240

Dumont, 143, 144, 163; failed in radio broadcasting, 148

Du Pont, 16; early data retention practices at, 119; early user of graphs, 125; meetings at, 124

Dynamic Random Access Memory (DRAM), 3

e-mail, history of, 264; how used, 275, 277; non-work traffic on, 272

Earnings per share (EPS), 234–236

Eccles, W.H., 188

Eckert-Mauchly Computer Corporation, 190; bought by Remind Rand, 200

Economics of software, described, 295–296

Economy, consumption of chips by, 209; how helped computer usage in U.S., 204–208; in U.S. fertile for computer sales, 197; impact of Internet on, 244

Edison, Thomas, 14, 18; hired by Orton, 78; invented stencil method, 123–124

Edison Electric Illuminating Company, 133

Education, purpose in colonial times, 41

EDVAC, project described, 190–191

Eisenhower, Milton, developed U.S. government's information strategies (World War II), 161

Elekrictats Gelleschaft (AEG), 20

Electronic games, 213

Electronic mail (e-mail), history of, 264; how used, 275, 277; non-work traffic on, 272

Electronic media, co-exists with print media, 167–168

Electronics, as power in Information Age, 4–5; creation and use of infrastructure, 282–283; effect on processing of information, 4; IBM hires engineers expert in (1950s), 26; in many media forms (1910s–1930s), 141; stimulates economic growth in U.S., 145

Emerson, competed with RCA, 23

Employment, effect of electronic media on, 169–170

ENIAC, 191; unveiling of (1946), 189–190

Engineers, why they could develop computers, 187–188

Enterprise resource planning (ERP), facilitated by advantages of information transparency, 248

Entrepreneurs, new U.S. wave of caused by PCs, 34–35

Epson, made printer for IBM PC (1981), 237

ERA, 190; bought by Remington Rand, 200

ERPE, 151

Ethernet, 238; developed by Metcalfe (1973), 229

Ethnic access to PCs, 266

Europe, enters computer market, 200; origins of electric-based industries in, 20–21; percent of global semiconductor market, 186; received computer technology from U.S. via Japan, 29–30; role in PC business, 204

Eveready Hour, 158

Exports, of U.S. computer chips and office appliances, 185

Factory, 1916 issue on shop conferences, 124

Fairbanks, Douglas, 150

Fairchild Semiconductor, early history, 31; early maker of chips, 30

Family, brought together by Internet, 259; shared experiences via radio, 153–154

Family Opportunity Act (1982), significance of, 270

Faraday, Michael, 188
Fast Mail, effect on Vail's management
 thinking, 99; service described (1870s), 72
Federal Communications Commission (FCC),
 172–173; enhanced competition, 287;
 influence in evolution of national radio
 broadcasting, 149; role in creation of ABC,
 22: supports a few national broadcasters,
 141, 171; TV standards, 163–166
Federal Express, use of bar codes, 211
Federal Radio Commission, 148
Felt & Tarrant Manufacturing Company,
 121
Fiber optics, part of new digital
 infrastructure, 215
Fidelity Investments, use knowledge
 management software, 249
File cabinets, part of a larger file organizing
 process, 118
Files, managerial control processes for, 118–
 119
Financial accounting, computer applications,
 232–236
Fireside chats, radio success of, 156
First Amendment, 49
Fitzgerald, F. Scott, view of film industry,
 155
Fleming, Ambrose, 140
Fleming valve, 138
Flint, Charles R., 19
Flowcharts, developed, 192
FM, radio band, 155, 164; TV and, 165–
 166
Forbes, William, invested in Bell Company,
 91; made president of Bell Telephone
 Company (National Telephone Company),
 14, 91–92, 284
Ford, John, role during World War II,162
Forms, expanded use of (late 1800s–early
 1900s), 117
FORTRAN, 192
Fox, makes "talkies," 150
France, builds network of optical telegraphy,
 74; number of telephones in, 100
Franco-Anglo rivalry (1700s–1800s), effect on
 U.S., 7–8
Franklin, Benjamin, 8, 188; appointed
 Postmaster General, 6, 57; pro–status quo,
 42
Free speech, in England and its colonies, 42–
 44; role in early U.S., 49–52
Fujitsu, 204; invested in Amdahl, 29
Furchtgott-Roth, Harold W., quoted, 207
Futures market, made possible by telegraph,
 82

Gag Rule, failed, 50, 52
Galambos, Louis, quoted on AT&T, 285
Galvin, James, in World War II, 162
Games, 293; extent of software sales of, 262;
 played on computers at work, 272;
 software mainly for boys, 265
Gates, William (Bill), 204, 213, 293, 295;
 initial relations with IBM, 33; moves to
 workstation market, 35; provided operating
 system to IBM, 202
Gateway 2000, 34, 202
Gender inequality, in home use of computers,
 265–266
General Electric (GE), 22, 23, 146, 189, 200,
 285; acquires NBC (1986), 25; during
 World War II, 162; electric-based
 products, 20, 21; had development lab, 181;
 licensed transistor, 178; made vacuum
 tubes, 143, 144; member Radio Trust, 143,
 144; radio history of, 22; sets up RCA, 141;
 withdraws from computer business, 28–29;
 withdraws from TV business, 145
Geographical information systems (GIS), 248
Genealogy, Internet used for, 275
Gilded Age, Western Union dominated
 telegraph during, 77–79
Gilder, George, views on value of connected
 computers, 243–244
Global Positioning System (GPS), 251
Glorious Revolution, 43
Gold & Stock Company, 77
Goldberg, Beverly, quoted, 245
Gould, Jay, 92; competed against Western
 Union, 77; quoted, 83
Gore, Al, promoted school use of Internet,
 267
Gosden, Freeman, 154
Government, discussion forums offered by,
 278; early U.S. policy toward creation of
 information and its dissemination, 49–50;
 home electronic contact with, 274–275;
 official documents mailed for free, 61;
 relation with national networks unravel
 (1950s–1970s), 171–173; role in supporting
 distribution of early newspapers, 8–9;
 supports intellectual property protections,
 206–207
Graham, Margaret, 20, 21, 23–25; quoted,
 285
Grain exchanges, used telegraph, 13
Grant, Ulysses S., 283
Gray, Elisha, 87–88; hired by Orton, 78
Great Britain, connected to U.S. with
 telegraph cable, 75; controlled international
 telegraph cables, 145–146

Great Depression, increased demand for information, 127; reduces radio industry sales, 23

Green, Norvin, 79; quoted, 82; views on role of telegraphy, 78–79, 81

Greene, Robert J., 246

Grove, Andrew, 31; named *Time* Man of the Year, 186–187

GUIDE, founded (1956), 201

H.E. Butt Grocery Company (HEB). *See* Continuous Replenishment (CRP)

Hackers, contributions of, 175

Hale, James W., 70

Hall, E.J., 95

Hall of Records, created at Du Pont (1910), 119

Hamilton, Alexander, 58

Harndon, William, 70

Harvard College, 39

Harvard Mark computers, 189

Harvard University, computer project at, 189

Hazard, Ebenezer, 57

Hectograph methods, 123

Hearst newspapers, 138

Henry, Joseph, 188

Henry, Patrick, pro–status quo, 42

Hewlett-Packard (H-P), 30, 202, 229, 238; allied with Intel, 185; developed server capabilities, 242; PC role of, 34

Hertz, 25

Higher education, public support for, 214

Hitachi, 29; supplies computers to Olivetti, 30

Hollerith, Herman, 19, 131–133, 188

Hollywood, evolution in 1920s, 150; role in support of World War II, 161–162

Home shopping, online, 272–274

Homes, effect of telephone on, 101–102; patterns of information use in, 270; three eras of computing in, 260–265; PCs uses in, 37, 257–280; number of radios in (1930), 149; shared experiences facilitated by radio, 153–154; target market for early telephones, 89–90

Honeywell, 19, 26, 28, 200; licensed transistor, 78

Hoover, Herbert, quoted, 157; used radio, 156

House Unamerican Activities Committee, 157, 160; effect on entertainment industry, 170

Households. *See* Homes

"Hub-and-spoke" mail sorting scheme, role of (1800–1860s), 62

Hubbard, Gardner Greene, 81; foe of Western Union, 78–79; role of in early telephone business, 13–14, 88–92, 283–284

"Human relations" school of management, drives need for business machines, 18; emergence of, 127–129

Hughes, Howard, sale of RKO film studio, 167

Hygrade (later Sylvania), 143, 144

HyperText Markup Language (HTML), an open standard, 243; introduced (1991), 241

IBM. *See* International Business Machines Corporation

IBM Journal of Research and Development, 201

Ideology, of informed citizens, 105

IEEE Computer Society, founded (1951), 201

Illinois Central Railroad, used telegraph, 85

Immigration, extent of (1905–1914), 15

Independents, telephone companies attached to AT&T network, 98, 99

Industrial Age, arrival of and information flows during, 6–15; foundations of compared to those of Information Age, 3–7, 282, 289–290; how powered, 3–4; information infrastructure recast for, 104–105; maturation of, 15–37; work in contrasted to that of Information Age, 246–247

Industrial and instrument manufacturers, major users of chips, 185

Industrial relations, emergence of ideology of, 127–129

Industrialization, effect of cotton gin on, 7

Industry associations, for information technology, 201

Industry-specific technologies, significance and role of, 210–211

Informate, phrase defined, 240

Information, demand for in late 1800s/early 1900s, 125–129; diffusion in British colonies and U.S., 39–42, 48; early interest in cost of, 56; early needs of management for, 17–19; electronically delivered pervades all aspects of U.S. culture (1907–1960s), 139; flow of in colonial times, 5–6, 44; flow of in late 1800s, 111–113; general significance and role in American history, 52–53, 298–299; in early corporations, 17–19; increase in supply of (late 1800s/early 1900s), 125–129; market place at birth of U.S., 47–51; nature of in early U.S., 51–54; need for graphical presentations (early 1900s), 124–125; need for helped radio

Information (*continued*)
broadcasting, 149; overview of
infrastructure of (1780s–1920), 55–57;
personnel management created demand
for, 127–129; powered by electronics, 4;
railroads had great need for, 130; telephone
as new infrastructure, 13–15; why bias
toward entertainment, 174
Information Age, as environment explained,
56–57; foundations of, 282; how Americans
viewed speed of access to, 56;
infrastructure of, 4, 56; makes Americans
believe in emancipatory potential of
communications, 104; origins of, 20–37;
significance of postal system to, 63; work
in contrasted to that of Industrial Age, 246–
247, 289–290
Information Management Systems (IMS),
220
Information processing workers, number in
the U.S. (1990s), 198
Information Resource Management (IRM), in
Information Age, 246
Information technology (IT), costs and
benefits of (1990s), 250–251; metrics of
performance, 252–254; origin of the
phrase, 217; role in business, 36; stages
theory on management of, 217–218
Information technology architecture,
relationship to organizations, 218, 220,
227
Information Technology industry,
deregulation created competition, 244
Information Theory, Shannon's contributions
to, 189; Turing's ideas, 188
Informed citizenry, belief led to first
American communications revolution, 104
Infrastructure, across centuries, 281–282;
under construction in U.S. for
information, 215
Innovation, how done in semiconductor
industry, 184–185; made possible by
systems of information, 288–289
Insurance industry, had great need for, 130–
133
Integrated circuits (ICs), defined, 180; four
types, 186; global market, 186; uses for,
185–186
Intel, 293–294; allied with Hewlett-Packard,
185; chip market share (1994), 34; designed
IC for cars, 248; how grew to major size,
33; introduces chips (1972), 188; origins of,
31; significance of, 186–187
Internal Revenue Service (IRS), uses Internet
to reach taxpayers, 274, 276–277

International Business Machines Corporation
(IBM), 189, 197, 295; allied with NexGen,
185; antitrust wars, 207; challenges
Windows NT, 238; developed server
capabilities, 242; development lab of, 181;
dominated computer industry, 200–204;
early uses of its computers, 220; EPS of,
234; history as a computer company, 20,
25–37; how came to dominate computer
business, 25–30, 32–35; industry rank, 252–
253; licensed transistor, 178; origins of, 19;
PCs of 1981, 32–35; 195, 237, 255;
punched-card business of, 134; significance
in creating computer industry, 286;
significance of not using proprietary
software, 295; unbundles software (1969),
295; vendor of tabulating equipment, 130
International Business Machines (IBM)
computers, IBM 650, 191, 193; IBM 701,
191; IBM 704, 191; NORC, 191; PC, 202–
203; 237, 255; RS/6000, 238; SSEC, 191;
System 360, 26, 28–29, 192, 193, 201, 228,
292
International Computers Ltd. (ICL), 200;
supplied computers by Fujitsu, 30
International Federation for Information
Processing (IFIP), founded (1960), 201
Internet, 35, 294; as historical extension of
earlier information infrastructure, 298;
beginnings of, 240–241; compared to
Vacuum Tube Era, 174–175; extent of
deployment in homes, 264–265;
government use to reach citizens, 274–275;
helped create software as discontinuity
from past experiences, 296; home access,
263–265; home shopping on, 272–274;
impact on business, government and
public, 205, 256, 282; origins of, 35–37;
role of, 242–245; UNIX linked to, 229; use
by children, 267, 270–271; use in homes,
258–259
Internet Explorer, 36
Interstate Commerce Act, created Interstate
Commerce Commission (1887), 130
Intranets, being built, 294
Inventory applications, role of computers,
210–211
Iowa, high rate of per capital telephone use
in, 103
Iowa State, 214
Iron, replaces wood, 4
Isuzu, used GIS, 248

Jackson, Andrew, constraint of information
flows during presidency of, 50, 68; made

Manufacturing sector, evolution of management in, 109–113; extent of computer deployment in, 209; firms created appetite for information technology, 107; how telegraphy helped management of, 86

March of Time, in World War II, 161

Market value, of companies using information technology, 253–254

Marshall Fields, 133

Mass culture, electronic origins of, 23; facilitated by electronic information, 138–140; Hollywood influences (1930s), 155

Mass markets, how electronic media mobilized, 157–159

Massachusetts, Committee of Correspondence, 45; has early press, 39–40

Massachusetts Institute of Technology (MIT), 214; computer development work at, 188–189

Matsushita, 25, 286; licensed products, 21; made monitor for IBM PC (1981), 237; sells U.S. technology back to U.S. firms, 173

MATH-MATIC UNIVAC, 192

McBride, Mary Margaret, radio program of, 166

McCallum, Daniel C., 17; commented on use of telegraph used, 85; developed accounting methods, 109; telegraph at New York and Erie Railroad, 12

McCarthy, Joseph, 157, 170

McLean, John, 74; quoted, 63; role as U.S. Postmaster General (1820s), 59

McLeish, Archibald, 162

McLuhan, Marshall, medium is "the message," 139; quoted, 168; views about TV, 167–169

McReynolds, James C., 98

MCI Communications, moved into long-distance phone service, 287

Meat-packing firms, telegraphy crucial to, 86

Melchip, licensed transistor, 178

Memphis Bell, 162

Mercantile exchange, how facilitated by telegraph, 83

Merchants, major uses of telegraph, 82–83; supported private mail delivery vendors, 70–71

Metcalfe, Henry, quoted, 110–111

Metcalfe, Robert, 111; developed Ethernet (1973), 229; founded 3Com Corporation, 237; urged use of cards for accounting data, 119

Metcalfe's Law, 243

Metropolitan Life Insurance Company, telephone rivals pneumatic tubes, 101

Mexican War, 66

Michigan Central Railroad, 14

Microcomputer (Micro) Era, 30–35, 218; technologies of, 223–225

Microcomputers, origins compared to radio's, 21–22

Microprocessor, for PCs, 34; origins of, 31–32. *See also* chips

Microsoft, 204, 213, 237, 256, 293; antitrust war, 207; benefited from technical standards, 194; CarPoint used Internet, 245; introduced MS-NET (1984), 237–238; market value of, 252–253; role and significance of, 34–35; role in software industry, 297; software products of, 291

Microsoft Windows, impact of standardization on, 194; NT, 242

Milton, John, quoted, 42–43

Mimeograph, developed by A.B. Dick, 123–124; made copies, 18

Minicomputers, revenues by company from (1994), 27; role defined, 229; supplier firms created for, 30

MIPS Computer Systems, founded (1984), 238

Money, flowed through early postal system, 63

Moore, Gordon, 30; quoted, 31

Morgan, J. Pierpont., 14, 96; brings Vail back to AT&T, 95, 284

Morill Act, 51

Morse, Samuel F.B., applies for telegraph patent, 188; invented telegraph, 11–12, 74; ties to Alfred Vail, 283; wanted Post Office Department to take over telegraph, 75

Mosaic, Internet software introduced (1993), 241; origins of, 36

Motion Picture Committee Cooperating for the National Defense, role of, 161

Motion pictures, arrival of sound, 150–152; contributed to national unity, 155–156; how vacuum tubes affected, 144; RFO and RCA, 23; role in advertising, 159

Motorola, chip market share (1994), 34; early maker of chips, 30, 31

Movie studios, movies go to TV, 167–168

Murrow, Edward R., 160, 167; discredits McCarthy, 170

Napoleonic Wars, 7

National Association of Educational Broadcaster (NAEB), 168

National Association of Office Appliance
    Manufacturers, 125–126
National Bell Telephone Company, formed
    from Bell Company, 91
National Broadcasting Company (NBC), 148,
    172; early TV at, 23–24; in color TV, 145;
    mission of, 152–153; origins of, 22; profits
    of (1930–1931), 158; sold to GE (1986), 25
National Carbon Company, 158; radio ad of,
    153
National Cash Register Corporation (NCR),
    26, 28, 189; antitrust wars, 207; explored
    entering punched-card business, 19; had
    development laboratory, 181; origins of
    cash register, 18; transistor licensed by, 178
National Intelligencer, reaches national
    audience, 65
National Science Foundation (NSF), 241
National Semiconductor Corporation,
    established, 31; number of products of, 186
National Telephone Company, created, 14
National Television Standards Committee
    (NTSC), 155; 163–166
Navigator, software dominates WWW, 36
NEC Corporation, see Nippon Electric
    Company
NetDay program, 267
Netscape, browser encouraged households to
    use Internet, 264; origins of, 36
NetWare, 35
Network Era, defined, 218, 219; organizations
    in, 245–246; transition to, 241–242
Networks, advantages of Internet
    architecture, 243; convergence of software
    toward, 294–295; development of Ethernet,
    229; early uses of, 236; economic value of,
    252–253; power of (1950s–1960s), 171
Neumann, John von, 189; 190–191
Neutrality Acts, radio used to influence
    public opinion regarding, 160
New Deal, legislation stimulates demand for
    punched-card equipment, 134; policy
    toward advertising, 159; programs
    stimulate need for business machines, 18
New Orleans, 13
"New Series Project," 29
New York, colony has early press, 40
New York & Erie Railroad, 17; early user of
    telegraph, 84–85; joined to other rail lines,
    10
New York Associated Press, 13, 83
New York Central Railroad, Hollerith worked
    with, 132–133; used telegraph, 85
New York Edison Company, 133
New York Stock Exchange, 13

New York Tribune, 65
New Yorker, 278–279
News, how telegraphy changed transmission
    of, 83; volume transmitted by telegraph
    and mail (1844–1860), 80
Newspapers, bought radio stations, 158–159;
    British colonial government oversight of,
    40; compared to early radio, 149; extent of
    distribution in colonial times, 41; how post
    office helped them, 8, 61; percent of postal
    traffic (1700s–1800s), 8, 60–61; readers in
    1700s, 5; popularity relative to movies, 151;
    role in early U.S., 64–65, 138; significance
    of role in cable TV, 286–287; supported
    private mail delivery vendors, 71; tried to
    keep radio from reporting news (1930s),
    157
Newsweek, quoted, 160
NexGen, allied with IBM, 185
Nile's Register, 65
Nippon Electric Company (NEC), 204, 286;
    enters computer business, 20; supplied
    Machines Bull, 30
Noble, David, quoted, 128
Nolan, Norton & Co., research on what could
    be automated (1980s), 232
Nolan, Richard, 20, 35–36, 217–256
Noorda, Ray, 237
Norris, William, 30
Novell, 34, 35, 204, 256, 294; challenges by
    Microsoft, 35; introduced Sharenet X
    (1983), 237
Noyce, Robert, 30; creates an IC (1959), 188;
    patented integrated circuits (chips), 31
Numbers, early technologies to help analyze,
    120–121

Office appliances, teaches users about
    potential of mechanical calculation, 187
Office equipment, types of (1926), 126; use
    of, 113–126
Office of Facts and Figures, role of, 162
Office of Scientific Research and
    Development , 162
Office of War Information, role of, 161, 162
Office supply industry, activities of, 113–135
Office workers, ideal market for office
    machines in U.S., 197–199
Olivetti, 200; supplied computers by Hitachi,
    30
Olsen, Kenneth, origins of DEC and, 30
On-line services, offered to home users, 263
Operating systems, role of, 291; software
    defined, 192
Optical telegraphy, history of, 74–75

Oracle, 34, 35, 213, 294

Organizations, and IT architecture, relationship between, 218, 220, 227; effect of PCs on, 239–240; influence of Internet on structure of, 245–246

Orton, William, disagreed with Hubbard on role of telegraphy, 79; entered phone business (1877), 90–91; management style contrasted with Vail's, 99; role as president of Western Union, 77–79; turns down telephone patents, 88

Osborne, 194

Otis, James, 45

Owens-Illinois Kimble Division, 144

Pacific Telegraph Act (1860), 75

Packard and Bell, 34

Paine, Thomas, 51; publication of *Common Sense*, 6, 45–46

Paley, William, forms CBS, 22, 148; in World War II, 162

Paramount Pictures, 151

Patents, early phone patents defended, 284; history of radio, 21–23; promotes computer development, 206–207; telephone, 87, 88, 92–93; U.S. government controlled wireless during World War I, 141

Patterson, James Henry, mentored Watson, 19; role at NCR, 18; sold cash registers (1880s), 115–116

Payroll applications, used punched-card technology, 133

PDP series, 292; success of, 30

Pearl Harbor, attack on stops U.S. TV broadcasting, 164

Pearlstine, Norman, on role of Grove, 186–187

"Peewee" radio, 143

Pennsylvania Railroad, joined to other railroads, 10; used comptometers, 122

Pennsylvania State University, 214

Pennsylvania Steel Company, 133

Performance, information technology benchmarks, 252–254

Peripherals, revenues by company (1994), 27

Personal computers (PC), adopted by companies, 238–240; applications listed, 204; arrival of, 194–195, 202–203; consequences of IBM's initial product offering, 31–35; cost of additional components per user, 196; effect of IBM's on information technology industry, 237; extent of deployment, 212, 257; IBM's impact on U.S. microcomputers, 25–26; in homes, 257–280; largest users of chips

(1990s), 186; most extensive use of chips, 209; networking of, 241–242; number acquired, 193; percent of cost due to chips, 185; revenues by company (1994), 27; significance of, 32–35, 255, 286; software for, 292–297; why diffusion rates varied between home and work, 280

Personnel departments, creation of, 127–129

Philadelphia, has early press, 40

Philco, 129; competed with RCA, 23

Philips, 25, 172, 286; competes with Telefunken, 20–21; licensed transistor, 178

Phonograph, RCA and, 22–23

Pickford, Mary, 150

Piore, Emmanuel R., 26

Plankalkul, 192

Plant, Harold C., 210

Pneumatic tubes, competes with telephone, 101

Poduska, William, 238

Point-of-sale (POS) terminals, role of, 210

Politics, British encourage free speech (1700s), 43–47; critical role of information in early U.S., 47–48; ideology of freedom of expression in colonial times, 42–45; use of electronic media in, 156–157. *See also* Jackson and New Deal

Poney Express, 75

Popular Electronics, 260

Portable radios, 160

Post Office Act (1792), described, 58–59, 80, 104; early facilities described, 63–65; number of and expansion, 59–60; revenues compared to Western Union's (1866–1920), 81; terms and results of, 8

Postal system, creation of, 8, 47, 57–53, 68–79; growth of (1787–1860), 53; initial reaction to arrival of railroads, 10–11; Jackson's policies, 50; organization of influenced Vail, 99; post-Civil War era, 80; purpose in early U.S., 49; rates dropped due to railroads, 10–11

Postal Telegraph Company, competed against Western Union, 77

Power and the Land (1938), 156

Powers, James, 131–133

Press books, 118

Press copying, technique described, 116–117

Prime Computer, 35, 202, 229, 238

Print media, co-exists with electronic media, 167–168

Printing press, initial uses, 5, 39, 49; intended for elites (1700s), 40–41; purpose in

Software, arrival of, 290–298; demand
stimulated by PCs, 34; distribution of, 295–
296; economics of, 296–297; IBM's
revenues from (1994), 26–27; majority
information discontinuity caused by, 281–
282; Microsoft's revenues from (1994), 26–
27; origins of, 192; protected by law, 207–
208; revenues by company (1994), 27; rise
of as an industry, 203–204, 290–298;
significance of, 282

Sony, 25, 286; licensed products, 21; sells
U.S. technology back to U.S., 173; TI
enters Japanese market, 31

Sound, arrival in motion pictures, 150–152

Soviet radio, U.S. radio rivalry with (1920s),
150–151

Spain, number of telephones in, 100

Spanish-American War, sentiment wiped by
newspapers, 138

SPARC system, introduced (1987), 238

Speculation, role of telegraphy in, 82

Sperry Rand, 26, 200. *See also* Remington
Rand

Sports, role of early radio, 149

Sports Illustrated, partners with CNN, 295

Sprint, moved into long-distance phone
service, 287

Sproull, Lee, 20, 37, 257–280

Spyglass, origin of, 36

Stagecoach, significance in mail delivery, 62–
63, 71

Stamp Act, protest against, 44

Standardization, contribution of IBM S/360
to, 192–194; Ethernet becomes a, 229

Standards, emergence of telephone, 90;
established for TV (1941), 23; for TV, 163–
166; IBM S/360 and S/370 became
computers, 29; of digital computer design
(1940s–1980s), 190–191; open architecture
of IBM PC, 32–33; open Internet, 243;
role in software, 292; role of UNIX, 229;
used by AT&T to control markets (early
1900s), 96

State Street Corporation, uses near real-time
information delivery, 248

Stanton, Frank, 171

Stationery, internal vs. external business, 123

Steam, as power in U.S., 4

Stencil methods, used for business
communications, 123

Stephenson, George, 10–11

Stock exchange, early users of telegraph, 13

Storing and retrieving, emergence of new
technologies for (1800s), 117–120

Storrow, James J., 14

Sun Microsystems, 35, 255; developed server
capabilities, 242; founded, 238; revenues of
(1994), 26–27

Supercomputers, CDC introduces, 30

Surveys, on changing role of CIOs, 246; on
number of Internet users (1996–1997), 241

Sweden, number of telephones in, 100

Sylvania, 160; competed with RCA, 23

Synnott, Bill, 239

System, 29, 112; 370; emergence of
managerial, 110–111; key to understanding
continuity of U.S. information
infrastructure, 288–289; tabulating
equipment configured as, 19, 133

Tabulating technology, use in large
organizations, 129–135

Talkies, arrival caused unemployment, 169;
arrival of sound in movies, 150–151

Tandem, 229

Tandon, 237

Tandy, 32

Tapscott, Don, on youth attitudes toward
computers, 213

Taxes, Britain's practices toward newspapers,
5–6; withholding encourages use of
calculators (1913), 121

TCP/IP, 238; becomes standard, 242, 243;
importance of, 229

Technology, evolves, 175; motives for
developing, 178; of computers (1940s-
1960s), 191–192; variants related to each
other, 214–215

Telecommunications, cause of deregulation in
U.S., 244

Telecommunications Act (1996), 214

Tele-Communications, Inc (TCI), acquired
by AT&T (1998), 288

Telecommuting, pattern of, 271–272

Telefunken, created, 20–21

Telegraph, 138–139; compared to typewriter,
86; costs compared to mail, 80–81; creation
of industry, 74–79; critical to Industrial
Age, 282–283; effect on manufacturing, 86;
expansion statistics, 76–77; flow of
information by, 13; railroads and, 11–15;
rivals Post Office, 79–80; role of, 68–79;
usage statistics, 81–82; use by business for
standard types of information, 123

Telegraphic train-dispatching, described, 85–
86

Telephone, as possible source of mass
entertainment, 138; cost of residential
service, 103; critical to Information Age,
282–286; deployment in U.S. (1876–1920),

Yankolovich, Daniel, 168–169

Yates, JoAnne, 239; explained early use of mechanical aids to calculation, 187; focus of her chapter, 16–19; on consequences of standardization, 194

Yoffie, David B., defines "digital convergence" and significance of, 287

Young people, attitude toward computers, 213

Young, Owen D., 146; formed RCA, 21

Y2K problem, cause of, 296

Zanuck, Darryl, 155

Zenith, 148; boycotted color TV, 145; compared with RCA, 23; returns to color TV (1961), 24

Zimmerman, Andrew, quoted, 240–241

Zuboff, Shoshana, 240

Zworykin, Vladimir K., 23, 163